Applied Computing in Medicine and Health

Applied Computing in Medicine and Health

Edited by

Dhiya Al-Jumeily

Abir Hussain

Conor Mallucci

Carol Oliver

AMSTERDAM • BOSTON • HEIDELBERG • LONDON
NEW YORK • OXFORD • PARIS • SAN DIEGO
SAN FRANCISCO • SINGAPORE • SYDNEY • TOKYO

Morgan Kaufmann is an imprint of Elsevier

Acquiring Editor: Todd Green
Editorial Project Manager: Amy Invernizzi
Project Manager: Priya Kumaraguruparan
Cover Designer: Maria Inês Cruz

Morgan Kaufmann is an imprint of Elsevier
225 Wyman Street, Waltham, MA 02451, USA

ISBN: 978-0-12-803468-2

British Library Cataloguing in Publication Data
A catalogue record for this book is available from the British Library

Library of Congress Cataloging-in-Publication Data
A catalog record for this book is available from the Library of Congress

For Information on all MK publications
visit our website at www.mkp.com

Contents

List of Contributors

Haya Al-Askar
Salman Bin Abdulaziz University, Department of Computer Science,
Saudi Arabia, KSA

Mohammed Al-Jumaily
Dr Sulaiman Al Habib Hospital, Dubai, UAE; Liverpool John Moores University,
Liverpool, UK

Obinna Anya
IBM Research — Almaden, San Jose, CA, USA

Douglas Arnold
NeuroRx Research Inc., Montreal, Canada

Farath Arshad
Centre for Health and Social Care Informatics — CHaSCI, Liverpool John Moores
University, Liverpool, UK

Stephen Attard
Paediatrics (Neurology) at Mater Dei Hospital, Malta

Nizar Bouguila
Concordia Institute of Information Systems Engineering, Concordia University,
Montreal, Canada

Sandra C. Buttigieg
Department of Health Services Management, University of Malta, Malta

Vincent Cassar
Department of Management, University of Malta, Malta

B. Chandra
Computer Science Group, Department of Mathematics, Indian Institute of
Technology, Delhi, India

Chelsea Dobbins
Applied Computing Research Group, Liverpool John Moores University,
Liverpool, UK

Stephen Fairclough
School of Natural Sciences and Psychology, Liverpool John Moores University,
Liverpool, UK

Anthony Farrugia
Department of Management, University of Malta, Malta

Paul Fergus
Applied Computing Research Group, Liverpool John Moores University, Liverpool, UK

Joe Gallagher
Health Research Group, University College Dublin, Ireland

Hong-Mei Gao
Professor, Department of Logistic Management and Engineering, Tianjin Agricultural University, Tianjin, China

Rozaida Ghazali
Faculty of Computer Science and Information Technology, Universiti Tun Hussein Onn Malaysia, Johor, Malaysia

Ali Ghuname
Al Dar University College, Dubai, UAE

Hani Hamdan
CentraleSupélec, L2S UMR CNRS 8506, Gif-sur-Yvette, France

Lisa Hammond
NHS Liverpool Community Health, Wavertree Technology Park, Liverpool, UK

Ciara Heavin
Health Information Systems Research Centre, University College Cork, Ireland

Tutut Herawan
Universitas Teknologi Yogyakarta & AMCS Research Center, Yogyakarta, Indonesia

De-Shuang Huang
Institute of Machine Learning and Systems Biology, Tongji University, Shanghai City, China

Shamaila Iram
University of Salford, Greater Manchester, UK

Princy Johnson
School of Engineering, Liverpool John Moores University, Liverpool, UK

Nawsher Khan
Department of Computer Science, Abdul Wali Khan University, Mardan, Pakistan

Ayodele Lasisi
Faculty of Computer Science and Information Technology, Universiti Tun Hussein Onn Malaysia, Johor, Malaysia

Yu-Chuan Liu
Assistant Professor, Department of Information Management, Tainan University of Technology, Tainan, Taiwan

Áine MacDermott
Al Dar University College, Dubai, UAE

Sam Mcpartland
Primary Care Commissioning IM&T Team, Informatics Merseyside, Liverpool, UK

Nonso Nnamoko
Centre for Health and Social Care Informatics — CHaSCI, Liverpool John Moores University, Liverpool, UK

Yvonne O' Connor
Health Information Systems Research Centre, University College Cork, Ireland

Siobhan O' Connor
School of Nursing, Midwifery & Social Work, University of Manchester, UK

John O' Donoghue
Global eHealth Unit, Department of Primary Care and Public Health, Imperial College London, UK

Michael Osadebey
Department of Electrical and Computer Engineering, Concordia University, Montreal, Canada

Pat Patterson
NHS Liverpool Community Health, Wavertree Technology Park, Liverpool, UK

Muhammad Irfan Qamar
IBM Canada Ltd., Canada

Naeem Radi
Al Khawarizmi International College, Abu Dhabi, UAE

Sami Ur Rahman
Department of Computer Science and Information Technology, University of Malakand, Pakistan

Martin Randles
School of Computer Science, Liverpool John Moores University, Liverpool, UK

Habib Shah
Faculty of Computer and Information Systems, Islamic University Madina, KSA

Hissam Tawfik
Department of Mathematics and Computer Science, Liverpool Hope University, UK

Francois-Benoit Vialatte
Laboratoire SIGMA, ESPCI ParisTech, Paris, France

Editor Biographies

Dr. Dhiya Al-Jumeily is a Principal Lecturer in applied computing and leads the Applied Computing Research Group (ACRG) at the faculty of Engineering and Technology, in Liverpool John Moores University. He is the Head of Enterprise for the Faculty. Dr. Al-Jumeily has extensive research interests covering a wide variety of interdisciplinary perspectives concerning the theory and practice of applied computing in medicine, machine learning, and health care. He has published well over 150 peer-reviewed scientific publications, four books, and three book chapters, in multidisciplinary research areas, including technology enhanced learning, applied artificial intelligence, neural networks, signal prediction, telecommunication fraud detection, AI-based clinical decision making, medical knowledge engineering, human—machine interaction, intelligent medical information systems, and wearable and intelligent devices and instruments. But his current research passion is decision support systems for self-management of health and disease. He is the founder and chair of the International Conference Series on Developments in eSystems Engineering DeSE (www.dese.org.uk) since 2007.

Dr. Abir Hussain is a Reader in the Faculty of Engineering and Technology in Liverpool John Moores University. Dr. Hussain gained her BSc degree at the Department of Electronic and Electrical Engineering at Salford University. She then joined the control systems center at UMIST to complete her MSc degree in Control and Information Technology. The MSc dissertation was in collaboration with the Department of Paper Science, where fractal simulations of martial damage accumulation in cellulosic fibers were investigated. Then she pursued a PhD research project at the Control Systems Centre at UMIST. Her PhD was awarded in 2000 for a thesis titled Polynomial Neural Networks and Applications to Image Compression and Signal Prediction.

Dr. Conor Mallucci is a consultant neurosurgeon at the Walton Centre for Neurology and Neurosurgery Liverpool. Dr. Mallucci also works at the Royal Liverpool Children's Hospital, Alder Hey, as a consultant pediatric neurosurgeon. Dr. Mallucci's research interest is hydrocephalus, brain, and spinal tumors.

Mrs. Carol Oliver is a PRINCE2 Practitioner with more than 20 years' experience in supporting higher education research and development. Mrs. Oliver has supported different research projects and managed the organization of a well-known international research conference.

Author Biographies

CHAPTER 1

Shamaila Iram works as a research fellow in the School of Built Environment at the University of Salford, United Kingdom. She received her PhD in Computer Science from Liverpool John Moores University in 2014. During her PhD, she got an opportunity to work in the SIGMA Laboratory at ESPCI ParisTech, France, for a few months. There, she worked on the early detection of Alzheimer using electroencephalographic signals. Previously, in 2010, Shamaila had obtained her MSc degree in Computing and Information Systems from Liverpool John Moores University, with Distinction. Her research interests are Big Data Analysis, Machine Learning, Signal Processing, and Artificial Intelligence.

— **UK**

Francois Vialatte is an associate professor at ESPCI ParisTech, Brain Plasticity Lab (Paris, France). He is also working as a team leader for brain—computer interface projects in the SIGMA Laboratory. His research interests are model signal processing, neuroscience, modeling, time-frequency analysis (wavelets, bump modeling), machine learning (LDA, neural networks, SVM). Previously, he worked as a senior researcher in signal processing for neuroscience in Riken BSI (lab. ABSP), Japan.

— **France**

Irfan Qamar is a senior IT professional currently working as an Enterprise Infrastructure Consultant at IBM Canada, Ltd. In his current role, he provides consulting services to some leading financial industry clients. Before IBM, he worked for Hewlett Packard as a consultant. Irfan works with various middleware and database-related technologies. He holds a bachelor's degree in Computer Science from York University, Toronto.

— **Canada**

CHAPTER 2

Chelsea Dobbins is a senior lecturer at the School of Computer Science at Liverpool John Moores University. She received her PhD in Computer Science, focusing on Human Digital Memories and Lifelogging, from Liverpool John Moores University in 2014. Her research interests include machine learning, mobile computing, lifelogging, human digital memories, pervasive computing, Big Data, artificial intelligence, and physiological computing.

— **UK**

Stephen Fairclough is a Professor of psychophysiology in the School of Natural Sciences and Psychology at Liverpool John Moores University. He received his PhD from Loughborough University in 2000. His research interests include physiological computing, cardiovascular psychophysiology and human factors psychology.

— UK

CHAPTER 3

B. Chandra is Professor of the Computer Science Group, Department of Mathematics, in the Indian Institute of Technology, Delhi, and previously was the Department Chair from 2004 to 2007. Her specialization is in the area of data mining, neural networks, machine learning and feature selection for gene expression data. She has been a visiting professor for a year at the University of Pittsburgh and at the Penn State University, United States. She has also been a visiting scientist at NIST, Gaithersburg, Maryland, during the summer of 2012. She has been the chairman of many sessions in data mining and machine learning in international conferences organized in United States, United Kingdom, Canada, Singapore, and France.

— India

CHAPTER 4

Michael Osadebey received the BSc degree in Physics and postgraduate diploma in electrical engineering from the University of Port-Harcourt and Rivers State University of Science and Technology, in Nigeria, in 1997 and 2000, respectively. He has an MSc in engineering (electronics) and biomedical engineering from Umea University, Umea, Sweden, and Tampere University of Technology, Tampere, Finland, in 2006 and 2009, respectively. Osadebey is currently a PhD candidate at Concordia University, Montreal, Canada. Mr. Osadebey works as a magnetic resonance image (MRI) reader at NeuroRx Research Inc., a clinical research organization based in Montreal, Canada. His duties at NeuroRx research include the application of advanced image analysis software in the analysis of MRI images of multiple sclerosis patients undergoing clinical drug trials treatment.

— Canada

Nizar Bouguila received his engineering degree from the University of Tunis in 2000 and MSc and PhD degrees from Sherbrooke University in 2002 and 2006, respectively, all in Computer Science. He is currently an Associate Professor with the Concordia Institute for Information Systems Engineering (CIISE) at Concordia University, Montreal, Quebec, Canada. His research interests include image processing, machine learning, data mining, 3D graphics, computer vision, and pattern recognition. In 2007, he received the Best PhD Thesis Award in engineering and natural sciences from Sherbrooke University, was awarded the prestigious Prix d'excellence de l'association des doyens des etudes superieures au Quebec (Best PhD

Thesis Award in Engineering and Natural Sciences in Quebec), and was a runner-up for the prestigious NSERC Doctoral Prize.

— **Canada**

Douglas Arnold, MD, is currently Professor in the Department of Neurology and Neurosurgery at McGill University, Director of the Magnetic Resonance Spectroscopy Unit in the Brain Imaging Center at the Montreal Neurological Institute, and president of NeuroRx Research, a central nervous system imaging clinical research organization. He has special expertise in advanced magnetic resonance imaging (MRI) acquisition and analysis techniques, particularly as they relate to understanding the evolution of multiple sclerosis (MS) and neurodegeneration. Dr. Arnold combines advanced image processing of conventional structural images with nonconventional MRI acquisition techniques such as magnetization transfer imaging and magnetic resonance spectroscopy to understand how inflammation in MS relates to injury to myelin and neurons. He also uses these techniques to understand how new therapies for MS affect the pathobiology of the disease. Dr. Arnold received his medical degree from Cornell University. He completed his residency in Neurology at McGill University and a postdoctoral fellowship in Magnetic Resonance at the University of Oxford.

— **Canada**

CHAPTER 5

Obinna Anya is a research staff member at IBM Research, Almaden. His research lies in the areas of human—computer interaction, collaborative workplaces, social informatics, and agent-based modeling with a focus on user analytics to inform the design of sociocomputational systems and environments for network-enabled organizations of the future. His current work investigates interaction and emergence in these kinds of systems. Obinna holds a PhD in Computer Science, an MSc in Distributed Systems—both from the University of Liverpool—and a BSc in Computer Science from the University of Nigeria, Nsukka. He has previously worked as a research scientist at Liverpool Hope University, where he was the lead researcher on a British Council—sponsored project titled Context-Aware Information Systems for e-Health Decision Support.

— **USA**

Hissam Tawfik is an associate professor of computer science and the program leader for the MSc Computer Science, MBA (Information Technology), and Computer Science PhD programs at Liverpool Hope University. He holds an MSc and PhD in Computer Engineering from University of Manchester and has an established research track, with more than 100 refereed journal and conference publications in the areas of biologically inspired systems, virtual reality, e-health, user-centered systems, intelligent transportation systems, and applied modeling and simulation for building layout and urban planning. Hissam leads the Intelligent and Distributed Systems

(IDS) Group at Liverpool Hope, serves on various editorial boards and review committees for international journals and conferences, and is a conference chair and organizer of the International Conference Series on Developments in eSystems Engineering DESE (www.dese.org.uk). He has previously collaborated on a number of EU-funded research projects, as well as a British Council—funded project titled Context-Aware Information Systems for e-Health Decision Support (in collaboration with the British University in Dubai), where he was the principal investigator.

— UK

CHAPTER 6

Paul Fergus is a senior lecturer in computer science in the School of Computer Science at Liverpool John Moores University, a visiting professor at Al Dar University College in Dubai, and a visiting professor at Supelec in France. Paul received a BSc (Hons) degree in Artificial Intelligence from Middlesex in 1997, an MSc in Computing for Commerce and Industry from the Open University in 2001, and a PhD in Computer Science from Liverpool John Moores University in 2005. Paul has more than five years' experience as a senior software engineer in industry and has worked on several development projects for the Prison Service, Ericsson, Nokia, NMC, Nissan, and Pilkington Glass. He has been an active research for more than 10 years and has published more than 130 papers on topics that include artificial intelligence, semantic web, signal processing, bioinformatics, and data science.

— UK

De-Shuang Huang received his BSc, MSc, and PhD degrees, all in Electronic Engineering, from the Institute of Electronic Engineering, Hefei, National Defense University of Science and Technology, Changsha, and Xidian University, Xian, China, in 1986, 1989, and 1993. During 1993—1997, he was a postdoctoral student in Beijing Institute of Technology and in National Key Laboratory of Pattern Recognition, Chinese Academy of Sciences, Beijing, China. In 2000, he joined the Institute of Intelligent Machines, Chinese Academy of Sciences, as the Recipient of "Hundred Talents Program" of CAS. From September 2000 to March 2001, he worked as a research associate in the Hong Kong Polytechnic University. In 2004, he worked as the university fellow in the Hong Kong Baptist University. From 2005 to March 2006, he worked as a research fellow in Chinese University of Hong Kong. From March to July 2006, he worked as a visiting professor in Queen's University of Belfast, United Kingdom. In 2007, 2008, and 2009, he worked as a visiting professor in Inha University, Korea. At present, he is the head of the Machines Learning and Systems Biology Laboratory, Tongji University. Dr. Huang is currently a senior member of the IEEE. He has published more than 200 papers.

— China

Hani Hamdan is a Professor in the Department of Signal Processing and Electronic Systems of the Ecole Supérieure d'Electricité (SUPELEC). He received his Engineering Diploma in Electricity and Electronics option Computer Science and

Telecommunication in 2000 from the Faculté de Génie of the Université Libanaise in Beirut, Lebanon; his Masters in Industrial control in 2001 from the Faculté de Génie of the Université Libanaise in collaboration with the Université de Technologie de Compiègne (UTC), France; and earned his PhD in Systems and Information Technologies in 2005 from the UTC. Between March 2002 and August 2005, he worked as a research engineer in computer science at the pole ICM (Ingénierie, Contrôles non destructifs et Mesure) of CETIM (CEntre Technique des Industries Mécaniques) in Senlis, France. During this period, he developed clustering and classification methods for real-time monitoring by acoustic emission of pressure vessels. From 2004 to 2005, he was president-elect of the Mouvement Associatif Doctoral of the UTC. From 2005 to 2006, he was researcher at CNRS (French National Center for Scientific Research), where he worked on the analysis and synthesis of speech. From 2006 to 2008, he was an assistant professor at the Université Paris-Nord (Paris 13), where he conducted research in classification, automatic control, and data analysis. He is author or coauthor of more than 50 scientific papers. His current research interests include signal processing, automatic control, and pattern recognition.

— **France**

CHAPTER 7

Haya Al-Askar is an assistant professor in the College of Computer Science and Engineering at Prince Sattam University, Saudi Arabia. Haya gained her PhD in Computer Science from Liverpool John Moores University in 2014. She also gained an MSc in Applied Artificial Intelligence from the University of Exeter in 2009. Haya's research interests include computer applications in education and teaching, artificial intelligence applications, computer application programs, and data analysis.

— **Saudi Arabia**

Naeem Radi is the CEO of the Al Khawarizmi University College in the United Arab Emirates. His main area of research involves the design of image processing algorithms for image compression. Dr. Radi has published many journal and conference papers and reports on many aspects of this research and has also acted as the session chair and on program committees for many international conferences. He serves as professional fellowship for BCS and as a professional member for IEEE.

— **UAE**

Áine MacDermott is a PhD research student in the School of Computer Science at Liverpool John Moores University. She achieved a first class BSc. (Hons) in the field of Computer Forensics in 2008. She gained her Associate Fellowship of Higher Education Academy (AFHEA) qualification in 2014, and is a DeSE Series Conference Coordinator based in the United Kingdom, working with Al Dar University College in Dubai. Her research interests include critical infrastructure protection, cloud security, network security, computer forensics, and e-health.

— **UAE**

CHAPTER 8

Martin Randles is currently a researcher, principal lecturer, and program leader for software engineering in the School of Computing and Mathematical Sciences at LJMU. He gained a BSc (Hons) in Mathematics from the University of Manchester in 1983. After a number of years in business and commerce, he achieved an MSc with distinction in Computing and Information Systems from LJMU in 2003. A PhD, in providing self-management in large-scale systems, followed this in 2007. Martin's research interests include the application of mathematical techniques to computer science, the control and management of large-scale complex systems, and autonomic computing. He has published widely in these fields in high-quality journals and conference proceedings.

— UK

Princy Johnson gained a Bachelor of Engineering in Electronics and Communication Engineering from GCT, Coimbatore, India, followed by a Master of Engineering in Applied Electronics from Guindy Engineering College, Madras, India, both with distinction. Funded through Commonwealth Scholarship, she received her PhD from King's College London in 2000. She has worked as a research and development engineer at Nortel Networks UK Ltd for two years, during which she had a patent issued for a novel reconfigurable OADM. Dr. Johnson is at Liverpool John Moores University, and her research interests include energy-efficient techniques and protocols for mobile wireless and sensor networks. She is currently developing an active EU research consortium on this topic. She is an active member of IEEE since 2001.

— UK

Naeem Radi is the CEO of the Al Khawarizmi University College in the United Arab Emirates. His main area of research involves the design of image processing algorithms for image compression. Dr. Radi has published many journal and conference papers and reports on many aspects of this research and has also acted as the session chair and on program committees for many international conferences. He serves as professional fellowship for BCS and as a professional member for IEEE.

— UAE

CHAPTER 9

Anthony Farrugia is a visiting lecturer at the Department of Management, Faculty of Economics, Management and Accountancy (FEMA). Anthony is currently reading a doctoral degree in medical decision-type expert mobile systems in neurology with Liverpool John Moores University, United Kingdom. Anthony's main interests include intelligent e-businesses, mobile health, artificial intelligence, and data mining for businesses, web, and mobile application development. Anthony also lectures on eTourism at the Institute of Tourism Studies in Switzerland (Malta). He is a chief commercial operations officer and cofounder of "Sourcecode Malta," which provides web and mobile development software services. Anthony is also an external academic member of the Applied Computer Research Group with LJMU, United Kingdom (www.appliedcomputing.org.uk). Recently, Anthony developed and launched a student teachers ePortfolio web application (STeP), which is currently being used by students following a BEd (Hons) degree at the University of Malta.

— **Malta**

Stephen Attard, MD, MRPCHCH, DCH, MSc (Cardiff), is resident specialist in pediatrics with a special interest in neurology and neurophysiology at the Department of Paediatrics, Mater Dei Hospital. He is a member of the BPNA and visiting lecturer at the University of Malta. Early in his pediatric career, Dr. Attard was involved in the development of a community-based service catering for children with psychosocial difficulties and at risk of abuse. In 2000, he was elected member of the Royal College of Pediatrics and Child Health. As Fellow at the Neuroscience Department at Great Ormond Street Hospital in London between 2002 and 2003, Dr. Attard worked with Prof. Brian Neville, the late Prof. Robert Surtees, Prof. Helen Cross, Dr. Lucinda Carr, and Dr. Stewart Boyd. Dr. Attard's research interests include the health care needs and quality of life of children with spina bifida, cerebral function monitoring for neonatal encephalopathy and seizures, the epidemiology of childhood visual impairment, attendances at pediatric A&E for neurological complaints, and the application of databases in pediatric neurology. He is currently involved in the setting up of the Maltese Cerebral Palsy Registry in collaboration with SCPE.net (Surveillance of Cerebral Palsy in Europe) and the use of headache diaries to monitor and manage pediatric headache.

— **Malta**

Mohammed Al-Jumaily is a Consultant Neurosurgeon at Al Habib Hospital, Dubai Healthcare City, United Arab Emirates. Additionally, he is also Lead for Clinical Research at Liverpool John Moores University, United Kingdom. In 2002, he received his MSc in Neurobiology and his PhD in Neurobiology in 2007. Since 2010, Mohammed has been a Fellow of the Royal College of Surgeons of Edinburgh in Neurosurgery. Clinical interests include minimally invasive spine surgery, endoscopic spinal surgery, primary and metastatic spine tumors, to name a few.

— **Dubai**

Sandra C. Buttigieg, MD, PhD (Aston), FFPH (UK), MSc, MBA, is an associate professor and head of department of Health Services Management, Faculty of Health Sciences at the University of Malta. She lectures on the Master Degree Programs in Health Services Management, Public Health, and Family Medicine. She is also an honorary senior research fellow at the School of Social Policy, College of Social Sciences, University of Birmingham, United Kingdom, and an honorary research fellow at Aston University, Birmingham, United Kingdom.

— **Malta**

Vincent Cassar, BA (Hons), MSc (Wales), PhD (Lond), CPsychol (UK), CSci (UK), is a chartered organizational psychologist with the British Psychological Society and a chartered scientist with the British Science Council. Vince is Senior Lecturer in the Department of Management (University of Malta) and Honorary Teaching Fellow at Birkbeck College (University of London). He has worked in the past with HFI (London), Sirota Inc (United States/United Kingdom), as a self-employed consultant and as a Talent Management Consultant at P5+ (EMD). His current research interests include psychological contract, occupational health and stress, and EBMgt. He has presented and published his studies in several peer-reviewed journals such as *Work & Stress*, *Journal of Managerial Psychology*, and *Journal of Vocational Behaviour* to name a few. He also acts as a reviewer for several peer-reviewed journals such as *Human Relations*, *Journal of Business Psychology*, and American Academy of Management's OB and Entrepreneurship section, and is a member of several international professional bodies. He is a member of the editorial board of the *European Journal of Economics and Management*. He was President of the Malta Association of Work and Organizational Psychology between 2011 and 2013 and Deputy Chair of MCAST between 2013 and 2014. He is currently a director on the Board of IPS Ltd and a member of the Senior Appointments Advisory Committee (OPM).

— **Malta**

Ali Ghuname, BSc (Hons), MSc (UK), is founder, vice chairman, and board of director in Al Dar University College. He is a health and informatics researcher, senior and leader in education development and organization of higher education sector since 1990. His research interests focus on smart solutions in E-Systems engineering and agile solutions and development. Mr Ghuname is a member of the IEEE and the British Computer Society (BCS). He has extensive leadership experience in quality assurance and assessment in a higher education environment, accreditation, improvement, and restructuring. Additionally, Mr Ghuname has experience in the field of curriculum development in information technology and business. He is part of the steering committee of the International Conference Series on Developments in eSystems Engineering DeSE (www.dese.org.uk) since 2011, and is the Local Organizing Chair Middle East for the 2015 conference in Dubai.

— **UAE**

CHAPTER 10

Yvonne O'Connor is an information systems postdoctoral researcher on the FP7 Supporting LIFE project within the Health Information Systems Research Center (HISRC), Business Information Systems at University College Cork, Ireland. The Supporting LIFE project explores the potential of mobile health use in developing countries by community health workers. In particular, her research focuses on (a) community health workers' decision-making processes and (b) health-related outcomes associated with a decision support system, namely, electronic community case management. She has published in a number of national and international journals and conferences. Outside of research, Yvonne is currently lead user interface (UI) analyst for the Supporting LIFE project. This work involves prototyping and designing graphic UIs for both the Supporting LIFE application and website. Yvonne received a first-class BSc (Hons) (2008) and a PhD (2013) in Business Information Systems, both from University College Cork, Ireland.

— **Ireland**

Siobhan O'Connor is a lecturer in adult nursing at the University of Manchester, United Kingdom. She received her BSc Nursing (2009—2013) and BSc Business Information Systems (2000—2004) from University College Cork, Ireland. Her multidisciplinary background led her to undertake doctoral studies in primary care informatics at the University of Glasgow (2014—2017). She has published in a number of national and international journals and conference proceedings in the nursing informatics and eHealth field. Her research interests focus on the use of mobile solutions to support patients and front-line health professionals in community settings for disease management, self-management, and education and training. She is currently working on an Innovate UK—funded program, Delivering Assisted Living Lifestyles at Scale, exploring the digital health engagement process.

— **UK**

Ciara Heavin is a college lecturer and a senior researcher in Business Information Systems and codirector of the BSc Business Information Systems, University College Cork, Ireland. She lectures systems analysis and design, web development (HTML 5.0, CSS, JavaScript, and PHP), data modeling, database development and opportunity assessment, and recognition in high-technology firms. Research interests include the development of ICT industries, primarily focusing on Ireland's software industry, specifically investigating knowledge management (KM) in software SMEs. More recently, she has undertaken funded research in the investigation, development, and implementation of innovative technology solutions in health care systems. Reviewer for a number of top journals and conferences and a member of three conference organizing committees, Ciara is managing editor of the *Journal of Decision Systems* since November 2011.

— **Ireland**

Joe Gallagher is a Clinical Lecturer in Medicine at the University College Dublin (UCD) and clinical director of the Global Health Group. He received his medical degree from Trinity College Dublin and subsequently membership of the Royal College of Physicians in Ireland and Irish College of General Practitioners. He has worked in a rural clinic in Malawi and is involved in projects in Malawi, Zambia, and Uganda. He is also an investigator in the Chronic Cardiovascular Disease Management Group in UCD. He has published in a number of national/international journals and conference proceedings in the area of cardiovascular disease, primary care, and mHealth for both developed and developing countries and is a reviewer for a number of international journals. His main research areas include primary care, health system design, heart failure prevention, rheumatic heart disease, and acute childhood illness.

— **Ireland**

John O'Donoghue is a senior lecturer in eHealth at Imperial College London and Deputy Director of its Global eHealth Unit. He is also the eHealth principal investigator within the Global Health Research Group at University College Dublin. He received his BSc in Computer Science and a research MSc in Real-Time Systems and Simulation from the Department of Mathematics and Computing, Cork Institute of Technology, Ireland, and a PhD from the Department of Computer Science at University College Cork, Ireland. He has published in a number of national/ international journals and conference proceedings in the area of eHealth and mHealth for both developed and developing countries. His main research areas include pervasive data management, quality of data, health informatics, and medical based information systems. He was the recipient the Massachusetts Institute of Technology (MIT) Ballou/Pazer DQ/IQ award, which recognizes a body of research that demonstrates a significant contribution to the field of Information Quality (IQ).

— **UK**

CHAPTER 11

Ayodele Lasisi is presently a doctoral degree candidate at the Faculty of Computer Science and Information Technology, Universiti Tun Hussein Onn Malaysia (UTHM). He holds an MSc degree with distinctions at International Islamic University Malaysia (IIUM) with specialization in Computer Networking & Linux Administration. He completed his BSc (Hons) degree in Computer Science from Babcock University (BU) in Nigeria. His research interests include computer security, artificial immune system and artificial intelligence, data communications and networking, data mining, and data classification. He has published in international journals and conference proceedings and has served in various capacities at international conferences. He is also a member of the Nigerian Computer Society (NCS) and Nigerian Institute of Management (NIM).

— **Malaysia**

Rozaida Ghazali is currently an associate professor at the Faculty of Computer Science and Information Technology, Universiti Tun Hussein Onn Malaysia (UTHM). She graduated with a PhD degree from the School of Computing and Mathematical Sciences at Liverpool John Moores University, United Kingdom, in 2007, on the topic of Higher Order Neural Networks for Financial Time series Prediction. Earlier in 2003, she completed her MSc degree in Computer Science from Universiti Teknologi Malaysia (UTM). She received her BSc (Hons) degree in Computer Science from Universiti Sains Malaysia (USM) in 1997. In 2001, Rozaida joined the academic staff in UTHM. Her research area includes neural networks, swarm intelligent, fuzzy logic, optimization, data mining, time series prediction, and data classification. She has successfully supervised a number of PhD and master's students and published more than 90 articles in various international journals and conference proceedings. She acts as a reviewer for various journals and conferences. She has also served as a conference chair and as a program committee member for numerous international conferences.

— **Malaysia**

Tutut Herawan received his PhD in computer science in 2010 from Universiti Tun Hussein Onn Malaysia. He is currently a senior lecturer at the Department of Information System, University of Malaya. His research area includes rough and soft set theory, DMKDD, and decision support in information system. He has successfully co-supervised two PhD students and published more than 200 articles in various international journals and conference proceedings. He is on the editorial board and acts as a reviewer for various journals. He has also served as a program committee member and co-organizer for numerous international conferences/workshops.

— **Malaysia**

CHAPTER 12

Yu-Chuan Liu was born in 1965 and received his PhD from the Institute of Astronautics and Aeronautics, National Cheng-Hung University, Taiwan, in 1993. He has served as R&D engineer and manager in machinery and liquid crystal display industries. Most of his experiences were focused on computer-integrated manufacturing and management information systems. Dr. Liu joined the faculty of Department of Information Management, Tainan University of Technology, Taiwan, since 2002. He is interested in the research topics of e-business for industry, production management and operation research, and ICT applications in agriculture, and the research results include several patents on the agro-product traceability system and research projects from government and industries with a total budget over US$700,000. Results of the mobile traceability data construction system of this chapter has won the silver prize of the 2012 National Invention and Creation Award in Taiwan and the golden prize of the 2014 Taipei International Invention Show and Technomart Invention Contest.

— **Taiwan**

Hong-Mei Gao was born in 1968 and received her PhD from the College of Economics and Management, Northeast Forestry University, China, in 2007. Prof. Gao has been a faculty member of the Department of Logistics Management and Engineering, Tianjin Agricultural University, China, since 2007. Her research interests include logistics for agro-product, warehouse and distribution management, and planning and management for logistic center. Prof. Gao has won the second prize for the 2011 Tianjin education achievement and first prize of the 2010 Tianjin R&D achievement. She is also the project coordinator of the 2013 national spark program for the traceability of the agro-product supply chain of the Ministry of Science and Technology of PRC, and the 2013 program of the Tianjin Municipal Science and Technology Commission for the smart food safety system development.

— **China**

CHAPTER 13

Nonso Nnamoko achieved a BEng (Hons) in Electrical and Electronic Engineering from Enugu State University of Science and Technology, Nigeria, in 2003. This was followed by five years' industrial experience and career development in various organizations, most notably Freeway Computers UK, where he worked as a computer technician. This was followed with an MSc in Computing and Information Systems from Liverpool John Moores University in 2010. Currently he is nearing completion of a PhD in the area of Artificial Intelligence in Healthcare also at Liverpool John Moores University.

— **UK**

Farath Arshad graduated as one of the first eight psycholinguists in the country in 1984 from Essex University. This was followed with an MSc in Cognition, Computing and Psychology from University of Warwick, and a PhD in the area of computing and its applications in education from Leeds University in 1990. Subsequently, upon completion of a research fellowship at Leeds, she spent some time in The Netherlands working for a government research center in applications of artificial intelligence, in information and communication technologies, medicine, and human—computer interface. Following a career break, Farath returned to academia at LJMU and helped establish CHaSCI. She headed this multifaculty center, which coordinates informatics research within health and social care, until March 2015. Additionally, Farath is a non-executive director and deputy chair of Warrington NHS Primary Care Trust (WPCT) Board.

— **UK**

Lisa Hammond achieved a BA (Hons) in Community Care, followed by an MSc in Adult nursing from Liverpool University between 1984 and 1989. Lisa worked as the clinical lead for integrated care within Liverpool Community Health for two years before taking her present position as program manager for discharge at Aintree University Hospital.

— **UK**

Sam McPartland is the transformational change manager and is part of the IMerseyside Team working on the MI program. Sam has been actively working with

Philips and Health Care Gateway to provide development of Integrated Community and GP Systems with Telehealth. This has involved working with key stakeholders such as community matrons and general practitioners to process map the requirements of use cases that would facilitate existing communication flows to enable technology developments in support of this process.

— **UK**

Patricia Patterson worked in various departments within the NHS, most notably within Liverpool Community Health as a matron at Everton Road. She retired in July 2012 after an incredible 44 years in the NHS.

— **UK**

CHAPTER 14

Habib Shah is assistant professor of the Department of Computer and Information Systems at Islamic University of Madinah Munawarah, Kingdom of Saudi Arabia. During 2014—2015, he was an Assistant Professor at the Department of Computer Science and Information Technology, University of Malakand, KPK, Pakistan. Prior to coming to Johor, he was a part-time lecturer at the University Tun Hussein Onn Malaysia (UTHM). From 2010 to 2014, he worked at Graduate Research Assistant in UTHM, Malaysia. He received a BSc from the University of Malakand in 2005, and a Master in Computer Science from the Federal Urdu University of Arts Science and Technology, Karachi, Pakistan. He received his PhD in Information Technology from the UTHM, Malaysia, in 2014. His research interests include soft computing, data mining, artificial neural networks, learning algorithms, swarm intelligence, classification, time series prediction, clustering, as well as numerical function optimizations. He has more than 20 publications in international journals and outstanding conferences.

— **Saudi Arabia**

Rozaida Ghazali is currently an associate professor at the Faculty of Computer Science and Information Technology, Universiti Tun Hussein Onn Malaysia (UTHM). She graduated with a PhD degree from the School of Computing and Mathematical Sciences at Liverpool John Moores University, United Kingdom, in 2007, on the topic of Higher Order Neural Networks for Financial Time series Prediction. Earlier in 2003, she completed her MSc degree in Computer Science from Universiti Teknologi Malaysia (UTM). She received her BSc (Hons) degree in Computer Science from Universiti Sains Malaysia (USM) in 1997. In 2001, Rozaida joined the academic staff in UTHM. Her research area includes neural networks, swarm intelligent, fuzzy logic, optimization, data mining, time series prediction, and data classification. She has successfully supervised a number of PhD and master's students and published more than 90 articles in various international journals and conference proceedings. She acts as a reviewer for various journals and conferences. She has also served as a conference chair and as a program committee member for numerous international conferences.

— **Malaysia**

Tutut Herawan received his PhD in computer science in 2010 from Universiti Tun Hussein Onn Malaysia. He is currently a senior lecturer at the Department of Information System, University of Malaya. His research area includes rough and soft set theory, DMKDD, and decision support in information system. He has successfully co-supervised two PhD students and published more than 200 articles in various international journals and conference proceedings. He is on the editorial board and acts as a reviewer for various journals. He has also served as a program committee member and co-organizer for numerous international conferences/workshops.

— **Malaysia**

Sami ur Rahman is Head of the Department of Computer Science at University of Malakand. He got his PhD degree in Medical Imaging from the University of Technology Darmstadt, Germany, in 2012. His research interests are image processing, medical imaging, and education visualization.

— **Pakistan**

Nawsher Khan is an Assistant Professor at Department of Computer Science, Abdul Wali Khan University Mardan, KPK, Pakistan. He was a Post-Doctoral Research Fellow at the University of Malaya, Kuala Lumpur, Malaysia, in 2014. He got his doctoral degree from the University Malaysia Pahang (UMP) Malaysia in 2013. He published more than 25 articles in various international journals and conference proceedings during his PhD and postdoctoral programs. He received his bachelor's degree in computer science from the University of Peshawar, Pakistan, and master's degree in computer science from Hazara University, Pakistan. Since 1999, he has worked in various educational institutions. In 2005, he was appointed in NADRA (National Database and Registration Authority) under the Interior Ministry of Pakistan and in 2008 has worked in (NHA) National Highways Authority.

— **Pakistan**

Acknowledgment

Thank-you to the many individuals without whose contribution and support this book would not have been possible. The Editors would like to offer their sincere gratitude to the chapters' authors for contributing their time and expertise to this book. We also wish to acknowledge the valuable contributions of the reviewers toward improving the quality, coherence, and presentation of the book chapters.

We would like to thank those who offered support, for the insightful discussions we had, and their assistance in writing, editing, and proofreading the chapters. Above all, we want to thank our families for their support and encouragement through the duration of the book's preparation and thank them for their patience and understanding while we worked to meet deadlines.

We would also like to thank Ms Áine MacDermott for helping us compose the final manuscript through proofreading, editing, and organizing the book chapters, and for the great support she provided throughout.

Introduction

Applied Computing is the practice of embedding the realization of Computer Science's latest technological advancements into industrial, business, and scientific intelligent solutions. Applied Computing stretches to a variety of computing fields, requiring an extensive knowledge of the specialized subject area and in many cases large teams of trained individuals to put into production. Artificial Intelligence (AI) is considered as one of the major fields of Applied Computing. AI has been introduced as an important tool in the implementation of Health and Medicine—centered solutions as real-world applications.

Within Heath and Medicine, the research into AI techniques has emerged significantly for clinical decision-making purposes. Clinical decision support systems that are based on intelligent techniques are increasingly used in the health care industry. These systems are intended to help physicians in their diagnostic procedures, making decisions more accurate and effective, minimizing medical errors, improving patient safety, and reducing costs. This book introduces different methods and techniques for clinical decision support systems with the aim of identifying a basic criterion for adequate use of intelligent techniques within such systems.

TECHNOLOGY IN HEALTH

Medicine is a discipline where the reliance on its professionals for help and support is of no equivalence. With the advancement of technology and the rapid growth of medical knowledge in research and development, the expectations of individuals and the community for the highest quality of health care has increased exponentially. This has challenged doctors and medical practitioners who now have limited time to dedicate to each patient, while in the meantime need to engage in the latest developments in their own specialization.

Traditionally, medical decisions have been determined mainly based on the physician's unaided memory as well as rapid judgments of the patient's symptoms and conditions. This has required doctors and physicians to keep up-to-date with the latest research and literature to ensure that they investigate medical cases with up-to-date knowledge.

Medical professional bodies and health care providers have established a realization for the need to develop their own professional training courses and recertification procedures for the purpose of ensuring that doctors have the ability to memorize the most relevant knowledge. However, fundamental limitations of human memory and recall mechanisms, coupled with the exponential growth in knowledge, meant that most of what is known could not be memorized by most individuals.

As such, an opportunity has been presented in developing computer tools and systems to assist in storing and retrieving the appropriate medical knowledge needed by the practitioners and professionals in dealing with some challenging conditions. These systems can also be used and utilized by the professionals to assist in diagnostic decisions and therapeutic and decision-making techniques.

The potential for computing techniques, methods, and tools to support clinicians and health care professionals with assistance, expert advice, and critical decision making was predicted more than four decades ago. Despite decades of research in this field, computer applications, intelligent computer applications, and computer decision support systems receive limited use in health care systems. The various reasons include usability, lack of technology and tools, and problems in integrating such tools with the demanding work that health care institutions provide.

Current advances in technology are providing and making it possible for researchers to develop intelligent applications or refine methods, techniques, and algorithms to develop sophisticated computer applications in various medical fields. In addition, studies show that computer applications and specifically intelligent systems in the field of health and medicine has now become a fast-developing research area that is combining sophisticated computing methods with the insights of expert medical consultants to produce better application tools for refining today's health care systems. These developments are attributing to better health care provision, as well as lowering the cost of health care, which is a major concern in many European countries and the United States. With the rapid development of new technology, data is becoming available immediately, as a result, pressuring clinicians to keep up with the newest developments in their field. Coupled with time constraints, this can lead clinicians and medical staff to take rapid decisions for diagnosing patients, which could consequently lead to misdiagnoses and unnecessary treatments.

ARTIFICIAL INTELLIGENCE IN MEDICAL DIAGNOSIS

Research shows that AI has contributed significantly in the evolution of biomedicine and medical informatics. With the advent of the latest computing technologies and tools, the complexity for developing medical diagnostic systems to act as decision support has increased. This is due to the various tools AI provides that could be used extensively in medical diagnosis to classify, learn, adapt, and modify data sets. These techniques include fuzzy logic, case-based reasoning, artificial neural network (ANN), genetic algorithms, principal components analysis (PCA), and Bayesian networks.

In medical diagnosis, recent work applied fuzzy logic to diagnose pediatric asthma, breast cancer, coronary heart disease, thyroid, diabetes, and ovarian cancer. Case-based reasoning was used for liver disease diagnosis while artificial neural networks were implemented to diagnose heart valve diseases. Expert Systems (ES) are used to diagnose breast cancer, detect lesions in mammograms, and to determine iron deficiency anaemia in women. ES were also developed to diagnose epilepsy from ECG signals, to diagnose and classify dengue patients and in lung cancer diagnosis. Other research shows the implementation of Bayesian networks to discover the human immunodeficiency virus and to predict accurately coronary artery disease. In addition, work presenting a combination of genetic algorithms with other AI techniques to diagnose lung cancer and liver disease is also apparent.

Different AI techniques are applied to diagnose different medical conditions. In literature, it is also evident that AI techniques are used in particular diseases, such as the case to diagnose breast cancer. An interesting finding is that in many medical cases, researchers have utilized more than one AI technique to accomplish their diagnosis. Researchers may use a particular AI technique in their intelligent system to classify a general medical condition while adding another additional technique to accurately predict the diagnosis. Current literature also shows applications of modified or tailored AI techniques to diagnose medical health conditions while in other cases researchers tried to find more accurate intelligent computational methods such as artificial immune systems in addition with other techniques to classify and predict the health condition.

The latest research shows successful diagnosis of diverse medical conditions with the use of different AI computational methods and paradigms. It is clearly evident that the field of medical science is showing an increase in the number of intelligent systems being developed that learn from new cases while in operation. These learning intelligent machines are used to assist clinicians and medical staff to diagnose more precisely their patients' health conditions. As researchers continue to develop these intelligent methods and techniques, computer applications in medicine will only intensify, get more complex, and perform accurate diagnosis.

THE IMPORTANCE OF DATA ANALYTICS

The careful collection and recording of evidence relating to patients and their illnesses has been an important and critical issue for many years. In recent years, many research groups, health care organizations, and health societies have started to collect large quantities of data about wellness and illness in different ways and forms, for example, data-centric health care. It is possible with the advances in applied computing to enable physicians to provide the best that is possible for their patients with realistic use of resources and reduction in cost, while enhancing the quality of health care.

Critical investment in translating key methods and insights into working systems is required to enable this vision of true evidence-based health care. This is in addition to the realization that key conception opportunities require advances in core computer science research and engineering. The promise to enhance the quality and effectiveness of health care to enhance the quality and longevity of life can be realized by the collection and systematic analysis of data collected on health and illness. This practice would provide new insights on wellness and illness that can be operationalized.

Automation and provision of decision support for accurate triage and diagnosis can be realized within the pipeline of data, to prediction, to action, to generating well-calibrated predictions about health outcomes, to produce effective plans for chronic disease management, and to formulate and evaluate larger-scale health care policies. Data can be transformed into predictive models by utilizing data-centric methods. Forecasts with well-characterized accuracies about the future or diagnoses about states of a patient that we cannot inspect directly can be generated using predictive models. Procedures can harness such forecasts or diagnoses to generate recommendations for actions in the world, and decisions about when it is best to collect more information about a situation before acting, considering the costs and time delays associated with collecting more information to enhance a decision.

Clinical and biomedical discovery is dependent on the collection and systematic analysis of large quantities of data. Methods for learning from data can provide the foundations for new directions in the clinical sciences via tools and analysis that identify subtle but important signals in the fusing of clinical, behavioral, environmental, genetic, and epigenetic data.

Building insights via analysis and visualizations can be enabled by computational procedures, which can only play an active role in framing and designing clinical studies, and in the proposal and confirmation of biomedical hypotheses. Especially, within such methods as those that identify statistical associations among events or observations and help to confirm causal relationships. The cost-effective optimization of health care delivery has many gains, and even more value can come by enabling fundamental scientific breakthroughs in biomedicine.

DECISION SUPPORT SYSTEM (DSS)

A decision support system (DSS) is an indispensable component in many different sectors. It is an interactive computerized system that enables decision makers to compile and examine the relevant information in order to provide a proper and reliable foundation for underpinning decision making. The decision support system in general terms may cover a variety of systems that aid decision making, including very simplified software systems and sophisticated knowledge based on AI systems. The clinical decisions taken by health care professionals are usually mainly dependent upon intelligent data analytics, clinical guidance, medical evidence, instructions, and principles derived from medical science. Clinical decision support systems (CDSS) would improve the use of knowledge for supporting decision making and therefore enhance the quality of health care service being delivered to the patient.

The advance of intelligent data-driven methods for informed health care decision making will also help support professionals to make informed decisions from current best-practice knowledge bases. In general, CDSS purpose would be used to review and convert the clinical input into a type of information using numerical and logical techniques. This would aid doctors and nurses in making diagnosis and treatment decisions. CDSS use is not yet widespread in hospitals and clinics; however, they have the potential to improve storing and retrieval of medical records, analysis of patient history for many purposes, including diagnosis, evaluation of real-time information collected from the monitors, use of medicines together with the treatment plan, and handling large amount of information and knowledge.

AI techniques have recently seen an increased trend in utilization within the field of CDSS. This is in an effort to enhance the accuracy and effectiveness of disease diagnosis and consequently prevent or at least minimize medical errors. Many studies have shown the effectiveness of applying AI within CDSS, where the intelligent agent as presented in the literature is one of the main components in the information architecture of a CDSS. Many researchers have considered the intelligence module as a fundamental part of CDSS and that the adoption of a CDSS with an embedded intelligence module would have the ability to learn over time. Research has shown that adopting AI within CDSS would support a considerable scope of decision making, particularly the decisions blanketed by uncertainty. It would also manage domains where the decision procedures tend to be more complicated and need specialist knowledge as well as evaluate the consequences of the proposed solution.

A system that combines clinical decision support systems with intelligent techniques would exceed the traditional CDSS and have many necessary characteristics, including an improved and supported decision-making process through enhanced outlook on intelligent behavioral patterns and an increased ability to learn and create new clinical knowledge.

The techniques implemented by systems based on intelligence strategies can either be a single technique that deals with certain problems or utilization of a combination of two or more techniques to tackle complex problems that involve a level of uncertainty and ambiguity. The challenge would be in the adaptation of suitable criteria for the adequate use of intelligent techniques. As such, a revision of current trends become necessary to define a general guideline that deals with issues relating to the evaluation of intelligent CDSSs. This is particularly through the provision of a basic guideline that assists the system designer in making an optimal selection between the various intelligence techniques to be applied within CDSS.

WHY THIS BOOK

This novel and unique book brings together specialists, researchers, and practitioners from the field of computer science, software engineering and medicine to present their ideas, research, findings, and principles of different tools and techniques in the development of advanced systems to support health care and medical practitioners for health-related decision making. The book is composed of 14 chapters, each chapter written by authors specialized in those critical fields. The foundation of the book is complemented by research collaborations established by the Applied Computer Research Group (ACRG) of Liverpool John Moores University (LJMU), international researchers in the field, and international medical practitioners. The book is also supported by a series of international conferences in the development of e-systems engineering, which is the vehicle of delivering the outcome of cutting-edge research in this crucial area of Applied Health Informatics.

It is very critical to realize that the time is just right for this book to be compiled and published. Health authorities are cutting costs, treatments and medicines are becoming increasingly expensive, and waiting times for procedures and referrals are all escalating. We need to seriously ask ourselves, Why? The answer is not just down to the volume and lack of specialists but more importantly incorrect diagnosis and lack of supporting information. Statistics for misdiagnosis is frightening; patients are seeking second opinions, even traveling to another country for consultations and advice. Although medical research is advancing at a rapid rate, governments and budgets are not. Therefore, it is evident that there is a vital requirement for developing systems that can support health care and streamline the health care process.

This book can be used as a reference to help understand the theories that underpin intelligent systems to support health and medicine. The reliance on the knowledge of human experts to build expert computer programs is helpful for several reasons: the decisions and recommendations of a program can be explained to its users and evaluators in terms that are familiar to the experts; additionally, as we hope to duplicate the expertise of human specialists, and in this case for health and medical disciplines, we can measure the extent to which our goal is achieved by a direct comparison of the output behavior to that of the human experts.

To summarize, these are the direct benefits of this book to the reader:

- Developers and researchers can use the book in the process of developing expert computer systems that can be used for clinical proposes. This should allow the possibility of providing an inexpensive dissemination of the best medical expertise to geographical regions where that expertise is lacking. This should allow a consultation to be made to nonspecialists who are not within easy reach of expert medical consultants.
- The book should allow physicians and researchers to enhance their understanding and knowledge and enable researchers to put together the latest medical expertise within their field, giving them a systematic structure for teaching their expertise to students and researchers in this field.
- It should also allow us to test applied computing theories and techniques in a real-world domain and to use that domain to suggest novel solutions for further applied computing research within health care applications.

This book is aimed at practitioners and academics whose interest is in the latest developments in applied computing and intelligent systems concepts, strategies, practices, tools, and technologies.

THE ORGANIZATION OF THE BOOK

This book is intended as a comprehensive presentation of ongoing investigations and analysis of current challenges and advances related to Applied Computing by focusing on a particular class of applications: AI methods and techniques in Health and Medicine. The book aims to cover different chapters by different authors from a wide variety of interdisciplinary perspectives concerning the theory and practice of Applied Computing in medicine, human biology, and health care. Particular attention is given to; AI-based clinical decision making, medical knowledge engineering, knowledge-based systems in medical education and research, intelligent medical information systems, intelligent databases, intelligent devices and instruments, medical AI tools, reasoning and metareasoning in medicine, and methodological, philosophical, ethical, and intelligent medical data analysis.

Chapter One presents a framework for the early diagnosis of neurodegenerative diseases (NDDs) using signal processing and signal classification techniques. The problem with NDDs is that they are incurable, hard to detect at an earlier stage because of non-obvious symptoms, and also hard to discriminate at a later stage because of pattern similarities of different NDDs. This work has highlighted the importance of machine learning and signal processing in the early diagnosis of life-threatening diseases such as Alzheimer's, Parkinson's, Huntington's, and ALS. In this chapter, the issues with the early diagnosis of NDDs and also with their possible solutions are presented. The analysis and classification of gait signals is presented using a set of well-known classifiers; linear, nonlinear, and Bayes. Results are presented from various dimensions using more than one performance evaluation technique. In addition, a novel combination of classifiers to improve the accuracy is proposed and demonstrated. The work has presented novel and significant findings that can be used in clinical practices for the early diagnosis of NDDs.

Chapter Two starts by defining wearable technology for lifelogging, which provides an ideal platform for the identification and quantification of negative emotion. Making these data available can be used to encourage reflective thought and facilitate the development of protective coping strategies. This type of technology permits the user to capture multimodal data sources pertaining to everyday behavior. This chapter also explores how lifelogging technologies can be used to monitor the physiological process of inflammation that is associated with negative emotion and deleterious consequences for long-term health. These technologies furnish the user with a platform for self-reflection, enhanced awareness, and the formulation of coping strategies. Development of this technology faces a number of significant challenges, including (1) obtaining measures that are clinically relevant, (2) capturing the context of an event to enable sufficient self-reflection, and (3) designing user interfaces that deliver insight without creating health anxiety or hypochondria. This chapter explores these challenges in detail and offers guidance on the design of a lifelogging technology that promotes effective self-reflection and protective coping.

Chapter Three provides a detailed description of various feature selection algorithms that are suited for gene selection in microarray data. Microarray is the array of DNA molecules that permit many hybridization experiments to be performed in parallel. Both supervised and unsupervised feature selection methods are described in detail. The pros and cons of using supervised versus unsupervised feature selection methods have been illustrated using benchmark micro array data sets. In the category of supervised feature selection algorithms, both filter and wrapper approaches have been dealt with. This chapter presents detailed simulation for each of the filter-based feature selection algorithms (using fivefold cross-validation) on benchmark micro array data sets. Performance of different filter-based feature selection algorithms are also demonstrated on top-ranking genes.

Chapter Four proposes a new and novel approach to correct intensity inhomogeneity in MRI images of the brain. Anatomic structural map, an equivalent of digital brain atlas, guides the algorithm for automatic operation. The structural map is generated directly from the test image. Accurate information from the structural map is combined with distorted intensity-level attributes of the test image to detect outliers in regions of interest (ROIs) generated by K-means clustering. The number of ROIs is the number of tissue classes specified by the user in K-means clustering. Outliers in each ROI are merged with voxels in the appropriate tissue class. Intensity levels of the new set of voxels in each tissue class are rescaled to conform to intensity levels of uncorrupted voxels. A review of current bias field correction strategies is presented by explaining their design techniques, importance, and limitations, respectively. The methodology of the proposed approached is conveyed. Additionally, results of testing the proposal on real magnetic resonance images are displayed, followed by a discussion of the results and concluding remarks.

Chapter Five describes the opportunities and challenges that the method of leveraging Big Data and pervasive analytics for elderly care presents. It is argued that though potentially viable as an approach to raise elderly care to a level where the uniqueness of each elderly person is adequately recognized, it does pose enormous social, ethical, and technical challenges that research cannot afford to ignore. A review of the research challenges in personalized services for elderly care is provided, in addition to an overview of the state-of-the-art and future challenges in the area of Big Data analytics for elderly care. Based on the discussion, ACTVAGE, a lifestyle-oriented context-aware framework for supporting personalized elderly care and independent living, is proposed. The framework combines systematic capture of past lifestyles and knowledge of current activities and user context, and applies rigorous analytics to build a complete picture of the elderly person's lifestyle and needs. A formal representation of the lifestyle concept is built for system design. Based on the representation, required services, including social networking, self-diagnosis and monitoring, advisory, entertainment, exercise and dietary, reminder and local events services, are developed to offer individually tailored and lifestyle-oriented support for active ageing and independent living.

Chapter Six provides a comprehensive discussion of intrapartum hypoxia and presents relevant literature in the area. Uterine contractions produced during labor have the potential to damage a fetus by diminishing the maternal blood flow to the placenta, which can result in fetal hypoxia. In order to observe this phenomenon in practice, labor and delivery are routinely monitored using cardiotocography monitors. The cardiotocography recordings are used by obstetricians to help diagnose fetal hypoxia. However, cardiotocography capture and interpretation is time consuming and subjective, often leading to misclassification that result in damage to the fetus and unnecessary caesarean sections. Therefore, correct classification is dependent on qualified and experienced obstetric and midwifery staff and their understanding of the classification method used, which can be difficult. Alternatively, objective measures may help to mitigate the effects of misclassification. For example, automatic detection of correlates between uterine contractions and fetal heart rate can be used to reduce unnecessary medical interventions, such as hypoxia and caesarean section during the first stage of labor, and is instrumental in vaginal delivery in the second. The challenge is to develop predictive algorithms capable of detecting, with high accuracy, when a child is genuinely compromised before medical intervention is considered. This chapter can be considered as a work in progress that has mapped out a possible work plan for dealing with CTG data and how it might be used in a machine learning environment to predict normal and pathological records in the CTG-UHB data set.

Chapter Seven discusses the dynamical neural network architectures for the classification of medical data. Extensive research indicates that recurrent neural networks, such as the Elman network, generated significant improvements when used for pattern recognition in medical time-series data analysis and have obtained high accuracy in the classification of medical signals. The aim of this chapter is to provide a literature survey of various applications of dynamical neural networks in medical related problems. Medical signals recorded in various applications contain noise that could be the result of measurement error or due to the recording tools. Data preprocessing will be discussed in this chapter to extract the features and to remove the noises. A case study using the Elman, the Jordan, and Layer recurrent networks for the classifications of uterine electrohysterography signals for the prediction of term and preterm delivery for pregnant women are presented.

Chapter Eight imbues clinical decision support with such features as a consequence of a more formal approach to their definition, design, implementation, and testing. Accountability is maintained through a formally design audit process, whereas robustness of decision analysis and system operation is autonomously handled by the system itself. This is extremely important in mobile decision support use by clinicians and in increasing confidence in the use of such systems. It can be noted, from the foregoing discussion, that there are (at least) two separate concerns to be handled, namely, concerns of system operation governance, accountability, and robustness and concerns of decision process governance, accountability, and robustness. Traditionally such concerns would be divided and handled separately in the software development process. In this case, however, there are evidently many cross-cutting concerns that do not fit neatly into one or the other concern. In addition, in a mobile setting, the role of a decision support system is not limited to presenting data analysis; it may also present relevant documentation and online information or provide alerts using the Internet. This chapter proposes, analyses, and assesses a formal representation and reasoning technique for mobile medical decision support systems that handles the separate and cross-cutting concerns of the systems by using a formal calculus of first order logic. The work is evaluated using a Breast Cancer prognosis system previously developed with health care professionals.

Chapter Nine provides and highlights the importance of using mobile technologies in health care management. In addition, the chapter presents the current practices when managing patients diagnosed with hydrocephalus, a medical condition causing headaches. The development of a NeuroDiary application is discussed, which is currently being tested as a software mobile application for collecting data from patients with hydrocephalus. The second phase development of the NeuroDiary is conveyed by adding the intelligent capability to the system, for the purpose of assisting clinicians in the diagnosis, analysis, and treatment of hydrocephalus. The authors are in the process of developing an intelligent system, which will be accessible on Android, Windows, and Apple phones to reach a wider audience of users while at the same time providing a reliable solution that addresses the needs of hydrocephalus patient management.

Chapter Ten provides for the first time a detailed step-by-step breakdown of the implementation process for mobile health (mHealth) in developing countries. A vast array of research exists that focuses on barriers of mHealth adoption in such domains. However, the majority of these papers embrace the concept of adoption to cover the entire process of implementation. This chapter acknowledges that various phases of implementation exist. As a result, the researchers identify potential barriers for each phase of mHealth implementation in developing countries. By examining existing literature, this study reveals that various sociocultural and technological factors across individuals and organizations collectively can hinder mHealth implementation in developing regions. Existing research indicates that the focus of mHealth in these constituencies, a nascent area of research, places too much emphasis on the benefits associated with mHealth implementation.

Subsequently, this chapter endeavors to outline the barriers that should assist with overcoming common obstacles in the successful implementation of mHealth initiatives in developing countries.

Chapter Eleven presents different computer-aided algorithms channeled at disease diagnosis to solve the problems associated with the voluminous diseases reported and recorded. Although these algorithms have proven successful, the negative selection algorithm provides a new pathway to adequately distinguish disease-impaired patients from the healthy ones. The Variable Detector (V-Detector) by generating sets of detectors randomly with the aim of maximizing the coverage area of each detectors, is compared with Sequential Minimal Optimization (SMO), Multi-Layer Perceptron (MLP), and Non-Nested Generalized Exemplars (NNGE) on the detection of disease, and experimental results shows that the V-Detector generated the highest detection rates of 98.95% and 74.44% for Breast Cancer Wisconsin and BUPA Liver Disorder data sets, and also performed significantly with the Biomedical data at detection rate of 71.64%. Thus, the V-Detector can achieve the highest detection rate and lowest false alarm rates.

Chapter Twelve covers the application of IT for the food processing industry in the fields of smart packaging and materials, automation and control technology, standards and their application scenarios, and production management principles. Although some field data can be automatically acquired and transmitted by sensor networking, most agricultural activity information is recorded by manual handwriting for the traceability information systems. An end-to-end mobile application system that records the farming activities by using smart devices to capture information of farming operations is developed. The information for farming activities is coded in two-dimensional labels of Quick Response (QR) codes. By scanning the proper operation labels, the corresponding farming data can be captured and uploaded simultaneously to the back-end web server. The proposed mobile farming information can be implemented either as the mobile data collection tool for public traceability or a private traceability system. These two applications are verified through implementation projects in Tainan and Tianjin. The results showed that the mobile farming information can be successfully implemented. Food traceability can be more credible because of the reliability of collected farming data.

Chapter Thirteen describes and analyzes the process of incorporating a telehealth system that was proposed as part of a 6-month pilot research project within the NHS Liverpool UK. The proposed system was developed to offer remote management facility patients with Long Term Conditions (LTC). The implementation relied upon clinicians who otherwise operate a conventional care delivery method which is more hospital based. The study reflects the aim of the pilot study, which sought to strengthen the quality of primary care delivered to patients, but also to educate clinicians on the use of telehealth systems. In addition, the study provides detailed insight into user experience of the system. For both patients (including carers) and clinicians involved in the pilot project, a quantitative and qualitative exercise was carried out through paper-based questionnaire and one-to-one semi-structured interviews, respectively. The sources for this analysis include information from related research and documents from the funding institutions who worked closely with the researchers to structure and deliver the overall project.

Chapter Fourteen proposes two hybrid algorithms, namely GGABC and HGABC, for breast cancer classification tasks. The simulation results from the breast cancer data set demonstrate that the proposed algorithms are able to classify women's breast cancer disease with a high accuracy and efficiently from standard algorithms. Furthermore, the proposed GGABC and HGABC algorithms are successfully used to balance the high amount of exploration and exploitation process. Besides breast cancer classification, the proposed methods may also be used for breast cancer diagnosis and medical image processing. The two proposed bio-inspired learning algorithms are explained; the experimental setup and results for cancer prediction are also conveyed and discussed.

Early Diagnosis of Neurodegenerative Diseases from Gait Discrimination to Neural Synchronization

Shamaila Iram[1], Francois-Benoit Vialatte[2], Muhammad Irfan Qamar[3]

University of Salford, Greater Manchester, UK[1]; Laboratoire SIGMA, ESPCI ParisTech, Paris, France[2]; IBM Canada Ltd., Canada[3]

E-mail: S.Iram@salford.ac.uk, francois.vialatte@espci.fr, irfanqamar@gmail.com

INTRODUCTION

Advancements in machine learning provoke new challenges by integrating data mining with biomedical sciences in the area of computer science. This emergent research line provides a multidisciplinary approach to combine engineering, mathematical analysis, computational simulation, and neuro-computing to solve complex problems in medical science. One of the most significant applications of machine learning is data mining. Data mining provides a solution to find out the relationships between multiple features, ultimately improving the efficiency of systems and designs of the machines. Data-mining techniques provide computer-based information systems to find out data patterns, generate information for the hidden relationships, and discover knowledge that unveils significant findings that are not accessible by traditional computer-based systems.

Neurodegenerative diseases (NDDs) are accompanied by the deterioration of functional neurons in the central nervous system. These include Parkinson, Alzheimer, Huntington, and amyotrophic lateral sclerosis (ALS) among others. The progression of these diseases can be divided into three distinct stages: retrogenesis, cognitive impairment, and gait impairment. Retrogenesis is the initial stage of any NDD which starts with the malfunctioning of the cholinergic system of the basal forebrain that further extends to the entorhinal cortex and hippocampus [1]. During retrogenesis, the patient's memory is severely affected as a result of the accumulation of pathologic neurofibrillary plaques and tangles in the entorhinal cortex, hippocampus, caudate, and substantia nigra [2]. This stage is known as cognitive impairment. Finally, a patient cannot maintain his or her healthy, normal gait because of disturbances in the corticocortical and corticosubcortical connections in the brain, for example, frontal connection with parietal lobes and frontal lobes with the basal ganglia, respectively [3].

Early detection or diagnosis of life-threatening and irreversible diseases such as NDDs (Alzheimer, Parkinson, Huntington, and ALS) is an area of great interest for researchers from different academic backgrounds. Diagnosing NDDs at an earlier stage is hard, where symptoms are often dismissed as the normal consequences of aging. Moreover, the situation becomes more challenging where the symptoms or data patterns of different NDDs turn out to be similar, and discrimination among these diseases becomes as crucial as the treatment itself. In this chapter, we claim the significance of analyzing gait signals for discriminating movement disorders in different NDDs for accurate diagnosis and timely treatment of patients as well as an early diagnosis of these diseases using EEG signals.

One significant tool for the discrimination of different NDDs is gait signals. Hausdorff *et al.* [4] suggested that understanding the relationship between loss of motor neurons and perturbation in the stability of stride-to-stride dynamics can help us to monitor NDD progression and in assessing potential therapeutic interventions. Furthermore, they claimed a reduced stride-interval correlation with aging in Huntington disease. Later in 2010, the same gait signals were used by Yunfeng and Krishnan [5] to estimate the probability density functions (PDFs) of stride intervals and its two subphases for Parkinson disease. Moreover, Masood *et al.* used the same data set of gait signals for the discrimination of different NDDs [6].

The other important tool for early diagnosis and treatment of neurological and neurodegenerative diseases is the electroencephalographic (EEG) signals. Hans Berger was the first to measure EEG signals in humans, and even today the EEG is extensively used to evaluate neurological diseases [7]. The EEG signals originate from the cerebral cortex and evoked by auditory and somatosensory stimuli.

The goal here is to implement a data-mining approach with innovative ideas, using gait and EEG signals as a discriminative and diagnostic tool, to design a diagnostic and therapeutic system for early diagnosis of life-threatening diseases such as Alzheimer, Parkinson, Huntington, and ALS.

RESEARCH CHALLENGES

This section provides a detailed insight into the challenges and the problems that need to be looked into, from two different perspectives—challenges with the early diagnosis of NDDs and issues related to machine learning.

ISSUES WITH THE EARLY DIAGNOSIS OF NDDS

NDDs, especially Alzheimer disease (AD), are the most prevalent form of dementia, and according to statistics, 5%−10% of the population above the age of 65 years are affected by these diseases [8]. The clinical symptoms of the disease are characterized by progressive amnesia, linking it with the continuous and gradual loss of cognitive power and, finally, paralyzing the person by affecting the motor neurons. NDDs triggered by the deterioration of neuronal cells due to accumulation of neurofibrillary tangles and pathological proteins (such as α-synuclein, tau proteins, etc.) and also the senile plaques in corticocortical and corticosubcortical parts of the brain [2]. Because the occurrence of memory loss can be related to one of the aging factors, the ability to predict or diagnose a NDD turns out to be impossible at an earlier stage.

The loss of cognitive power is generally associated with a decrease of functional synchronization of different parts of the brain. Hence, loss of functional interaction between cortical areas could be considered a possible symptom of any NDD. Finding the synchronization in terms of coherence and correlation can possibly provide significant information in the early diagnosis of NDDs. However, the compactness of EEG signals due to various frequency bands makes this task less straightforward. Still more research is required to find out the exact role of each frequency band in the early diagnosis of these diseases.

ISSUES RELATED TO THE MACHINE LEARNING APPROACH

In the context of machine learning, data mining offers many challenges that need to be considered to get optimal results from a classifier. These factors can affect the mining process in terms of computation time, extraction and selection of appropriate features, and implementation of new approaches that can help us get the expected results. This section briefly states those challenges:

- **Skewed data sets:** Learning of a classifier from an imbalanced data set usually generates biased results. In this case, a classifier becomes more sensitive (highly trained) for the majority class and less sensitive (less trained) for the minority class. Ultimately, the results obtained from such classification make the situation more complicated, especially when the data are being processed from a real-time environment—biomedical, genetics, radar signals, intrusion detection, risk management, and credit card scoring [9].
- **Handling missing data:** There are many reasons behind missing entries in a data set. A damage in the remote sensor network, failure of gene microarray to yield gene expression, fingerprints, dust or manufacturing defects, and missing applicable tests while diagnosing patients, for example, can lead to missing entries in a data set, as described by Marlin [10]. Feature extraction and classification based on such data sets can lead to unreliable results. Problems of missing data should be investigated before starting a computation process.
- **Multiclass data sets:** The problem of skewed data sets becomes even more complicated when it comes to multiclass data sets. Practically speaking, in real-world environments, mostly the data sets come from a multiclass domain, for instance, protein fold classification [11]. These multiclass data sets pose new challenges as compared to simple two-class problems. Zhou et al. [12] argue that handling multiclass data sets is much harder than handling two-class problem domains. Jeopardizing the problem further, almost all classifier evaluation techniques are designed for two-class problems and happen to be unfit for multiclass problems.

- **Extraction and selection of relevant features:** The accuracy of a classifier is directly dependent on the variables that are provided for the classification. The analysis of gait as well as EEG signals and extraction of relevant information is not an easy task. Gait signals may be contaminated with other muscle movement signals or by the environmental data. Similarly, EEG signals may contain the signals of eye movements or externally generated signals (power line, electrode movement, etc.). In the presence of these artifacts, discrimination or classification leads to wrong results. This problem calls for pre-processing steps to get clean signals before classification. Once the signals are extracted, the next challenge is the selection of the most relevant features among others. This not only saves computation time but also reduces the complexity of the system.
- **Data Filtering:** Previous studies focus on the analysis of compact EEG signals without filtering them into narrow frequency bands. However, this lack of filtration does not provide optimal information about the frequency band, which is more important for detecting Alzheimer (or other NDDs) at its earlier stage.
- **Selection of a Classifier:** In the field of pattern recognition, the main focus is the successful classification of the features with the maximum possible accuracy rate. A classifier with a specific set of features may or may not be an appropriate option for another set of features. Moreover, different classification algorithms achieve varying degrees of success in different kinds of applications [13]. For this reason, selection of an appropriate classifier becomes a challenging task. Indeed, further research is needed to generalize the performance of the classifiers.

NEURODEGENERATIVE DISEASES

Neurodegenerative disease is an umbrella term used to describe medical conditions that directly affect the neurons within the brain [14]. These include Parkinson, Alzheimer, Huntington, and ALS. Patients with these kinds of disease experience cognitive decline over a long period, and symptoms include gait abnormalities, problems with speech, and memory loss due to progressive cognitive deterioration [15].

ALZHEIMER DISEASE

The changes in the brain that accompany these symptoms are the "tangles" and "plaque" of a toxic protein—amyloid beta (Aβ). These pathological neurofibrillary tangles accumulate in the entorhinal cortex and the hippocampus in the brain, areas that are responsible for the short- and long-term memory of a person [16]. Neuroscientists have reported that in order to keep memory alive, the communication between these two parts is very essential, and any hurdle between these two regions breaks the circuit and leads toward memory disturbance and eventually memory loss [2].

PARKINSON DISEASE

Parkinson disease is characterized by the dopaminergic deterioration process of the nerve cells of substantia nigra [17], a part of the brain responsible for the production of "dopamine"—a chemical that works as a neurotransmitter for controlling movements in different parts of the body. The degenerative process starts from the base of the brain, leading to the destruction of olfactory bulbs, followed by the lower brain stem and subsequently substantia nigra and midbrain [18]. Eventually, it destroys the limbic system and frontal neocortex, resulting in cognitive and psychiatric symptoms.

HUNTINGTON DISEASE

A specific part of the brain, PolyQ, has the Huntington gene with 11−34 repeated sections of glutamine—responsible for the production of cytoplasmic protein called Huntington. When the PolyQ region generates more sections of glutamine, a mutant Huntington protein is produced, which is the actual cause of Huntington disease [19]. This disease is an incurable hyperkinetic motor disorder. The primary symptoms of this disease are jerky and shaky movements, called chorea [20].

AMYOTROPHIC LATERAL SCLEROSIS

To date, it is believed that the actual cause of this disease is a mutant gene, superoxide dismutase 1 (*SOD1*), that affects the motor neurons of the brains. Moreover, toxicity in cerebrospinal fluid (CSF) is also considered a cause of neuron degeneration [21]. Motor neurons are the nerve cells that are responsible for voluntary movement of the muscles [22]. Weakness in arms and leg muscles is the initial symptom of ALS, which is followed by severe attacks to chest muscles, leaving patients unable to breathe [23].

CLASSIFICATION ALGORITHMS FOR NDDs

Several methods have been proposed and used for detection of NDDs. Most approaches focus on cognitive decline, biomarkers, and direct analysis of metabolites or genes [24]. However, in recent years, early detection and neuroimaging techniques [25], including genetic analysis, have been commonly used to detect potentially life-threatening diseases like cancer, cystic fibrosis, and neurologic diseases. Mini-Mental State Examination (MMSE) and symptom quantification are other well-known techniques commonly used to diagnose NDDs. Nonetheless, the use of computer algorithms and visualization techniques are considered fundamental to support the early detection process.

Although these approaches provide obvious benefits, current applications for classifying medical data still lack consistency in terms of revealing hidden significant information, especially from real-time clinical data. The main limitation with the approaches is that they only consider a small number of classifiers. Furthermore, many of them fail to include relevant and important features, such as age and gender, that can have a significant impact on results. Moreover, overall accuracy depends on a single set of variables, although other variables potentially could have greater impact on performance evaluation [26]. The approach posited here considers all well-established classification algorithms and uses a large-scale feature set. Each variable in the array has its own significant relationship with the progression of specific diseases. Moreover, rather than relying on base-level classifiers, a new strategy is described based on the fusion of classifiers. In this way, it will be possible to explore any new dimensions that may emerge from the results.

CLASSIFIER FUSION STRATEGY

The classifier fusion strategy incorporates several distinct processes—data gathering, feature extraction, and feature evaluation—as illustrated in Figure 1.1. Combining these processes provides a system for processing gait data to support the early detection of specific NDDs. Industry-led data sets with toolsets designed for processing large biomedical data are used to provide a solution for the early detection of NDDs that performs better than several well-known approaches. Using this unique configuration, new toolsets are provided for real-time symptomatic data analysis of NDDs to support diagnostic and treatment strategies.

Data Gathering and Data Preprocessing

In this study, gait data for healthy subjects and patients with Huntington, Parkinson, and ALS, extracted from Physionet[1] data sets, are used. The data sets contain data for 16 healthy control subjects (14 females, 2 males), 15 Huntington patients (9 females, 6 males), 15 Parkinson patients (5 females, 10 males), and 13 patients with ALS (3 females, 10 males). Patients with NDDs all have movement problems and are at the final stages of the disease.

As a preprocessing step, relevant features are extracted from integrated data. After completing this stage, all extracted features are meaningful and ready for classification. In this study, 3000 "motion vector" values for left and right foot strides of each subject were extracted over a 10-second period. The mean values obtained from the motion vectors are used to eliminate erroneously recorded data.

Imbalanced Data Sets and Resampling of Data

Learning from imbalanced data sets is an important and controversial topic, which is addressed in our research. These kinds of data sets usually generate biased results [27]. For instance, imagine a medical data set with 50 true negative values (majority class) and 20 true positive values (minority class). If half is selected for training and the remainder for testing (25 healthy and 10 sick persons), we find

---

[1]www.physionet.org

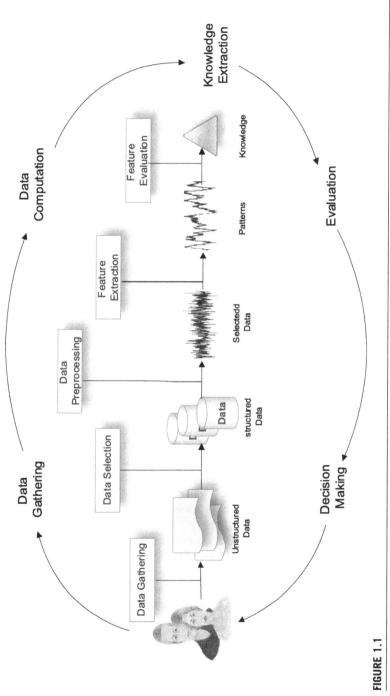

FIGURE 1.1

Data Mining Process.

that the accuracy is 90%. The result suggests that the classifier performs reasonably well. However, what happens is that when all the negative values are accurately identified (healthy persons) and only 5 of the 10 positive values (sick persons) are classified correctly. In this situation, the classifier is more sensitive to detecting the majority class patterns but less sensitive to detecting the minority class patterns. This is because the training data are imbalanced. In other words, the classifier concludes that 5 of the 10 unhealthy people are healthy when this is not the case. These kinds of results ultimately cause more destruction if the data come from real-time environments, such as biomedicine, genetics, radar signals, intrusion detection, risk management, and credit card scoring [9].

In order to solve the imbalanced data set problem, it is necessary to resample data sets. Different resampling techniques are available to achieve this, including undersampling and oversampling [28]. *Undersampling* is a technique wherein we reduce the number of patterns within the majority class data set to make it equivalent to other classes. In *oversampling*, more data are generated within the minority class. In this study, as a result of a short number of data sets for each class consequently, *oversampling* is adopted.

There are eight features in each class, which include signals for the right foot, signals for the left foot, age, height, weight, body mass index, time, and walking speed. For each variable, the minimum and maximum values are calculated. Then, random pseudo-numbers between these values are generated to produce 20 equal patterns for each class.

Feature Classification

The data set containing the eight features described in the previous section provides the feature sets required to diagnose NDDs accurately. More specifically, this data set is used to *select a classifier, train it, test it,* and finally *evaluate* the result to determine if the correct classification is performed.

The computation is directly proportional to the number of features considered in the data set. Figure 1.2 demonstrates a *scatter plot* using only three selected features and shows the complexity of classification of gait patterns for each subject. In this instance, Features 1 and 2 are associated with *right and left foot movement signals*, whereas Feature 3 represents *age*, which is considered an important factor in disease progression.

Using the defined feature set, several classifiers have been evaluated for consideration in the final classifier fusion strategy. The principal goal is to use classifiers that perform the best. The classifiers considered are the linear discriminant classifier (ldc), quadratic discriminant classifier (qdc), and the quadratic Bayes normal classifier (udc) for density-based classification. For linear classification, an additional four classifiers are selected, which are the logistic linear (loglc), Fisher's (fisherc), nearest means (nmc), and the polynomial (polyc). A linear classifier predicts the class labels based on a weighted linear combination of features or the predefined variables. The Parzen (parzenc), decision tree (treec), support vector machine (svc), and k-nearest neighbor (knnc) classifiers have been selected for nonlinear

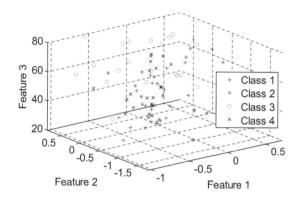

FIGURE 1.2

Dimensional Scatter Plot of Selected Features where Class 1, Class 2, Class 3, and Class 4 represent "healthy", "Huntington", "Parkinson" and "ALS", respectively.

classification of our data sets. The results produced by all 11 classifiers are illustrated in Figure 1.3.

The results illustrated in Figure 1.3 were evaluated using a confusion matrix table to determine the performance of each classifier. In this instance, the confusion matrix technique was used to determine the distribution of errors across all classes. The estimate of the classifier is calculated as the trace of the matrix divided by the total number of entries. Additional information that a confusion matrix provides is the point where misclassification occurs. This shows the true-positive, false-positive, true-negative, and false-negative values. Diagonal elements show the performance of the classifier, whereas off-diagonal elements represent the errors.

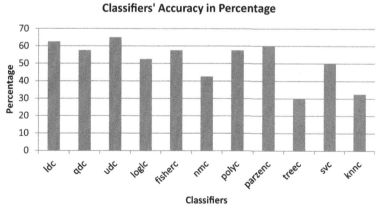

FIGURE 1.3

Classification Accuracy of Classifiers Tested.

Building on the previous set of results described previously, this section considers the three best-performing classifiers for inclusion in the fusion classifier strategy. From the 11 classifiers, tested the linear discriminant classifier (ldc), the quadratic Bayes normal classifier (udc), and the Parzen Classifier (parzenc) provide the best results with accuracies of 62.5%, 65%, and 60%, respectively. These base classifiers were selected and included in the fusion strategy. Figure 1.4 demonstrates the classifiers fusion strategy, in general.

Figure 1.5 describes the scenario and illustrates the simulated results obtained during the evaluation of gait signals using the 11 base-level classifiers. The results obtained from the three best-performing classifiers are stored in a single array, and their error rates are computed. The mean error rate for the three classifiers is 0.42. The same three classifiers are then combined into a cell array using six different rules. The mean error rate for the combined classifiers is 0.40, which is slightly less than the mean of the base-level classifiers.

The base classifier evaluation and fusion classifier strategy was implemented using Matlab. The base-level classifiers are combined into a cell array using a set of fixed combining rules. Six different rules were analyzed: *minimum selection (minc), maximum selection (maxc), median selection (medianc), mean selection (meanc), product combiner (prodc)*, and *voting selection (votec)*. The evaluation of a cell array of trained classifiers *(v and vc)* is done by testing the *(testset)* set.

Evaluation

This section presents the results for experiments performed on the fusion classifier strategy. In this study, the multiclass receiver operating characteristic (ROC) analysis technique is used. This technique is useful for analyzing several different classes, in our case four different classes. First, the classifiers are evaluated in Matlab using the *testc* routine, which provides several performance estimates for a trained classifier on a test data set. The mean value produced by the test results for individual classifiers is 0.42, which is an error rate. In comparison, the mean value for

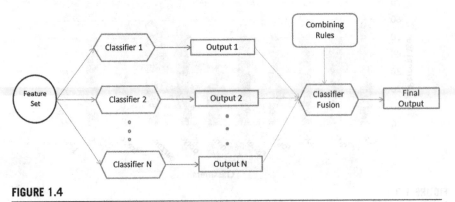

FIGURE 1.4

A Classifier Fusion Strategy.

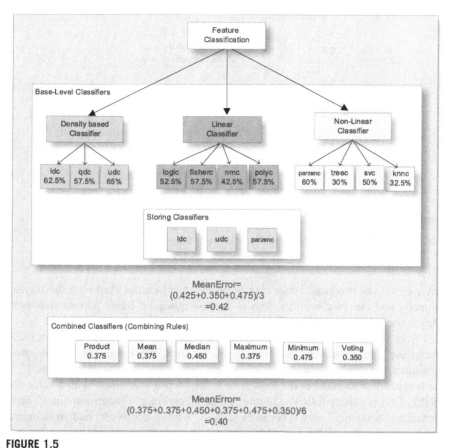

FIGURE 1.5

Summary of Feature Classification by Base-Level Classifiers and Fusion Strategy.

combined classifiers is 0.40, which is obtained by combining different classification rules. This has clearly shown that the combined classification technique works better than the individual use of classifiers. Moreover, the results depict that the voting combination rule works more efficiently than other combining rules used. Using the voting combination rule, the prediction of the base-level classifiers is combined according to a static voting scheme, which does not change when changes are made to the training set.

Figure 1.6 shows the results of the ROC analysis for the base-level classifiers, where the quadratic Bayes normal classifier shows the least error rate compared to all other classifiers. In this case, Error I represents the false-positive values, whereas Error II presents the false-negative values that show the system's failure to predict any disease and label the objects as healthy persons. As can be noted from Figure 1.6, the uncorrelated quadratic Bayes normal classifier generated

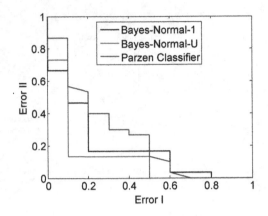

FIGURE 1.6

ROC Analysis to Compare Base-Level Classifier Techniques.

fewer errors and produced better classification when benchmarked with the Bayes normal-1 and Parzen classifiers. This is because quadratic Bayes normal classifier (Bayes normal-U) uses uncorrelated variables.

Figure 1.7 shows the results when classifiers are combined using various combining rule algorithms that include the product, the mean, the median, the maximum, the minimum, and the voting combining rules. As shown in Figure 1.7, the best result that produces the least error is the "voting combiner" with a value of 35.0%. This is closely followed by the "product combiner," "mean combiner," and "maximum combiner," with other rules such as "median combiner" and "minimum combiner" showing 45.0% and 47.5% errors, respectively.

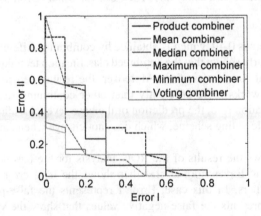

FIGURE 1.7

ROC Analysis to Compare Combining Techniques.

NEURAL SYNCHRONIZATION AND DATA COLLECTION

Synchronization, precisely speaking, is a coordination of "rhythmic oscillators" for a repetitive functional activity, whereas neural synchronization is putatively considered a mechanism where brain regions simultaneously communicate with each other to complete a specific task such as perception, cognition, and action. Any disturbance in the brain, caused by a disease or any other infection, can greatly affect the synchronization of the brain. Quantitative analysis of EEG signals provides a better insight into the synchronization between different parts of the brain. For instance, decreased synchrony has been detected in the EEG signals of AD patients compared with healthy persons [5].

Mild cognitive impairment (MCI) is characterized by an impaired memory state of the brain, probably leading toward mild Alzheimer disease (MiAD) or Alzheimer disease (AD). This prodromal stage of AD is under a great influence of research since a long time [29]. Statistics report that 6%−25% of MCI transform to AD annually and 0.2%−4% of healthy persons develop AD [30], revealing that MCI is a transitional state of MiAD and AD.

Various synchrony measurement techniques have already been discussed to detect any perturbation in the EEG signals of AD patients [31]. For instance, both linear such as coherence and nonlinear such as phase synchronization methods are widely used to quantify synchronization in EEG signals [32]. A comparison of occipital interhemispheric coherence (IHCoh) for normal older adults and AD patients reveals a reduced occipital IHCoh both for lower and higher bands of alpha [33]. Almost similar findings were reported by Locatelli *et al.* [34], who noticed a significant increase in delta coherence between the frontal and posterior regions in AD patients whereas a decrease in alpha coherence was shown in the temporoparieto-occipital areas. Spontaneous phase synchronization of different brain regions is calculated by using Kuramoto's parameter (ρ), which is particularly useful for measuring multichannel data sets.

Despite the considerable success of the above-mentioned techniques to analyze disruption in the EEG signals of Alzheimer patients, further investigations are still required to fulfill the clinical requirements. For instance, in order to detect Alzheimer at its earlier stage, we need to focus on those areas where Alzheimer attacks at first and then we need to check its synchronization with the rest of the brain regions. Furthermore, additional novel and comprehensive methods are still required to check the validity of aforementioned techniques on EEG signals to detect any perturbation in the brain signals of Alzheimer patients.

For our early experiments, to understand the structure and hidden patterns of EEG signals, we have collected EEG data from various healthy subjects at ESPCI ParisTech SIGMA laboratory, France. The age of the subjects was between 25 and 40 years.

The signals are extracted by the placement of an electrode cap on the scalp of our subject. The electrodes are placed according to the International 10-20 system. A gel is injected within these electrode holes on the scalp to increase the conductivity between the scalp and the electrodes. After inserting the gel, the electrodes are placed on the cap to collect the EEG. The EEG system we use in the SIGMA lab is actiCap EEG system with 16 electrodes, amplified by a V-Amp 16 amplifier, both from Brain Products. The electrodes used are active, and the data are filtered using the Vision Recorder software from Brain Products. The data are afterwards analyzed using Matlab.

Figure 1.8 shows the position of the electrodes on the cap to receive EEG signals from the brain of the subjects. Different parts of the brain are differentiated with different colors, dotted lines, and also with integers. For instance, integer 1, which is written on the orange part, denotes the frontal part of the brain. This part includes five channels—FP1, FP2, FPz, F3, and F4. The left temporal is denoted by integer 2, and it is highlighted with blue color. This part includes three (3) channels—F7, T3, and T5. Similarly, the central part of the brain is denoted by integer 3, and it is highlighted with green color. This part has 5 channels—Fz, C3, Cz, C4, Pz. The fourth part is the right temporal, which is denoted by integer 4 and is highlighted

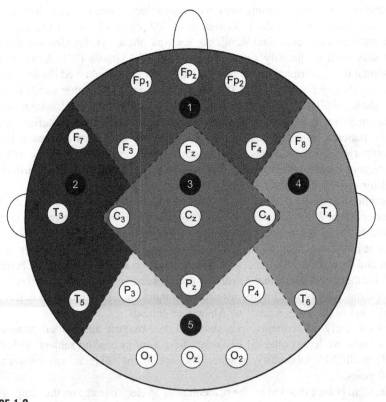

FIGURE 1.8

The 21 channels used for EEG recordings.

by pink color. This part constitutes of three (3) channels—F8, T4, T6. Similarly, the last part, which is denoted by integer 5, is the occipital region. This part is highlighted with yellow color, and it consists of five channels—P3, P4, O1, O2, and Oz.

NEURAL SYNCHRONY MEASUREMENT TECHNIQUE

In this section, we briefly review the synchrony measurement techniques that we have implemented on our data sets, which include phase synchrony, cross-correlation, and coherence.

PHASE SYNCHRONY (HILBERT TRANSFORM)

The oscillation of two or more cyclic signals where they tend to keep a repeating sequence of relative phase angles is called phase synchronization. Synchronization of the two periodic nonidentical oscillators refers to the adjustment of their rhythmicity, that is, the phase locking between the two signals. It refers to the interdependence between the instantaneous phases $\varphi_1(t)$ and $\varphi_2(t)$ of the two signals $x_1(t)$ and $x_2(t)$, respectively. It is usually written as

$$\varphi_{n,m} = n\varphi_1(t) - n\varphi_2(t) = constant \tag{1}$$

where n and m are integers indicating the ratio of possible frequency locking, and $\varphi_{n,m}$ is their relative phase or phase difference. To compute the phase synchronization, the instantaneous phase of the two signals should be known. This can be detected using analytical signals based on Hilbert Transform.

$$z(t) = x(t) + i\tilde{x}(t) \tag{2}$$

Here $z(t)$ is a complex value, where $x(t)$ is a real time series and $\tilde{x}(t)$ is its Hilbert transform.

The Hilbert transform can be calculated as

$$\tilde{x}(t) = \frac{1}{\pi} PV \int_{-\infty}^{\infty} \frac{x(\tau)}{t - \tau} dt \tag{3}$$

Here PV denotes the Cauchy principle value. The instantaneous phase $\varphi_1(t)$ and $\varphi_2(t)$ for both signals can be calculated with the formula

$$\varphi(t) - arctan\frac{\tilde{x}(t)}{x(t)} \tag{4}$$

CROSS-CORRELATION

Cross-correlation is a mathematical operation used to measure the extent of similarity between two signals. If a signal is correlated to itself, it is called auto-correlated.

If we suppose that $x(n)$ and $y(n)$ (why not $S1(t)$ and $S2(t)$ make a uniform signals suggestion) are two time series, then the correlation between is calculated as

$$\widehat{R}_{xy}(m) = \begin{cases} \sum_{n=0}^{N-m-1} x_{n+m} y_n & m \geq 0 \\ \widehat{R}_{yx}(-m) & m < 0 \end{cases} \tag{5}$$

Cross-correlation returns a sequence of length $2*N - 1$ vector, where x and y vectors are of length N ($N > 1$). If x and y are not of the same length, then the shorter vector is zero-padded. Cross-correlation returns values between -1 and $+1$. If both signals are identical to each other the value will be 1; if they are totally different to each other then the cross-correlation coefficient is 0, and if they are identical with the phase shift of 180o then the cross-correlation coefficient will be -1 [35].

MAGNITUDE SQUARED COHERENCE

The coherence functions estimates the linear correlation of signals in frequency domain. The magnitude squared coherence is defined as the square of the modulus of the mean cross power spectral density (PSD) normalized to the product of the mean auto PSDs. The coherence $C_{xy}(f)$ between two channel time series is computed as

$$C_{xy}(f) = \frac{|P_{xy}(f)|}{P_{xx}(f)P_{yy}(f)} \tag{6}$$

$P_{xy}(f)$ is the cross PSD estimate of x and y. $P_{xx}(f)$ and $P_{yy}(f)$ are the PSD estimates of x and y, respectively.

$P_{xy}(f)$ is the cross PSD estimate of x and y. $P_{xx}(f)$ and $P_{yy}(f)$ are the PSD estimates of x and y, respectively.

For discrete signals x and y, cross PSDs ($P_{xy}(f)$) can be calculated with the given formula:

$$P_{xy}(f) = \lim_{T \to \infty} E\left\{ \left[F_x^T(w)\right]^* F_y^T(w) \right\} \tag{7}$$

Here, cross spectral density, which is also known as cross power spectrum, is the Fourier transform of the cross-correlation function.

$$P_{xy}(f) = \int_{-\infty}^{\infty} R_{xy}(t)e^{-jwt}dt = \int_{-\infty}^{\infty} \cdot \left[\int_{-\infty}^{\infty} (x(t)).y(T+t)dT \right] e^{-jwt}dt \tag{8}$$

Where $R_{xy}(t)$ is the cross-correlation of $x(t)$ and $y(t)$. On the other side, auto PSDs ($P_{xx}(f)$, and $P_{yy}(f)$) for $x(t)$ and $y(t)$ can be calculated from the auto correlation instead of cross-correlation functions.

$$P_{xx}(f) = \lim_{T \to \infty} E\left\{ \left[F_x^T(w) \right]^* F_x^T(w) \right\} \qquad (9)$$

$$P_{yy}(f) = \lim_{T \to \infty} E\left\{ \left[F_y^T(w) \right]^* F_y^T(w) \right\} \qquad (10)$$

DATA DESCRIPTION AND DATA FILTERING

The data sets we are analyzing have been recorded from three different countries of European Union. Specialist at the memory clinic referred all patients to the EEG department of the hospital. All patients passed through a number of recommended tests; MMSE, The Rey Auditory Verbal Learning Test, Benton Visual Retention Test, and memory recall tests. The results are scored and interpreted by psychologists and a multidisciplinary team in the clinic. After that, each patient is referred to the hospital for EEG assessment to diagnose the symptoms of AD. Patients were advised to be in a resting state with their eyes closed during the test. The sampling frequency and number of electrodes for three data sets are all different. Detailed information is as follows.

DATABASE A

The EEG data set A contains 17 MiAD patients (10 males; aged 69.4 ± 11.5 years) and 24 healthy subjects (9 males; aged 77.6 ± 10 years). They all are of British nationality. These data were obtained using a strict protocol from Derriford Hospital, Plymouth, United Kingdom, and has been collected using normal hospital practices. EEG signals were obtained using the modified Maudsley system which is similar to the traditional International 10-20 system. EEGs were recorded for 20 seconds at a sampling frequency of 256 Hz (later on sampled down to 128 Hz) using 21 electrodes.

DATABASE B

This EEG data set was composed of 5 MiAD patients (2 males; aged 78.8 ± 5.6 years) as well as 5 healthy subjects (3 males; aged 76.6 ± 10.0 years). They all are of Italian nationality. Several tests, for instance; MMSE, the Clinical Dementia Rating Scale (CDRS), and the Geriatric Depression Scale (GDS) were conducted to evaluate the cognitive state of the patients. The MMSE result for healthy subjects is 29.3 ± 0.7, whereas for MiAD patients it is 22.3 ± 3.1. EEGs were recorded for 20 seconds at a sampling frequency of 128 Hz using 19 electrodes at the University of Malta, Msida MSD06, Malta.

DATABASE C

This data set consists of 8 MiAD patients (6 males; aged 75 ± 3.4 years) and 3 healthy subjects (3 males; aged 73.5 ± 2.2 years). They all are of Romanian

Nationality. The AD patients have been referred by a neurologist for EEG recordings. The time series are recorded for 10 to 20 minutes at a sampling frequency of 512 Hz using 22 electrodes. The signals are notch filtered at 50 Hz. Further details about the data can be found in [51].

For the current study, we have obtained a version of the data that is already preprocessed of artifacts by using independent component analysis (ICA), a blind source separation technique (BSS).

DATA FILTERING INTO FIVE FREQUENCY BANDS

EEG time series are classified into five frequency bands. Each frequency band has its own physiological significance.

- Delta (δ: $1 \leq f \leq 4$ Hz): are characterized for deep sleep and are correlated with different pathologies.
- Theta (θ: $4 \leq f \leq 8$ Hz): play an important role during childhood. High theta activities in adults are considered abnormal and associated with brain disorders.
- Alpha (α: $8 \leq f \leq 12$ Hz): usually appear during mentally inactive conditions and under relaxation. They are best seen during eyes are closed and mostly pronounced in occipital location.
- Beta (β: $12 \leq f \leq 25$ Hz): are visible in central and frontal locations. Their amplitude is less than alpha waves and they mostly enhance during tension.
- Gamma (γ: $25 \leq f \leq 30$ Hz): are best characterized for cognitive and motor functions.

Bandpass filter is applied to each EEG channel to extract the EEG data in specific frequency bands $[F : (F + W)]$ Hz. Butterworth filters were used (of second order) as they offer good transition band characteristics at low coefficient orders; thus, they can be implemented efficiently [36].

DIFFERENT APPROACHES TO COMPUTE EEG SYNCHRONY

Different approaches have already been implemented to measure the synchrony between different parts of the brain for Alzheimer patients, MCI patients and healthy subjects. Dauwels *et al.* [35] have proposed two unique methods to compute synchrony, which they named Local and Global synchrony measures. In the Local synchrony, they computed the synchrony of different regions (left and right temporal, frontal, central, and occipital) separately and then compared the results of one region with the other. In the Global approach, synchrony measures are applied to all 21 channels simultaneously. They named this computation "large-scale synchrony measure" since each region spans several tens of millimeters.

Taking inspiration from these concepts, we have presented advanced and novel approaches to compute EEG synchrony for Alzheimer patients, for all parts of the brain in optimized and narrow frequency bands. In this chapter, we present average and principal components analysis (PCA)–based EEG synchrony measure for Alzheimer and healthy subjects as shown in the Figure 1.9. A detailed description of these methods is provided in the next sections.

AVERAGE SYNCHRONY MEASURE

Average EEG synchrony takes its name because the likelihood of synchronization between two parts of the brain is calculated by computing the average of synchrony measures for all channel pairs between two respective parts. This means that first we apply neural synchrony measurement technique on each channel pair (time series of two channels) of two different regions for all frequency bands and then we take the average of those results.

For instance, we apply phase synchrony measure on each channel pair of left and right temporal ((F_7–F_8), (F_7–T_4), (F_7–T_6), (T_3–F_8), (T_3–T_4), (T_3–T_6), (T_5–F_8), (T_5–T_4), (T_5–T_6)) and then we take the average result of right temporal–left temporal. Similarly, we compare the left temporal with frontal ((F_7–FP_1), (F_7–FP_2), (F_7–FP_z), (F_7–F_3), (F_7–F_4), (T_3–FP_1), (T_3–FP_2), (T_3–FP_z), (T_3–F_3), (T_3–F_4), (T_5–FP_1), (T_5–FP_2), (T_5–FP_z), (T_5–F_3), (T_5–F_4)), left temporal–central ((F_7–F_z), (F_7–C_3), (F_7–C_z), (F_7–P_z), (T_3–F_z), (T_3–C_3), (T_3–C_z), (T_3–C_4), (T_3–P_z), (T_5–F_z), (T_5–C_3), (T_5–C_z), (T_5–C_4), (T_5–P_z)), and left temporal–occipital ((F_7–P_3), (F_7–P_4), (F_7–O_1), (F_7–O_2), (F_7–O_z), (T_3–P_3), (T_3–P_4), (T_3–O_1), (T_3–O_2), (T_3–O_z), (T_5–P_3), (T_5–P_4), (T_5–O_1), (T_5–O_2), (T_5–O_z)).

Working on the same lines, we compare the right temporal (F_8, T_4, T_6) with rest of the brain area. For instance, we apply phase synchrony measure on each channel pair of right and left temporal ((F_8–F_7), (T_4–F_7), (T_6–F_7), (F_8–T_3), (T_4–T_3), (T_6–T_3), (F_8–T_5), (T_4–T_5), (T_6–T_5)) and then we take the average result of right temporal–left temporal. Similarly, we compare the right temporal with frontal ((F_8–FP_1), (F_8–FP_2), (F_8–FP_z), (F_8–F_3), (F_8–F_4), (T_4–FP_1), (T_4–FP_2), (T_4–FP_z), (T_4–F_3), (T_4–F_4), (T_6–FP_1), (T_6–FP_2), (T_6–FP_z), (T_6–F_3), (T_6–F_4)), right temporal–central ((F_8–F_z), (F_8–C_3), (F_8–C_z), (F_8–P_z), (T_3–F_z), (T_4–C_3), (T_4–C_z), (T_4–C_4), (T_4–P_z), (T_6–F_z), (T_6–C_3), (T_6–C_z), (T_6–C_4), (T_6–P_z)), and right temporal–occipital ((F_8–P_3), (F_8–P_4), (F_8–O_1), (F_8–O_2), (F_8–O_z), (T_4–P_3), (T_4–P_4), (T_4–O_1), (T_4–O_2), (T_4–O_z), (T_6–P_3), (T_6–P_4), (T_6–O_1), (T_6–O_2), (T_6–O_z)).

The same procedure has been repeated for rest of the synchrony measures, that is, cross-correlation and coherence. After getting the results, we compare the neural synchronization of AD patients and healthy subjects, for all three measurement techniques (phase synchronization, cross-correlation and coherence), by Mann–Whitney U test.

PCA-BASED SYNCHRONY MEASURE

The basic purpose of PCA is to reduce the dimensionality of a data set to convert it to uncorrelated variables providing maximum information about a data point,

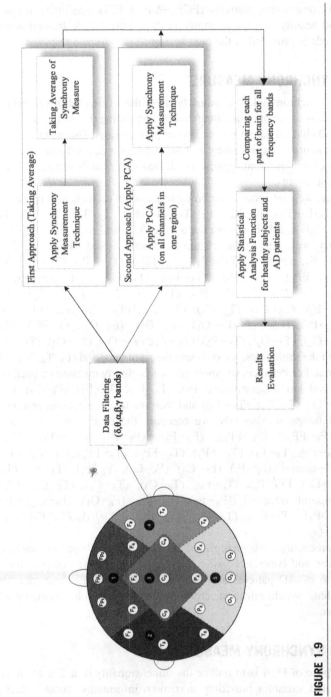

FIGURE 1.9

Average vs. PCA based Synchrony Measure.

eliminating interrelated variables. In other words, it transforms highly dimensional data set (of m dimensions) into low-dimensional orthogonal features (of n dimension), where $n < m$.

In this method, instead of applying synchrony measurement techniques directly on the filtered data, first we apply the PCA technique on all channels of one region. This eliminates any redundant information that a region might provide. For instance, we apply PCA on all three channels of left temporal (F_7, T_3, T_5) and, consequently, it provides a single signal without any redundant information. It is noteworthy here that still we have a signal into five narrow frequency bands (δ, θ, α, β, γ) for each part. This means that for left temporal, after the application of PCA on three channels (F_7, T_3, T_5), we have a single signal, say LT, for all these frequency bands: LT_δ, LT_θ, LT_α, LT_β, LT_γ. Similarly, after applying PCA to right temporal (RT), we have the following signals: RT_δ, RT_θ, RT_α, RT_β, RT_γ. For frontal, central, and occipital, the signals are as (F_δ, F_θ, F_α, F_β, F_γ), (C_δ, C_θ, C_α, C_β, C_γ), and (O_δ, O_θ, O_α, O_β, O_γ) respectively.

After the application of PCA, now we have a single comprehensive signal in five frequency bands in each part. Proceeding toward the findings of neural synchronization, we apply the neural synchrony measure, say phase synchrony, on EEG time series of two regions. We calculated phase synchrony between left and right temporal ((LT_δ–RT_δ), (LT_θ–RT_θ)–, (LT_α–RT_α), (LT_β–RT_β), (LT_γ–RT_γ)), left temporal–frontal ((LT_δ–F_δ), (LT_θ–F_θ)–, (LT_α–F_α), (LT_β–F_β), (LT_γ–F_γ)), left temporal–central ((LT_δ–C_δ), (LT_θ–C_θ)–, (LT_α–C_α), (LT_β–C_β), (LT_γ–C_γ)), and left temporal–occipital ((LT_δ–O_δ), (LT_θ–O_θ)–, (LT_α–O_α), (LT_β–O_β), (LT_γ–O_γ)).

Similarly, we have compared right temporal with the rest of the brain areas; right temporal–left temporal ((RT_δ–LT_δ), (RT_θ–LT_θ)–, (RT_α–LT_α), (RT_β–LT_β), (RT_γ–LT_γ)), right temporal–frontal ((RT_δ–F_δ), (RT_θ–F_θ)–, (RT_α–F_α), (RT_β–F_β), (RT_γ–F_γ)), right temporal–central ((RT_δ–C_δ), (RT_θ–C_θ)–, (RT_α–C_α), (RT_β–C_β), (RT_γ–C_γ)), and right temporal–occipital ((RT_δ–O_δ), (RT_θ–O_θ)–, (RT_α–O_α), (RT_β–O_β), (RT_γ–O_γ)).

The same procedure has been repeated for rest of the synchrony measures, that is, cross-correlation and coherence. After getting the results, we compare the neural synchronization of MiAD patients and healthy subjects for all three measurement techniques (phase synchronization, cross-correlation and coherence) by Mann–Whitney U test.

STATISTICAL ANALYSIS

To investigate whether there is a significant difference between the EEG signals of MiAD patients and control subject and also to prove the probable significance of our proposed methodology, we apply the Wilcoxon rank sum (Mann–Whitney) test on our data sets. The rank sum function is a nonparametric test that allows to check whether the statistics at hand, in our case synchrony results, take different values from two different populations. Lower p-values indicate higher significance in terms of large difference in medians of two populations.

Results are compared in two different perspectives:

1. Investigating three different synchrony measures at a time will help us to compare which measure works better for EEG signals.
2. Second, we are able to compare two different methods for three synchrony measures and for three different data sets.

RESULTS AND DISCUSSION

The aim of the present study is to find the relationship of EEG synchronization with AD, and thus to explore further dimensions in the disconnection theorem of cognitive dysfunction in AD. And also, we aim to propose a better method to detect any change in EEG synchrony that can be considered as a biomarker for the early detection of AD.

First we discuss all three synchrony measures with PCA based method. As shown in the Table 1.1, the p-values for cross-correlation in the RT-C region are 2.47×10^{-4}, 1.46×10^{-4}, 0.009 for delta, theta, and alpha bands, respectively. In the LT-O region, the smallest p-values for delta and theta bands are 8.50×10^{-5} and 6.8×10^{-5} respectively. The second best measure that has given us remarkable results is phase synchrony, where we get 0.0067, 0.0403, and 0.0585 p-values for delta, theta, and alpha bands, respectively, in the RT-C region. We get 0.0041 and 0.0271 p-values for delta and alpha bands, respectively, in the LT-O region. Lastly, the coherence function shows significant results in the RT-C region for delta band, p-value $= 0.0378$, and in the LT-O region with p-values 9.8×10^{-4} and 0.05 for delta and alpha bands, respectively. Coherence function does not provide significant results and hence contradicts *Bahar* theory [37], where the control group showed higher values of evoked coherence in delta, theta, and alpha bands in the left frontoparietal electrode pairs compared with AD patients.

Similarly, we have found 8 significant values below 0.01 ($p < 0.01$) and 11 significant values below 0.05 ($p < 0.05$) for the PCA-based method whereas only 2 values below 0.01 ($p < 0.01$) and 8 values below 0.05 ($p < 0.05$) in case of the Average method for phase synchrony measure. Similarly, for cross-correlation measure, although the difference is not very high, the PCA method still has shown more significant values. For example, the number of p-values below 0.01 ($p < 0.01$) are 26 whereas almost all 35 values are below 0.05 ($p < 0.05$); on the other hand, for the Average method, 22 values are below 0.01 whereas 30 values are below 0.05 ($p < 0.05$), as shown in the Table 1.2. As aforementioned, coherence function does not perform better compared with other two synchrony measures, but again we found more significant results in case of the PCA method (2 values below 0.01 and 7 values below 0.05) compared with the Average method, wherein we found only one significant value below 0.01 and 7 significant values below 0.05.

Table 1.1 P-Values at Different Frequency Bands in Different Brain Connections

Synchrony Measure	Brain-Connections	Frequency regions	P-values
Cross Correlation	RT-C	Delta (δ)	2.47×10^{-4}
		Theta(θ)	1.46×10^{-4}
		Alpha(α)	0.009
	RT-O	Delta (δ)	6.9×10^{-5}
		Theta(θ)	2.7×10^{-5}
		Alpha(α)	0.0029
	RT-F	Delta (δ)	5.01×10^{-4}
		Theta(θ)	6.8×10^{-5}
		Alpha(α)	0.0062
	LT-C	Delta (δ)	4.3×10^{-5}
		Theta(θ)	3.8×10^{-5}
		Alpha(α)	0.0192
	LT-O	Delta (δ)	8.5×10^{-5}
		Theta(θ)	6.8×10^{-5}
		Alpha(α)	0.0052
	LT-F	Delta (δ)	2.2×10^{-4}
		Theta(θ)	5.4×10^{-5}
		Alpha(α)	0.0091
	LT-RT	Delta (δ)	3.3×10^{-4}
		Theta(θ)	6×10^{-5}
		Alpha(α)	0.0253
Phase Synchrony	RT-C	Delta (δ)	0.0067
		Theta(θ)	0.0403
		Alpha(α)	0.05
	RT-O	Delta (δ)	0.0041
		Alpha(α)	0.0271
Coherence	RT-C	Delta (δ)	0.0378
	RT-O	Delta (δ)	0.0378
		Alpha(α)	0.0192

Results revealed that cross-correlation (xcorr) synchrony in right temporal—occipital (RT−O) for theta (θ), alpha (α), and beta (β) ranges provides an optimal information for the early diagnosis of Alzheimer patients. Also, phase synchrony measure in left temporal—frontal (LT−F) and left temporal-right temporal (LT−RT) regions provides significant information for theta (θ) and beta (β) ranges. The provided results support our hypothesis that a decrease in synchronization between temporal regions have a direct link with the progression of AD. These findings will help clinicians for the early diagnosis of AD patients.

Table 1.2 Total Number of Significant Values in Case of PCA and Average Method

Synchrony Measure	Method	P < 0.01 (Total Values)	P < 0.05 (Total Values)
Cross correlation	PCA	26	35
	Average	22	30
Phase Synchrony	PCA	8	11
	Average	2	8
MS Coherence	PCA	2	7
	Average	1	4

CONCLUSION

This chapter has presented a framework for the early diagnosis of NDDs using signal processing and signal classification techniques. The problem with the NDDs is that they are incurable, hard to detect at earlier stages because of nonobvious symptoms, and also hard to discriminate at later stages because of pattern similarities of different NDDs. Because there is no single authentic remedy available for such diseases, scientists find a lot of interest in finding those hidden patterns that can help us in the early diagnosis of NDDs. This chapter has highlighted the importance of machine learning and signal processing in the early diagnosis of life-threatening diseases such as Alzheimer, Parkinson, Huntington, and ALS. In this thesis, we have presented the issues with the early diagnosis of NDDs and also with their possible solutions. The analysis and classification of gait signals is presented using a set of well-known classifiers—linear, nonlinear, and Bayes. Results are presented and elaborated from various dimensions using more than one performance evaluation technique. In addition, we have proposed and demonstrated a novel idea of combining classifiers to improve the classification accuracy. The latter half of the thesis presented the implementation of neural synchrony measurement techniques using EEG signals to calculate synchronization in different parts of the brain for Alzheimer and non-Alzheimer patients. The chapter has presented novel and significant findings that can be used in clinical practices for the early diagnosis of NDDs.

REFERENCES

[1] Rogers J, Webster S, Lue L-F, Brachova L, Harold Civin W, Emmerling M, Shivers B, Walker D, McGeer P. Inflammation and Alzheimer's disease pathogenesis. Neurobiol Aging 1996;17:681−6.
[2] Braak H, Braak E. Neuropathological stageing of Alzheimer-related changes. Acta Neuropathol 1991;82:239−59.
[3] Hebert LE, Beckett LA, Scherr PA, Evans DA. Annual Incidence of Alzheimer disease in the United States projected to the years 2000 through 2050. Alzheimer Dis Assoc Disord 2001;15:169−73.

[4]   Hausdorff M, Lertratanakul A, Cudkowicz E, Peterson L, Kaliton D, Goldberger L. Dynamic markers of altered gait rhythm in amyotrophic lateral sclerosis. J Appl Physiol 2000;88:2045–53.

[5]   Yunfeng W, Krishnan S. Statistical analysis of gait rhythm in patients with Parkinson's disease. IEEE Trans Neural Syst Rehabil Eng 2010;18:150–8.

[6]   Banaie M, Pooyan M, Mikaili M. Introduction and application of an automatic gait recognition method to diagnose movement disorders that arose of similar causes. Expert Syst Appl 2011;38:7359–63.

[7]   Berger H. Über das Elektrenkephalogramm des Menschen. Archiv für Psychiatrie Nervenkrankheiten 1929;87:527–70.

[8]   Ferri CP, Prince M, Brayne C, Brodaty H, Fratiglioni L, Ganguli M, Hall K, Hasegawa K, Hendrie H, Huang Y, Jorm A, Mathers C, Menezes PR, Rimmer E, Scazufca M. Global prevalence of dementia: a Delphi consensus study. The Lancet 2005;366:2112–7.

[9]   Ganji F, Abadeh S, Hedayati M, Bakhtiari N. Fuzzy classifcation of imbalanced data sets for medical diagnosis. In: 17th Iranian Conference of Biomedical Engineering (ICBME); 2010. p. 1–5.

[10]   Marlin BM. Missing data problems in machine learning. University of Toronto; 2008.

[11]   Zhao X-M, Li X, Chen L, Aihara K. Protein classification with imbalanced data. Proteins 2008;70:1125–32.

[12]   Zhi-Hua Z, Xu-Ying L. Training cost-sensitive neural networks with methods addressing the class imbalance problem. IEEE Trans Knowledge Data Eng 2006;18:63–77.

[13]   Ani A, Deriche M. A New Technique for Combining Multiple Classifiers using The Dempster-Shafer Theory of Evidence. J Artificial Intelligence Res 2002;17:333–61.

[14]   Meriggi P, Castiglioni P, Rizzo F, Gower V, Andrich R, Rabuffetti M, Ferrarin M, Di Rienzo M. Potential role of wearable, ambulatory and home monitoring systems for patients with neurodegenerative diseases and their caregivers. In: 5th International Conference on Pervasive Computing Technologies for Healthcare; 2011. p. 316–9.

[15]   Harter A, Hopper A, Steggles P, Ward A, Webster P. The Anatomy of a Context-Aware Application. Wireless Networks 2002;8:187–97.

[16]   Armstrong RA, Cairns NJ, Patel R, Lantos PL, Rossor MN. Relationships between β-amyloid (Aβ) deposits and blood vessels in patients with sporadic and familial Alzheimer's disease. Neurosci Lett 1996;207:171–4.

[17]   Beck J. Parkinson's Disease Foundation. 2012. Available: http://www.pdf.org/en/about_pd.

[18]   Hou J-GG, Lai EC. Non-motor Symptoms of Parkinson's Disease. Int J Gerontol 2007; 1:53–64.

[19]   Neela D, Rangarajan K. Hybrid Workflow Net Based Architecture for Modeling Huntington's Disease. In: Bio-Inspired Computing: Theories and Applications (BIC-TA), 2011 Sixth International Conference on; 2011. p. 319–23.

[20]   Wang Y, Chen Q, Hu W. Behavior Selection Mechanism of Two Typical Brain Movement Disorders: Comparative Study Using Robot. In: International Conference on Digital Manufacturing and Automation; 2010. p. 319–23.

[21]   Matías-Guiu J, Galán L, García-Ramos R, Barcia JA, Guerrero A. Cerebrospinal fluid cytotoxicity in lateral amyotrophic sclerosis. Neurología (English Edition) 2010;25: 364–73.

[22]   Dugdale DC. Amyotrophic lateral sclerosis and other motor neuron diseases. 2010. Available: http://www.ncbi.nlm.nih.gov/pubmedhealth/PMH0001708/.

[23] Madarame T, Tanaka H, Inoue T, Kamata M, Shino M. The development of a brain computer interface device for amyotrophic lateral sclerosis patients. In: IEEE International Conference on Systems, Man and Cybernetics; 2008. p. 2401−6.

[24] Woon WL, Cichocki A, Viallate F, Musha T. Techniques for early detection of Alzheimer's disease using spontaneous EEG recordings. In: Presented at the IOP Publishing; 2007.

[25] Wang L, Zang Y, He Y, Liang M, Zhang X, Tian L, Wu T, Jiang T, Li K. Changes in hippocampal connectivity in the early stages of Alzheimer's disease: Evidence from resting state fMRI. NeuroImage 2006;31:496−504.

[26] Knauer U, Meffert B. Evaluation based combining of classifiers for monitoring honeybees. In: Presented at the Workshop on Applications of Computer Vision (WACV), Germany; 2009.

[27] Ghanem AS, Venkatesh S, West G. Multi-class Pattern Classification in Imbalanced Data. In: Presented at the Proceedings of the 20th International Conference on Pattern Recognition; 2010.

[28] Fernández A, García S, Jesus MJd, Herrera F. A study of the behaviour of linguistic fuzzy rule based classification systems in the framework of imbalanced data-sets. Fuzzy Sets Syst 2008;159:2378−98.

[29] Babiloni C, Frisoni GB, Pievani M, Vecchio F, Lizio R, Buttiglione M, Geroldi C, Fracassi C, Eusebi F, Ferri R, Rossini PM. Hippocampal volume and cortical sources of EEG alpha rhythms in mild cognitive impairment and Alzheimer disease. NeuroImage 2009;44:123−35.

[30] Frisoni GB, Padovani A, Wahlund LO. The predementia diagnosis of Alzheimer disease. Alzheimer Dis Assoc Disord 2004;18:51−3.

[31] Gallego-Jutgla E, Elgendi M, Vialatte F, Sole-Casals J, Cichocki A, Latchoumane C, Jaesung J, Dauwels J. Diagnosis of Alzheimer's disease from EEG by means of synchrony measures in optimized frequency bands. In: International Conference of the IEEE Engineering in Medicine and Biology Society; 2012. p. 4266−70.

[32] Breakspear M. Nonlinear phase desynchronization in human electroencephalographic data. Hum Brain Mapp 2002;15:175−98.

[33] Anghinah R, Kanda PA, Jorge MS, Lima EE, Pascuzzi L, Melo AC. Alpha band coherence analysis of EEG in healthy adult's and Alzheimer's type dementia patients. Arq Neuropsiquiatr 2000;58:272−5.

[34] Locatelli T, Cursi M, Liberati D, Franceschi M, Comi G. EEG coherence in Alzheimer's disease. Electroencephalogr Clin Neurophysiol 1998;106:229−37.

[35] Dauwels J, Vialatte F, Cichocki A. A Comparative Study of Synchrony Measures for the Early Detection of Alzheimer's Disease Based on EEG. In: Neural information processing, vol. 4984. Berlin: Springer; 2008. p. 112−25.

[36] Oppenheim AV, Schafer RW, Buck JR. Discrete-time signal processing. 2nd ed. Upper Saddle River, NJ: Prentice Hall; 1999.

[37] Güntekin B, Saatçi E, Yener G. Decrease of evoked delta, theta and alpha coherences in Alzheimer patients during a visual oddball paradigm. Brain Res 2008;1235:109−16.

Lifelogging Technologies to Detect Negative Emotions Associated with Cardiovascular Disease

2

Chelsea Dobbins[1], Stephen Fairclough[2]

Applied Computing Research Group, Liverpool John Moores University, Liverpool, UK[1];
School of Natural Sciences and Psychology, Liverpool John Moores University, Liverpool, UK[2]
E-mail: C.M.Dobbins@ljmu.ac.uk, S.Fairclough@ljmu.ac.uk

INTRODUCTION

Human emotion provides a powerful and important aspect to life experience that is fundamental to our understanding of ourselves and critical in motivating behavior [1,2]. However, not all emotional experiences are positive and beneficial for health and well-being. For instance, the repeated experience of negative emotions, such as depression, anger, or anxiety, can have long-term damaging consequences for health [3]. Frequent and repeated episodes of such negative emotion are associated with inflammatory changes through a number of physiological systems in the human body, which may be clinically relevant for the future development of coronary heart disease [4] and hypertension (high blood pressure) [5]. However, this tendency may be accelerated for those individuals who have a predisposition toward the experience of negative emotion [6]. For example, a number of adverse cardiac events, such as myocardial ischemia and ventricular arrhythmia, may be triggered by episodes of extreme anger [7-9]. Negative emotional states are associated with psychological stress, which can trigger a process of inflammation within the body that is linked to the development of cardiovascular disease (CVD) [10]. The allostatic model of stress and disease [11] provides an exemplar of how psychological stress can damage long-term health via a process of "wear and tear" that is cumulative and attritional [12]. Furthermore, the detrimental impact of negative emotion on human physiology may occur without any conscious awareness on the part of the individual [13]. As such, the process of recognizing and reducing those activities or behaviors that produce negative feelings is important for the maintenance of good health and well-being. There is emerging evidence to indicate that effective coping strategies may ameliorate the impact of negative emotions on health [11]. However, these strategies require insight and high self-awareness in order to be developed and deployed in an effective fashion. Therapeutic systems designed to promote self-awareness, such as cognitive–behavioral therapy (CBT), focus on detailed record-keeping to promote such awareness about the relationship between behaviors and consequences for behavior change goals [2]. As such, there is a role for technology to play in the process of record-keeping, improved self-awareness and the promotion of effective coping strategies.

NEGATIVE EMOTION AND CARDIOVASCULAR HEALTH

CVD generates vast economic effects and is the leading cause of disability and premature death globally, causing over 36 million deaths worldwide [14-16]. In 2010 in the United States, CVD and stroke have been estimated to have cost the economy $315.4 billion in direct (e.g., cost of physicians and other professionals, hospital services, prescribed medications, home health care, and other medical durables) and indirect (e.g., lost productivity that results from premature mortality) costs [17]. Alternatively, in the United Kingdom, both indirectly and directly, CVD alone costs the health services £8.7 billion and the UK economy £30 billion annually, yet 80%–90% of premature CVD is preventable [15,18]. This disease is the United Kingdom's biggest killer, causing almost 200,000 deaths every year, in the United States it claims over 600,000 people and in Europe over 4 million deaths and over 1.9 million deaths in the European Union (EU) are caused annually by CVD, costing the EU economy almost €196 annually [15,18-20].

Negative emotions are an everyday phenomenon that are both pervasive and difficult to avoid. Everyone will experience feelings of anger, sadness, or anxiety at some time. However, what differentiates between individuals is the frequency of those emotional experiences and the severity of each episode. Most of us have an intuitive sense that negative emotion is detrimental for health and well-being in the long term, particularly the health of the cardiovascular system, but the significance of this connection may be underestimated by the general population. For example, one large-scale, international study concluded that psychosocial factors (including depression and stress) were stronger predictors of myocardial infarction than diabetes, obesity, smoking, and hypertension [21]. Similarly, the tendency to direct anger and aggressive feeling toward another person has a linear relationship with hypertension. Everson and colleagues [22] reported that an increase of 1 point on the Anger Out scale resulted in a 12% increased likelihood of hypertension over a 4-year period. An increased incidence of coronary heart disease has also been associated with higher levels of anxiety [23].

The experience of negative emotion appears to have a detrimental effect on cardiovascular health that is both cumulative and attritional. This pattern of long-term "wear and tear" on human physiology was described by McEwen [24] in connection with the experience of stress. He argued that major physiological systems in the human body, such as the autonomic nervous system, the endocrine system, the immune system, etc., could be locked into a pattern of sustained activity due to chronic exposure to stressful stimuli. This type of chronic stress has significant consequences for biological ageing, as well as the long-term health of the individual and mortality [25].

The pattern of sustained change in major physiological systems associated with stress are also found in connection with negative emotional states. People suffering from depression are characterized by increased heart rate and reduced heart rate variability due to alterations in the way in which the autonomic nervous system is controlled [26]. The sinoatrial node, which regulates the beating action of the heart, is controlled jointly by inputs from the sympathetic nervous system and the parasympathetic nervous system; the former increases the heart rate, whereas the latter has the opposite effect. Depression tends to impair input from the parasympathetic nervous system, leading to a faster heart rate. This pattern is enhanced in depressed patients by increased circulation of adrenaline and cortisol in the bloodstream, both of which reinforce the influence of the sympathetic nervous system [26]. As well as the autonomic nervous system and the endocrine system, the immune system is also influenced by episodes of depression; levels of pro-inflammatory cytokines are increased, which has consequences for both mood (e.g., a tendency toward negative emotion) and behavior (e.g., reduced appetite and physical activity) [27]. Like the allostatic load model, advanced by McEwen [28], repeated and sustained periods of depression have a corrosive impact on cardiovascular health via a pattern of sustained physiological disruption.

The deleterious impact of anger on cardiovascular health stems from an over-stimulation of the sympathetic nervous system. This alteration in autonomic activity leads to increased vasculature constriction, which increases blood pressure and heart rate; there is also evidence for elevated levels of adrenaline and cortisol in the bloodstream well as alterations in the ventricular function of the heart [3]. Although the physiological manifestation of anger within the cardiovascular system is straightforward, estimating its impact on cardiovascular health is complicated by individual differences with respect to the expression and experience of anger. A prospective study of almost 8000 participants, studied over 10—15 years, indicated that high levels of cynicism and low levels of control over the expression of anger were the strongest predictors of subsequent CVD [29].

Anxiety is a negative emotional experience that is commonly linked to situations that provoke fear, apprehension, and uncertainty in the individual. This negative state is associated with over activation of sympathetic nervous system and elevated adrenaline and cortisol. Anxiety has also been linked to abnormal patterns of cardiac control and coronary vasospasm (i.e., rupturing of atherosclerotic plaques on the arterial wall) [26]. The experience of anxiety has been linked to increased incidence of coronary heart disease [23] and elevated incident hypertension [30]; however, the link between anxiety and hypertension has been disputed [31]. It has been argued that the psychological mechanism of rumination (i.e., uncontrollable, repetitive, and intrusive thoughts about a distressing topic) is fundamental to the experience of anxiety and the influence of this negative emotion on cardiovascular health [32].

It should be noted that all three negative emotional states contain significant overlap both with respect to their conceptual definition and associated measures [33]. For example, anxiety and depression are often positively correlated, and one wonders whether a general factor of negative affectivity (i.e., the propensity to experience negative emotion) would be the most appropriate psychological concept on which to base the study of cardiovascular health. Camacho [34] have explicitly described a continuum from anxiety to depression as an inflammatory emotional state; in other words, an experience of negative emotion that is strongly associated with inflammation and dysregulation of the major physiological systems. A prospective study reported a strong link between anxiety/depression and CVD, but this association was not replicated for anger [35]. It is also important to consider the time course of the relationship between negative emotion and cardiovascular health. Episodes of negative emotion that are short-term and acute may cause specific cardiovascular events, such as an arrhythmia, whereas the process of atherosclerosis is cumulative and gradual and takes place over a long period of time [36].

This short review has emphasized the convergence of three negative emotional states on the physiological systems of the human body. Depression, anger, and anxiety all create a shift toward sympathetic dominance in the autonomic nervous system. This increase of catabolic activity creates a series of coordinated changes across the heart, lungs, vasculature, viscera etc. The same pattern is also associated with elevated adrenaline and cortisol in the bloodstream and a rise in levels of pro-inflammatory cytokines. Hence, negative emotions promote a sustained increase of metabolic activity and an inflammatory process, which can be highly damaging for the long-term health of the individual. It should be noted that many of the physiological changes described above occur without any conscious awareness on the part of the individual. It has also been argued that negative emotions may exert significant effects on the cardiovascular system even when the person is sleeping [37]. Objective measurement in combination with pervasive monitoring technology may be the only way to unveil the influence of negative emotional states on physiological systems and could act as an important data source for interventions that are designed to improve health in the long-term.

LIFELOGGING TECHNOLOGY

Between 2000 and 2050, it is projected that the world population will increase by 47%, from 6.1 to 8.9 billion [38]. As a result, the life expectancy of adults worldwide is also increasing, and so addressing the costs of demographic change is high up the political agenda [39]. A challenge is ensuring that healthy life expectancy (HLE), that is, the average amount of years that we live without disease/injury, increases at the same rate as life expectancy, and enabling people to work for longer [40]. As a result of changes in lifestyle, diet, and ageing, behavior-related, or noncommunicable diseases (NCDs), including CVD, cancer, and diabetes, are also rising [39]. As we age, the potential economic and societal costs of NCDs increases, thus affecting economic growth worldwide [39].

The effective use of advanced technological systems represents one approach to reducing the profound economic and societal costs of disease on the global population. Lifelogging is a technology that supports the necessary self-reflection required to develop an effective coping strategy via the continuous recording of behavior from data from the body. Data are continuously gathered from multiple sources (e.g., from wearable cameras and body sensors) to capture patterns of daily activity in a permanent and comprehensive format. Although this practice of recording objective data on daily patterns of behavior is known as lifelogging, the outcome of this process is often referred to as a lifelog or human digital memory (HDM). As technology advances, and sensors become more prevalent within our environment, we have access to an increasing range of data. Through unique addressing schemes, the Internet of Things (IoT) has enabled a range of mobile devices to interact with each other and cooperate with their neighbors in order to provide a comprehensive source of information [41]. Currently, there are more connected devices than people on the planet: approximately 25 billion connected devices compared to the world's population of 7.2 billion, with this number set to increase twofold to 50 billion by 2020 [42] as shown in Figure 2.1.

Furthermore, over the next decade, the IoT is projected to generate $14.4 trillion of value from factors including reduced costs, employee productivity, waste elimination, customer experience, and innovation (reducing time to market) [43]. This availability of a myriad of connected sensing devices has enabled lifelogs to become richer with information, and their use in various application domains is also increasing.

The data arising from a lifelog can be consulted and used as the basis for self-reflection and insight. For instance, cross-referencing the daily occurrence of negative emotional episodes with physiological markers (e.g., electrocardiogram [ECG] and pulse velocity) and lifelogging data, (e.g., time of day, location, and photographs) enables great insight into behavior. For example, during the context of driving, the occurrence of traffic congestion at a particular junction, raises blood pressure without any awareness on the part of the driver [44]. The repetition of this daily behavior over a sustained period would contribute to the development

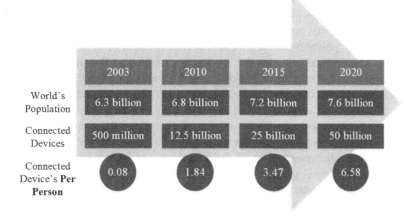

FIGURE 2.1

Growth of the Internet of Things.

of CVD. However, if the individual could review those moments when anger increased and view the magnitude of change in the cardiovascular system, this would lead to a profound insight into the context of this behavior and the significance of psychophysiological pathways. Armed with this insight, the driver may adapt his behavior via a change in behavior, such as avoiding a particular location at a particular time of day in the future. The availability and range of measures that are available greatly increase the sophistication of self-monitoring, and the availability of such data can be used to increase self-awareness and self-knowledge. However, this benign influence of lifelogging technology depends on a number of factors, including (1) the confidence users have in the sensitivity and validity of the resulting data, (2) the insight provided by these systems and the additional benefit or utility that is provided by the availability of these data, and (3) the interface/visualization of data, which determines the ease with which insight can be obtained.

This chapter will explore lifelogging technologies, the effectiveness of technological coping strategies to alleviate anger and anxiety and the human—computer interaction (HCI) issues that the area faces. The chapter will conclude with a summary of the key challenges facing this category of technology.

BACKGROUND
LIFELOGGING TECHNOLOGIES

The concept of logging and storing all of ones accumulated digital items was first proposed in 1945, by Vannevar Bush [45], with the concept of the Memex. Subsequently, fundamental advancements in technology have enabled this idea to be realized and has been an inspiration for many computer scientists, such as Steve Mann, the pioneer of wearable lifelogging systems [46,47], and more recently by Microsoft with their commercial wearable camera device, the SenseCam™ [48].

The use of mobile phones and cameras for the collection of data related to the surroundings of an individual have been explored in previous research [49,50]. This work indicated that the use of such visual imagery is the preferred representation for autobiographical memories because it is an efficient form of data representation [51]. One central argument of the current chapter is that lifelogging can support positive self-regulation of health via representation and feedback of implicit behavior. This position is supported by Doherty et al. [52], who found that the act of reviewing lifelogging data prompted their participants to make changes to their lifestyle, for example, increased level of exercise, spending more time with their children. However, these hardware platforms are limited in the sense that the physiological changes underpinning the experiences were not included. These data are important because they provide insight into those unconscious physiological processes that support everyday behavior and experience. Furthermore, these data can yield an objective index of emotional experience and promote positive strategies for coping by bridging the gap between conscious experience and the unconscious physiological activity.

Recent research into the area of affective computing has demonstrated that emotional states can be recognized from physiological signals [53-55]. These data are highly personalized and unique to every individual. The incorporation of physiological data into a lifelog would allow users to access an objective representation of how an emotional episode, such as an outburst of anger, is manifested in the body. The development of smaller sensors and wireless communications is revolutionizing the ubiquity of monitoring and the availability of physiological data for personal use [56]. One such approach has been the Affective Diary [57,58], which is a digital diary where users can write notes while the application allows "body memorabilia" to be recorded from sensors [58]. This system has been used to explore the emotional aspect to creating diaries and is designed to support self-reflection [59]. However, manually uploading logged data into the application, and visualizing data in the form of "somewhat ambiguously shaped and coloured figures" both represented disadvantages for uses of the Affective Diary [58]. The AffectAura [55] takes a different approach and represents itself as an "emotional prosthetic" that allows users to reflect on their emotional states over long periods of time. The AffectAura has been designed as a technology probe to explore the potential power of a reflective process based upon a pairing of affective data with knowledge of workers' information and data interaction artifacts. Data are collected from a variety of devices, including a webcam, Kinect, and microphone. Supervised machine learning was used to develop an affect recognition engine based on the resulting database. These categorized data are displayed in a timeline format, which captured the ebb and flow of affects, represented by a series of bubbles. The results of an evaluation indicated that users were able to leverage cues from AffectAura to construct stories about their days, even after they had forgotten these particular incidents or their related emotional tones [55]. Using the k-nearest neighbor (kNN) classifier, AffectAura predicted emotional status across the emotional states of valence, arousal, and engagement and achieved a modest prediction accuracy of 68% across all three states [55]. Other related research includes the lifelogging system developed by the Hernandez et al. [51] lifelogging mirror system that enabled an individual to capture and reflect on their daily activities. This system was composed of a number of wearable devices that capture physiological signals, acceleration, and photographs. These data are subsequently displayed in an interactive digital mirror interface to aid reflection. This interface consisted of two components: a digital mirror, which was used to display the information and a "gesture recognition system" to browse the data. In order to interact with the system, via the gesture system, a Kinect camera has been attached below the mirror, which allowed the user to navigate through their data by waving their arms (up, down, left and right) in front of the camera [51]. As such, photos are linked to the physiological data and the user may search the resulting data on a daily timeline.

HUMAN—COMPUTER INTERACTION

Capturing physiological data through multimodal sensors enables the psychophysiological context of an event or emotional episode to be recorded. However, displaying this type of context via a human—computer interface cannot be considered "intelligent" and effective unless the system is capable of perceiving and expressing this type of context [60]. Furthermore, using these data to create an intuitive interface that promotes self-awareness and positive behavior change represents a second level of challenge for the system designer.

There are a number of HCI issues pertaining to the design of lifelogging interfaces, and a number of studies have been conducted in this area. For example, Impact used a website to visualize step counts to represent physical activity and self-annotated notes of the context of this behavior to represent the activity level of the user [61]. UbiFit Garden combined a mobile sensing platform (MSP) with a visual metaphor via a smartphone interface that was designed to increase users' levels of physical activity [61,62]. Feedback was provided by the visualization of a garden, with the flowers in this digital garden growing and blooming as the user became more active. Furthermore, a large yellow butterfly appeared when a weekly goal had been completed and a series of smaller butterflies have been used as indications of recent goal attainments, which acted as a reward and a reminder of past successes [62]. Fish n' Steps also attempted to increase levels of physical activity by measuring the step count of the user via pedometers and linking these data with an interactive game that involved caring for a virtual pet. The daily step count from the users was used to grow and sustain the emotional well-being of a fish in an aquarium, and this visualization was used to motivate users to become more physically active [63].

Other types of lifelogging interfaces have moved away from physical activity and toward more traditional journal-keeping activities. Footprint Tracker is a lifelogging tool that combines photographs, location, temporal, and social context cues into a two-panel display. A timeline interface was used to highlight the presence of data within a particular period, and this was supplemented with a data panel to display the relevant information [64]. A study of Footprint Tracker concluded that this kind of diary format increased participants' ability to recall and reflect on their daily activities. The emphasis of Footprint Tracker on realism and the requirement for unobtrusive devices should be noted for diary or journal applications [64].

Other types of lifelogging applications emphasize psychological well-being as well as physical fitness. The DStress system is designed to reduce stress by setting goals and activities for the user to undertake [65]. The goals of the system are achieved by providing feedback to the user with respect to:

1. Type of stress-reduction activity (exercise, meditation)
2. Instructions on how to execute these activities
3. Techniques for logging progress with activities
4. Reminders about activities and logging
5. A record of past activities.

The system was used by 77 participants over a period of 1 month to determine the effectiveness of the application with respect to stress reduction. A survey technique was used to collect information before and after the study to evaluate its effectiveness as an intervention. The system included an element of adaptive personalization by modifying the level of difficulty for goals for the user, with respect to their previous performance. The study found that being adaptive was beneficial as it was able to maintain a suitable level of difficulty for users to get the greatest benefit [65]. The EmoTree represents a similar application [66] that incorporated data from an ECG into the data stream. This system was designed to detect emotional triggers for overeating and was based on the rationale that increased stress was associated with undesirable behavior. The application included an intervention that was delivered via the mobile application, which was designed to assist participants in adjusting from a state of stress to a state of relative calm. The interface is designed as a tree that displays the collection of physiological data and the deliverance of emotion to the user. The user's emotional state is aggregated as the background color to indicate positive or negative valence of affect [66]. Evaluation of this system was undertaken via three studies that (1) gathered emotional eating patterns via participants self-reporting emotions and food intake every hour, (2) investigated intervention techniques by including a deep breathing intervention exercise into the app that is triggered when the user self-reports stress/anxiety emotions, and (3) detected emotional states using wearable ECG, electrodermal activity (EDA), and a three-axis accelerometer and a two-axis gyroscope body sensors [66]. The authors reported that all participants became more aware of their eating habits, and 87.5% became more aware of their emotions via their interaction with the application. However, only 37.5% reported a change in behavior as a result of the first study. This work is interesting because of the low conversion from recording behavior to implementing changes, as "logging made participants more aware, it seemed that most needed something extra to incentivise real change" [66]. It also seems that in the case of the second study, this intervention worked relatively well, but it was reported that personalization would have been more beneficial. The third study aimed to move toward this idea with the introduction of wearable technology. Using a machine learning approach of Gaussian process regression (GPR) produced an accuracy of 75% for classifying arousal and 72.62% for valence [66].

As individuals collect more personal information, the topic of HCI becomes more intrinsic to lifelogging applications. This area offers as a way of visualizing our data to derive knowledge and understanding, as well as promoting positive behavioral changes. However, the creation of such applications and tools poses new challenges in HCI and enables diverse disciplines, such as ubiquitous computing, data visualization, and psychophysiology, to collaborate on the design of these systems [67].

RESEARCH CHALLENGES

The challenge for these technologies is to access data that are highly relevant for the health of the individual, in the long term, and presenting those data to the individual via an interface that effectively leads to positive behavioral change. This will require various components to work concurrently so that data can be unobtrusively

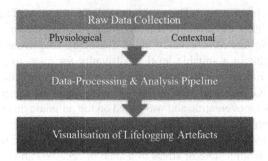

FIGURE 2.2

High-level schematic of an effective lifelogging system to promote positive behavioral changes.

collected, processed, analyzed, and effectively visualized to promote such changes as conveyed in Figure 2.2.

In achieving this, the following is an overview of the key research challenges that face the development of this type of system.

OBTAINING CLINICALLY RELEVANT MEASUREMENTS

The potential health benefits of lifelogging technology will be determined by the choice of sensor and associated measures that are utilized in a mobile ambulatory monitoring platform. It is important for lifelogging technology to embrace those biological markers that are indicative of inflammation and predictive of disease, for example, circulating levels of C-reactive protein (CRP) and interleukin 6 (IL-6) in the bloodstream [11]. Measurement of inflammation may be achieved via proxy measures, for example, measurement of heart rate variability (HRV) is possible via a conventional ECG, and this variable is significantly correlated with levels of both CRP and IL-6 [68-70]. Similarly, pulse wave velocity (PWV), which may be calculated by combining an ECG with a photoplethysmographic sensor attached to the finger, is associated with local arterial stiffness—an early marker of atherosclerosis [71].

Body sensor networks can be created for the capture of medically relevant data that are composed of multiple wearable sensors [72]. Technological advances in the design of wearable devices have allowed sensor apparatus to become smaller, weigh less, and consume less power; therefore, physiological data can be collected unobtrusively [73]. For instance, pulse and respiratory rates have been successfully collected using different sensors in Google Glass [73]. Such systems consist of three main entities: (1) the hardware that is used to collect such information, (2) the communication protocols that are used to transmit data to a central location, and (3) data analysis techniques to extract clinically relevant information from the raw data [72]. However, each element in this data collection pipeline incorporates a number of challenges. For instance, multiple pieces of hardware are required, such as a number of wearable sensors/devices and cameras, to capture signals from the body and the environment. Furthermore, synchronizing data streams from multiple devices, in real time and in a mobile environment, is challenging. Physiological data must be filtered, and artifacts identified in order to isolate the contribution of such factors on cardiovascular physiology. However, in principle, the inclusion of multiple sensors should make it easier to detect such artifacts. Additionally, transmitting these data securely, efficiently, and reliably over wireless networks presents further issues to ensure that the data packets are not intercepted and modified [74]. The reliable transmission of personal physiological data over public networks is a cause for concern as outsiders can gain access to such networks and potentially comprise the privacy and the reliability of the data [74]. These data need to be protected securely as any system that uses physiological data requires data to be free of errors, which could occur by intentional manipulation, for processing and diagnosis [75].

CAPTURING CONTEXT

The success of lifelogging systems depends on an intelligent integration of information about context with physiological data [75]. Human memory operates by associating linked items together; as such, capturing context is important for augmenting recall and understanding of past events [76]. The enrichment of lifelogs with context-related metadata, such as the presence of other people, location data, sounds, and physiological data, would provide multiple cues for the recall and reflection on information held in a digital memory [77].

Smartphone technology has revolutionized the development of lifelogging systems that are used to remotely monitor the user [72]. The global smartphone market has experienced tremendous growth in recent years, with shipments increasing by 40%, to more than 1 billion units, in 2013 [78]. These devices are seen as the preferred platform to capture context-related data as they are seen as a "ready to use" platform that does not require significant configuration but is capable of gathering a wealth of contextual information about the user, including call/message logs, captured images, and music preference [72,79]. Additionally, a number of sensors, including Global Positioning System (GPS), Bluetooth and motion sensors (e.g., accelerometer), permit location, proximity of other devices, and activity to also be recorded [79]. Such sensor-based systems are integral in forming awareness of context because they provide (1) insight into physiological changes over time, (2) the ability to correlate activity with physiological data, and (3) prediction of future trends of the user's health [75].

One of the fundamental challenges of implementing a context-aware system is the problem of identifying the relevant context for data capture [75]. Supervised machine learning can be used to address this issue by training the system on a specific set of criteria [75]. For instance, once the markers of anger have been identified, the system can be trained to recognize those physiological signs and correlate them with other pieces of data (e.g., location, photos). However, the heterogeneous and distributed nature of these data represents a challenge for the integration of multiple streams into a single timeline. These data must be synchronized to capture specific episodes of emotion through a number of different sensors using a number of frequencies. Further research is required to determine the level of synchronization required to achieve the level of data integration in order to describe an episode of anger as one example. Once anger has been determined, these algorithms require training in order to distinguish between episodes that yield high or low levels of inflammation.

PROCESSING AND VISUALIZING BIG DATA SETS OF PERSONAL INFORMATION TO DELIVER INSIGHT

Lifelogging produces vast amounts of data; for instance, SenseCam, a wearable camera developed by Microsoft, is capable of capturing 3000 images per day [80]. When other devices and pieces of information are included, this set of personal big data will expand rapidly. As a result, this complex set of heterogeneous data is composed of many items of unstructured data that requires adequate storage facilities and needs to provide us with useful information. Mining such large sets of data for useful information often requires techniques that go beyond searching traditional relational databases [81]. Previously, this type of structured data had the advantage of being easily entered, stored, queried, and analyzed and the result was searchable by simple, straightforward algorithms. However, lifelogging produces a new era of information that is more unstructured. Such data cannot be readily classified and does not reside in a traditional row—column database, such as text and multimedia content (e.g., weblogs, social media, e-mail, sensors, photographs, audio files, and presentations) [81]. With so many different ways to generate an index, it becomes more challenging to decide on one to use. However, sophisticated algorithms can be used to mine and organize these data for useful information, and patterns begin to emerge from aggregating multiple sources of information [81]. Intrinsically, the goal of collecting and mining such personal big sets of data is to discover and extract critical pieces of information that provides the user with control for decision making [82]. Presenting this information to users will enable them to reflect on their behavior through their personal data. However, as more and more data are generated daily, there comes a point of saturation where the user will become overwhelmed by their data. Perhaps the idea of a "self-forgetting" system could be the solution where physiological data could be used as an indicator to mark certain periods for retention, or data mining techniques could be used to indicate periods of interest so that other times could be "forgotten" or erased.

The current chapter is concerned with a lifelogging system whose design goal is to provide a platform that supports self-reflection to reduce the onset of CVD. In order to achieve this goal, data must be processed efficiently and displayed in an informative and clear manner. The system interface is a powerful tool that can generate either a positive (e.g., tolerant/content) or negative (e.g., anger/disgust) effect on the user's experience of the entire system [1]. For instance, if an interface is overly complicated, fails to perform its task (e.g., crashes regularly) or if the appearance is not adaptive can lead to the generation of negative emotions [1]. These are important points to consider when designing a system that is meant to reduce anger and stress. Data must be presented in a way that intuitively supports self-reflection, without being overwhelming, causing alarm or inciting further negative emotions. As such, the area of big data visualization poses several types of challenges. In order to convey information and derive knowledge from complex and large data sets, it is important to employ techniques that are both aesthetically pleasing and functional [83]. However, trying to achieve this often leads to tools that have poor performance in terms of functionality, scalability, and response time [83]. It is important to recognize that effective visualization techniques may not transfer across different tasks [84]. For instance, Epstein et al. [84] have explored displaying location and activity data that was generated from a smartphone in a number of ways, including tables, graphs, captions, maps, Sankey diagrams, and as a timeline. Their study concluded that participants generally preferred tabular and graphical presentations, which summarized data in an easily consumable format and that these methods were more useful at "discovering factors that influence their behavior ($p<0.01$) and for finding patterns ($p<0.01$)" [84]. However, these findings are fairly preliminary. In order to support self-reflection, reducing CVD requires more complex items of data that need to be displayed effectively to encourage this task.

This approach will enable the promotion of positive coping strategies by bridging the gap between conscious experience and data representing unconscious processes. Utilizing such technologies to monitor behavior provides a very powerful graphical illustration of our health and well-being. Bringing together lifelogging and physiological data capture enables the context of situations to be derived and markers for anger to be determined. This technology enables the user to quantify the impact that everyday periods of anger has on the markers of cardiovascular health by reflecting the triggers for associated behavior. The individual is subsequently empowered to reevaluate the situation and change his or her behavior accordingly.

SUMMARY

From a societal perspective, logging, visualizing, and reflecting on periods of inflammation has the potential to reduce the long-term probability of developing CVD. The availability of smaller and more powerful sensors, wearable devices, and the explosion of the "quantified self" movement has also been a driving force that has brought lifelogging to the forefront of researchers and consumers [85]. By 2016, it is predicted that wearable fitness and personal health devices will be a $5-billion market [85,86].

Currently, it is straightforward to log overt aspects of behavior, such as facial expressions, location, and movement. However, combining those markers with covert changes in cardiovascular physiology, which cannot be perceived directly by the user, would make sure applications are more powerful. Hence, it will be extending a person's awareness of their bodies and how their reactions to situations directly impact on physiological systems. This is a very exciting avenue to pursue. As we become more self-aware, we will be able to reevaluate or lifestyles and prevent the onset of certain diseases. The area of lifelogging is growing rapidly and as such presents us with unique opportunities to develop novel solutions, which include much richer data capturing and processing capabilities.

ACKNOWLEDGEMENTS

This research has been undertaken as part of the project "Development of a Multimodal Lifelogging Platform to Support Self-Reflection & Monitor Inflammation Associated with the Experience of Negative Emotions" that has been supported by the UK Engineering and Physical Sciences Research Council (EPSRC) under Research Grant EP/M029484/1.

REFERENCES

[1] Voeffray C. Emotion-sensitive Human-Computer Interaction (HCI): State of the art - Seminar paper. Emotion Recognition 2011:1−4.
[2] Hollis V, Konrad A, Whittaker S. Change of Heart: Emotion Tracking to Promote Behavior Change. In: Proceedings of the SIGCHI Conference on Human Factors in Computing Systems (CHI 2015); 2015.
[3] Suls J. Anger and the Heart: Perspectives on Cardiac Risk, Mechanisms and Interventions. Prog Cardiovasc Dis 2013;55(6):538−47.
[4] Samuels MA. The Brain-Heart Connection. Circulation 2007;116(1):77−84.
[5] Sesso HD, Buring JE, Rifai N, Blake GJ, Gaziano JM, Ridker PM. C-Reactive Protein and the Risk of Developing Hypertension. J Am Med Assoc Dec. 2003;290(22):2945−51.
[6] Williams JE, Paton CC, Siegler IC, Eigenbrodt ML, Nieto FJ, Tyroler HA. Anger proneness predicts coronary heart disease risk: prospective analysis from the atherosclerosis risk in communities (ARIC) study. Circulation 2000;101(17):2034−9.
[7] Kop WJ, Verdino RJ, Gottdiener JS, O'Leary ST, Bairey Merz CN, Krantz DS. Changes in Heart Rate and Heart Rate Variability Before Ambulatory Ischemic Events. J Am Coll Cardiol 2001;38(3):742−9.
[8] Lane RD, Laukes C, Marcus FI, et al. Psychological Stress Preceding Idiopathic Ventricular Fibrillation. Psychosom Med 2005;67(3):359−65.
[9] Strike PC, Steptoe A. Behavioral and Emotional Triggers of Acute Coronary Syndromes: A Systematic Review and Critique. Psychosom Med 2005;67(2):179−86.
[10] O'Donovan A, Neylan TC, Metzler T, Cohen BE. Lifetime exposure to traumatic psychological stress is associated with elevated inflammation in the Heart and Soul Study. Brain Behav Immun 2012;26(4):642−9.
[11] Ganzel BL, Morris PA, Wethington E. Allostasis and the human brain: Integrating models of stress from the social and life sciences. Psychol Rev 2010;117(1):134−74.
[12] McEwen BS. Physiology and Neurobiology of Stress and Adaptation: Central Role of the Brain. Physiol Rev 2007;87:873−904.

[13] Brosschot JF. Markers of chronic stress: Prolonged physiological activation and (un)conscious perseverative cognition. Neurosci Biobehav Rev 2010;35(1):46–50.

[14] World Health Organization. Global status report on noncommunicable diseases 2010. 2011.

[15] Townsend N, Wickramasinghe K, Bhatnagar P, Smolina K, Nichols M, Leal J, et al. Coronary Heart Disease Statistics 2012. In: British Heart Foundation. 18th ed. 2012. p. 1–211.

[16] World Health Organization. Prevention of Cardiovascular Disease: Guidelines for assessment and management of cardiovascular risk. 2007.

[17] Go AS, Mozaffarian D, Roger VL, Benjamin EJ, Berry JD, Blaha MJ, et al. Heart Disease and Stroke Statistics—2014 Update: A Report From the American Heart Association. Jan. 2014.

[18] British Heart Foundation. Modelling the UK burden of Cardiovascular Disease to 2020: A Research Report for the Cardio & Vascular Coalition and the British Heart Foundation. 2008.

[19] Nichols M, Townsend N, Scarborough P, Rayner M, Leal J, Luengo-Fernandez R, et al. European Cardiovascular Disease Statistics 2012. In: European Heart Network. 4th ed. 2012. p. 1–129.

[20] Centers for Disease Control and Prevention (CDC). Heart Disease Facts and Statistics. 2014. Available: http://www.cdc.gov/heartdisease/statistics.htm (accessed: 13-Jan-2015).

[21] Charlson FJ, Stapelberg NJ, Baxter AJ, Whiteford HA. Should Global Burden of Disease Estimates Include Depression as a Risk Factor for Coronary Heart Disease? BMC Med 2011;9(1):47.

[22] Everson SA, Goldberg DE, Kaplan GA, Julkunen J, Salonen JT. Anger Expression and Incident Hypertension. Psychosom Med 1998;60(6):730–5.

[23] Janszky I, Ahnve S, Lundberg I, Hemmingsson T. Early-Onset Depression, Anxiety, and Risk of Subsequent Coronary Heart Disease : 37-Year Follow-Up of 49,321 Young Swedish Men. J Am Coll Cardiol 2010;56(1):31–7.

[24] McEwen BS. Protective and Damaging Effects of Stress Mediators. N Engl J Med 1998; 338(3):171–9.

[25] Karlamangla AS, Singer BH, Seeman TE. Reduction in Allostatic Load in Older Adults Is Associated With Lower All-Cause Mortality Risk: MacArthur Studies of Successful Aging. Psychosom Med 2006;68(3):500–7.

[26] Sirois BC, Burg MM. Negative Emotion and Coronary Heart Disease: A Review. Behav Modif 2003;27(1):83–102.

[27] Elderon L, Whooley MA. Depression and Cardiovascular Disease. Prog Cardiovasc Dis 2013;55(6):511–23.

[28] McEwen BS. Physiology and Neurobiology of Stress and Adaptation: Central Role of the Brain. Physiol Rev 2007;87(3):873–904.

[29] Haukkala A, Konttinen H, Laatikainen T, Kawachi I, Uutela A. Hostility, Anger Control, and Anger Expression as Predictors of Cardiovascular Disease. Psychosom Med 2010;72(6):556–62.

[30] Roest AM, Martens EJ, de Jonge P, Denollet J. Anxiety and Risk of Incident Coronary Heart Disease: A Meta-Analysis. J Am Coll Cardiol 2010;56(1):38–46.

[31] Player MS, Peterson LE. Anxiety Disorders, Hypertension, and Cardiovascular Risk: A Review. Int J Psychiatry Med 2011;41(4):365–77.

[32] Thurston RC, Rewak M, Kubzansky LD. An Anxious Heart: Anxiety and the Onset of Cardiovascular Diseases. Prog Cardiovasc Dis 2013;55(6):524–37.

[33] Suls J, Bunde J. Anger, Anxiety, and Depression as Risk Factors for Cardiovascular Disease: The Problems and Implications of Overlapping Affective Dispositions. Psychol Bull 2005;131(2):260–300.

[34] Camacho A. Is anxious-depression an inflammatory state? Med Hypotheses 2013;81(4): 577–81.

[35] Kubzansky LD, Cole SR, Kawachi I, Vokonas P, Sparrow D. Shared and unique contributions of anger, anxiety, and depression to coronary heart disease: a prospective study in the normative aging study. Ann Behav Med 2006;31(1):21–9.

[36] Kop WJ. The integration of cardiovascular behavioral medicine and psychoneuroimmunology: New developments based on converging research fields. Brain Behav Immun 2003;17(4):233–7.

[37] Brosschot JF. Markers of chronic stress: Prolonged physiological activation and (un)conscious perseverative cognition. Neurosci Biobehav Rev 2010;35(1):46–50.

[38] United Nations. World population to 2300. 2004.

[39] National Institute on Aging. National Institutes of Health, U.S. Department of Health and Human Services, and World Health Organization. Global Health and Aging 2011.

[40] The International Longevity Centre UK. The Economic Value of Healthy Ageing and Working Longer Notes based on the ILC-UK and Actuarial Profession joint debates Supported by Prudential. 2010.

[41] Atzori L, Iera A, Morabito G. The Internet of Things: A survey. Comput Networks 2010;54(15):2787–805.

[42] Evans D. The Internet of Things: How the Next Evolution of the Internet Is Changing Everything. 2011.

[43] Bradley J, Barbier J, Handler D. Embracing the Internet of Everything To Capture Your Share of $ 14.4 Trillion. 2013.

[44] Fairclough SH, van der Zwaag M, Spiridon E, Westerink J. Effects of mood induction via music on cardiovascular measures of negative emotion during simulated driving. Physiol Behav 2014;129:173–80.

[45] Bush V. As We May Think. The Atlantic MonthlyJULY 1945.

[46] Mann S. Wearable Computing: A First Step Toward Personal Imaging. Computer 1997; 30(2):25–32.

[47] Mann S, Fung J, Aimone C, Sehgal A, Chen D. Designing EyeTap Digital Eyeglasses for Continuous Lifelong Capture and Sharing of Personal Experiences. In: Proceedings of CHI 2005 Conference on Human Factors in Computer Systems; 2005.

[48] Hodges S, Williams L, Berry E, Izadi S, Srinivasan J, Butler A, et al. SenseCam: A Retrospective Memory Aid. UbiComp 2006 Ubiquitous Comput 2006;4206:177–93.

[49] Hamm J, Stone B, Belkin M, Dennis S. Automatic Annotation of Daily Activity from Smartphone-based Multisensory Streams. In: Mobile Computing, Applications, and Services; 2013. p. 328–42.

[50] Doherty AR, Pauly-Takacs K, Caprani N, Gurrin C, Moulin CJA, O'Connor NE, et al. Experiences of Aiding Autobiographical Memory Using the SenseCam. Hum Comput Interact 2012;27(1-2):151–74.

[51] Hernandez J, McDuff D, Fletcher R, Picard RW. Inside-Out: Reflecting on your Inner State. In: 2013 IEEE International Conference on Pervasive Computing and Communications Workshops (PERCOM Workshops); 2013. p. 324–7.

[52] Doherty AR, Caprani N, Conaire CÓ, Kalnikaite V, Gurrin C, Smeaton AF, et al. Passively Recognising Human Activities Through Lifelogging. Comput Human Behav 2011;27(5):1948–58.

[53] Ivonin L, Chang H-M, Chen W, Rauterberg M. Unconscious emotions: quantifying and logging something we are not aware of. Pers Ubiquitous Comput 2012;17(4):663−73.

[54] van den Broek EL, Janssen JH, Westerink JHDM. Guidelines for Affective Signal Processing (ASP): from lab to life. In: 3rd International Conference on Affective Computing & Intelligent Interaction, ACII 2009, 10−12 Sept 2009, Amsterdam, The Netherlands; 2009.

[55] McDuff D, Karlson A, Kapoor A, Roseway A, Czerwinski M. AffectAura: An Intelligent System for Emotional Memory. In: Proceedings of the 2012 ACM annual conference on Human Factors in Computing Systems - CHI '12; 2012. p. 849−58.

[56] Pantelopoulos A, Bourbakis NG. A Survey on Wearable Sensor-Based Systems for Health Monitoring and Prognosis. IEEE Trans Syst Man Cybern C Appl Rev 2010; 40(1):1−12.

[57] Lindström M, Ståhl A, Höök K, Sundström P, Laaksolathi J, Combetto M, et al. Affective Diary − Designing for Bodily Expressiveness and Self-Reflection. In: CHI '06 extended abstracts on Human factors in computing systems; 2006. p. 1037−42.

[58] Ståhl A, Höök K, Svensson M, Taylor AS, Combetto M. Experiencing the Affective Diary. Pers Ubiquitous Comput 2009;13(5):365−78.

[59] Machajdik J, Hanbury A, Garz A, Sablatnig R. Affective Computing for Wearable Diary and Lifelogging Systems: An Overview. In: 35th Annual Workshop of the Austrian Association for Pattern Recognition (OAGM/AAPR); 2011.

[60] Cambria E, Hupont I, Hussain A, Cerezo E, Baldassarri S. Sentic Avatar: Multimodal Affective Conversational Agent with Common Sense. Towar. Auton. Adapt. Context. Multimodal Interfaces. Theor Pract 2011;(Issues 6456):81−95.

[61] Li I, Dey AK, Forlizzi J. Using Context to Reveal Factors that Affect Physical Activity. ACM Trans Comput Interact Mar. 2012;19(1):1−21.

[62] Consolvo S, McDonald DW, Toscos T, Chen MY, Froehlich J, Harrison B, Klasnja P, LaMarca A, LeGrand L, Libby R, Smith I, Landay JA. Activity Sensing in the Wild: A Field Trial of UbiFit Garden. In: Proceeding of the Twenty-Sixth Annual CHI Conference on Human Factors in Computing Systems - CHI '08; 2008. p. 1797−806.

[63] Lin JJ, Mamykina L, Lindtner S, Delajoux G, Strub HB. Fish'n'Steps: Encouraging Physical Activity with an Interactive Computer Game. UbiComp 2006: Ubiquitous Computing 2006:261−78.

[64] Gouveia R, Karapanos E. Footprint Tracker: Supporting Diary Studies with Lifelogging. In: Proceedings of the SIGCHI Conference on Human Factors in Computing Systems - CHI '13; 2013. p. 2921−30.

[65] Konrad A, Bellotti V, Crenshaw N, Tucker S, Nelson L, Du H, et al. Finding the Adaptive Sweet Spot: Balancing Compliance and Achievement in Automated Stress Reduction. In: Proceedings of the SIGCHI Conference on Human Factors in Computing Systems (CHI 2015); 2015.

[66] Carroll EA, Czerwinski M, Roseway A, Kapoor A, Johns P, Rowan K, et al. Food and Mood: Just-in-Time Support for Emotional Eating. In: 2013 Humaine Association Conference on Affective Computing and Intelligent Interaction; 2013. p. 252−7.

[67] Li I, Dey A, Forlizzi J, Höök K, Medynskiy Y. Personal Informatics and HCI: Design, Theory, and Social Implications. In: Proceedings of the 2011 Annual Conference Extended Abstracts on Human Factors In Computing Systems - CHI EA '11; 2011. p. 2417−20.

[68] Haensel A, Mills PJ, Nelesen RA, Ziegler MG, Dimsdale JE. The relationship between heart rate variability and inflammatory markers in cardiovascular diseases. Psychoneuroendocrinology 2008;33(10):1305−12.

[69] Lampert R, Bremner JD, Su S, Miller A, Lee F, Cheema F, et al. Decreased heart rate variability is associated with higher levels of inflammation in middle-aged men. Am Heart J 2008;156(4):759. e1-7.

[70] Kemp AH, Quintana DS. The relationship between mental and physical health: Insights from the study of heart rate variability. Int J Psychophysiol 2013;89(3):288—96.

[71] Koivistoinen T, Virtanen M, Hutri-Kähönen N, Lehtimäki T, Jula A, Juonala M, et al. Arterial pulse wave velocity in relation to carotid intima-media thickness, brachial flow-mediated dilation and carotid artery distensibility: The Cardiovascular Risk in Young Finns Study and the Health 2000 Survey. Atherosclerosis 2012;220(2):387—93.

[72] Patel S, Park H, Bonato P, Chan L, Rodgers M. A review of wearable sensors and systems with application in rehabilitation. J Neuroeng Rehabil 2012;9(1):21.

[73] Hernandez J, Li Y, Rehg JM, Picard RW. BioGlass: Physiological Parameter Estimation Using a Head-Mounted Wearable Device. In: EAI 4th International Conference on Wireless Mobile Communication and Healthcare (Mobihealth); 2014. p. 55—8.

[74] Rawat KS, Massiha GH. Secure Data Transmission Over Wireless Networks: Issues And Challenges. Annual Technical Conference IEEE Region 2003;5:65—8.

[75] Viswanathan H, Chen B, Pompili D. Research Challenges in Computation, Communication, and Context Awareness for Ubiquitous Healthcare. IEEE Commun Mag 2012; 50(5):92—9.

[76] Doherty AR, Smeaton AF. Automatically Augmenting Lifelog Events Using Pervasively Generated Content from Millions of People. Sensors 2010;10(3):1423—46.

[77] Olsson T, Soronen H, Väänänen-Vainio-Mattila K. User needs and design guidelines for mobile services for sharing digital life memories. In: Proceedings of the 10th international conference on Human computer interaction with mobile devices and services; 2008. p. 273—82.

[78] CCS Insight. Global Smartphone Market Analysis and Outlook: Disruption in a Changing Market. 2014.

[79] Belimpasakis P, Roimela K, You Y. Experience Explorer: A Life-Logging Platform Based on Mobile Context Collection. In: 2009 Third International Conference on Next Generation Mobile Applications, Services and Technologies; 2009. p. 77—82.

[80] Kelly L, Jones GJF. Examining the utility of affective response in search of personal lifelogs. 5th Workshop on Emotion in Human-Computer Interaction, held at the 23rd BCS HCI Group conference September 1, 2009, Cambridge, UK.

[81] Wu X, Zhu X, Wu GQ, Ding W. Data Mining with Big Data. IEEE Trans Knowl Data Eng 2014;26(1):97—107.

[82] Kaisler S, Armour F, Espinosa JA, Money W. Big Data: Issues and Challenges Moving Forward. In: 2013 46th Hawaii International Conference on System Sciences; 2013. p. 995—1004.

[83] Philip Chen CL, Zhang C-Y. Data-intensive applications, challenges, techniques and technologies: A survey on Big Data. Inf Sci 2014;275:314—47.

[84] Epstein D, Cordeiro F, Bales E, Fogarty J, Munson SA. Taming Data Complexity in Lifelogs: Exploring Visual Cuts of Personal Informatics Data. In: Proceedings of the 2014 Conference on Designing Interactive Systems (DIS); 2014. p. 673.

[85] Khan S, Marzec E. Wearables: On-body computing devices are ready for business. Tech Trends 2014: Inspiring Disruption. Deloitte, Ed. 5th ed. New York: Deloitte University Press; 2014. p. 54—64.

[86] McIntyre A, Ekholm J. Market trends: Enter the wearable electronics market with products for the quantified self 2013.

Gene Selection Methods for Microarray Data

3

B. Chandra

Computer Science Group, Department of Mathematics, Indian Institute of Technology, Delhi, India

E-mail: bchandra104@yahoo.co.in

INTRODUCTION TO GENE SELECTION

Microarray has become a powerful tool for biomedical research, as work in the area has been increasing exponentially. Microarray can be explained as an array of DNA molecules that permit many hybridization experiments to be performed in parallel. DNA microarray technology has made it easy to monitor the expression levels of thousands of genes under particular experimental environments and conditions. DNA microarray data [13] includes a gene expression matrix in which each column represents expression levels of each gene from a single experiment and each row represents the expression of a gene across all experiments.

In microarray data, genes represent the features. Feature selection in the case of microarray data refers to gene selection. Feature selection/gene selection has gained a lot of importance in the last decade since large amounts of genomic data are produced constantly. Microarray data can be effectively used for classification of different types of cancer. The problem encountered in cancer microarray data is that there are very few samples in contrast to the number of genes that denote the features. It is a challenging task to select the important genes that lead to various types of cancer. It has been observed that identifying informative genes that have the greatest power of classification is essential for categorizing different tumor types [10]. The nature of relatively high dimensionality but small sample size in microarray data can cause the problem of "curse of dimensionality" and overfitting of training data. Hence, gene selection is all the more important for efficient sample classification [8].

Feature selection forms a preprocessing step for any machine learning task. The aim of feature selection is to choose a subset of features by eliminating redundant features that do not provide useful information. It is a process of selecting the best possible subset of features based on certain criteria that improves the functionality of the classifier. A good feature subset can

- lead to better classification and model comprehensibility,
- simplify data description,

45

- improve prediction accuracy and performance, and
- reduce computational cost.

Gene selection can be carried out in a supervised or unsupervised manner.

UNSUPERVISED AND SUPERVISED GENE SELECTION

Supervised methods require the genes and related conditions to be associated with labels that provide information about a preexisting classification. The class label might correspond to disease subtype. In this case, the sample classification is carried out by analyzing microarray data in the supervised mode. Unsupervised gene selection methods help in discovering genes that are important without knowing the sample type. This is especially useful for the study of DNA microarray data for new diseases.

Because gene selection in microarray data refers to feature selection, in the rest of the manuscript, gene selection and feature selection will be used interchangeably. The following section describes the general categories of feature selection.

APPROACHES TO FEATURE SELECTION

Feature selection algorithms can be categorized into three main types: filter, wrapper, and embedded approach [11]. The filter approach [19,20] relies on the general characteristics of data to evaluate and select feature subsets. Different evaluation criteria, namely, distance, information, dependency, and consistency, are used. The disadvantages of using a filter approach are that each feature is dealt with independently and that interactions between the features are not taken into account. The selected features are independent of the learning methods, and hence filter based methods are widely used. ReliefF [20], chi-square test [22], CFS [12] t-test, Laplacian score [14], maximum relevance minimum redundancy (mRMR) [7], trace ratio [25], effective range based gene selection [5], and maximum weight minimum redundancy [31] are some of the well-known filter approach algorithms that have been described in the next section.

The wrapper approach [6,34] selects the feature subset based on a classifier, and ranks feature subset using prediction accuracy. It is computationally very expensive as this allows the use of standard optimization techniques like sequential forward selection (SFS) [33] and backward feature selection [23], sequential forward floating selection (SFFS), sequential backward floating selection (SBFS) [27], and greedy search and randomized search like genetic algorithm [35]. The embedded approach [15] performs feature selection as a part of the learning algorithm and is usually specific to given learning machines.

FILTER BASED SUPERVISED FEATURE SELECTION ALGORITHMS

Some of the well-known supervised filter based feature selection methods have been discussed in this section.

Relief

Relief [18] is a feature selection algorithm applied only for binary classification. It does not use a heuristic approach and has linear time complexity in number of training instances and number of features. It revolves around the idea of how well, with respect to given attributes, an instance discriminates with other nearest instances. In this algorithm, the discriminating quality of each attribute called weight of features is estimated. The procedure is given below.

1. For the estimation of quality, an instance R_i is randomly selected and its two nearest neighbors are searched as follows:
    Nearest hit H, i.e., nearest neighbor from the same class as R_i.
    Nearest miss M, i.e., nearest neighbor from the other class.
    Let I_1 and I_2 denote two instances. The difference function with respect to a particular feature f_i is defined as follows. For a feature having discrete values,

$$\text{diff}(f_i, I_1, I_2) = 0 \quad \text{if} \quad \text{value}(f_i, I_1) = \text{value}(f_i, I_2).$$
$$\qquad\qquad\qquad 1 \quad \text{if} \quad \text{value}(f_i, I_1) \neq \text{value}(f_i, I_2). \tag{1}$$

and for a feature having continuous values,

$$\text{diff}(f_i, I_1, I_2) = |\text{value}(f_i, I_1) - \text{value}(f_i, I_2)| / (\max(f_i) - \min(f_i)) \tag{2}$$

where $\text{value}(f_i, I_1) = $ numerical value of feature f_i at instance I_1.

2. Each feature is given zero weight initially, and it is updated at each iteration. The updating rules are given below:
    Decrement Rule: When a feature value is different for two instances of the same class, it becomes undesirable. Hence its weight is decremented in the case of quality estimation with the help of nearest hit neighbor.
    Increment rule: When a feature value is different for two instances of different class, it becomes desirable. In this case, the weight of the feature is incremented with the help of nearest miss neighbor. Hence the updating equation for feature weights takes care of both decrement and increment rules. The feature weights are updated as follows:

$$W[f_i] = W[f_i] - \text{diff}(f_i, R_i, H)/m + \text{diff}(f_i, R_i, M)/m \tag{3}$$

3. Weight updation for features is continued m times, where m is a prespecified user input.
4. Only those features are selected whose weight exceeds a predefined threshold λ.

Muni et al. [24] used Relief algorithm for selecting important genes in microarray data. Because Relief can be used only for binary classification problems, an extension to this algorithm called ReliefF was developed. ReliefF is used for selecting features for a multiclass problem.

ReliefF

ReliefF [21] starts with the random selection of any instance R_j and then searches for K nearest neighbors from the same class called nearest hit H_j and also K nearest neighbors from each of the classes (other than its own) called nearest miss $M_j(C)$

where C denotes the class. The selection of K nearest neighbors instead of one nearest neighbor as in Relief algorithm helps in improving the reliability of quality of attribute. ReliefF is also capable of handling missing data in the data set.

In order to deal with the multiclass problem, the average of all the differences obtained with hit and miss classes are taken. Because there is a large number of terms belonging to miss classes, the sum of $\mathrm{diff}(f_k, R_i, M_j(C))$ will dominate $\mathrm{diff}(f_k, R_i, H_i)$, for kth feature f_k, the weighted average over all the classes is taken, where weight is proportional to the number of samples in each class (see equations (4) and (5)). This ensures that the weights $W_h[f_i]$ and $W_m[f_i]$ are in [0, 1]. Weight updation for hit and miss classes is given by

$$W_m[f_i] = \sum_{C \neq \mathrm{class}(R_i)} \left\{ \left[\frac{p(C)}{1 - p(\mathrm{class}(R_i))} \sum_{j=1}^{K} \mathrm{diff}\left(f_k, R_i, M_j(C)\right) \right] \Big/ (m * K) \right\}$$

$$\sum_{C \neq \mathrm{class}(R_i)} \frac{p(C)}{1 - p(\mathrm{class}(R_i))} = 1 \tag{4}$$

$$W_h[f_i] = \sum_{j=1}^{K} \mathrm{diff}\left(f_k, R_i, H_j\right) / (m * K) \tag{5}$$

where m denotes the number of random instances taken and $p(C)$ denotes the probability of occurrence of class C.

The algorithm is as follows;

```
Input:
     a) Training instances comprising of n features and class value
     b) Feature set F
     c) Threshold value λ.
Output:
     W: weights of selected features
     S: Selected features with weight > λ
  1. Initialization: For each attribute W[fᵢ] = 0, S = φ;
  2. for t = 1 to m
  3. Randomly select an instance Rₜ
  4. Find K nearest hits instance Hⱼ
  5. for each class C ≠ class(Ri) do
  6. from class C find K nearest misses Mj(C).
  7. for i = 1 to n
```

$$W[f_i] = W[f_i] - W_h[f_i] + W_m[f_i]$$

```
  8. for i = 1 to n
  9. if W[fᵢ] > λ
 10. Add fᵢ into set S.
 11. end
     return set S.
```

Bolón et al. [3] have used ReliefF successfully for gene selection in microarray data.

Simulation Results on Microarray Data Using ReliefF

Benchmark microarray data sets from the site http://www.gems-system.org/ were taken for illustrating the performance of ReliefF in terms of classification accuracy of samples. A description of the data sets is as follows:

11_Tumors: This data set [30] consists of 11 types of human tumors, namely, ovary, bladder/ureter, breast, colorectal, gastroesophageal, kidney, liver, prostate, pancreas, lung adeno, and lung squamous.

Leukemia1: This data set [10] consists of three type of tumors, namely, acute myelogenous leukemia (AML), acute lymphoblastic leukemia (ALL) B cell, and ALL T cell.

Leukemia2: This data set [1] comprises of three types of tumors, namely, AML, ALL, and mixed-lineage leukemia (MLL).

Lung_Cancer: This data set [2] is composed of various types of lung cancer and one normal tissue. The lung cancer types are adeno, squamous, COID, and SMCL.

SRBCT: It consists of four cancer categories [17] of small, round blue cell tumors (SRBCT). The cancer types are EWS, RMS, BL, and NB.

Brain_Tumor1: It has five types of human brain tumor, namely, medulloblastoma, malignant glioma, AT/RT, normal cerebellum, and PNET [26].

Prostate_Tumor: This data set consists of prostate tumor tissues and normal tissues [29].

DLBCL: DLBCL data set [28] comprises of two categories, namely, diffuse large B-cell lymphomas (DLBCL) and follicular lymphomas. Number of samples, genes, and classes in each of the data sets is given in Table 3.1.

In order to ensure robust gene selection, genes were selected using 5-fold cross-validation, and the classification accuracy (using Naive Bayes' classifier) obtained for the top 50 and 100 selected genes is reported in Tables 3.2 and 3.3. The last column in Tables 3.2 and 3.3 denotes the average accuracy.

Table 3.1 Description of data sets

Data set	Classes	Genes	Samples
11_Tumors	11	12534	174
Leukemia1	3	5328	72
Leukemia2	3	11226	72
Lung_Cancer	5	12601	203
SRBCT	4	2309	83
Brain_Tumor1	5	5921	90
Prostate_Tumor	2	10510	102
DLBCL	2	5470	77

Table 3.2 Accuracy obtained by ReliefF for the top 50 genes

Data set	1	2	3	4	5	Average
11_Tumors	74.29	60.00	68.57	74.29	79.41	71.31
Brain_Tumor1	50.00	94.44	77.78	61.11	66.67	70.00
DLBCL	80.00	86.67	86.67	75.00	81.25	81.92
Leukemia1	85.71	100.00	80.00	93.33	85.71	88.95
Leukemia2	100.00	92.86	93.33	85.71	93.33	93.05
Lung_Cancer	85.00	82.93	85.37	87.50	92.68	86.70
Prostate_Tumor	90.00	90.48	90.00	95.00	100.00	93.10
SRBCT	75.00	88.24	100.00	81.25	94.12	87.72

Table 3.3 Accuracy obtained by ReliefF for the top 100 genes

Data set	1	2	3	4	5	Average
11_Tumors	71.43	70.59	82.86	57.14	60.00	68.40
Brain_Tumor1	66.67	83.33	66.67	61.11	83.33	72.22
DLBCL	86.67	81.25	100.00	80.00	68.75	83.33
Leukemia1	93.33	85.71	92.86	100.00	92.86	92.95
Leukemia2	80.00	93.33	78.57	92.86	78.57	84.67
Lung_Cancer	82.93	95.12	80.00	90.24	90.00	87.66
Prostate_Tumor	85.71	100.00	95.00	85.71	100.00	93.29
SRBCT	100.00	100.00	100.00	94.12	82.35	95.29

When all the features were used, the average classification accuracy obtained using 5-fold cross-validation is shown in Table 3.4.

It is observed that gene selection definitely plays an important role in sample classification microarray data because there is a marked increase in classification accuracy for each of the data sets using the top 50 and 100 genes.

Table 3.4 Accuracy obtained using all features

Data set	Average
11_Tumors	26.94
Brain_Tumor1	38.89
DLBCL	41.50
Leukemia1	54.19
Leukemia2	33.43
Lung_Cancer	52.63
Prostate_Tumor	61.71
SRBCT	76.03

CHI-SQUARE TEST

Chi-square test [22] is used to determine whether there is significant difference between the expected frequency and the observed frequency in gene expression levels in a microarray data set. The expression levels of genes are discretized. If the frequency of occurrence of a gene expression value is different for different classes, it indicates that the gene is important for sample classification. For a gene f, the χ^2 value is computed as

$$\chi_f^2 = \sum_{x_i \in f} \sum_{c_j \in C} \left(O(x_i, c_j) - E(x_i, c_j)\right)^2 / E(x_i, c_j) \tag{6}$$

where $O(x_i, c_j)$ is the number occurrences of a particular gene expression value x_i for class c_j and $E(x_i, c_j)$ is the expected number of occurrences of that gene expression value x_i when class is c_j. $E(x_i, c_j)$ is given by

$$E(x_i, c_j) = \left(n(x_i) * n(c_j)\right)/n \tag{7}$$

where

$n(x_i)$ = number of occurrences of value x_i in gene f
$n(c_j)$ = number of instances of class c_j
n = total number of instances in the data set

Features having higher χ^2 values are selected. Chi-square test has been successfully used for gene selection in microarray data [36].

Simulation Results of Chi-Square Feature Selection on Benchmark Microarray Data Sets

Performance of chi-square test for gene selection has been evaluated on eight microarray data sets described before. 5-fold cross-validation was used for selecting the features. Accuracy is given in Tables 3.5 and 3.6. The average classification accuracy for each of the data sets for both the top 50 and 100 genes is much higher than the average accuracy reported in Table 3.4 when all the genes are used.

Table 3.5 Accuracy obtained by chi-square test for the top 50 genes

Data set	1	2	3	4	5	Average
11_Tumors	74.29	62.86	80.00	74.29	73.53	72.99
Brain_Tumor1	83.33	83.33	77.78	66.67	66.67	75.56
DLBCL	93.33	93.75	93.75	100.00	73.33	90.83
Leukemia1	100.00	92.86	100.00	92.86	100.00	97.14
Leukemia2	92.86	78.57	85.71	73.33	93.33	84.76
Lung_Cancer	85.00	90.00	78.05	75.61	87.80	83.29
Prostate_Tumor	85.71	90.00	100.00	85.00	90.48	90.24
SRBCT	94.12	100.00	94.12	100.00	87.50	95.15

Table 3.6 Accuracy obtained by chi-square test for the top 100 genes

Data set	1	2	3	4	5	Average
11_Tumors	71.43	79.41	65.71	74.29	80.00	74.17
Brain_Tumor1	77.78	66.67	83.33	83.33	83.33	78.89
DLBCL	100.00	93.33	87.50	100.00	73.33	90.83
Leukemia1	85.71	86.67	93.33	92.86	100.00	91.71
Leukemia2	80.00	100.00	85.71	85.71	73.33	84.95
Lung_Cancer	80.49	92.68	85.37	82.50	92.50	86.71
Prostate_Tumor	80.00	90.00	100.00	100.00	80.95	90.19
SRBCT	100.00	94.12	100.00	100.00	88.24	96.47

t-TEST

t-test is used for gene selection when there are two samples. This test is used to determine if the mean values of two samples are different from each other. It is based on the assumption that if the mean value of the expression levels for a gene for different samples is different, the gene is important. For each gene, the *t* value is computed as

$$t = \left(\bar{f}_1 - \bar{f}_2 \right) \Big/ \sqrt{\frac{s_1^2}{n_1} + \frac{s_2^2}{n_2}} \tag{8}$$

where $\bar{f}_1$ is the mean of gene expression vales for class 1 and $\bar{f}_2$ is the mean of gene expression for class 2; s_1^2 and s_2^2 denote the variance of gene expression values for sample 1 and sample 2, respectively. The corresponding number of instances in each sample is given by n_1 and n_2. The gene having a higher *t* value is more important for sample classification. Hence, genes having higher *t* values are selected. The disadvantage of the method is that it can be used only for a two-class problem.

Simulation Results on Two-Class Microarray Data Sets Using *t*-Test

Following are the 5-fold cross-validation results and the average accuracies for two-class DLBCL and prostate tumor data sets (See Tables 3.7 and 3.8). Since feature selection using *t*-test can be used only for a two-class problem, the classification accuracy of samples are reported only for two data sets having two classes. The same observation is made that in microarray data sets, gene selection plays an important role in classification.

Table 3.7 Accuracy obtained by *t*-test for the top 50 genes

Data set	1	2	3	4	5	Average
DLBCL	93.75	86.67	86.67	60.00	87.50	82.92
Prostate_Tumor	90.48	95.00	95.24	90.00	95.00	93.14

Table 3.8 Accuracy obtained by *t*-test for the top 100 genes

Data set	1	2	3	4	5	Average
DLBCL	93.33	87.50	86.67	81.25	100.00	89.75
Prostate_Tumor	95.24	95.24	90.00	85.00	90.00	91.10

ReliefF is highly dependent on the choice of *m* and *K*. Further, it does not take into account the interdependence among the features. The mRMR algorithm was developed to overcome some of the drawbacks.

MAXIMUM RELEVANCE MINIMUM REDUNDANCY

mRMR algorithm [7] was developed specially for gene selection in microarray data. mRMR is a supervised filter based feature selection algorithm that finds relevance and redundancy simultaneously among the selected features. Relevancy of features implies features that provide information toward distinguishing class information. Redundant features are those that do not provide any extra information. Hence, computation of redundancy is equally important. mRMR feature selection algorithm is different for discrete and continuous variables.

mRMR Feature Selection for Discrete Variables

S is the subset of n features that has maximal relevance, A is the subset that satisfies the maximal mean value of all mutual information $I(f_i, C)$ between individual features f_i and class vector C.

$$\max \mathrm{A}(S, C), \text{ where } A = \frac{1}{n}\sum_{f_i \in S} I(f_i, C) \tag{9}$$

$$I(f_i, C) = \sum_{c_k \in C}\sum_{f_{i_v} \in f_i} p(f_{i_v}, c_k)\log \frac{p(f_{i_v}, c_k)}{p(f_{i_v})\,p(c_k)} \tag{10}$$

where f_{i_v} denotes the particular feature value f_i and c_k is the class label. $p(f_{i_v}, c_k)$ stands for the joint probability of f_{i_v} and c_k, and $p(f_{i_v})$ and $p(c_k)$ are the marginal probabilities.

The feature selected using maximum relevance may be highly dependent. It is imperative to remove redundant features. Minimal redundancy condition is obtained as

$$\min R(S), \ R = \frac{1}{n^2}\sum_{f_i, f_j \in S} I(f_i, f_j) \tag{11}$$

Thus, mutually exclusive features can be obtained.

mRMR maximizes relevance, A, and minimizes redundancy, R, at the same time using the following

$$\Omega = \max(A - R) \tag{12}$$

This method is termed as mutual information difference (MID), as A and R are combined using difference method. Yet another approach of maximizing relevance and minimizing redundancy at the same time has been proposed [7] by defining:

$$\theta = \max(A/R) \tag{13}$$

and the method is called mutual information quotient (MIQ).

The mRMR (MID) algorithm is as follows:

1. For each feature f_i compute the mutual information $I(f_i, C)$ using equation (10)
2. Find the feature fj such that $f_j = \arg_{f_i} \max I(f_i, C)$
3. Initialize selected feature set S as $S = \{f_j\}$
4. Find the feature fj not in S such that

$$f_j = \arg_{f_i} \max \left[I(f_i, C) - \frac{1}{|S|} \sum_{f_j \in S} I(f_i, f_j) \right]$$

5. Include f_j in S
6. Repeat steps 4 and 5 till the number of features in S is less than k, the number of features to be selected.

The mRMR (MIQ) algorithm is as shown below:

1. For each feature f_i, compute the mutual information $I(f_i, C)$ using equation (10)
2. Find the feature f_j such that $f_j = \arg_{f_i} \max I(f_i, C)$
3. Initialize selected feature set S as

$$S = \{f_j\}$$

4. Find the feature f_j not in S such that

$$f_j = \arg_{f_i} \max \left[I(f_i, C) \Big/ \frac{1}{|S|} \sum_{f_j \in S} I(f_i, f_j) \right]$$

5. Include f_j in S
6. Repeat steps 4 and 5 till the number of features in S is less than k, the number of features to be selected.

mRMR for Continuous Variables

There also exists two methods for computing the mRMR values of continuous variables. The methods are as follows:

FCD: For continuous data, F statistic between the features and the class variable C is chosen as the score of maximum relevance. The F test value (V) is given by

$$V(f_i, C) = \left[\sum_j n_j \left(\overline{f}_i^j - \overline{f}_i \right) \middle/ (M - 1) \right] \middle/ \sigma^2 \qquad (14)$$

where n_j is the number of instances in the jth class, $\overline{f}_i^j$ is the mean value of f_i belonging to jth class, $\overline{f}_i$ is the mean value of f_i over all the classes, M is the total number of classes and

$$\sigma^2 = \left[\sum_j (n_j - 1) \sigma_j^2 \right] \middle/ (N - M) \qquad (15)$$

where N is the total number of instances and σ_j^2 is the variance of jth class. Hence, for the feature set S, the maximum relevance is given as

$$\max RV, \ RV = \frac{1}{|S|} \sum_{f_i \in S} V(f_i, C) \qquad (16)$$

Minimum redundancy is found using the correlation between the features. Using the Pearson correlation coefficient, minimum redundancy is computed as follows:

$$\min RD, \ RD = \frac{1}{|S|^2} \sum_{i,j} \left| \mathrm{corr}\left(f_i, f_j \right) \right| \qquad (17)$$

where $\mathrm{corr}(f_i, f_j)$ is correlation between features f_i and f_j. Absolute value of the correlation has been considered to take into account both positively and negatively correlated features.

mRMR maximizes relevance, RV, and minimizes redundancy, RD, at the same time using the following

$$\max \ (RV - RD)$$

This method is termed as F test with correlation using difference (FCD), as RV and RD are combined using the difference method. Yet another way of maximizing relevance and minimizing redundancy at the same time is by defining

$$\max \ (RV/RD)$$

which is termed as F test with correlation using quotient (FCQ).

mRMR has been used for feature selection in gene expression data by Unler et al. (2011). The algorithm is as shown below:

1. For each feature f_i compute the F test value $V(f_i, C)$ using equation (14)
2. Find the feature f_j such that $f_j = \mathrm{arg}_{f_i} \max V(f_i, C)$
3. Initialize selected feature set S as

$$S = \{f_j\}$$

4. Find the feature f_j not in S such that

$$f_j = \arg_{f_i} \max \left[V(f_i, C) - \frac{1}{|S|} \sum_{f_j \in S} \text{corr}(f_i, f_j) \right]$$

5. Include f_j in S
6. Repeat steps 4 and 5 till the number of features in S is less than k, the number of features to be selected.

Additionally, the mRMR (FCQ) algorithm is explained:

1. For each feature f_i, compute the F test value $V(f_i, C)$ using equation (14)
2. Find the feature f_j such that $f_j = \arg_{f_i} \max V(f_i, C)$
3. Initialize selected feature set S as

$$S = \{f_j\}$$

4. Find the feature f_j not in S such that

$$f_j = \arg_{f_i} \max \left[V(f_i, C) - \frac{1}{|S|} \sum_{f_j \in S} \text{corr}(f_i, f_j) \right]$$

5. Include f_j in S
6. Repeat steps 4 and 5 till the number of features in S is less than k, the number of features to be selected.

Zhang et al. [37] developed a Gene selection algorithm by combining ReliefF and mRMR.

Simulation Results on Microarray Data Sets Using mRMR (MID & MIQ, FCD & FCQ)

The following tables give the classification accuracy for various Microarray Data sets by selecting features using 5-fold cross-validation. Average accuracy is depicted in the last column. Compared with the average accuracy when all the genes are used as depicted in Table 3.4, the accuracy reported in Tables 3.9 to 3.12 are much higher.

Table 3.9 Accuracy obtained by mRMR MID for the top 50 genes

Data set	1	2	3	4	5	Average
11_Tumors	54.29	77.14	77.14	70.59	71.43	70.12
Brain_Tumor1	83.33	72.22	77.78	88.89	77.78	80.00
DLBCL	86.67	93.33	100.00	93.33	81.25	90.92
Leukemia1	80.00	93.33	92.86	100.00	78.57	88.95
Leukemia2	92.86	92.86	100.00	93.33	93.33	94.48
Lung_Cancer	90.24	85.00	82.93	82.50	95.12	87.16
Prostate_Tumor	76.19	85.00	85.00	90.00	90.48	85.33
SRBCT	88.24	100.00	93.75	94.12	87.50	92.72

Table 3.10 Accuracy obtained by mRMR MIQ for the top 100 genes

Data set	1	2	3	4	5	Average
11_Tumors	80.00	82.86	74.29	88.57	58.82	76.91
Brain_Tumor1	83.33	88.89	88.89	61.11	83.33	81.11
DLBCL	86.67	93.33	87.50	93.33	100.00	92.17
Leukemia1	80.00	100.00	100.00	78.57	92.86	90.29
Leukemia2	100.00	100.00	85.71	100.00	80.00	93.14
Lung_Cancer	87.50	92.50	87.80	82.93	82.93	86.73
Prostate_Tumor	90.00	85.71	100.00	66.67	95.00	87.48
SRBCT	100.00	100.00	93.75	76.47	81.25	90.29

Table 3.11 Accuracy obtained by mRMR FCD for the top 50 genes

Data set	1	2	3	4	5	Average
11_Tumors	80.00	74.29	68.57	58.82	71.43	70.62
Brain_Tumor1	77.78	77.78	77.78	88.89	88.89	82.22
DLBCL	81.25	93.33	81.25	93.33	86.67	87.17
Leukemia1	100.00	100.00	85.71	100.00	92.86	95.71
Leukemia2	93.33	86.67	92.86	92.86	78.57	88.86
Lung_Cancer	77.50	80.49	77.50	78.05	85.37	79.78
Prostate_Tumor	90.00	85.00	85.71	95.24	95.00	90.19
SRBCT	100.00	94.12	94.12	100.00	100.00	97.65

Table 3.12 Accuracy obtained by mRMR FCD for the top 100 genes

Data set	1	2	3	4	5	Average
11_Tumors	74.29	71.43	73.53	71.43	71.43	72.42
Brain_Tumor1	77.78	50.00	77.78	83.33	66.67	71.11
DLBCL	73.33	100.00	87.50	87.50	93.33	88.33
Leukemia1	100.00	100.00	100.00	93.33	100.00	98.67
Leukemia2	93.33	85.71	92.86	86.67	85.71	88.86
Lung_Cancer	80.00	87.50	80.49	78.05	90.24	83.26
Prostate_Tumor	90.48	100.00	100.00	85.71	75.00	90.24
SRBCT	100.00	100.00	100.00	93.75	100.00	98.75

TRACE RATIO

Trace ratio [25] is a graph-based feature selection algorithm that uses Fisher score and Laplacian score as the evaluation criterion. Two undirected graphs, namely, G_w and G_b for within-class and between-class affinities are constructed using Fisher score, their corresponding adjacency matrices being A_w and A_b. Within-class relationship will be higher if both instances x_i and x_j of the data set X belong to the same class. Hence, the feature subset selection should minimize

$$\sum_{ij}||c_i - c_j||^2 (A_w)_{ij} \tag{18}$$

for the same class and maximize otherwise. On the other hand, between-class relationship will be higher if both data x_i and x_j belong to different classes. Hence, the selected feature subset selection should maximize:

$$\sum_{ij}||c_i - c_j||^2 (A_b)_{ij} \tag{19}$$

for different classes and minimize otherwise, where c_i is class of the instance x_i.

Fisher score or Laplacian score is used to find the weight matrices A_w and A_b depending on whether it is supervised or unsupervised feature selection. In Fisher score:

$$(A_w)_{ij} = \begin{cases} \dfrac{1}{n_{c_i}}, & \text{if } c_i = c_j; \\ 0, & \text{if } c_i \neq c_j; \end{cases} \tag{20}$$

$$(A_b)_{ij} = \begin{cases} \dfrac{1}{n} - \dfrac{1}{n_{c_i}}, & \text{if } c_i = c_j; \\ \dfrac{1}{n}, & \text{if } c_i \neq c_j; \end{cases} \tag{21}$$

where c_i denotes the class label of the ith instance x_i and n_{c_i} denotes the number of records belonging to class c_i.

In Laplacian score, the adjacency matrix is computed as

$$(A_w)_{ij} = \begin{cases} e^{-\dfrac{||x_i - x_j||^2}{t}}, & \text{if } x_i \text{ and } x_j \text{ are neighbours;} \\ 0, & \text{otherwise;} \end{cases} \tag{22}$$

which denotes the radial distance. t denotes any constant

$$A_b = \frac{1}{1^T D_w 1} D_w 1 1^T D_w \tag{23}$$

In order to combine both the objectives in a single function, ratio of the two is taken and maximized. The ratio is given by

$$\tau(M_p) = \frac{\sum_{ij}||c_i - c_j||^2 (A_b)_{ij}}{\sum_{ij}||c_i - c_j||^2 (A_w)_{ij}} \tag{24}$$

$$\tau(M_p) = \frac{tr\left(M_p^T X L_b X^T M_p\right)}{tr\left(M_p^T X L_w X^T M_p\right)} \tag{25}$$

where

$M_P = [m_{i_1}, m_{i_1}, \ldots m_{i_k}]$ denotes the selection matrix, where $i_1, i_2, \ldots i_k$ are the first k elements of a permutation of $[1, 2, \ldots, n]$, that is, the feature number. Where m_{i_r} denotes a column matrix, with all zeros except 1 in the rth position, and tr denotes the trace of the matrix. L_w and L_b are Laplacian matrices of the form

$$L_w = D_w - A_w$$
$$L_b = D_b - A_b$$

D_w and D_b are diagonal matrices defined as

$$(D_w)_{ii} = \sum_{ij}(A_w)_{ij} \tag{26}$$

$$(D_b)_{ii} = \sum_{ij}(A_b)_{ij} \tag{27}$$

Let, $P = X L_b X^T, Q = X L_w X^T$. The score of a feature set is computed according to the Trace ratio criterion for a particular selection matrix M_p

$$\lambda = \tau(M_p) = \frac{tr\left(M_p^T P M_p\right)}{tr\left(M_p^T Q M_p\right)} \tag{28}$$

Score of each feature f_i is computed as

$$S(f_i) = m_i^T (P - \lambda Q) m_i \tag{29}$$

where m_i is the column vector with all zeros except 1 at the ith position.

The trace radio algorithm is explained below:

A_w: adjacency matrix for within-class relationship
A_b: adjacency matrix for between-class relationship
S: selected feature set.

1. Compute A_w and A_b using (20) and (21) or using (22) and (23).
2. Compute D_w and D_b using (26) and (27), respectively.
3. Compute L_w and L_b as

$$L_w = D_w - A_w$$
$$L_b = D_b - A_b$$

4. Select initial set S of k features randomly and construct selection matrix

$$Mp = [m_1, \ m_2, \ ....m_k]$$

5. Compute $\lambda = \frac{tr(M_p^T P \, M_p)}{tr(M_p^T Q M_p)}$

    where $P = XL_bX^T$ and $Q = XL_wX^T$

6. Compute score of each feature f_i as

$$V_2(f_i) = m_i^T (P - \lambda Q) \, m_i$$

7. Select the new top k features based on V_2 score
8. If selected features in step 7 are same as features in S, return.

    Else, modify S to contain selected feature in step 7, compute M_p and go to step 5.

Simulation Results of Trace Ratio on Benchmark Microarray Data Sets

Classification accuracy obtained using 5-fold cross-validation for eight microarray data sets are given in Tables 3.13 and 3.14. Average accuracy is reported in the

Table 3.13 Accuracy obtained by trace ratio for the top 50 genes

Data set	1	2	3	4	5	Average
11_Tumors	74.29	68.57	65.71	67.65	62.86	67.82
14_Tumors	48.39	43.55	21.31	45.16	40.98	39.88
Brain_Tumor1	83.33	83.33	72.22	72.22	72.22	76.67
DLBCL	87.50	93.75	86.67	93.33	86.67	89.58
Leukemia1	92.86	100.00	92.86	64.29	80.00	86.00
Leukemia2	100.00	92.86	93.33	85.71	93.33	93.05
Lung_Cancer	85.71	92.86	93.33	85.71	86.67	88.86
Prostate_Tumor	95.24	95.00	85.71	100.00	75.00	90.19
SRBCT	100.00	100.00	100.00	94.12	88.24	96.47

Table 3.14 Accuracy obtained by trace ratio for the top 100 genes

Data set	1	2	3	4	5	Average
11_Tumors	82.86	68.57	62.86	61.76	77.14	70.64
14_Tumors	36.07	50.82	46.77	35.48	27.42	39.31
Brain_Tumor1	83.33	77.78	72.22	88.89	83.33	81.11
DLBCL	93.75	93.75	86.67	93.33	86.67	90.83
Leukemia1	92.86	100.00	92.86	100.00	100.00	97.14
Leukemia2	92.86	85.71	86.67	92.86	86.67	88.95
Lung_Cancer	82.50	92.68	85.37	82.50	78.05	84.22
Prostate_Tumor	90.48	95.00	85.71	100.00	80.00	90.24
SRBCT	100.00	100.00	93.75	94.12	88.24	95.22

last column and it shows that gene selection has an important role to play in sample classification.

EFFECTIVE RANGE BASED GENE SELECTION

Effective range based gene selection was proposed by Chandra et al. [5] for selection of genes in micro array data in order to overcome limitations of earlier algorithms. The method can be effectively used for ranking of features and also for generating weights. This is based on uniquely defined effective ranges of genes (features). Let $F = \{f_1, f_2, ..., f_n\}$ be the feature set of Data set D of size n and dimension n and $C = \{C_j\}$ be the class set $j = 1, 2, ..., N$. The effective range (R_{ij}) of C_j for f_i is given by

$$R_{ij} = \left[r_{ij}^-, r_{ij}^+ \right] = \left[\mu_{ij} - \left(1 - p_j\right)\gamma\sigma_{ij}, \; \mu_{ij} + \left(1 - p_j\right)\gamma\sigma \right] \quad (30)$$

μ_{ij} = mean of f_i for C_j.
σ_{ij} = standard deviation of f_i for C_j.
r_{ij-} = lower bounds of the effective range
r_{ij+} = upper bounds of the effective range
p_j = prior probability of C_j

The value of γ is determined statistically by the Chebyshev inequality, which is defined as follows:

$$P\left(\left| X - \mu_{ij} \right| \geq \gamma\sigma_{ij} \right) \leq \frac{1}{\gamma^2} \quad (31)$$

which is true for all distributions.

The steps for the algorithm are described below.

1. Effective ranges R_{ij} is computed for all classes and each feature f_i.
2. The effective lower value of ranges of classes are sorted in the ascending order.
3. Overlapping area (OA_i) among classes of feature f_i is found, which is given as

$$OA_i = \sum_{j=1}^{l-1} \sum_{k=j+1}^{l} \varphi_i(j, k) \quad \text{where} \quad \varphi_i(j, k) = \begin{cases} r_{ij}^+ - r_{ik}^- & \text{if } r_{ij}^+ > r_{ik}^- \\ 0 & \text{otherwise} \end{cases} \quad (32)$$

4. Find the area coefficient and normalized area coefficient of feature f_i, which are given by

$$AC_i = \frac{OA_i}{\max_j \left(r_{ij}^+\right) - \min_j \left(r_{ij}^-\right)} \quad (33)$$

$$NAC_i = AC_i / \max(AC_j), \quad \text{for } j = 1, ..., d \quad (34)$$

5. Find the weight (w_i) of the ith feature f_i as

$$w_i = 1 - NAC_i$$

select the features for which $w_{ij} > \theta$, where θ denotes the threshold.

Simulation Results of ERGS on Benchmark Microarray Data Sets

Following are the simulation results giving the classification accuracy of samples using 5-fold cross-validation for feature selection. When compared to the accuracy given in Table 3.4 (with all the features) (See Tables 3.15 and 3.16), the accuracies using the top 50 and 100 genes are much higher.

Table 3.15 Accuracy obtained by ERGS for the top 50 genes

Data set	1	2	3	4	5	Average
11_Tumors	74.29	55.88	60.00	77.14	71.43	67.75
14_Tumors	38.71	29.51	32.79	35.48	32.26	33.75
Brain_Tumor1	72.22	50.00	72.22	72.22	77.78	68.89
DLBCL	86.67	80.00	80.00	100.00	87.50	86.83
Leukemia1	100.00	85.71	100.00	86.67	92.86	93.05
Leukemia2	92.86	86.67	92.86	73.33	92.86	87.71
Lung_Cancer	92.68	85.37	80.00	90.24	80.00	85.66
Prostate_Tumor	95.24	95.00	90.00	95.00	80.95	91.24
SRBCT	88.24	100.00	100.00	100.00	93.75	96.40

Table 3.16 Accuracy obtained by ERGS for the top 100 genes

Data set	1	2	3	4	5	Average
11_Tumors	57.14	65.71	58.82	85.71	74.29	68.34
14_Tumors	35.48	27.42	41.94	31.15	36.07	34.41
Brain_Tumor1	83.33	77.78	55.56	83.33	83.33	76.67
DLBCL	73.33	93.33	80.00	93.75	87.50	85.58
Leukemia1	100.00	92.86	93.33	100.00	92.86	95.81
Leukemia2	92.86	100.00	86.67	100.00	92.86	94.48
Lung_Cancer	85.37	92.68	85.00	92.50	92.68	89.65
Prostate_Tumor	80.00	90.00	85.71	95.00	100.00	90.14
SRBCT	94.12	100.00	94.12	93.75	88.24	94.04

MAXIMUM WEIGHT MINIMUM REDUNDANCY

The maximum weight minimum redundancy (MWMR) feature selection algorithm [31] uses the Fisher, Laplacian, or constraint score for computing the relevance of features. It uses Pearson correlation coefficient or mutual information as redundancy measures. It can be used as a supervised feature selection algorithm if the Fisher score is used as a relevance measure and as an unsupervised algorithm if the Laplacian score is used. The MWMR selects the feature subset in which the features are most relevant for the classification/clustering task by ensuring that the correlation among the features are minimal. It chooses the optimal subset of features such that features have maximum weight and minimum redundancy. Unlike ReliefF, one can specify the number of features to be selected a priori.

Mathematical Formulation of the MWMR Framework

The aim in MWMR algorithm is to construct an objective function that helps in finding a feature subset with maximum weight and minimum redundancy. Let the data set be denoted by $X = [x_1, x_2, ... x_d]$ containing d instances. Each instance contains n rows (features) denoted by f_i ($i = 1, ..., n$). The weights of features are computed using one of the three feature weighting algorithms (Fisher, Laplacian, and Constraint scores) and stored in a vector $W = [w_1, w_2, ..., w_n]$ where $w_i > 0$ denotes the weight of ith feature. Similarly, the redundancy among features is computed using the Pearson correlation coefficient. Correlation among features stored in an $n \times n$ matrix R where R_{ij} denotes the correlation between f_i and f_j. R_{ii} has been assigned 0. Mutual Information is also used as a redundancy measure.

Let k be the number of features to be selected and $v = [v_1, v_2, ..., v_n]$ be an indicator vector, where v_i is the indicator of the presence of ith feature in the selected subset. If $v_i = 1$, then ith feature is present in the selected feature set otherwise $v_i = 0$. The objective is to find optimal v such that weight of selected features are maximum and the correlation among features are minimum:

$$\max_v \left(\frac{v^T w}{k} - \frac{v^T R v}{k(k-1)} \right) \tag{35}$$

$$\text{s.t.} \sum_i v_i = k, \; v_i \in \{0, 1\}$$

These two conditions have been incorporated to restrict the number of selected features to k. Because it is difficult to solve the above optimization problem with v_i being either 0 or 1, the optimization problem is reformulated as

$$\max_v \left(\frac{v^T w}{k} - \frac{v^T R v}{k(k-1)} \right) \tag{36}$$

$$\text{s.t.} \sum_i v_i = k, \; v_i \in [0, 1]$$

This ensures that the features corresponding to top k v_i's are selected in the desired subset. Standard methods of solving quadratic programming problems cannot be used to solve the above problem because of an extra constraint $v_i \in [0, 1]$. Hence pairwise updating algorithm has been to solve the optimization problem. The Lagrangian function of equation (36) can be written as

$$L(v, a, \beta, \gamma) = \left(\frac{v^T w}{k} - \frac{v^T R v}{k(k-1)} \right) - a \left(\sum_i v_i - k \right) + \sum_i \beta_i v_i + \sum_i \gamma_i (1 - v_i) \tag{37}$$

where a, β, γ are Lagrange multipliers, and all are nonnegative. The solution that maximizes equation (36) must satisfy the necessary Karush−Kuhn−Tucker (KKT) conditions:

$$\begin{cases} \left(\frac{w}{k} - \frac{2Rv}{k(k-1)} \right)_i - a + \beta_i - \gamma_i = 0 \\ \sum_i \beta_i v_i = 0 \\ \sum_i \gamma_i (1 - v_i) = 0 \end{cases} \tag{38}$$

where

$\left(\frac{w}{k} - \frac{2Rv}{k(k-1)} \right)_i$ is the ith element of vector $\left(\frac{w}{k} - \frac{2Rv}{k(k-1)} \right)$

The KKT condition (38) can be rewritten as

$$\left(\frac{w}{k} - \frac{2Rv}{k(k-1)} \right)_i \begin{cases} \leq a & \text{when} \quad v_i = 0 \\ = a & \text{when} \quad v_i \in (0, 1) \\ \geq a & \text{when} \quad v_i = 1 \end{cases} \tag{39}$$

The term $\left(\frac{w}{k} - \frac{2Rv}{k(k-1)} \right)_i$ is called the reward of the ith feature, which is denoted as $r_i(v)$. As k is constant, the reward of a feature represents the relation between the weight of the feature and the average correlation with the other selected features. The term *reward* indicates that if the weight of a feature is large and the average correlation of feature f_i with the other selected features is small, then the reward will be large.

The original set is partitioned into three disjoint sets according to value v_i.

$S_1 = \{f_i \mid v_i = 0\},$
$S_2 = \{f_i \mid v_i \in (0,1)\}$ and
$S_3 = \{f_i \mid v_i = 1\}.$

The property of S_1, S_2, and S_3 is that if v_i is the optimal solution of the problem (36), then there exists a constant λ such that

1. $\forall\ f_i \in S_1 \quad r_i(v) \leq \lambda$
2. $\forall\ f_i \in S_2 \quad r_i(v) = \lambda$
3. $\forall\ f_i \in S_3 \quad r_i(v) \geq \lambda$

Pairwise updating algorithm is adopted for determining the optimal v. v_i is updated according to

$$v_l^{\text{new}} = \begin{cases} v_l & \text{if } l \neq i \text{ and } l \neq j \\ v_l + \delta & \text{if } l = i \\ v_l - \delta & \text{if } l = j \end{cases} \tag{40}$$

δ is computed by

$$\delta = \begin{cases} \min(v_j, 1 - v_i) & \text{if } 2R_{ij} - R_{ii} - R_{jj} \geq 0 \text{ and } r_i(v) > r_j(v) \\ \min\left(v_j, 1 - v_i, \dfrac{k(k-1)(r_j(v) - r_i(v))}{2R_{ij} - R_{ii} - R_{jj}}\right) & \text{if } 2R_{ij} - R_{ii} < 0 \text{ and } r_i(v) > r_j(v) \\ \min(v_j, 1 - v_i) & \text{if } 2R_{ij} - R_{ii} - R_{jj} > 0 \text{ and } r_i(v) = r_j(v) \end{cases}$$

$$\tag{41}$$

On iterative computing δ and updating of the pairwise element of v, the objective function of MWMR can be increased. The MWMR algorithm is as follows:

```
Input:
      W: weight matrix
      R: correlation matrix
Output:
      Indicator vector v
1. Initialize v using either maximum weight or minimum redundancy strategy.
2. Select fᵢ ∈ S₁US₂, having largest reward rᵢ(v).
3. Select fⱼ ∈ S₂US₃, having smallest reward rⱼ(v).
4. If rⱼ(v) > rᵢ(v)
      compute δ using equation (41) and update vᵢ and vⱼ using equation (40).
5. Else if rⱼ(v) = rᵢ(v)
      If 2 Rᵢⱼ - Rᵢᵢ - Rⱼⱼ > 0
         Compute δ using equation (41) and then update vᵢ and vⱼ using
equation (40).
6. Else if 2 Rᵢⱼ - Rᵢᵢ - Rⱼⱼ = 0
         Check whether there exists an f₀ ∈ S₁US₂ and fₚ ∈ S₂US₃ such that
            2 Rᵢⱼ - Rᵢᵢ - Rⱼⱼ > 0 and r₀(v) = rₚ(v)
```

If the pair (f_o, f_p) can be found,
        compute δ using equation (41) and update v_o and v_p
according to equation (40).

Simulation Results of MWMR on Benchmark Microarray Data Sets

Sample classification accuracy for all the eight microarray data sets using MWMR feature selection algorithm (using Fisher score) is given in Tables 3.17 and 3.18. The accuracy using features selected with MWMR in all the microarray data sets for the top 50 and 100 genes is much superior compared to that using all the features.

COMPARISON OF ACCURACY FOR MICROARRAY DATA SETS USING SUPERVISED FILTER BASED FEATURE SELECTION ALGORITHMS

Figures 3.1(a) to (h) gives the comparison of accuracy using the top 50 and 100 genes for various data sets using different filter based feature selection algorithms.

For 11_Tumors, Brain Tumor_1, DLBCL, Leukemia (1 and 2), Prostrate Tumor and Lung Cancer data sets, features selected using MWMR are able to classify the samples better even with the top 50 selected genes. For Brain Tumor_1, the mRMR_FCD algorithm requires only the top 50 genes for classification. For DLBCL, SRBCT and Prostrate Tumor effective range based gene selection (ERGS) technique performs well in terms of classification accuracy, with only the

Table 3.17 Accuracy obtained by MWMR for the top 50 genes

Data set	1	2	3	4	5	Average
11_Tumors	71.43	71.43	74.29	74.29	55.88	69.46
Brain_Tumor1	66.67	72.22	77.78	83.33	72.22	74.44
DLBCL	87.50	86.67	93.33	80.00	100.00	89.50
Leukemia1	100.00	100.00	92.86	100.00	93.33	97.24
Leukemia2	92.86	92.86	93.33	100.00	92.86	94.38
Lung_Cancer	73.17	90.24	87.50	82.93	97.50	86.27
Prostate_Tumor	100.00	75.00	100.00	85.00	100.00	92.00
SRBCT	100.00	94.12	81.25	100.00	93.75	93.82

Table 3.18 Accuracy obtained by MWMR for the top 100 genes

Data set	1	2	3	4	5	Average
11_Tumors	42.86	48.57	74.29	71.43	67.65	60.96
Brain_Tumor1	72.22	61.11	83.33	77.78	61.11	71.11
DLBCL	80.00	100.00	93.33	80.00	68.75	84.42
Leukemia1	92.86	92.86	85.71	100.00	100.00	94.29
Leukemia2	100.00	85.71	93.33	92.86	80.00	90.38
Lung_Cancer	85.37	90.24	90.00	78.05	72.50	83.23
Prostate_Tumor	90.48	90.00	95.00	85.71	85.00	89.24
SRBCT	100.00	82.35	93.75	94.12	100.00	94.04

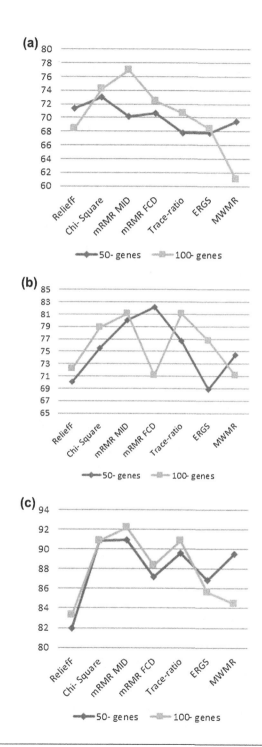

FIGURE 3.1

(a) 11 tumors. (b) Brain Tumor 1. (c) DLBCL. (d) Leukemia 1. (e) Leukemia 2. (f) Lung cancer. (g) Prostate Tumor. (h) SRBCT.

(d)

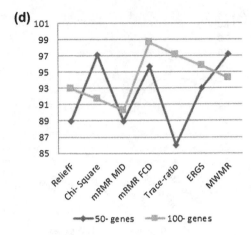

(e)

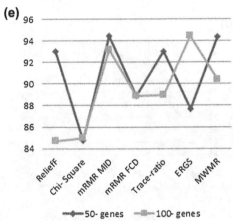

(f)

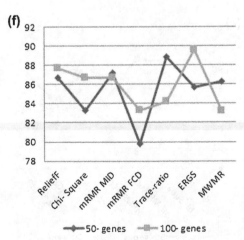

FIGURE 3.1

cont'd.

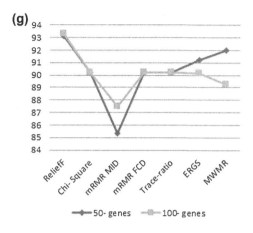

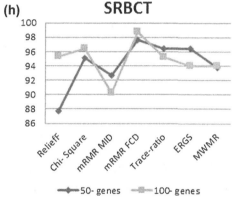

FIGURE 3.1

cont'd.

top 50 selected genes. In the case of ReliefF except 11_Tumors, the classification accuracy is lower when the top 100 genes are selected as opposed to the top 50 genes. For the DLBCL data set, both the top 50 genes and the 100 genes selected by all the feature selection algorithms perform equally well.

It was also observed that for all the data sets, the classification accuracy is increased to a great extent using the top 50 and 100 selected genes as compared to that when all the genes are considered.

FEATURE SELECTION ALGORITHMS BASED ON WRAPPER APPROACH

In the case of the wrapper approach, feature selection is based on a classifier. Following are some details of the wrapper approach.

SEQUENTIAL FORWARD SELECTION

The steps followed in SFS [33] are as follows:

1. The most important feature $S_1 = f_i$ is selected first using some criterion.
2. Then pairs of features are formed with f_i and the best pair is selected as $S_2 = \{f_i, f_i\}$.
3. Set of 3 features are formed using S_2 and the best set of 3 features is selected as $S_3 = \{f_i, f_j, f_k\}$.
4. This process is repeated until a predefined number of features are selected.

The disadvantage of SFS is that the new features are added continuously in the selected features set. It does not give flexibility to remove the features that have been already added in case they have become obsolete after the addition of new features.

SEQUENTIAL BACKWARD SELECTION

The sequential backward selection (SBS) process [23] follows the reverse process as compared to SFS. The steps are as follows.

1. For all the n features, a predefined criterion function is found.
2. At each step, one feature is deleted at a time and the criterion function is found for all subsets containing $n - 1$ features.
3. Based on the criterion function, the feature that performs worst is discarded.
4. The same procedure is followed with the remaining $n - 2$ features, and finally the selection process stops until a predefined number of features are left.

The disadvantage of SBS is that if a feature has been discarded it cannot be added again. Its usefulness cannot be evaluated again and brought back to selected features subset.

SIMULATION RESULTS ON BENCHMARK MICROARRAY DATA SETS USING SFS AND SBS

Following are the 5-fold cross-validation results for the microarray data sets described before using SFS and SBS algorithms.

Wrapper approaches are generally computationally expensive (See Tables 3.19 and 3.20). For the microarray data sets mentioned in Table 3.1, filter based feature selection algorithms perform better compared to SFS wrapper approach for most of the data sets except in the case of Lung Cancer and Prostate_Tumor. For prostate_-tumor SFS performs better than mRMR_MID, MWMR both for top 50 and 100 selected genes. SFS performs better than mRMR_MIQ for top 50 selected genes but worse than that for the top 100 selected genes. Performance of SBS is worse than all filter based feature selection algorithms for most of the data sets except in the case of lung cancer.

Table 3.19 Accuracy obtained using SFS

Data set	1	2	3	4	5	Average
11_Tumors	70.06	71.85	63.22	67.76	45.89	63.76
Brain_Tumor1	79.29	64.46	73.46	66.68	66.71	70.12
DLBCL	87.47	84.09	83.90	93.40	68.70	83.51
Leukemia1	101.68	82.75	82.68	79.87	82.33	85.86
Leukemia2	52.52	73.29	78.42	81.80	60.56	69.32
Lung_Cancer	83.51	94.89	80.65	103.48	85.19	89.54
Prostate_Tumor	74.21	94.69	100.43	82.85	97.81	90.00
SRBCT	82.01	97.02	59.10	81.38	82.36	80.37

Table 3.20 Accuracy obtained using SBS

Data set	1	2	3	4	5	Average
11_Tumors	67.65	62.86	57.14	71.43	42.86	60.39
Brain_Tumor1	66.67	72.22	77.78	61.11	66.67	68.89
DLBCL	73.33	81.25	73.33	93.33	62.50	76.75
Leukemia1	93.33	85.71	78.57	73.33	78.57	81.90
Leukemia2	57.14	71.43	73.33	86.67	64.29	70.57
Lung_Cancer	78.05	92.68	80.00	97.50	82.93	86.23
Prostate_Tumor	70.00	95.00	95.24	80.00	90.48	86.14
SRBCT	76.47	94.12	56.25	88.24	81.25	79.26

SEQUENTIAL FORWARD FLOATING SELECTION

The SFFS was proposed [27] as an improvement over SFS. Following lines describe the algorithm in detail. Let X denote set of selected features and d denote the number of features to be selected. SFFS consists of three steps which are given as follows.

1. Initialize X to empty set.
2. Use SFS to select the most significant feature and add it to X. If X consists of d features, then stop else go to step 2.
3. Find the least significant feature x in X. If x was just added to X in step 1, then go to step 1. Else remove feature x from X and go to step 3.
4. Find the least significant feature x in X. If X consists of at least 3 features and the value of $J(X - x)$ is greater than the best value of J found so far, then remove x from X and repeat step 3. Else, go to step 1.

SEQUENTIAL BACKWARD FLOATING SELECTION

The SBFS was proposed [27] as an improvement over SBS. Description of the algorithm is given as follows. Let X denote set of selected features and d denotes the number of features to be selected. Initialize X to complete data set set Y. Size of Y is D. SBFS consists of three steps which are given as follows.

1. Use SBS to select the most insignificant feature in X and remove it from X. If X consists of d features, then stop else go to step 2.
2. Find the most significant feature x in $Y-X$. If x was just removed from X in step 1, then go to step 1. Else add feature x to X and go to step 3.
3. Find the most significant feature x in $Y-X$. If X consists of at most $D-3$ features and the value of $J(X+x)$ is greater than the best value of J found so far, then add x to X and repeat step 3. Else, go to step 1.
4. So far, the well-known supervised feature selection algorithms have been discussed. Very often the class label is not known especially when the data belongs to a new domain. Hence unsupervised feature selection algorithms may be required to select features in unlabeled data.

UNSUPERVISED FILTER BASED FEATURE SELECTION ALGORITHMS

Following are some widely known unsupervised feature selection algorithms. Unsupervised feature selection algorithms are often helpful when the class labels are not present. In the context of microarray data, it is useful when the disease type is not known and only the gene expressions of various samples are known. This is useful for selecting important features in an unknown disease.

LAPLACIAN SCORE

This is an unsupervised filter based feature selection algorithm. The Laplacian method [14] is based on the observation that in many real-world classification problems, data from the same class are often close to each other. The importance of a feature is evaluated by its power of locality preserving, or Laplacian, score. In order to model the local geometric structure, we construct a nearest neighbor graph. Laplacian score seeks those features that respect this graph structure.

The Laplacian score of a feature indicates its relevance to preserve locality. The Laplacian score is based on the observation that two instances that are close to each other generally belong to the same class. Laplacian score uses the nearest neighbor graph to obtain the local structure of the data and obtains the Laplacian score value of each feature. Features having higher Laplacian score values are selected.

Let the data set consist of m instances. First, the nearest neighbor graph (M) is constructed, where each node of graph M denotes an instance. For each pair of instances, say x_i and x_j, if x_i is one of the k-nearest neighbor of x_j or x_j is one of the k-nearest neighbors of x_i, then an edge is put between nodes i and j in the graph M.

Similarity weight matrix W is obtained using a nearest neighbor graph M. If two nodes, say i and j, are connected by an edge in the graph M, then $W(i, j) = \exp\left(-\frac{|xi-xj|^2}{\sigma}\right)$ for some constant σ, otherwise $W(i, j) = 0$.

For each feature, f, the Laplacian score is computed as follows:

1. Construct a diagonal matrix D such that the diagonal entries are given by row sum of W and all other entries are 0.

2. Define the transformed feature as

$$\tilde{f} = f - \frac{f^T DI}{I^T DI} I \tag{42}$$

where $I = [1, 1, ..., 1]^T$.

3. The Laplacian score is obtained by

$$\text{Laplacian score } (f) = \frac{\tilde{f}^T L \tilde{f}}{\tilde{f}^T D \tilde{f}} \tag{43}$$

where $L = D - W$

Hwang et al. [16] used the Laplacian score for selecting the relevant genes for a new disease. They ranked all the genes based on Laplacian scores and selected the best matching genes. Ferreira et al. [9] used Laplacian score feature selection for comparison with a similarity measure for feature selection in high-dimensional data.

MULTICLUSTER FEATURE SELECTION

Multicluster feature selection (MCFS) [4] is an unsupervised feature selection method, and it selects those features that preserve the multicluster structure of the data. It uses spectral analysis and correlation. Further, spectral analysis is used because it helps in manifold learning.

Let the data set with N instances be denoted by $X = [x_1, ..., x_N]$ and let D denote the number of features. Let d denote the top-ranking features to be selected that preserve the multicluster structure of the data. The steps are described below:

Initially, a nearest neighbor graph G is constructed using X. G consists of N vertices where each vertex corresponds to an instance in X. Initially, there is no edge between any pair of vertices in G. In the next step, for each instance, k nearest neighbors are searched. An edge is placed in the graph G between the instance and k of its nearest neighboring instances. Weight matrix W is computed using G, where the entries in W indicate the extent to which two neighboring instances are closer to each other. W is computed using any of the following methods:

a. 0−1 weighing

$$W(i, j) = \begin{cases} 1 & \text{If nodes } i \text{ and } j \text{ are connected in } G \\ 0 & \text{otherwise} \end{cases} \tag{44}$$

b. Heat Kernel weighing

$$W(i, j) = \begin{cases} \exp\left(-\frac{|x_i - x_j|^2}{\sigma}\right) & \text{If nodes } i \text{ and } j \text{ are connected in } G \\ 0 & \text{otherwise} \end{cases} \tag{45}$$

c. Dot product weighing

$$W(i, j) = \begin{cases} (x_i^T x_j) & \text{If nodes } i \text{ and } j \text{ are connected in } G \\ 0 & \text{otherwise} \end{cases} \tag{46}$$

Matrix W captures the similarity structure of the data at local level. A diagonal matrix M is obtained where the diagonal entries of M correspond to the row sum of W. Using M and W graphs, the Laplacian is computed as

$$L = M - W \tag{47}$$

The generalized eigenvalue problem is obtained as

$$Ly = \lambda M y \tag{48}$$

Let $\lambda_1, \lambda_2, \ldots$ and λ_k be the smallest k eigenvalues of equation (48) and y_i be the eigenvector corresponding to the eigenvalue λ_i. Because each eigenvector represents the multicluster structure of the data and the relevant features preserve multicluster structure of the data, linear combination of relevant features can be used to approximate the eigenvectors. To obtain the weights of each feature, least squares regression problem with L_1 constraint on parameters (weights) is solved, where an eigenvector y_i is the dependent variable and features are independent variables. The regression parameters are denoted by vector w_i, which contains the required feature weights. The regression problem is given by

$$\min_{w_i} ||y_k - X^t w_i||_2^2 \ s.t. ||w_i||_1 \leq d \tag{49}$$

Because there are k eigenvectors given by $\{y_1, y_2, \ldots, y_k\}$, equation (49) can be solved by using any of the k eigenvectors as the dependent variable. Solving all the k regression problems, k solutions (weight vectors) are obtained and are given by $\{w_1, \ldots, w_k\}$, which denote the k feature weight vectors. Because w_i assigns a weight to every feature, a procedure is devised to compute the final weight of each feature using all the possible feature weight vectors. The final weight of a feature is denoted by an MCFS score; the procedure to compute the MCFS score is given below.

For a feature f_j, the MCFS score is computed as the maximum weight value over all the k weight vectors. Let $A = [w_1, w_2, \ldots, w_k]$, then the MCFS score of the jth feature is computed as

$$\text{MCFS}(j) = \max(A_j)$$

where A_j denotes the jth row of the matrix A.

A feature having higher MCFS score is better at preserving the multicluster structure of the data. Hence, features are sorted by the descending MCFS score, and the top d features are selected. Wang et al. [32] used MCFS for comparison with a feature selection method based on eigenvalues of a Laplacian matrix.

SIMULATION RESULTS OF LAPLACIAN SCORE AND MCFS UNSUPERVISED FEATURE SELECTION

Sample classification accuracy using unsupervised feature selection algorithm Laplacian score and MCFS algorithm for various microarray data sets discussed before is

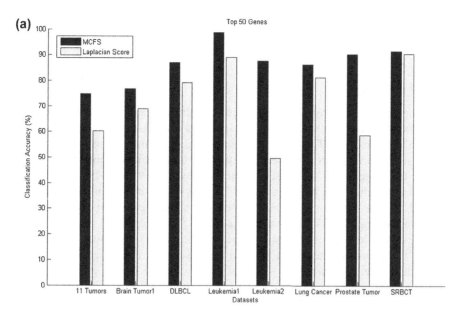

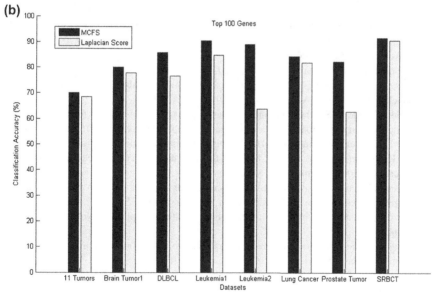

FIGURE 3.2

(a) Top 50 genes. (b) Top 100 genes.

shown in the following histograms (Figure 3.2(a) and (b)) for the top 50 and 100 selected genes.

CONCLUSIONS

This chapter presents various feature selection methods suited for gene selection in microarray data. Both supervised and unsupervised feature selection methods have been described in detail. The pros and cons of using supervised versus unsupervised feature selection methods have been illustrated using benchmark microarray data sets. In the category of supervised feature selection algorithms, both filter and wrapper approaches have been dealt with. The chapter presents detailed simulation for each of the filter based feature selection algorithms (using 5-fold cross-validation) on benchmark microarray data sets. Performance of different filter based feature selection algorithms have been demonstrated on top-ranking genes. Finally, the simulation results of wrapper approaches have been compared with that of filter based approaches.

REFERENCES

[1] Armstrong SA, Staunton JE, Silverman LB, Pieters R, den Boer ML, Minden MD, et al. MLL translocations specify a distinct gene expression profile that distinguishes a unique leukemia. Nat Genet 2002;30(1):41–7.

[2] Bhattacharjee A, Richards WG, Staunton J, Li C, Monti S, Vasa P, et al. Classification of human lung carcinomas by mRNA expression profiling reveals distinct adenocarcinoma subclasses. Proc Natl Acad Sci USA 2001;98(24):13790–5.

[3] Bolón-Canedo V, Sánchez-Maroño N, Alonso-Betanzos A. Distributed feature selection: an application to microarray data classification. Appl Soft Comput 2015;30:136–50.

[4] Cai D, Chiyuan Z, Xiaofei H. Unsupervised feature selection for multi-cluster data. In: Proceedings of the 16th ACM SIGKDD international conference on Knowledge discovery and data mining. ACM; 2010.

[5] Chandra B, Manish G. An efficient statistical feature selection approach for classification of gene expression data. J Biomed Inform 2011;44(4):529–35.

[6] Devijver PA, Josef K. In: Pattern recognition: a statistical approach, vol. 761. London: Prentice Hall; 1982.

[7] Ding C, Peng H. Minimum redundancy feature selection from microarray gene expression data. J Bioinform Comput Biol 2005;3(2):185–205.

[8] Dougherty ER. Small sample issues for microarray-based classification. Comp Funct Genomics 2001;2(1):28–34.

[9] Ferreira AJ, Figueiredo MAT. Efficient feature selection filters for high-dimensional data. Pattern Recogn Lett 2012;33(13):1794–804.

[10] Golub TR, Slonim DK, Tamayo P, Huard C, Gaasenbeek M, Mesirov JP, et al. Molecular classification of cancer: class discovery and class prediction by gene expression monitoring. Science 1999;286(5439):531–7.

[11] Guyon I, Elisseeff A. An introduction to variable and feature selection. J Machine Learn Res 2003;3:1157–82.

[12] Hall MA. Correlation-based feature selection for machine learning [dissertation]. Hamilton, New Zealand: The University of Waikato; 1999.

[13] Harrington CA, Rosenow C, Retief J. Monitoring gene expression using DNA microarrays. Curr Opin Microbiol 2000;3(3):285−91.

[14] He X, Deng C, Niyogi P. Laplacian score for feature selection. Advances in neural information processing systems; 2005.

[15] Huang J, Yunze C, Xiaoming X. A hybrid genetic algorithm for feature selection wrapper based on mutual information. Pattern Recogn Lett 2007;28(13):1825−44.

[16] Hwang T, Zhang W, Xie M, Liu J, Kuang R. Inferring disease and gene set associations with rank coherence in networks. Bioinformatics 2011;27(19):2692−9.

[17] Khan J, Wei JS, Ringner M, Saal LH, Ladanyi M, Westermann F, et al. Classification and diagnostic prediction of cancers using gene expression profiling and artificial neural networks. Nat Med 2001;7(6):673−9.

[18] Kenji K, Rendell LA. A practical approach to feature selection. In: Proceedings of the Ninth International Workshop on Machine Learning; 1992.

[19] Kenji K, Rendell L. The Feature Selection Problem: Traditional Methods and a New Algorithm. In: AAAI-92 Proceedings; 1992.

[20] Kononenko I, Šimec E, Robnik-Šikonja M. Overcoming the myopia of inductive learning algorithms with RELIEFF. Appl Intell 1997;7(1):39−55.

[21] Kononenko I. Estimating attributes: analysis and extensions of RELIEF. Machine Learning: ECML-94. Berlin: Springer; 1994.

[22] Liu H, Setiono R. Chi2: Feature selection and discretization of numeric attributes. In: 2012 IEEE 24th International Conference on Tools with Artificial Intelligence. IEEE Computer Society; 1995.

[23] Marill T, Green DM. On the effectiveness of receptors in recognition systems. Information Theory IEEE Trans 1963;9(1):11−7.

[24] Muni DP, Pal NR, Das J. Genetic programming for simultaneous feature selection and classifier design. IEEE Trans Syst Man Cybern B Cybern 2006;36(1):106−17.

[25] Nie F, Xiang S, Jia Y, Zhang C, Yan S. Trace Ratio Criterion for Feature Selection. AAAI 2008;2:671−6.

[26] Pomeroy SL, Tamayo P, Gaasenbeek M, Sturla LM, Angelo M, McLaughlin ME, et al. Prediction of central nervous system embryonaltumour outcome based on gene expression. Nature 2002;415(6870):436−42.

[27] Pudil P, Novovičová J, Kittler J. Floating search methods in feature selection. Pattern Recogn Lett 1994;15(11):1119−25.

[28] Shipp MA, Ross KN, Tamayo P, Weng AP, Kutok JL, Aguiar RCT, et al. Diffuse large B-cell lymphoma outcome prediction by gene-expression profiling and supervised machine learning. Nat Med 2002;8(1):68−74.

[29] Singh D, Febbo PG, Ross K, Jackson DG, Manola J, Ladd C, et al. Gene expression correlates of clinical prostate cancer behavior. Cancer Cell 2002;1(2):203−9.

[30] Su AI, Welsh JB, Sapinoso LM, Kern SG, Dimitrov Petre, Lapp H, et al. Molecular classification of human carcinomas by use of gene expression signatures. Cancer Res 2001;61(20):7388−93.

[31] Wang J, Wu L, Kong J, Li Y, Zhang B. Maximum weight and minimum redundancy: a novel framework for feature subset selection. Pattern Recogn 2013;46(6):1616−27.

[32] Wang Z, Qiu P, Xu W, Liu Y. Spectral feature selection and its application in high dimensional gene expression studies. In: Proceedings of the 5th ACM Conference on Bioinformatics, Computational Biology, and Health Informatics. ACM, New York; 2014.

[33] Whitney AW. A direct method of nonparametric measurement selection. IEEE Trans Comput 1971;100(9):1100–3.

[34] Yang Y, Pedersen JO. A comparative study on feature selection in text categorization. ICML, vol. 97. 1997.

[35] Yang J, Honavar V. Feature subset selection using a genetic algorithm. In: Feature extraction, construction and selection. New York: Springer; 1998. p. 117–36.

[36] Yeoh E-J, Ross ME, Shurtleff SA, Kent Williams W, Patel D, Mahfouz R, et al. Classification, subtype discovery, and prediction of outcome in pediatric acute lymphoblastic leukemia by gene expression profiling. Cancer Cell 2002;1(2):133–43.

[37] Zhang Y, Ding C, Li T. Gene selection algorithm by combining reliefF and mRMR. BMC Genomics 2008;9(Suppl. 2).

Brain MRI Intensity Inhomogeneity Correction Using Region of Interest, Anatomic Structural Map, and Outlier Detection

Michael Osadebey[1], Nizar Bouguila[2], Douglas Arnold[3]

Department of Electrical and Computer Engineering, Concordia University, Montreal, Canada[1]; Concordia Institute of Information Systems Engineering, Concordia University, Montreal, Canada[2]; NeuroRx Research Inc., Montreal, Canada[3]

E-mail: m_osadeb@encs.concordia.ca, nizar.bouguila@concordia.ca, doug@mrs.mni.mcgill.ca

INTRODUCTION

The magnetic resonance imaging (MRI) system is a popular imaging modality for diagnostic procedures and clinical research in the field of medicine. MRI images are important component of clinical trials of drugs for treatment of multiple sclerosis, Alzheimer, and other neurodegenerative diseases [1-3]. MRI system images exhibit high spatial and contrast resolution, which efficiently discriminates different anatomical structures within a physiological system. However, acquisition of high-quality images is dependent on generation of spatially homogeneous radio frequency field by the MRI system. The absence of a homogeneous field results in image corrupted by bias field. Bias field is the characterization of a specific tissue or homogeneous anatomic structure by nonuniform voxel intensities instead of uniform voxel intensities. Several factors are responsible for bias field. It includes improper acquisition parameter settings, nonuniform sensitivity of radiofrequency coils, nonuniformity of static field, gradient-induced eddy currents, and magnetization properties of the anatomic structure under investigation [4-6].

Bias field, like Rician noise, is a type of image degradation. Rician noise can result from imperfect system components and trade-offs in selection of acquisition parameters. Bias field is the result of combination of several factors including factors responsible for Rician noise. Bias field and Rician noise have different spatial variation within an image. At different levels of severity, Rician noise is uniformly distributed throughout an image but the distribution of bias field is random. Distribution and severity of bias field varies with MRI system magnetic field strength, optimality of selected acquisition parameters, individual patient anatomy, and each MRI slice within the volume data. As the magnetic field strength of an MRI system increases, spatial variation of bias field changes from locally smooth inhomogeneity to locally nonsmooth inhomogeneity [7-9].

Utility of MRI images for manual and automated diagnosis can be significantly reduced by the presence of bias field. Visual inspection of an MRI scan degraded by bias field is more challenging to a physician. It requires more time to discern between presence of an abnormal anatomic structure and artifact. State-of-the-art image analysis algorithms, which are based on voxel intensities, perform poorly by misclassifying tissue classes because different intensity levels are assigned to the same tissue class. It is therefore necessary to perform intensity inhomogeneity correction before manual or automatic image analysis.

In the past 30 years, researchers have made several contributions to correction of bias field in medical images. Despite the significant contributions, correction of intensity inhomogeneity is still an active research area because of increasing clinical interest on brain MRI images and development of high field MRI systems that produce more complex characteristics of bias field [10,11]. None of the current algorithms for correction of intensity inhomogeneity addresses the problem of correcting all the different characteristics of intensity inhomogeneity across different levels of magnetic field strength [12].

This chapter proposes a new and novel approach to correct intensity inhomogeneity in MRI images of the brain. Anatomic structural map, an equivalent of digital brain atlas, guides the algorithm for automatic operation. The structural map is generated directly from the test image. Accurate information from the structural map is combined with distorted intensity-level attributes of the test image to detect outliers in regions of interest (ROIs) generated by K-means clustering. The number of ROI is the number of tissue classes specified by the user in K-means clustering. Outliers in each ROI are merged with voxels in the appropriate tissue class. Intensity levels of the new set of voxels in each tissue class are rescaled to conform to the intensity levels of uncorrupted voxels.

This chapter is organized as follows. The following section describes the different mathematical models that explain the presence of bias field in MRI imaging process. The third, fourth and fifth sections review current bias field correction strategies by explaining their design techniques, importance, and limitations respectively. In the sixth section, we describe the methodology of our proposal. Results of testing our proposal on real MRI images are displayed in the seventh section. The results are discussed in the eighth section. The final section concludes this report.

MATHEMATICAL MODELS OF BIAS FIELD

Mathematical model that explains bias field in MRI systems is derived from the generally accepted mathematical model describing imaging process in different imaging modalities [13,14]. At location index l within an image consisting of L number of voxels, a voxel with observed intensity value I_l and the underlying uncorrupted signal x_l are related according to

$$I_l = b_l x_l + \varepsilon \tag{1}$$

where b_l and ε are spatially varying functions of the image coordinate denoting bias field and uniformly distributed random noise due to the imaging device, respectively. To account for signal variation within a specific tissue class j, the general model in equation (1) is reformulated as:

$$I_l = b_l\left(u_j + \varepsilon_l\right) + \varepsilon \tag{2}$$

The expression in equation (2) shows that signal emitted by an anatomic stricture belonging to a specific tissue class is a random variable corrupted with noise ε_l and distributed around a mean value u_j. Biological noise ε_l arising from a specific anatomic structure and noise ε due to the MRI device makes determination of bias field in equation (2) nontrivial. The model yields intractable equations when different anatomic structures are under consideration [15]. To simplify the model, the following two assumptions are made on bias field and the imaged object [16,17].

- The bias field is a slowly varying variable that can be approximated by a constant within a clearly defined neighborhood.
- The image is piecewise constant and can be approximated as the sum of all disjoint regions.

For computational convenience, the intratissue variability represented by the term $(u_j + \varepsilon_l)$ is neglected so that the general model is rephrased as [18,13]

$$I_i = b_i u_j + \varepsilon \tag{3}$$

Additional computational convenience would be to account for the intratissue signal variation but assume that that bias field is independent of image noise, so equation (2) becomes

$$I_i = b_i\left(u_j + \varepsilon_l\right) \tag{4}$$

The computational complexity of equation (4) is further reduced through logarithmic transformation, which turns the multiplicative bias field b into an additive bias field [19,20]:

$$log I_l = log b_l + log u_j + log e_l \tag{5}$$

Correction of intensity inhomogeneity, preceded by noise removal, is a two-step process. The first is an estimation of intensity inhomogeneity in the image domain followed by division in equations (1)–(4) or subtraction in the log domain in equation (5).

DESIGN TECHNIQUES OF CURRENT ALGORITHMS

Current bias field correction schemes can be classified into two classes according to the object of interest for source of information in the elimination of bias field.

PROSPECTIVE METHOD

In prospective methods, the imaging device is the object of interest because it is regarded as the source of intensity inhomogeneity. The bias field is corrected by ensuring correct acquisition parameters and acquisition protocols. This can be achieved by calibrating the MRI system with phantoms, special imaging sequences, and a combination of two different radio frequency coils [21,22].

Images of objects with uniform physical properties such as oil and water are used as phantoms. Intensity inhomogeneity of the image is estimated from the filtered and smoothed MRI image of the phantom [22].

Combination of surface and volume coils allows each individual coil to compensate for the deficiency of the other coil. The surface coil characterized by good signal-to-noise-ratio (SNR) but vulnerable to intensity inhomogeneity is compensated for with the presence of the volume coil, which has a poor SNR but is resistant to intensity inhomogeneity [23].

RETROSPECTIVE METHOD

Retrospective methods have the acquired image as object of interest and correct bias field using prior knowledge and properties measured from the acquired image. There are several categories of retrospective method. In this chapter, we review only four popular categories. They are low-frequency filtering, surface fitting, segmentation, and histogram.

- **Low-Frequency Filtering:** Low-pass filtering technique exploits the slowly varying property of bias field. Bias field and image details are assumed to be localized in the lower and upper ranges of the frequency domain, respectively. This property enables extraction of the bias field from the corrupt image. Homomorphic filtering, popular for nonuniform illumination correction, is in this category. This filtering method follows the mathematical model in equation (5) by computing bias-corrected image as the difference between log transformation of degraded image and log transformation of low-frequency filtered image [24]. A similar algorithm, homomorphic unmask filtering, corrects the bias field according to the mathematical model in equation (4) [22]. Wavelet decomposition is another low-pass filtering approach to correct intensity inhomogeneity. The degraded image is decomposed into approximate space and residual space. The approximate template in approximate space is regarded as consisting of multiscale sensitivity profiles of surface coil of the MRI system.

Bias field is determined from the sensitivity profile which gives optimal output from a suitably chosen filter [25,26].

- **Surface Fitting:** A surface fitting method fits parametric smooth functions such as polynomials and splines to image features that characterize the slowly varying intensity inhomogeneity. The image features may be intensities [27] or local gradients [28,29]. A popular surface fitting method is the parametric bias field correction referred to as PABIC. It is based on a parametric model of tissue statistics and polynomial model of the intensity inhomogeneity field. Estimation of bias field is formulated as nonlinear energy minimization [18].

- **Segmentation:** The segmentation method is based on the principle that accurate segmentation trivializes intensity inhomogeneity correction. It is widely acknowledged that alternating segmentation and intensity inhomogeneity steps optimizes the output of an image analysis task. Examples of segmentation methods include fuzzy c-means (FCM) [19], mixture models [30,31], and level set [16].

- **Histogram:** Histogram methods manipulate the intensity histogram of the image for correction of the bias field. There are three popular techniques under histogram-based bias field correction methods. The nonparametric nonuniformity normalization (N3) is in this category. Design of N3 is based on a multiplicative mathematical model and assumes that the histogram of an image represents probability distribution of a given signal. It corrects bias field by seeking the bias field that maximizes the frequency content of the histogram of an image [32]. Another approach in this category considers that intensity inhomogeneity increases the information content of an image. Entropy, a measure of information content, is extracted from the image intensity histogram and cast in an information minimization framework to correct the bias field [33].

Yet another approach seeks to manipulate histogram information in the local neighborhood of the image where the intensity inhomogeneity is assumed to be constant. Local neighborhoods of the image are obtained by dividing the image into subvolumes. Intensity inhomogeneity map is estimated by comparing each histogram in each locality of the test image to the corresponding locality in a histogram model [34].

IMPORTANCE OF CURRENT ALGORITHMS

The several volumes of research articles on correction of bias field reflect the importance of brain MRI in the study and examination of neurodegenerative diseases. Specific contributions of different algorithms in the correction of intensity inhomogeneity as stated in [14] are outlined below.

The old and popular homomorphic filtering approach is very simple to implement and can operate in real time. The design of FCM makes it robust to partial volume effect. Iteration between segmentation and bias field correction in segmentation-based techniques inherently improves the accuracy of the corrected bias field. Histogram-based methods are potentially suitable for automated operations because prior knowledge of the image and initialization is not required as in segmentation-based methods.

LIMITATIONS OF CURRENT ALGORITHMS

Limitations of current algorithms are inherent in their design formulation or derived from the adopted mathematical model. These limitations are categorized as algorithm and model limitations.

ALGORITHM LIMITATIONS

Phantom-based methods cannot correct for patient-induced inhomogeneities. Both phantom-based methods and combination of surface and volume coils for bias correction requires more acquisition time, which is often impractical in large-scale studies such as clinical trials [8,14]. Frequency spectrums of homogeneous regions that describe specific anatomic structures are in the same low range as bias fields. There is a high risk of eroding relevant anatomic structures when the filtering method of intensity homogeneity correction is applied [35]. The blind extrapolation of intensity inhomogeneity from a major tissue to the entire image in an intensity-based surface fitting method limits the accuracy of bias field correction. Gradient-based methods in the same class as surface fitting methods can give erroneous bias field estimate if the homogeneous image regions are not large enough or is dominated by abnormal tissue, such as the presence of a tumor [14]. Many current bias field correction techniques are not robust to images corrupted by little or no bias field [12].

MODEL LIMITATIONS

Since 1971, when the MRI system was invented, increased clinical interest in brain MRI encouraged the development of high magnetic field strength MRI systems. The operating magnetic field strength increased from 1.5 T to 7 T for humans and as much as 9.4 T and 14.1 T for animals. Use of higher magnetic field improves the signal-to-noise ratio and acquisition time but bias field, if present, can be significant, severe, and complex [10]. The common assumption of a smoothly varying multiplicative bias field adopted by most current algorithms is only an ideal expectation to make the problem of bias field correction tractable. Experience has shown that even with this assumption, the bias fields computed by most of these algorithms such as [36] and [32] are in general not smooth. Extra resources and sometimes heuristics approach is adopted to maintain smoothness [7]. In the past, Veltuizen et al. [37] were among those researchers who cast doubts on the reliability of adopting smooth multiplicative-intensity inhomogeneity field as the model of bias field. The doubt was made strong when the contribution of [38] demonstrated that the intensity inhomogeneity field is not necessarily globally smooth. The field may be locally smooth but not globally. In such situations, most of the current algorithms will be inefficient for the correct bias field.

METHODS
THEORY AND PROBLEM FORMULATION

A MRI image is a signal Y defined in an image domain Ω. The signal has three attributes, namely, intensity I, spatial location R, and entropy S. Entropy is derived from R. These attributes are in Ω, $\Omega_I \in \Omega$, $\Omega_S \in \Omega$, and $\Omega_R \in \Omega$. The signal represents M types of anatomic structures, so that there are M disjoint regions in the domain of each attribute:

$$\Omega_I = \left\{\Omega_{I,1}, \ldots\ldots\ldots, \Omega_{I,M}\right\} \tag{6}$$

$$\Omega_R = \left\{\Omega_{R,1}, \ldots\ldots\ldots, \Omega_{R,M}\right\} \tag{7}$$

$$\Omega_S = \left\{\Omega_{S,1}, \ldots\ldots\ldots, \Omega_{S,M}\right\} \tag{8}$$

For each attribute, regions representing each of the M anatomic structure can be segmented by suitable image-processing techniques. Intensity levels attributes are segmented by, for example, k-means clustering algorithm [39]. The entropy attribute is segmented by combining entropy filtering with thresholding. Spatial location attributes can be segmented by computing region property across the image.

Ideal MRI Image
The following holds true for an MRI image acquired using correct acquisition parameters and acquisition protocol:

$$\Omega = \Omega_I \cup \Omega_R \cup \Omega_S \tag{9}$$

$$\varnothing = \cap_{j=1}^{M} \Omega_{I,j} \tag{10}$$

$$\varnothing = \cap_{j=1}^{M} \Omega_{R,j} \tag{11}$$

$$\varnothing = \cap_{j=1}^{M} \Omega_{S,j} \tag{12}$$

$$\varnothing = \Omega_{I,j} \cap \Omega_{R,K} \quad j \neq k \tag{13}$$

$$\varnothing = \Omega_{I,j} \cap \Omega_{S,K} \quad j \neq k \tag{14}$$

MRI Image Corrupted by Bias Field
We make the following eight statements regarding MRI image corrupted by bias field:

1. The MRI signal has been processed and is without noise
2. The bias field signal, unlike noise signal, is not uniformly distributed throughout the image.

3. Like residual noise signals, there does exist residual bias field signals. They are insignificant and can be neglected since they do not adversely affect image quality and image analysis.
4. Henceforth, intensity levels not significantly affected by bias fields will be termed clean signals; otherwise, they are termed corrupt signals.
5. The domain defined by intensity attributes of each tissue class is the union of the set of clean voxels $\{I_j\}$ and set of corrupt voxels $\{I_k\}$:

$$\Omega_{I,j} = \{I_j\} \cup \{I_k\}, \quad j \neq k, \quad k = 1, \ldots\ldots, M \tag{15}$$

The expression in equation (15) implies that voxels associated with bias field in a particular tissue class belong to a different anatomic structure.

6. The corrupt voxels are in image locations termed outliers G. Outliers are voxel locations that are members of the set that violates expressions in equations (10)–(14):

$$\Omega_{I,j} \cap \Omega_{R,K} = G_{R,K}, \quad j \neq k \tag{16}$$

$$\Omega_{I,j} \cap \Omega_{S,K} = G_{S,K}, \quad j \neq k \tag{17}$$

7. Both corrupt and clean signals in each tissue class are described by a normal distribution.
8. The intensity level attribute of an image has tissue-specific numeric meaning [40], which potentially trivializes manual and automated analyses of an MRI scan. Presence of bias field distorts intensity levels and makes their meaning vague with respect to a tissue class. Nevertheless, spatial locations and spatial information of anatomic structures under investigation are not distorted.

OUR PROPOSED BIAS FIELD CORRECTION STRATEGY

We propose a three-step bias field correction strategy:

1. Create ROIs by clustering. The number of ROIs should be cleverly chosen to equal the number of anatomic structures under investigation.
2. Compensate for vagueness of intensity level attributes by seeking extra information from an anatomic structural map.
3. Detect voxel locations where the bias field is considered significant using the improved intensity level attributes.

ALGORITHM DESIGN

Implementation of our proposal is explained by the flow chart in Figure 4.1. The test image is at the top of the figure. Red-colored numbers in the figure depict each step for implementation of the algorithm. The first step thresholds the test image using

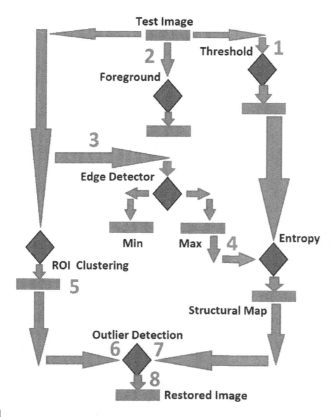

FIGURE 4.1

Flow chart of the bias field correction algorithm.

the Otsu method [41]. The Otsu method finds the threshold that minimizes intraclass variations within the image. We chose the Otsu method for thresholding because in many applications the Otsu method proved to be simple and effective [42]. Noise and voxels corrupted by bias field are eliminated. Only very strong edges representing image details are retained. The output of the Otsu method is one of two components to create an accurate template of the image. The second step extracts foreground voxels of the test image. In the third step, the test image is fed to multiscale canny edge detector. Canny edge detector [43] is the preferred edge detector because of its optimal performance in terms of robustness to noise, minimal response, and good location of edges [44]. The multiscale edge detector outputs two images. The first image is the edge image at the minimum edge scale. The other is the edge image at the maximum edge scale. In the fourth step, the edge image at maximum scale is combined with the Otsu image to produce a structural map of the test image. In the fifth step, ROIs in the image are generated by a k-means algorithm. The number of ROIs is chosen to equal the number of tissue classes. The choice of k-means instead of a more robust algorithm was motivated by its simplicity, an important requirement at the preliminary steps of the proposed algorithm. The sixth step test each ROI for outliers using entropy and spatial information from the structural map according to equations (16) and (17). Outliers are assigned to their appropriate tissue class j in the seventh step to produce new sets of voxels for each tissue class. The new set of voxels $x_j \in [p_{1j} \ p_{2j}]$ are rescaled by mapping to $x'_j \in [S_{1j} \ S_{2j}]$ [45].

$$x'_j = S_{1j} + \left(\frac{x_j - P_{1j}}{P_{2j} - P_{1j}} \right) (S_{2j} - S_{1j}) \qquad (18)$$

where p_{1j} and p_{2j} are the minimum and maximum values of reclassified voxels, respectively, and S_{1j} and S_{2j} are the minimum and maximum values of the initial set of clean voxels. The statistics of an initial set of clean voxels can be substituted with the statistics of a model for the tissue class, if available.

EXPERIMENTAL DESIGN

The proposed algorithm was tested on real MRI images. We chose not to use image simulators to validate our proposal because they lack the natural anatomic variability and image acquisition artifacts of real images [14]. Performance of the algorithm was evaluated qualitatively using visual inspection of corrected images. Visual quality assessment, though subjective, was preferred because it is the only performance evaluation criterion that validates all objective performance criteria. We choose to avoid comparative quantitative performance evaluation because of lack of publically available ground truth data.

SOURCE OF TEST DATA

Fifteen T1-weighted brain MRI images with different severity levels of bias fields were sourced from NeuroRx Research Inc. (www.neurorx.com). NeuroRx is a clinical research organization (CRO) dedicated to working with the pharmaceutical industry to facilitate clinical trials of new drugs for multiple sclerosis (MS) and other neurological diseases. The organization provides professional management including logistics of scan handling and tracking of all MRI-related study activities and promptly delivers precise MRI outcome measurements that are performed in a regulatory-compliant environment.

EXPERIMENTAL RESULTS

The result of applying our algorithm to different levels of severity and complexity of bias fields in brain MRI images are displayed in seven different figures (Figures 4.2−4.8).

DISCUSSION

This discussion is sectioned according to the figure number of the experimental results. Discussion based on Figure 4.2 is detailed because it explains each step in the implementation of the proposed algorithm.

SOURCE OF TEST DATA

Figure 4.2a is the test image corrupted by bias field. Test image voxel values originally acquired as int32 is converted to double precision gray level. After conversion, four duplicates of the image are made. The first duplicate after the Otsu method of thresholding is in Figure 4.2b. Foreground voxels extracted from the second duplicate are shown in Figure 4.2c.

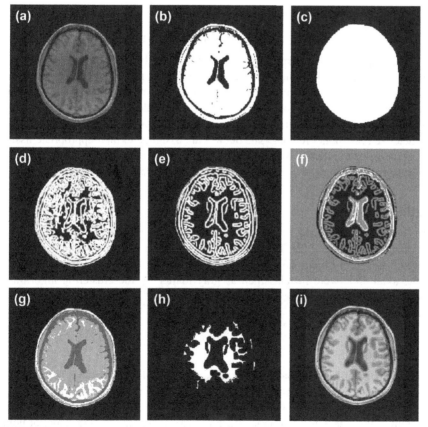

FIGURE 4.2

(a) Test image. (b) Otsu threshold. (c) Foreground. (d) Minimum scale edge image.
(e) Maximum scale edge image. (f) Anatomic structural map. (g) Region of interest.
(h) Outliers. (i) Restored image.

The third duplicate is fed to the multiscale edge detector, which outputs the edge image at the minimum and maximum scales. The local entropy of both edge images are displayed in Figure 4.2d and Figure 4.2e. Entropy image at the maximum scale in Figure 4.2e is combined with the output of Otsu thresholding to obtain an anatomic structural map of the MRI slice.

The structural map displayed in Figure 4.2f contains accurate tissue-specific spatial and entropy information. Voxel locations with low entropy, in dark color, represent homogeneous regions of a specific anatomic structure. Voxel locations with high entropy, in white color, are image details that separate homogeneous regions within and between tissue classes.

ROIs detected in the fourth duplicate of the test image are shown in Figure 4.2g. Corrupt voxel intensity levels, known as outliers, are identified by using entropy information in the tissue structural map shown in Figure 4.2h. Outliers $G_{S,k}$ are voxel locations in one of tissue classes j in the structural map that are members of the set determined by setting entropy threshold $s_{th} = 0.3$.

$$G_{S,k} = \{\Omega_{I,J} \cap \Omega_{S,K}\} \cap \{S : s < s_{th}\} \tag{19}$$

High image contrast generates an edge effect [46]. In this chapter, the edge effect is revealed as high entropy values recorded by entropy filter in small homogeneous regions around edges that demarcate gray matter and white matter tissues. This problem was addressed by area threshold $A_{th} = 100$. Area thresholding is also applied in identification of white matter regions to eliminate homogeneous regions within edges that characterize gray matter regions. The outliers are assigned to their appropriate tissue classes, rescaled to produce the restored image shown in Figure 4.2i. The visual quality of the restored image is very high compared to the degraded image.

FIGURE 4.3

The test image in Figure 4.3a has same anatomic structures (except ventricle) as the test image in Figure 4.2a. The tissue structural map is shown in Figure 4.3b. The ROI image in Figure 4.3c shows that white matter tissues around the midline of the axial slice were misclassified as gray matter by the clustering algorithm. The restored image in Figure 4.3d is of much higher quality than the degraded image.

FIGURE 4.4

The test image in Figure 4.4a is a typical example of a locally smooth but globally nonsmooth bias field. The tissue structural map is in Figure 4.4b. The ROI clustering algorithm correctly labeled white matter in Figure 4.4c though intensity levels are different within the same anatomic structure. This accurate labeling may not hold for a clustering algorithm, which is more robust than k-means algorithm. Intensity-level variation was corrected by invoking the intensity rescaling function incorporated in our proposed system. The restored image is shown in Figure 4.4d.

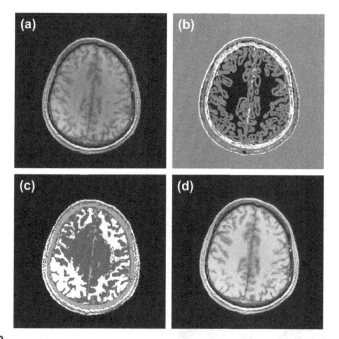

FIGURE 4.3

(a) Test image. (b) Anatomic structural map. (c) Region of interest. (d) Restored image.

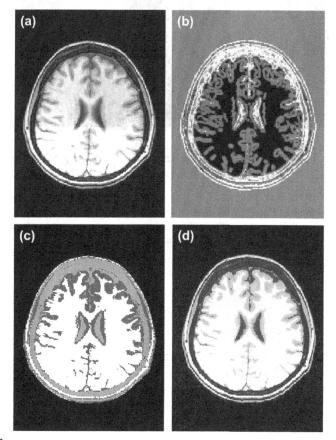

FIGURE 4.4

(a) Test image. (b) Anatomic structural map. (c) Region of interest. (d) Restored image.

FIGURE 4.5

The test image in Figure 4.5a has same level of severity as the test image in Figure 4.2a. The structural map in Figure 4.5b, the ROI in Figure 4.5c, and the restored image in Figure 4.5d indicate that the proposed algorithm demonstrates the same level of performance for the same level of severity of the bias field.

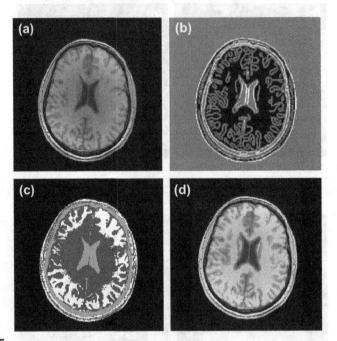

FIGURE 4.5

(a) Test image. (b) Anatomic structural map. (c) Region of interest. (d) Restored image.

FIGURE 4.6

The structural map in Figure 4.6b was generated from the test image in Figure 4.6a. Entropy and spatial information from the structural map was combined with the ROI in Figure 4.6c to restore the image. Visual assessment of restored image in Figure 4.6d shows that there are much more uniform intensity levels within tissue classes than the test image.

FIGURE 4.7

The test image in Figure 4.7a is in the same category of severity as the test image in Figure 4.4. Unlike Figure 4.4, our system detected presence of a bias field. The structural map and the clustered ROI are depicted in Figure 4.7b and Figure 4.7c, respectively. Intensity inhomogeneity was significantly reduced in the restored image of Figure 4.7d.

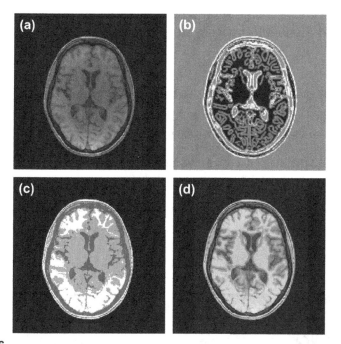

FIGURE 4.6

(a) Test image. (b) Anatomic structural map. (c) Region of interest. (d) Restored image.

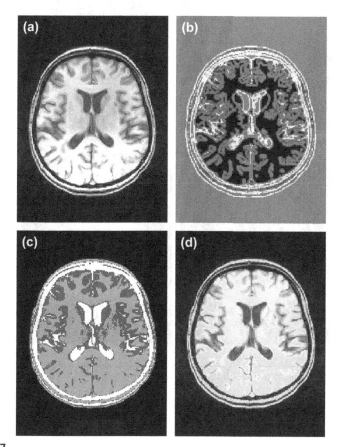

FIGURE 4.7

(a) Test image. (b) Anatomic structural map. (c) Region of interest. (d) Restored image.

FIGURE 4.8

The test image in Figure 4.8a is yet another example of locally smooth but globally nonsmooth bias field. The intensity level of white matter voxels toward the frontal lobe is obviously different from voxels of the same anatomic structure in other regions of the MRI slice image. As depicted in the bottom left figure, white matter voxels toward the frontal lobe was mislabeled as gray matter because of the presence of bias field. Information from the structural map in Figure 4.8b was combined with the ROI in Figure 4.8c to restore the image. The restored image shown in Figure 4.8d is superior in visual quality compared to the test image.

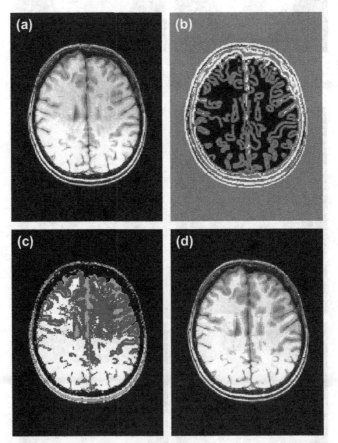

FIGURE 4.8

(a) Test image. (b) Anatomic structural map. (c) Region of interest. (d) Restored image.

CONCLUSION

The mathematical model adopted by current retrospective bias field correction algorithms follow two-step process to restore an image. First is estimation of the bias field followed by either division or addition in the image domain. Most algorithms are based on simplified mathematical models to avoid equations having intractable solutions. They assume smoothly varying multiplicative bias field for different ranges of magnetic field strength. This assumption limits their performance where the bias field is severe, complex and not necessarily globally smooth, particularly at higher magnetic field strengths. We hereby propose a new bias field correction algorithm that does not require the computationally intensive estimation of the bias field. Our proposal demonstrated excellent performance on brain MRI images that were degraded by different manifestations of bias field. This chapter pioneers the automatic generation of an anatomic structural map directly from the degraded MRI image of the brain. The anatomic structural map is a template that can be extended to a digital brain atlas. Current template-based bias field correction algorithms are guided to automatic operation by digital brain atlas derived externally from multiple subjects MRI images. Externally derived digital brain atlas requires incorporating additional resources such as additional image registration.

REFERENCES

[1] Arnold DL, Riess GT, Matthews PM, Francis GS, Collins DL, Wolfson C, et al. Use of proton magnetic resonance spectroscopy for monitoring disease progression in multiple sclerosis. Ann Neurol 1994;36(1):76–82.

[2] Gold R, Kappos L, Arnold DL, Bar-Or A, Giovannoni G, Selmaj K, et al. Placebo-controlled phase 3 study of oral bg-12 for relapsing multiple sclerosis. N Engl J Med 2012;367(24):2362–2.

[3] Aubert-Broche B, Fonov V, Weier K, Narayanan S, Arnold DL, Banwell B, et al. Is it possible to differentiate the impact of pediatric monophasic demyelinating disorders and multiple sclerosis after a first episode of demyelination? In: Durrleman S, Fletcher T, Gerig G, Niethammer M, Pennec X, editors. Spatio-temporal Image Analysis for Longitudinal and Time-Series Image Data. Lecture Notes in Computer Science. New York: Springer; 2015. p. 38–48. http://dx.doi.org/10.1007/978-3-319-14905-9.

[4] Guillemaud R, Brady M. Estimating the bias field of mr images. IEEE Trans Med Imaging 1997;16(3):238–51.

[5] Vovk U, Pernus F, Likar B. A review of methods for correction of intensity inhomogeneity in mri. IEEE Trans Med Imaging 2007;26(3):405–21.

[6] Wells III WM, Grimson WEL, Kikinis R, Jolesz FA. Adaptive segmentation of mri data. Medical Imaging. IEEE Trans 1996;15(4):429–42.

[7] Li C, Xu C, Anderson AW, Gore JC. MRI tissue classification and bias field estimation based on coherent local intensity clustering: a unified energy minimization framework. In: Prince JL, Pham DL, Myers KJ, editors. Information Processing in Medical Imaging; vol. 5636 of Lecture Notes in Computer Science. Berlin Heidelberg: Springer; 2009. p. 288–99. http://dx.doi.org/10.1007/978-3-642-02498-6.

[8] Rajapakse JC, Kruggel F. Segmentation of mr images with intensity inhomogeneities. Image Vis Comput 1998;16(3):165–80.

[9] Roy S, Carass A, Bazin P, Prince JL. Intensity inhomogeneity correction of magnetic resonance images using patches. In: SPIE Medical Imaging. International Society for Optics and Photonics; 2011. p. 79621F.

[10] Haacke EM, Brown RW, Thompson MR, Venkatesan R. Magnetic resonance imaging. Wiley-Liss; 2014.

[11] Van de Moortele P, Auerbach EJ, Olman C, Yacoub E, Uğurbil K, Moeller S. T 1 weighted brain images at 7 tesla unbiased for proton density, t 2 contrast and rf coil receive b 1 sensitivity with simultaneous vessel visualization. Neuroimage 2009;46(2):432–46.

[12] Arnold JB, Liow J, Schaper KA, Stern JJ, Sled JG, Shattuck DW, et al. Qualitative and quantitative evaluation of six algorithms for correcting intensity nonuniformity effects. Neuroimage 2001;13(5):931–43.

[13] Prima S, Ayache N, Barrick T, Roberts N. Maximum likelihood estimation of the bias field in mr brain images: Investigating different modelings of the imaging process. In: Proceedings of the 4th International Conference on Medical Image Computing and Computer-Assisted Intervention. MICCAI '01. London, UK: Springer-Verlag; 2001. p. 811–9.

[14] Vovk U, Pernus F, Likar B. A review of methods for correction of intensity inhomogeneity in mri. IEEE Trans Med Imaging 2007;26(3):405–21.

[15] Cui W, Wang Y, Lei T, Fan Y, Feng Y. Level set segmentation of medical images based on local region statistics and maximum a posteriori probability. Comput Mathematical Methods Med 2013;2013:1–12.

[16] Li C, Huang R, Ding Z, Gatenby JC, Metaxas DN, Gore JC. A level set method for image segmentation in the presence of intensity inhomogeneities with application to mri. IEEE Trans Image Process 2011;20(7):2007–16.

[17] Vokurka EA, Thacker NA, Jackson A. A fast model independent method for automatic correction of intensity nonuniformity in mri data. J Magn Reson Imaging 1999;10(4):550–62.

[18] Styner M, Brechbuhler C, Szckely G, Gerig G. Parametric estimate of intensity inhomogeneities applied to mri. IEEE Trans Med Imaging 2000;19(3):153–65.

[19] Ahmed MN, Yamany SN, Mohamed N, Farag AA, Moriarty T. A modified fuzzy c-means algorithm for bias field estimation and segmentation of mri data. IEEE Trans Med Imaging 2002;21(3):193–9.

[20] Liao L, Lin T, Li B. Mri brain image segmentation and bias field correction based on fast spatially constrained kernel clustering approach. Pattern Recogn Lett 2008;29(10):1580–8.

[21] Wicks DAG, Barker GJ, Tofts PS. Correction of intensity nonuniformity in mr images of any orientation. Magn Reson Imaging 1993;11(2):183–96.

[22] Axel L, Costantini J, Listerud J. Intensity correction in surface-coil mr imaging. AJR Am J Roentgenol 1987;148(2):418–20.

[23] Brey WW. Correction for intensity falloff in surface coil magnetic resonance imaging. Med Phys 1988;15(2):241.

[24] Johnston B, Atkins MS, Mackiewich B, Anderson M. Segmentation of multiple scle-
      rosis lesions in intensity corrected multispectral mri. IEEE Trans Med Imaging 1996;
      15(2):154–69.

[25] Han C, Hatsukami TS, Yuan C. A multi-scale method for automatic correction
      of intensity non-uniformity in mr images. J Magn Reson Imaging 2001;13(3):428–36.

[26] Lin F, Chen Y, Belliveau JW, Wald LL. A wavelet-based approximation of surface coil
      sensitivity profiles for correction of image intensity inhomogeneity and parallel imaging
      reconstruction. Hum Brain Mapp 2003;19(2):96–111.

[27] Zhuge Y, Udupa JK, Liu J, Saha PK, Iwanage T. Scalebased method for correcting back-
      ground intensity variation in acquired images. In: Proc. SPIE 4684, Medical Imaging
      2002: Image Processing, 1103; 2002.

[28] Meyer CR, Bland PH, Pipe J. Retrospective correction of intensity inhomogeneities in
      mri. IEEE Trans Med Imaging 1995;14(1):36–41.

[29] Hui C, Zhou YX, Narayana P. Fast algorithm for calculation of inhomogeneity
      gradient in magnetic resonance imaging data. J Magn Reson Imaging 2010;32(5):
      1197–208.

[30] Van Leemput K, Maes F, Vandermeulen D, Suetens P. Automated model-based bias
      field correction f mr images of the brain. IEEE Trans Med Imaging 1999;18(10):
      885–96.

[31] Gispert JD, Reig S, Pascau J, Vaquero JJ, Garcia-Barreno P, Desco M. Method for bias
      field correction of brain t1-weighted magnetic resonance images minimizing segmenta-
      tion error. Hum Brain Mapp 2004;22(2):133–44.

[32] Sled JG, Zijdenbos AP, Evans AC. A nonparametric method for automatic correction of
      intensity nonuniformity in mri data. IEEE Trans Med Imaging 1998;17(1):87–97.

[33] Likar B, Maintz JBA, Viergever MA, Pernus F. Retrospective shading correction based
      on entropy minimization. J Microsc 2000;197(3):285–95.

[34] Shattuck DW, Sandor-Leahy SR, Schaper KA, Rottenberg DA, Leahy RM. Magnetic
      resonance image tissue classification using a partial volume model. Neuroimage
      2001;13(5):856–76.

[35] Hou Z. A review on mr image intensity inhomogeneity correction. Int J Biomed
      Imaging 2006;2006:1–11.

[36] Wells WM, Grimson WEL, Kikinis R, Jolesz FA. Adaptive segmentation of MRI data.
      IEEE Trans Med Imaging 1996;15(4):429–42.

[37] Velthuizen RP, Heine JJ, Cantor AB, Lin H, Fletcher LM, Clarke LP. Review and eval-
      uation of mri nonuniformity corrections for brain tumor response measurements. Med
      Phys 1998;25(9):1655.

[38] Collewet G, Davenel A, Toussaint C, Akoka S. Correction of intensity nonuniformity in
      spin-echo t1-weighted images. Magn Reson Imaging 2002;20(4):365–73.

[39] Zalik KR. An efficient k-means clustering algorithm. Pattern Recogn Lett 2008;29(9):
      1385–91.

[40] Zhuge Y, Udupa JK. Intensity standardization simplifies brain mr image segmentation.
      Comput Vision Image Understanding 2009;113(10):1095–103.

[41] Otsu N. A threshold selection method from gray-level histograms. IEEE Trans Syst
      Man Cybern 1979;9(1):62–6.

[42] Chou C, Lin W, Chang F. A binarization method with learning built rules for document
      images produced by cameras. Pattern Recognit 2010;43(4):1518–30.

[43] Canny J. A computational approach to edge detection. IEEE Trans Pattern Anal Ma-
      chine Intell 1986;8(6):679–98.

[44] Bao P, Zhang L, Wu X. Canny edge detection enhancement by scale multiplication. IEEE Trans Pattern Anal Machine Intell 2005;27(9):1485–90.

[45] Nyul LG, Udupa JK. On standardizing the mr image intensity scale. Magn Reson Med 1999;42(6):1072–81.

[46] Jäger F. Normalization of Magnetic Resonance Images and its Application to the Diagnosis of the Scoliotic Spine, vol. 34. Logos Verlag Berlin GmbH; 2011:35.

Leveraging Big Data Analytics for Personalized Elderly Care: Opportunities and Challenges

5

Obinna Anya[1], Hissam Tawfik[2]

IBM Research – Almaden, San Jose, CA, USA[1]; Department of Mathematics and Computer Science, Liverpool Hope University, UK[2]

E-mail: obanya@us.ibm.com, tawfikh@hope.ac.uk

INTRODUCTION

Advances in several subfields of information and communication technology (ICT), including social computing, sensor networks, the Internet of Things, and intelligent information processing, have given rise to "a world of data" [1] with fast and pervasive analytics at scale. In recent years, there has been a growing interest in collecting and analyzing data about several aspects of our life—our shopping habits and travel records, our "likes," tweets, photos, digital clicks, and daily interactions and conversations with friends and family—via personal mobile devices, the social media, credit card swipes, wearable gadgets, smart buildings, intelligent vehicles, and advanced analytics applications. Although these pervasive data collection and analytics methods continue to grow and build digital profiles of us and our lifestyles, significant open questions remain as to what data should be collected, what insights should be drawn from them, and for what use.

Broadly speaking, one of such uses has been to support innovation and decision making, and one area where this has gained traction recently is the health care industry, particularly elderly care. Elderly people represent a growing proportion of the world's population. As noted by the World Population Ageing Report [2], the population of people in the world aged 60 and older has risen from 205 million in 1950 to almost 810 million in 2012, and is projected to double by 2050, reaching 2 billion (approximately 20% of the world's population and an increase of about 181% between 2010 and 2050). In addition, we are living longer. It is anticipated that we can expect to have an increase in life expectancy at birth from 86 years for males and 92 years for females by 2050 [3]. Building technologies to empower the elderly to stay healthy and active and, as importantly, participate in decisions pertaining to their health care is at the center of studies on personalized elderly care. Achieving this remains challenging primarily because of huge differences in individual care needs and the progressive nature of ageing [4].

Personalization entails processes that encourage and respect the contributions elderly persons can make to their own health—from the perspective of their values, goals, past experience, and knowledge of their own health needs—with the underlying goal of providing for them care that is "predictive, personalized, preventive and participatory" [5]. However, existing approaches often treat the elderly as compliant individuals, and deliver services through a series of discrete care episodes that hardly take account of the varied needs and lifestyles of the elderly [6]. With exabytes of data generated on a daily basis about our activities from digital footprints and online activities, recent research efforts are focusing on exploiting these massive data sets to address the challenge of personalized elderly care. But, despite the potential ability of Big Data to add to our knowledge of ourselves in novel ways and to enrich our understanding of people's latent needs and preferences [7-9], deriving valuable insight from Big Data poses numerous challenges.

In this chapter, we describe the opportunities and challenges that leveraging Big Data analytics for elderly care presents. It is argued that though potentially viable as an approach to raise elderly care to a level where the uniqueness of each elderly person is adequately recognized [10], it does pose inherent and enormous social, context-aware, and technical challenges that research cannot afford to ignore. We present a review of research in personalized services for elderly care and explore the challenges in the area of Big Data analytics for elderly care. Based on the discussion, ACTVAGE—a context-aware lifestyle-oriented framework for supporting personalized elderly care and independent living is proposed. The framework combines systematic capture of past lifestyles and knowledge of current activities and user context. It then applies rigorous analytics to build a complete picture of the elderly person's lifestyle and contextual needs in order to build a formal representation of the lifestyle concept for system design. Based on the representation, required services, including social networking, self-diagnosis and monitoring, advisory, entertainment, exercise, dietary, reminder, and local events services are developed to offer individually tailored and lifestyle-oriented support for active ageing and independent living.

THE CHALLENGE OF PERSONALIZATION IN ELDERLY CARE

The notion of personalized care has been an important factor underlying the provision of quality care [11] and a central consideration in the design of health and social services for the elderly [10,12,13]. Personalized care places emphasis on the individual needs of a person rather than on efficiencies of the care provider or the sophistication of technologies for care support; builds upon the strengths of a person as an individual rather than on their weaknesses as a care receiver; and honors their values, personal choices, and preferences [12,14-16]. An overarching goal was to support the elderly care receiver to maintain a sense of self [10]. However, considerable confusion surrounds the notion of personalized care—what it means as a concept, what it involves in practice, and how best to take account of it in the design of computational systems for elderly care. More comprehensive discussions of the conceptual analysis and practical dimensions of personalized care are available [4,17-22]. The goal here is to highlight how personalization of care has become a particularly huge challenge as we develop more automated care services and ICT-based solutions to support the elderly [23,24].

- *Difficulty in operationalizing the concept of personalization for system design:* A review of the literature in health care indicates, as noted earlier, that there is lack of consensus about the exact meaning of personalized care. There is also considerable ambiguity to date concerning the optimum method of measuring the process and outcomes of personalized care [19,20,25,26]. One of the reasons for this, as Armstrong [27] noted, is that there is an inherent difficulty in choosing a single descriptor to qualify the "object" of care, that is, the person that clinicians and carers deal with on an everyday basis. The identity, and hence personality, of any individual is "both multi-faceted (biological, psychological, social) and ever-changing." Elderly persons vary in their health and social care needs because they have unique circumstances and values and have different disease history and life experiences. They also vary in their personal wishes and desires, for example, preferred heating, lighting, exercise requirements, and audio levels. A key challenge becomes how to operationalize "personality" as a formal concept for system design to support the elderly through a care and treatment plan that recognizes the uniqueness of the individual and seeks to understand the world from the person's perspective while supporting their psychological, clinical, and social needs [10]. Big Data analytics can help in abstracting key events in a person's life so as to construct a computable account of their varying lifestyles and desires, especially for elderly persons with cognitive impairments.
- *Technologies for elderly care often appear unduly technology-centric:* The last decade or so has seen an explosion in technological innovation in the field of elderly care. However, adoption of technological solutions for elderly care does not appear to follow a similar growth trajectory [16,23,28]. As observed earlier, existing solutions often appear "fundamentally incompatible with ageing" [23] and deliver services through a series of technology-centric care episodes without consideration of the peculiar needs and preferences of the elderly, or what they can easily interact with [6,23,24]. In smart homes, for example, satisfying the needs of the user remains a major challenge in research and development [29]. Because of the huge focus on technology, as well as the speedy rate of advances in ICT, most technologies for everyday use are designed to last for a couple of years. For example, we change the way interfaces work,

often for cosmetic reasons without recognizing that the elderly, with memory impairment, will find it difficult to adapt to such rate of change. Our industry faces the challenge of how to design full-function technology devices with a constant interface, for example, large easy-to-read screen displays, regardless of upgrades or new versions, that the elderly will find easier to use [23]. Second, the elderly often organize their homes for their particular comfort needs. As such, the introduction of technology into such environment needs to be nonintrusive, with minimal impact and without unduly effecting the elderly person's interaction in that environment. Thus, any technology introduced must be adaptable to a wide range of environments and interactive behaviors as well as being as transparent as possible, for example, by adapting to personal lifestyles.

- *Customizing and adapting technology design for optimum user satisfaction:* Because ageing is a progressive process, technologies for elderly care need to keep track of developments in an elderly person, for example, new symptoms, in order to enable easy modification of care services [4]. As early as 1997 (when research in personalized computer support for the elderly was relatively gaining momentum), the French National Centre for Scientific Research—Science for Engineering consulted a group of experts on smart homes for the elderly to better identify research issues and define priorities (Estève [30] cited by [24]). The recommendations of the expert group, which have remained to a large extent a challenge to date, include allowing the elderly to express their values and choices, rather than outrightly treating them as compliant individuals, and to regard the elderly user's surrounding, for example, activities, family, and neighbors, as important in the task of determining user needs. A key variable, therefore, in technology adoption by the elderly, and hence in ensuring that designs meet user needs, is the technology's perceived usefulness to the user [31]. As such, the design of technologies for elderly care should be driven by an understanding of actual need for the technology, ease of learning to use the technology, the elderly person's cognitive and perceptual abilities, as well as other sociopsychological factors such as preferences, attitudes, beliefs, and involving the elderly user in the design process [28,31]. For the first time, the phenomenon of Big Data has provided us with cheap, large-scale data to ensure accurate understanding of the needs, beliefs, circumstances, and desires of the elderly person for system design. Using Big Data analytics, research can potentially build technologies that can relate new symptoms to an elderly person's lifestyle and past habits, as well as medical history and genetic makeup, and even predict new symptoms before they occur.
- *Building technologies that are dependable for elderly use:* Given the vulnerability of the elderly, care services and technologies for their use need to operate in a predictable and dependable way [4] in order to guarantee the health and safety of the elderly users. Approaches in Big Data analytics, for example, quantified self, can help in generating accurate mathematical models of elderly users in a way that ensures that provided care services are robust, dependable,

and exhibit desirable behaviors. As Big Data analytics evolves into a promising field for providing insight from very large data sets and improving outcomes, there is a need for a holistic approach that seeks not only to decipher who the elderly individual is [32] as the primary driver of care, but also to make the technologies usable for them.

Existing research approaches to developing personalized elderly care technologies can be broken down into two broad categories: (1) *monitoring and surveillance*, whereby electronic technologies are deployed to keep track of an elderly person's medical condition and daily activities, and automatically alert health care staff when intervention is required. Research in this category focuses primarily on *smart homes and the monitoring activities of daily living*. (2) *Assistive technologies*, which can range from a simple device to help a physically impaired old adult, for example, with Parkinson disease to turn on a tap without much risk, to a personal robot that is able to spoon-feed an elderly person or administer medication without the need for a health care staff. In what follows, we briefly discuss a number of research efforts in these areas. These efforts overlap, and it is not unlikely to find, for example, a project that integrates the concept of a smart home and the technique of activities of daily living monitoring [33], or a smart home that employs a robot care assistant [29]. Our goal here is to critically review research in these areas in relation to the key challenges of personalized elderly care as discussed above.

SMART HOMES

The smart home approach to personalized elderly care is one category of research in elderly care that has received a relatively high attention over the last decade or so, with many research and development projects ongoing and funded by international and governmental organizations. Examples of such projects include Life 2.0, OLDES, CAALYX, MATCH Home Care Project, and K4CARE.[1] See [4,29,34,35] for a more thorough review of research in smart homes. The smart home offers a cost-effective way for caring for the elderly in "their own homes" without institutionalizing them and provides a viable solution to technology-driven assistive living for the elderly [13,33]. A smart home is "any living or working environment that has been carefully constructed to assist people in carrying out required activities" [29]. Research in smart homes has thrived in part because of a reliance on home automation systems, and the availability of supporting technologies, such as personal computers, sensors, passive and active electronic "tags," and cellular phones. Existing works have concentrated on sensor networks, data collection and communication, and low-level ad hoc responsive assistance based on the simple processing of low-

---

[1]The Older People's e-Services at home project, http://www.oldes.eu/
http://www.match-project.org.uk/main/main.html
Complete Ambient Assisting Living Experiment, http://www.caalyx-mv.eu/
http://www.life2project.eu/

level raw sensor data using decision rules [33]. For example, if room temperature is below a specific value, start the air conditioner. Over the years, the task of building smart homes has integrated other approaches in health care for increased success. Telemedicine or "telehomecare", for example, where clinical consultations and treatments are provided virtually to an elderly in a smart home via ICT technologies has been used for disease prevention and monitoring of the elderly [36]. Others include "the intelligent room," which combines robotics, vision and speech technology, and agent-based architectures in order to provide computation and information services for people engaged in day-to-day activities with the goal of pulling the computer out into the real world of people [37]; "integrated home systems," which provides for the elderly a single human—machine interface to household systems and gadgets [38,39]); "rehabilitation integrated systems" for better access and ergonomics for the elderly [40]; and the "adaptive house," which uses advanced neural network to control such things as room temperature, heating, and lighting without previous programming by the residents [41]. Recent approaches leverage advances in context-awareness, for example, the context-sensitive rule-based architecture for a smart home environment [42]; social computing, for example, the aware community, which allows an elderly in a smart home to engage with other people via social networks [43] as well as mobile technologies, the service-oriented paradigm, and cloud-based infrastructures [44-46]. In addition, research in smart home has served as an environment for scientific study of home life, particularly the relationships between space and information, for example, through approaches that integrate learning into everyday activity in a smart home [44], in order to provide better personalized services for the elderly.

Despite the huge progress in smart home research, realizing the vision of smart home presents a number of challenges. Some of these challenges stem from the fact that at any specific time a smart home is required to generate data about the environment such as temperature and humidity; medication level; the status of doors, windows, and lights; and about the location and behaviors of its inhabitants, such as sleeping, cooking, watching TV, etc. As noted by [33], the central issue becomes how to fuse data from multiple sources in order to form a meaningful interpretation of a situation, in relation to other information sources such as electronic health records as well as information about user needs, and subsequently provide personalized care to the elderly inhabitant. A related challenge in smart homes is that the technologies often appear too intrusive and technologically too sophisticated and unusable for an elderly person [23]. Overall, existing smart homes hardly adapt to the personal lifestyles of the elderly.

MONITORING ACTIVITIES OF DAILY LIVING

Monitoring of activities of daily living (ADLs), also known as lifestyle monitoring or behavioral monitoring, is an approach to elderly care where changes in activity profiles of an individual are used as a proxy to highlight a change in the individual's health or care status [47]. Over the last decade, many studies on ADLs of elderly people have been carried out. For example, Gokalp and Clarke [48] present an excellent review of studies that monitored ADLs of elderly people; see also [49-51]. A key goal of ADL monitoring is to provide assisted living to the elderly person. Changes in daily activity level, including daily habits, movements, vital signs, etc. can provide important clues regarding functional ability, cognitive capability, loss of autonomy or independence, medication adherence, decline in health status, or progress of an existing illness, which could consequently be used as a basis to revise existing care plan [48]. Applications of ADL monitoring are based on four broad technologies: context-aware or ambient sensor technologies, telemonitoring technologies, wearable technologies, and combinatorial technologies [48,49,52]. Most studies reviewed have focused on technologies and strategies for monitoring. The predominant monitoring strategy is that of detecting changes in activity levels of the elderly person, such as changes in motion or location, changes in body temperature or blood pressure, and the rate of access to the door or usage of appliances, for example, TV, refrigerator. Little attention was given to determining how changes in activity profile compare to the individual's history of activity, or relate to the elderly person's actual preferences. Brownsell et al. [47] outline a number of interesting research questions that still pose a challenge to research in ADL monitoring, which include determining the primary purpose and role of lifestyle monitoring (assessment or long-term monitoring, or both; providing effective monitoring of a person's levels of activity using sensors; understanding sufficiently the link between health status and activity; identifying clearly the features of a particular person's life and activities to be monitored; determining how analysis of ADL monitoring would be utilized in actual clinical services; and finally, identifying the requisite service response to monitoring, as well as the organizational and operational issues associated with monitoring. Although research in monitoring ADLs of the elderly appears quite promising, with many commercial lifestyle-monitoring products on the market, mostly for short-term health and care assessments,[2] overall review suggests that monitoring ADLs remains relatively challenging, and there is little understanding about how to develop effective systems that would enable comprehensive care in a way that recognizes the individuality of an elderly person or seeks to understand the world from their own perspective.

ASSISTIVE ROBOT TECHNOLOGIES

Assistive robot technologies for elderly care have thrived largely as a result of growing advances in robotics and artificial intelligence and have led to personal robots that assist the elderly with daily tasks such as dressing and bathing, interact with them and provide companionship to ease the burden of loneliness, and even help them to communicate remotely with physicians and caregivers [3,29,53]. A number

---

[2]http://www.chubbcommunitycare.co.uk/products/info/quietcare-for-professional-assessment

of research projects in this category combine the smart home concept (discussed earlier) with robotic assistance. They are rapidly advancing from engineering prototypes to potential commercial realities and positioned for mass market adoption. Examples include Hector, a mobile assistive robot for the elderly created out of the CompanionAble Project[3] at the Intelligent Systems Research Laboratory, University of Reading, United Kingdom. Hector can work collaboratively with a smart home and remote control center to better support older people living at home, helping them stay independent for longer and avoid unplanned hospital admissions [3]. Other projects combine activity monitoring with robotics. For example, as part of an EU-funded research project, senior citizens in Italy, Spain, and Sweden have had their homes equipped with sensors to track their activity and health. Mobile telepresence robots, a wheeled videoconferencing system that can be piloted remotely, allow relatives and doctors check in with the elderly and interact with them [54].

There are two principal directions in robotics research (for elderly care), namely, task-oriented robotics and interaction-oriented robotics [55,56]. Task-oriented robots rely on physics and mechatronics to perform tasks in controlled specific environments. The most successful task-oriented robots serve in factory automation, where they typically assemble electronic devices or deal with heavy objects [56]. Task-oriented robots have been adapted for elderly care in smart homes, where they follow algorithms to perform well-defined tasks, such as alerting doctors and caregivers when medication has dropped below a certain level or when the elderly person has changed location within a smart home environment. Interaction-oriented robots, on the other hand, are designed to interact with elderly users and rely primarily on social behavioral theories. A central goal of research for the elderly was to explore important issues about what functions a robot assistant could provide to an elderly individual, as well as learning more about the way people interact with a robot when more "human-like" characteristics are introduced—many of which pose tremendous challenges from ethical and sociotechnical dimensions [57]. However, most work have been focused on technical testing of whether the technology does work, rather than on trying to understand how elderly people will choose to interact with the technology or have it adapted for them [29,33].

BIG DATA ANALYTICS FOR ELDERLY CARE

The goal of this chapter in discussing a review of challenges in personalized elderly care has been to show through such discussion why efforts to leverage Big Data analytics for elderly care should be tackled through a holistic approach that simultaneously takes into account the sociotechnical and context-aware challenges posed by personalized elderly care. As noted earlier, existing approaches to personalized elderly care, for example, smart homes, ADLs, and assistive robotics, appear overly

---

[3]http://www.companionable.net/

technology-centric, lack a formal specification of the concept of personalization, and often treat the elderly as compliant individuals and deliver care services without sufficient consideration of the actual needs and preferences of the elderly, or their values and lifestyles. For the first time in human history, research has at its disposal zettabytes (10^{21} gigabytes) of data, that have been obtained from almost every fabric of our daily life activities—from hospital visits, travels, friends and family interactions, to occupational activities and shopping patterns—that could potentially be harnessed to gain a near perfect understanding of an elderly person's lifestyles, values, beliefs, as well as a history of choices the person has made [58].

Big Data refers to data that are so diverse, complex, and large-scale combining both structured and unstructured information contents from multiple sources [59] so much that it is technically challenging, if not impossible, to be processed using existing traditional software and analytic methods, such as relational databases and management information systems. Boyd and Crawford [60] outline a definition that highlights so interestingly both the opportunities and challenges of Big Data in elderly care. According to the authors, Big Data is "a technological, cultural, and scholarly phenomenon" that rests on the interplay of three things, namely, (1) *technology*, taking advantage of increased computing power and algorithmic accuracy to gather, analyze, link, and compare large data sets; (2) *analysis*, drawing on large sets to identify patterns in order to make economic, social, technical, and legal claims; and (3) *mythology*, the computational turn in thought and research that large data sets offer a higher form of intelligence and knowledge that can generate insights that were previously impossible, with the aura of truth, objectivity, and accuracy. Data are not technically "neutral" [61], and if considered otherwise, become, in the words of Lisa Gitelman [62], an "oxymoron." Deriving actionable value from Big Data, therefore, requires that research takes cognizance of the contexts that have shaped the data collection, the forms of arguments and analysis that can, and are, made with the data, as well as a clear indication of what the data do not, and cannot, account for [63]. Big Data[4] for elderly care comes from three major sources. The first, popularly referred to as *Big Data*, involves analytics of multiple types of data across a population, typically over a period of time, potentially from multiple sources, of structured and unstructured nature, and of heterogeneous kinds of objects. This has been a by-product of ubiquitous smart technologies that have pervaded every aspect of our life. The second comes from what Cornell NYC Tech professor Deborah Estrin has called *small data*, the output of a whole host of pervasive tracking processes about any one individual, e.g. data from quantified self [61]. The third source of Big Data refers to what ethnographers, such as Tricia Wang [64], have called *thick data*, and includes more qualitative kinds of data, obtained, for example, from interviews and direct observational studies, which are needed to bridge and/or reveal knowledge gaps in quantitative and algorithmic

---

[4]In general, we use the term Big Data (capitalized) to refer to this phenomenon of large-scale data for analytics

Big Data. Besides the large volumes of data available to the health care industry, driven by digitization of EHRs, laboratory systems, physician notes, medical correspondence, regulatory requirements, and care plans [65-67], which many experts say double every five years, as well as data from social media and public health records, current approaches in the use of Big Data for elderly care tend to focus on the Big Data and small data categories. These approaches leverage ubiquitous sensor-enabled devices and such techniques as sociometeric badges [9] and the concept of quantified self[5] [68]. Though potentially capable of providing statistical regularities in a "measured life" [69] and a mathematical explanation for understanding human dynamics [9] and personal health [70], these techniques have been critiqued for their tendency to hide rather than reveal the very essence of what makes us who we are [63], as they may automatically affect how "the self is understood, experienced, and practiced more broadly" [71].

The biggest opportunity that Big Data offers for the personalization of elderly care lies not only in the availability of large volumes of data but also in the diversity of both the types and sources of data. This opportunity, it could be argued, will potentially be harnessed at the confluence of health care and personal location data, which according to a recent report from McKinsey Institute, constitute two of the five domains that would be greatly transformed by Big Data [72]. As noted earlier, one of the major challenges in personalized elderly is the difficulty in specifying the concept of personalization and operationalizing it for computational design. This is all the more challenging in view of the fact that elderly people usually suffer multiple age-related ailments, such as dementia and Parkinson disease, that impair considerably their cognitive and physical capabilities. In such cases, health care practitioners often resort to information from historical records and family members in order to gain an understanding of the patient. By digitizing, combining, and effectively using Big Data, the health care industry stands an unprecedented chance to gain a significant understanding of the elderly patient. This will lead to more targeted treatment outcomes and increase the chances of detecting diseases at earlier stages when they can be treated more easily and effectively. In addition, certain care outcomes, such as allergies, risks of infection or hospital-acquired illness; or the possibility of identifying patients who may choose elective surgery or benefit from proactive care or lifestyle changes; or the possibility of comorbid conditions due to environmental, family, or lifestyle factors, etc. can be more effectively estimated on the basis of historical data [13]. Big Data is deeply related to the phenomenon of e-Science [73], computationally intensive science that is usually carried out in highly distributed computing environments, using immense data sets and requiring grid computing. From this perspective, Big Data will potentially play a vital role as a part of e-Social Science in collecting, processing, and analyzing social and behavioral data [74] for personalized elderly care.

---

[5]Also known as the QS movement; http://en.wikipedia.org/wiki/Quantified_Self

REQUIREMENTS AND CHALLENGES FOR BIG DATA—DRIVEN ELDERLY CARE APPLICATIONS

Creating value from Big Data requires a holistic understanding of the nature of data in Big Data that gives rise to issues of variety or heterogeneity of data, incompleteness and inconsistency, timeliness, privacy, context, collaboration, and visualization, as well as challenges that arise as a result of the multistep processes in Big Data analytics and the tools ecosystem around Big Data [75]. Big Data in health care and elsewhere is characterized by five V's that constitute the five key dimensional challenges in Big Data analytics, namely, volume, velocity, variety, veracity, and value.[6] These pose nontrivial challenges in elderly care just as they do in other areas where Big Data analytics is being explored as a potential solution, for example, health care [66,76,77] and smart city [78]. Already, one of the greatest problems to the deployment of Big Data analytics in care is deciding what data is relevant [76]. As new forms of Big Data for elderly care, for example, QS, sociometric monitoring, and genome sequencing, begin to fuel this exponential growth, the problem of finding the needle in the haystack becomes significantly worse [75,77]. A downside of the growing size of Big Data, which presents a challenge to analytics, is that in most cases, for example in health care, up to 90% of the data generated are discarded [77]. Fortunately, advances in data provisioning and data management, such as cloud computing and virtualization, are facilitating the development of platforms for more effective capture and storage of large volumes of data on demand [79].

An associated challenge is the constant flow of new data streaming at unprecedented rates. Velocity of data increases as data are accumulated via various real-time devices, such as daily monitoring of glucose level in diabetic patients, QS, blood pressure reading, etc. Many systems for streaming data often perform the same functions; meaning that data must be rationalized and normalized, which adds to the analytics overhead. Similarly, because a wide range of systems are deployed for Big Data capture, data often come in enormous variety—structured, unstructured, and semistructured—a dimension that is both interesting and challenging to elderly care. The variety of data from multiple sources may define data values differently, thus increasing complexity and inconsistency of data. For example, only relatively small percentage of data streams about our daily activities, for example, from fitness devices, genetics, travel records, genomics, social media, and other sources can presently be organized and analyzed for meaningful and actionable insight [77]. Elderly care applications need more efficient and automatic ways of converting and combining varieties of data from multiple sources in order to enhance data relevancy and create value for personalized care.

Of the five-dimensional V's of Big Data, veracity is perhaps the most difficult to quantify, verify, and measure. Veracity or "data assurance" becomes arguably a critical issue because of the increase in the use of nonscientific methods and practices in

---

[6]Some authors use 3V's or 4V's to characterize the concept of Big Data; see for example [35].

Big Data gathering. Data without veracity creates vulnerability, and affects adversely the validity and reliability of analytics results. In a survey by IBM, about 30% of respondents expressed concern that as data currently stand, it is hard to know which information is accurate and which is out of date. One in three business leaders do not trust the information they use to make decisions. What's more, poor data quality costs the U.S. economy around $3.1 trillion each year, providing a huge incentive for the development of tools and systems that maintain the veracity of data [80]. Data quality issues are of acute concern in elderly care, as the use of inaccurate information at the point of care could be fatal. More research is needed to develop algorithms with the capability to understand poor heterogeneous data, for example, by automatically generating the right metadata to describe the recorded data.

Value, of course, is the goal of Big Data analytics. Developing an effective means of addressing the challenges posed by volume, velocity, variety, and veracity will ultimately lead to high data value and more useful insights for elderly care. Equally important is the need for analytics to place significant importance to every step in Big Data analytics, and developing tools to support them. Many studies show that out of the multiple steps of Big Data analytics, namely data acquisition, extraction and cleaning, integration, modeling and analysis, interpretation, and deployment, much research attention has focused on one or two steps, ignoring the rest [75]. Current approaches for extracting value from Big Data are varied, ad hoc, and highly application-dependent [81]. Other requirements and concerns in Big Data analytics, for example, privacy, data ownership, usability, choice of analytics platforms, architectural design, support for efficient data storage and real-time guarantees, virtualization requirements, and the dominance of the open source paradigm remain and have been variously addressed in the literature (see e.g. [75,77,81,82]). For example, although many countries and health care organizations have developed laws governing how data can be used and revealed in different contexts and for different purposes, there is still huge public concern about the inappropriate use of personal data, particularly through linking of data from multiple sources [75]. Privacy, like most of the other concerns discussed above, is both a technical and a sociological problem and can only be effectively addressed from both perspectives. However, the five V's represent an appropriate starting point for a discussion about the challenges of Big Data analytics for personalized elderly care.

THE ROLE OF CONTEXT

Like many health care applications for personalized support [49] and intelligent services [78], elderly care systems are highly dependent on their execution context. A common definition of context considers it as "any information that can be used to characterize the situation of an entity," where an entity refers to a person, place, or object that is considered relevant in an interaction sequence [83]. Context is critical in the design of care support systems for the elderly because of its ability to enable us to construct and maintain awareness of a person's activities, status, or context in different settings, yet it has remained a poor source of information in computing environments [83]. As a result, the term has been considered differently by different authors—as the surroundings of the interaction between the user and the application [84], what is needed to characterize and encode the situation of an entity [85], information about the activity or task the user is currently performing [86], or what is needed to understand what people do, and how and why they achieve and maintain a mutual understanding of the context for their actions [87].

In Big Data analytics, context provides a structure to ensure that discovery of patterns and relations from Big Data occur within the right contextual setting, which Sokol and Ames [88] refer to as situational awareness. By using situational data to gain knowledge of the complex and dynamic environments in which humans perform their tasks and adding a rich and correct cumulative context to Big Data analytics, analytic model accuracy is greatly enhanced. Context can provide metadata for making sense of Big Data and for addressing such concerns as privacy and consistency by offering a description of the entities that are relevant to a set of data—people, organizations, and relationships between the entities and events [88]. Dobre and Xhafa [78] outline a number of requirements for designing context-aware support in Big Data analytics applications, which include providing real-time guarantees for data provisioning, helping users augment their reality by providing information about mobility and locality, providing support communication and connectivity imperfection, and providing support for efficient data access, storage, and analytic scalability.

PROPOSED FRAMEWORK

Although research in personalized elderly care has not so far sufficiently addressed all the fundamental challenges of personalization in elderly care, a number of important successful results have been obtained, particularly in the area of context-aware support in monitoring and surveillance in smart homes and the development of situation-aware assistive technologies [49,50]. Leveraging the trend of research on context-aware user support, particularly the works of [85-87,89] and building on the unique capabilities of Big Data analytics in amassing and analyzing large-scale data about individual behaviors and lifestyles (as discussed earlier), we present in this section the conceptual framework of ACTVAGE, a context-aware lifestyle-oriented framework for supporting personalized elderly care and independent living. As shown in Figure 5.1, the proposed framework combines an understanding of user lifestyles, personal preferences and beliefs, as well as knowledge of user context in order to offer a model of ICT-enabled support for independent living.

The framework consists of four layers, namely, the *data layer*, the *analytics layer*, the *context-awareness layer*, and the *services layer* (see Figure 5.2). The approach will combine systematic data capture and rigorous analytics to uncover the actual and complete picture of the elderly person's lifestyles and build a formal representation of the lifestyle concept for system design. Lifestyle information is integrated with context-aware capabilities that are dynamically configurable using the

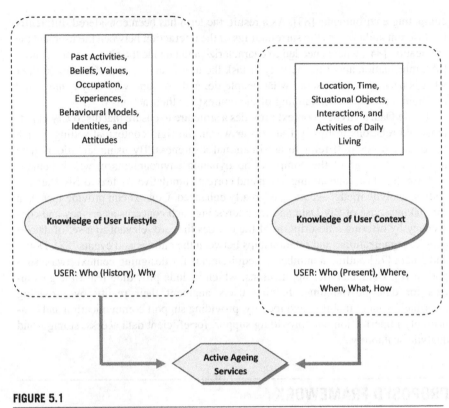

FIGURE 5.1

ACTVAGE, Conceptual Framework.

user's location, identity, time, and an understanding of user activities of daily living in order to provide personalized recommendations. Based on the recommendations, a set of *active ageing services* are developed, using the capabilities of mobile devices and cloud-based services, to offer individually tailored and lifestyle-oriented services for active ageing and independent living, including social networking, self-diagnosis and monitoring, advisory, entertainment, exercise and dietary, reminder and local events services. The e-services will leverage on advances in ICT, including pervasive computing and usability engineering, for the provisioning of rich and platform independent e-services.

In developing the conceptual design of ACTVAGE, we draw on the seven principles and best practices to guide the development of Big Data analytics systems [74,90,85]. Exploiting Big Data analytics, as noted by Chen and Zhang [74], requires not only new technologies but also new ways of thinking. In the remainder of this section, we describe the steps and activities of the proposed framework and illustrate its application.

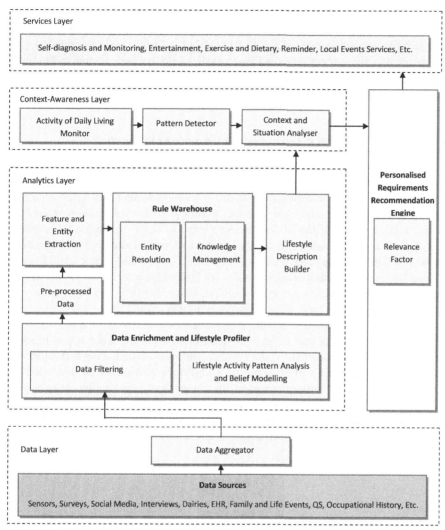

FIGURE 5.2

ACTVAGE, System Architecture.

STEP ONE: DATA AGGREGATION AND PROCESSING

The main tasks in this step include aggregating, filtering, and preprocessing data from large volumes and different sources that "informally" describes an individual's lifestyles. Later, the data is formalized in order to transform it into a formal model for the design of e-services. Various approaches for human-centered computing [91], for example, contextual inquiry, ethnography, and experience sampling, as well as some analytics-driven approaches such as QS and sociometric monitoring, will be employed bringing together elderly persons, health care staff, families, and communities to explore and understand the real-life experiences of using health care technologies for independent living and to elicit the actual needs and requirements for the design of active ageing services for personalized elderly care. Formal techniques for requirements gathering, including questionnaires, interviews as well as profiling and personas will be employed with a focus on specifically making the ACTVAGE system usable.

STEP TWO: LIFESTYLE MODELING AND FORMALIZATION

In this step, the data captured from the previous stage will be formalized in order to transform it into a formal model for the design of active ageing services. This stage will involve the use of modeling and simulation tools, including rule-based systems, as well as cognitive methods and the specification of a lifestyle ontology to enable proper representation of the lifestyle concept. The lifestyle ontology will be integrated with a context ontology for the creation of person-centered and context-aware e-services for the elderly patient that enables quality and independent living. Figure 5.3 shows an activity context model for building a context ontology. The hierarchical context model draws upon the CAPIM context [89], and aggregates the information—location, time, actor—necessary to detect the relevant attributes of a past activity into a unique set of data. In the model, we use the term *actor* to represent an elderly person or user to be supported. Information about the actor's history of events, social interests, beliefs, and personal attributes is used as context information in building the actor's lifestyle profile. Lifestyle profile will be implemented as *lifestyle graph*, where vertices represent life events, and edges represent relationships between life events. The vertices will consist of two types of life events: atomic events and composite events. Composite events are derived from atomic events. An example composite event in an actor's event history would be "attend Liverpool

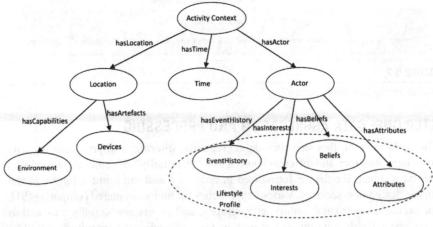

FIGURE 5.3

Activity Context Model for Capturing Lifestyle Events.

Community College." Multiple atomic events included in this composite event would include things the person did while at Liverpool Community College, for example, "was a chorister." The process of lifestyle modeling and formalization will draw on research in life event modeling (e.g., [92,93]) and will include computer-based knowledge representation formalisms such as (1) a behavior-aware and lifestyle ontology and (2) a lifestyle description language. The resultant computer-processable representation will be integrated with context ontology in order to provide a richer description of an elderly person's lifestyle, situations, and preferences for the development of a lifestyle-oriented e-services framework.

A key feature of this step is the use of behavioral and neurophysiological measures, as well as the formalization of the lifestyle concept using primarily cognitive methods, event modeling, and data mining, and activity pattern analysis. It involves the use of rule-based systems, agent-based modeling, as well as the specification of a lifestyle ontology to enable proper representation of the lifestyle concept. The use modeling would enable the creation of generic care and support workflows for elderly care. The integration of the lifestyle ontology with a context ontology allows for the creation of person-centered and context-aware e-services for the elderly patient that enables quality and independent living. A central goal here is to enable the transformation of the data acquired in step one into a formal model of user lifestyle for the design of active ageing e-services

STEP THREE: LIFESTYLE-ORIENTED CONTEXT-AWARE RECOMMENDATION

The next step of our approach is to add information about the user's current activities, location, time, etc. as context variables to the formal lifestyle model developed in the previous step (Figure 5.4). This step will be implemented using CAPIM, a context-aware computing platform developed by [89]. CAPIM includes services that are able to aggregate and semantically organize context data. The services react based on dynamically defined context-oriented workflows, such as those specified in elderly care plans and captured from monitoring activities of daily living. The platform includes an execution engine that supports context-aware actions for orientation, information, and recommendation. A key advantage of CAPIM is that it actively and autonomously adapts and provides the appropriate services or content to the user, using the advantages of contextual information without too much user interaction [78]. Enabling efficient mechanisms for provisioning context-sensitive data to users is an important challenge in these types of context-aware platforms, whereas provisioning context services in a nonintrusive manner remains a major advantage.

STEP FOUR: ACTIVE AGEING SERVICES COMPOSITION

This step will involve the development of lifestyle-oriented context-aware services that provide "back-end" behavior to be integrated into ACTVAGE prototype. These

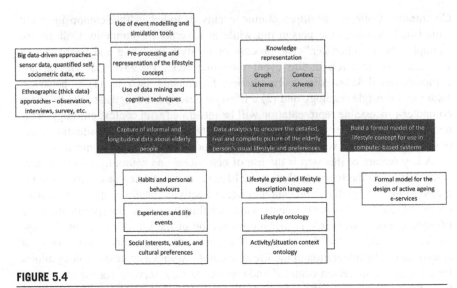

FIGURE 5.4

Description of the Lifestyle Data Capture and Formalization Process.

services will have the capability to monitor and influence user behavior and support independent living in line with personalized profile models defined during lifestyle profiling, as well as context information generated in step three. The development of these services will follow a traditional waterfall-type development lifecycle, and will involve two iterations of the following tasks: (1) interpretation and analysis of requirements (initially from the lifestyle profiling stage, and from testing/validation feedback on the second iteration); (2) identification of input, output, and processing requirements; (3) specification of software-level interfaces, and design of methodologies/algorithmic approaches that can achieve the requisite behavior; (4) implementation of a set of software services that underpin "active ageing" functionality in the ACTVAGE platform; and (5) testing of developed services against the lifestyle profiling stage requirements, live user requirements, and feedback to beta phase.

Although the lifestyle profiling stage will provide significant detail and design guidance in terms of the lifestyle description language and surrounding vocabulary; initially, the developed services are categorized as follows: (1) critical and/or monitoring services, (2) social networking or communications services, and (3) exercise/activity, dietary, and behavioral services. They will utilize the concepts and behaviors determined and formalized in the lifestyle profiling stage to provide customized lifestyle-oriented services for active ageing, using the architectural design and tools in Figure 5.5. In implementing the ACTVAGE services, emphasis will be placed on assessing how well and seamlessly the services integrate with typical home appliances that the elderly persons are accustomed to for consistency in system interfaces.

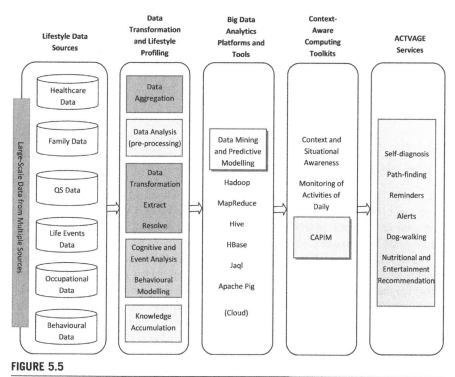

FIGURE 5.5

ACTVAGE, System Architecture—Showing Platforms and Tools for Implementation.

EXAMPLE SCENARIO

In order to demonstrate the applicability of our proposed framework, we illustrate using a hypothetical example of a dementia resident how ACTVAGE could be used in a real-world setting. Dementia is a condition related to ageing, with symptoms ranging from memory loss to decreased reasoning and communication skills [10]. As of 2010, the number of people with dementia was estimated at 35.6 million worldwide, and the number is expected to double every 20 years [94].

It is usually the norm that people with dementia, especially in rich economies where attaining great age is increasingly the case, are cared for in residential homes by professional (though not highly paid) carers whose job is typically viewed as having low status [10]. They are usually under pressure to balance work and administrative duties and are left with little time to gain sufficient understanding of their residents. In addition, these carers regularly encounter challenging behavior from the residents, including refusal to eat and take medication, inconsistent behaviors, and physical and verbal aggression that is difficult to diagnose and resolve [10]. No two residents are alike, and what has worked for one might not work for another. Existing solutions have leveraged techniques in person-centered care. However, there remains the need to gain an in-depth understanding of a dementia resident,

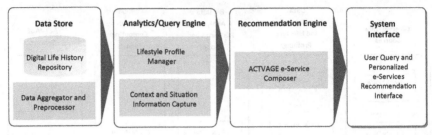

FIGURE 5.6

ACTVAGE System—Showing System Interface and Key System Components.

particularly in cases where families do not have much valuable information about the resident. Here, we discuss how the various steps in ACTVAGE could enable a carer gain an in-depth understanding of a dementia resident's life history, values, and interests for personalized care (see Figure 5.6).

The system acquires data using both Big Data and thin data driven approaches (Facebook and Twitter data) as well as thin based approaches (semistructured interviews) via the Data Aggregator (see Figure 5.4). The data sets acquired are preprocessed, transformed, and stored in the digital life history repository. As shown in Figure 5.5, the repository contains data about several aspects of a resident's past life events, interests, values, and preferences—modeled as a lifestyle graph (in step two). The Aggregator is designed to allow the carer and family members to remotely upload information about a resident using separate bespoke mobile apps and web applications, such as Digital Life Story.[7] Context information about user activity is captured via wall-mounted cameras. The carer is able to enter queries and perform data analysis aimed to construct user lifestyle profile using the analytics and query engine. Services are composed in the recommendation engine. The system interface allows the carer to perform these actions as well as to view and analyze system output.

DISCUSSION AND CONCLUSION

The power to generate continuously growing amounts of data, scaling up to unprecedented volumes and streaming in different varieties and at fast rates presents a unique opportunity to address the problem of personalized elderly care by enabling us to construct data-driven mathematical models of individual persons for analytics. This capability is made possible primarily by two factors. First, technologies for readily collecting vast amounts of data are becoming available in more and more application areas. Second, infrastructures for persistently storing these data and processing them are becoming a reality. Interestingly, this power has become available at a point in human history when the world is facing a growing increase in its ageing

---

[7]http://mylifesoftware.com/

population [2]. However, Big Data analytics equally brings several challenges to data processing and analysis. The features that define Big Data, such as volume, velocity, veracity, etc., and the multistep processes required to derive value from Big Data demand new processing and storage algorithms that go beyond what existing database and information processing systems offer. In addition, they pose system design and nontechnical challenges along several dimensions including sociological and context-awareness issues.

This chapter contributes to research efforts that aim to highlight the opportunities and challenges of Big Data analytics and lay out foundations for the design and development of applications that leverage the Big Data to address the problem of the world's ageing population. We present an overview of research in personalized elderly care, and explore the opportunities and challenges in leveraging Big Data analytics for personalized elderly care and independent living. In particular, we have focused our discussion of the opportunities and challenges to be addressed in relation to the five-dimensional V's of Big Data, as well as the multistep process of Big Data analytics, while acknowledging that other challenges remain that are not covered in this chapter. Based on this discussion, we propose ACTVAGE—a context-aware lifestyle-oriented framework for supporting personalized elderly care and independent living. The framework will potentially improve elderly care through the development of a model of ICT-enabled support for independent living that is grounded in an understanding of a history of user lifestyles and personal preferences, as well as knowledge of user activity context. By developing a set of lifestyle-oriented active ageing e-services, the proposed framework makes a novel contribution to elderly health care through an approach that exploits the lifestyle concept combined with context-aware user support, which itself has received considerable attention in ICT and computer science research, as a foundation for informing the design of ICT-enabled active ageing services and products. In addition, the approach will lead to the development of usable technologies for encouraging independent living, reducing reliance on institutionalized care, and promoting active social and healthy life into old age.

In a compelling paper, Choudhury et al. [95] present an approach that leverages Big Data, in particular Facebook data, to identify women at risk of postpartum depression at an early stage and provide them access to appropriate services and support. They employed statistical analysis and survey techniques to demonstrate the feasibility of Big Data as a tool to detect, characterize, and predict postpartum depression in new mothers, and as a result, recommend treatment plans to avoid recurrence. Like Choudhury and her colleagues, this chapter makes a case that Big Data has the potential to revolutionize care by providing us access to the vast amounts of data about individuals via self-reports, transaction data, and online activities as ground truth for developing ICT-based services for health care. We propose this innovative approach in a way that integrates digital life history with user activity context.

The chapter has focused on a high-level description of the ACTVAGE framework and lacks specific details about a number of the techniques included in the proposed framework, for example, life event modeling, ontology development, graph analytics, context information processing, and service composition. Future work will focus on developing specific details of the framework as well as prototype and evaluate systems based on it within a real-world application context. Our goal here is primarily to present the conceptual architecture of a new framework that combines knowledge of user lifestyle and knowledge of user activity context toward tackling the problem of personalized elderly care, and to show how the conceptualization was informed by meta-analysis of studies in personalized elderly care. As such, we have pointed to research studies, tools, and techniques that could be leveraged in developing and implementing solutions based on the proposed framework. In addition, we have illustrated the applicability of the framework to support elderly people living with dementia using a real-world example scenario. Integrating context and history of lifestyles into a single framework presents a lot of challenges. The value to be derived from Big Data is both analytically and technically bound to the context of production and use of the data, which as Dourish [87] notes is "a slippery notion" [p. 29]. Context is a central issue for Big Data analytics system. The power of Big Data to deliver on the promise of differentiated and useful insights lies precisely in the ability of analytics algorithms and systems to take into account both the context that has shaped data production and the context within which analytics-driven recommendations would be utilized. The overarching goal of the work described in this chapter is to lay a foundation for combining Big Data analytics with context-aware computing as a novel way to address the problem of personalized elderly care. The proposed framework will equally apply to many problem areas that leverage Big Data analytics.

REFERENCES

[1] Watkins AE, Scheaffer RL, Cobb GW. Statistics in Action: Understanding a World of Data. Wiley publishers; 2004.
[2] United Nations, World Population Ageing, Economic and Social Affairs; 2013.
[3] Hicks J. Hector: Robotic Assistance for the Elderly, Forbes Magazine; 2012. http://www.forbes.com/sites/jenniferhicks/2012/08/13/hector-robotic-assistance-for-the-elderly/ (accessed 27 January 2015).
[4] Wang F, Turner KJ. Towards Personalised Home Care Systems. In: Maglogiannis I, editor. Proceedings of the 1st International Conference on Pervasive Technologies related to Assistive Environments, L2.1-L2.7, ACM, New York, USA; July 2008.
[5] Overby CL, Tarczy-Hotnoch P. Personalized medicine: challenges and opportunities for translational bioinformatics. Per Med 2013;10(5):453–62.
[6] Tawfik H, Zhou S, editors. Special Issue on User-centred Health Informatics. Int J Healthcare Technol Manag; 2012.
[7] Brynjolfsson E, McAfee A. The Big Data boom is the innovation story of our time, Atlantic; 21 November, 2011. http://www.theatlantic.com/business/archive/2011/11/the-big-data-boom-is-the-innovation-story-of-our-time/248215/ (accessed 25 January 2015).
[8] Lohr S. The age of Big Data. New York Times; 11 February, 2012. http://www.nytimes.com/2012/02/12/sunday-review/big-datas-impact-in-the-world.html (accessed 03 February 2015).

[9]   Pentland A. Social Physics: How Good Ideas Spread-The Lessons from a New Science. New York: Penguin; 2014.

[10] Maiden N, et al. Computing Technologies for Reflective, Creative Care of People with Dementia. Communications ACM 2013;58(11):60−7.

[11] McCormack B, McCance T. Person-Centred Nursing: Theory, Models and Methods. London: Blackwell Publishing; 2010.

[12] McCormack B. A Conceptual Framework for Person-Centered Practice with Older People. Int J Nurs Pract 2003;9(3):202−9.

[13] Malanowski N, Ozcivelek R, Cabrera M. Active Ageing and Independent Living Services: The role of Information and Communication Technology, JRC Scientific and Technical Reports. European Commission; 2008.

[14] McCormack B, McCance TV. Developing a Conceptual Framework for Person-Centred Nursing. J Adv Nurs 2006;56(5):472−9.

[15] McCance T, McCormack B, Dewing J. An Exploration of Person-Centredness in Practice. Online J Issues Nurs 2011;16(2).

[16] Edvardsson D, Fetherstonhaugh D, Nay R. Promoting a Continuation of Self and Normality: Person-Centred Care as Described by People with Dementia, Their Family Members and Aged Care Staff. J Clin Nurs 2010;19(17−18):2611−8.

[17] McCance T, Gribben B, McCormack B, Laird EA. Promoting person-centred practice within acute care: the impact of culture and context on a facilitated practice development programme. Int Pract Dev J 2013;3(1).

[18] Kitwood T. Dementia Reconsidered: The Person Comes First. Buckingham: Open University Press; 1997.

[19] Nolan MR, Davies S, Brown J, Keady J, Nolan J. Beyond person-centred care: a new vision for gerontological nursing. J Clin Nurs 2004;13(3a):45−53.

[20] Brooker D. What is person centred care? Rev Clin Gerontol 2004;13(3):215−22.

[21] Augusto JC, Nugent CD, Martin S, Olphert C. Towards personalization of services and an integrated service model for smart homes applied to elderly care. In: Giroux S, Pigot H, editors. Proceedings of International Conference on Smart Homes and health Telematic. IOS Press; July 4-6, 2005. p. 151−8.

[22] Morgan S, Yoder LH. A Concept Analysis of Person-Centered Care. J Holist Nurs 2012; 30(1):6−15.

[23] Ebling MR. Pervasive Change Challenges Elders. IEEE Pervasive Computing 2014:2−4.

[24] Tawfik H, Anya O. Towards Lifestyle-Oriented and Personalised e-Services for Elderly Care. In: Proceedings of the 6th conference on Developments in eSystems Engineering (DeSE). UAE: IEEE; 2013. p. 357−60. http://dx.doi.org/10.1109/DeSE.2013.69.

[25] Williams B, Grant G. Defining people-centredness: Making the implicit explicit. Health and Social Care in the Community 1998;6(2):84−94.

[26] Mead N, Bower P. Patient-centredness: A conceptual framework and review of the empirical literature. Soc Sci Med 2000;51(7):1087−110.

[27] Armstrong D. A new history of identity: A sociology of medical knowledge. Basingstoke: Palgrave; 2002.

[28] Charness N, Boot WR. Aging and information technology use: Potential and barriers. Curr Direct Psychol Sci 2009;18:253−8.

[29] Chan M, Estève D, Escriba C, Campo E. A review of smart homes- present state and future challenges. Comput Methods Programs Biomed 2008;91(1):55−81.

[30] Estève D. Questionnement sur l'organisation de la recherche et de l'action de terrain dans le développement des soins a domicile. Rapport LAAS Mars; 1997.

[31] Rogers WA, Fisk AD. Toward a psychological science of advanced technology design for older adults. J Gerontol Psychol Sci 2010;65B(6):645−53.

[32] Rudder C. Dataclysm: Who We Are When We Think No One's Looking. New York: Crown Publishers; 2014.

[33] Chen L, Nugent CD. Situation Aware Cognitive Assistance in Smart Homes. J Mobile Multimedia 2010;6(3):263−80.

[34] Alam MR, Reaz MBI, Ali MAM. A Review of Smart Homes—Past, Present, and Future. IEEE Trans Syst Man Cybern 2012;42(6):1190−203.

[35] Robles RJ, Kim T. Review: Context Aware Tools for Smart Home Development. Int J Smart Home 2010;4(1):1−11.

[36] Demiris G. Electronic home healthcare: concepts and challenges. Int J Electr Healthcare 2004;1(1):4−16.

[37] Brooks RA. The Intelligent Room Project. In: Proceedings of the 2nd International Conference on Cognitive Technology (CT '97), Aizu, Japan; 1997. p. 271−8.

[38] Cooper M, Keating D. Implications for the emerging home systems technologies for rehabilitation. Med Eng. Phys 1996;18(3):176−80.

[39] Nisbet P. Integrating assistive technologies: current practices and future possibilities. Med Eng Phys 1996;18(3):193−202.

[40] Cherry AD, Cudd PA, Hawley MS. Providing rehabilitation integrated systems using existing rehabilitation technology. Med Eng Phys 1996;18(3):187−92.

[41] Mozer MC. The Neural Network House: An Environment that Adapts to its Inhabitants, Proc of the AAAI Spring Symposium on Intelligent Environments. Technical Report SS-98-02, AAAI Press, Menlo Park, CA; 1998. p. 110−4.

[42] Herbert J, O'Donoghue J, Chen X. A Context-Sensitive Rule-based Architecture for a Smart Building Environment. Int J Smart Home 2009;3(1).

[43] Wactlar H, Bertoty J, Walters R, Hauptmann A. The Aware Community. Int J Smart Home 2009;3(1):2009.

[44] Intille SS. Designing a Home of the Future. IEEE Pervasive Computing 2002:80−6.

[45] Páez DG, Aparicio F, Ascanio JR, Beaterio A. Innovative Health Services Using Cloud Computing and Internet of Things, Ubiquitous Computing and Ambient Intelligence. Lecture Notes Comput Sci 2012;7656:415−21.

[46] Ou Y, Shih P, Chin Y, Kuan T, Wang J, Shih S. Framework of Ubiquitous Healthcare System Based on Cloud Computing for Elderly Living, Proc. In: of Signal and Information Processing Association Annual Summit and Conference (APSIPA); 2013. p. 1−4. Asia-Pacific.

[47] Brownsell S, Bradley D, Blackburn S, Cardinaux F, Hawley MS. A systematic review of lifestyle monitoring technologies. J Telemed Telecare 2011;17(4):185−9.

[48] Gokalp H, Clarke M. Monitoring activities of daily living of the elderly and the potential for its use in telecare and telehealth: a review. Telemed J E Health 2013;19(12):910−23.

[49] Bricon-Soufa N, Newman CR. Context awareness in health care: A review. Int'l Journal of Med. Inf 2007;76:2−12.

[50] Al-Bashayreh MG, Hashim NL, Khorma OT. Context-Aware Mobile Patient Monitoring Frameworks: A Systematic Review and Research Agenda. J Software 2013; 8(7):1604−12.

[51] Hong J, Baker M. Wearable Computing. IEEE Pervasive Computing 2014:7−9.

[52] Ni Scanaill C, Carew S, Barralon P, Noury N, Lyons GM. A review of approaches to mobility telemonitoring of the elderly in their living environment. Ann Biomed Eng 2006;35:547−63.

[53] Rantz MJ, Marek KD, Aud M, Tyrer HW, Skubic M, Demiris G, et al. A technology and nursing collaboration to help older adults age in place. Nurs Outlook 2005;53(1):40−5.

[54] Knight W. Your Retirement May Include a Robot Helper, Computing News; 2014. http://www.technologyreview.com/news/531941/your-retirement-may-include-a-robot-helper/.

[55] Cowley SJ, Kanda T. Friendly machines: Interaction-oriented robots today and tomorrow. Alternation: Int J Study Arts Humanities Southern Africa 2005;12:79−106.

[56] Pineda LA, Meza IV, Avilés HH, Gershenson C, Rascón C, Alvarado M, et al. IOCA: An Interaction-Oriented Cognitive Architecture. Research in Computer Science 2011; 54:273−84.

[57] Anya O, Tawfik H, Nagar A, Westaby C. An Ethics-Informed Approach to the Development of Social Robotics. In: Weir D, Sultan N, editors. From Critique to Action: The Practical Ethics of the Organizational World. Newcastle: Cambridge Scholars Publishing; 2011. p. 231−53.

[58] IHTT. Transforming Health Care through Big Data 2013. http://c4fd63cb482ce6861463-bc6183f1c18e748a49b87a25911a0555.r93.cf2.rackcdn.com/iHT2_BigData_2013.pdf.

[59] Davenport T. Big Data at Work: Dispelling the Myths, Uncovering the Opportunities. Boston: Harvard Business Review Press; 2014.

[60] Boyd D, Crawford K. Critical Questions for Big Data: Provocations for a Cultural, Technological, and Scholarly Phenomenon. Inform Commun Soc 2012;15(5):662−79.

[61] Neff G. Why Big Data Won't Cure Us. Big Data 2013;1(3):117−23.

[62] Gitelman L. "Raw Data" Is an Oxymoron. Cambridge: MIT Press; 2013.

[63] Carr N. The Limits of Social Engineering. MIT Technology Review April 16 2014.

[64] Wang T. Big Data Needs Thick Data. Ethnography Matters; 2013. http://ethnographymatters.net/blog/2013/05/13/big-data-needs-thick-data/.

[65] Raghupathi W. Data Mining in Health Care. In: Kudyba S, editor. Healthcare Informatics: Improving Efficiency and Productivity. Boca Raton, FL: CRC Press; 2010. p. 211−23.

[66] Raghupathi W, Raghupathi V. Big Data analytics in healthcare: promise and potential. Health Information Science and Systems 2014;2(3). http://www.hissjournal.com/content/2/1/3.

[67] IBM. Data Driven Healthcare Organizations: Use Big Data Analytics for Big Gains; 2013. http://www-03.ibm.com/industries/ca/en/healthcare/documents/Data_driven_healthcare_organizations_use_big_data_analytics_for_big_gains.pdf.

[68] Wolf G. The Data-Driven Life. The New York Times; 28 April, 2010.

[69] Singer E. The Measured Life. MIT Technology Review; 2011. http://www.technologyreview.com/featuredstory/424390/the-measured-life/ (accessed 25 Feb 2015).

[70] Wolf G. The Quantified Self and the Future of Healthcare. The Health Care Blog; 2011. http://thehealthcareblog.com/blog/2011/05/12/the-quantified-self-and-the-future-of-health-care/.

[71] Sherman J. How Theory Matters: Benjamin, Foucault, and Quantified Self—Oh My!, EPIC Perspectives; 2015. https://www.epicpeople.org/how-theory-matters/ (accessed March 27 2015).

[72] Manyika J, Chui M, Brown B, Bughin J, Dobbs R, Roxburgh C, et al. Big Data: The Next Frontier for Innovation, Competition, and Productivity. McKinsey Global Institute; 2012.

[73] Hey T, Trefethen AE. The uk e-science core programme and the grid, Future Gener. Comput Syst 2002;18(8):1017−31.

[74] Chen CL, Zhang CY. Data-intensive applications, challenges, techniques and technologies: A survey on Big Data. Inform Sci 2014;275:314–47.

[75] Jagadish HV, Gehrke J, Labrinidis A, Papakonstantinou Y, Patel JM, Ramakrishnan R, et al. Big Data and Its Technical Challenges. Commun ACM 2014;57(7):86–94.

[76] Burghar C. Big Data and Analytics Key to Accountable Care Success. IDC Health Insights; 2012.

[77] Hinssen P. The age of data-driven medicine, Across Technology; 2012. http://datascienceseries.com/blog/download-the-age-of-data-driven-medicine.

[78] Dobre C, Xhafa F. Intelligent services for Big Data science. Future Generation Computer Systems Jul 2014;37:267–81.

[79] Su C-J, Chiang C-Y. IAServ: An Intelligent Home Care Web Services Platform in a Cloud for Aging-in-Place. Int J Environ Res Public Health 2013;10(11):6106–30.

[80] IBM. The Big Data and Analytics Hub; 2014. http://www.ibmbigdatahub.com/infographic/four-vs-big-data.

[81] Zicari RV. Big Data: Challenges and Opportunities. In: Akerkar R, editor. Big Data Computing. Boca Raton, FL: Chapman and Hall/CRC; 2013. p. 564.

[82] Marz N, Warren J. Big Data: principles and best practices of scalable realtime data systems. Manning; 2012.

[83] Dey AK. Understanding and Using Context. Pers Ubiquitous Comput 2001;5:4–7.

[84] Coutaz J, Crowley JL, Dobson S, Garlan D. Context is key. Commun ACM 2005;48: 49–53.

[85] Dey AK, Abowd GD, Salber D. A conceptual framework and a toolkit for supporting the rapid prototyping of context-aware applications. Hum Comput Interaction 2001; 16:97–166.

[86] Henricksen K. A Framework for Context-aware Pervasive Computing Applications. University of Queensland; 2003.

[87] Dourish P. What We Talk About When We Talk About Context. Pers Ubiquitous Comput 2004;8(1):19–30.

[88] Sokol L, Ames R. Analytics in a Big Data Environment, IBM. Redbooks; 2012.

[89] Dobre C. CAPIM: A Platform for Context-Aware Computing, Proc. of International Conf. on P2P, Parallel, Grid. Cloud and Internet Computing Oct. 2011;266:26–8.

[90] García AO, Bourov S, Hammad A, Hartmann V, Jejkal T, Otte JC, et al. Data-intensive analysis for scientific experiments at the large scale data facility. IEEE Symposium on Large Data Analysis and Visualization (LDAV) 2011:125–6.

[91] Beyer H. User-Centered Agile Methods. Hum Centered Inform 2010;3(1):1–71.

[92] Tambouris E, Vintar M, Tarabanis K. A life-event oriented framework and platform for one-stop government: The OneStopGov project. In: Proceedings of Eastern European eGov Days Conference; 2006.

[93] Wu LL. Event History Models for Life Course Analysis. In: Mortimer Jeylan T, Shanahan Michael J, editors. Handbook of the Life Course. New York: Kluwer Academic/Plenum Publishers; 2003. p. 447–502.

[94] Prince M, Bryce R, Albanese E, Wimo A, Ribeiro W, Ferri CP. The global prevalence of dementia: a systematic review and metaanalysis. Alzheimers Dement 2013;9(1): 63–75.e2.

[95] De Chaudhury M, Counts S, Horvitz EJ, Hoff A. Characterizing and predicting postpartum depression from shared facebook data. In: Proceedings of the 17th ACM conference on Computer supported cooperative work & social computing. New York: ACM Press; 2014. p. 626–38.

Prediction of Intrapartum Hypoxia from Cardiotocography Data Using Machine Learning

Paul Fergus[1], De-Shuang Huang[2], Hani Hamdan[3]

Applied Computing Research Group, Liverpool John Moores University, Liverpool, UK[1];
Institute of Machine Learning and Systems Biology, Tongji University, Shanghai City, China[2];
CentraleSupélec, L2S UMR CNRS 8506, Gif-sur-Yvette, France[3]
E-mail: p.fergus@ljmu.ac.uk, dshuang@tongji.edu.cn, Hani.Hamdan@centralesupelec.fr

INTRODUCTION

Assessment of fetal well-being throughout pregnancy, labor, and birth is widely regarded as a fundamental component of maternity care and essential for optimizing fetal outcome [1]. Therefore, misclassification may result in complications to both the mother and baby or unnecessary decisions to perform cesarean section. In the United Kingdom, the number of deliveries between 2012 and 2013 was reportedly 671,255—a 0.3% increase on the previous year.[1] Breaking this figure down, 1 in every 200 pregnancies results in stillbirth[1] and 300 babies die in the first four weeks of life [2]. Furthermore, according to the Royal College of Obstetricians and Gynaecologists (RCOG), 500 full term babies per year, alive at the onset of labor, are either stillborn, die within a week, or suffer from brain injuries, caused by childbirth complications.[2] In other cases, between one and seven fetuses in every 1000 experience hypoxia, caused by delivery-induced stress [3]. This may result in cardiopulmonary arrest; severe brain damage; lung and other vital organ damage, including long-term medical conditions, such as cerebral palsy, hearing, visual, and cognitive problems; and in severe cases death [4]. This problem is not specific to the United Kingdom. Worldwide, more than 130 million babies are born every year and about 3.6 million of them will die due to perinatal complication—around 1 million of them are thought to be intrapartum stillbirths [5].

A variety of methods are currently used to assess fetal well-being, including fetal movement counting and biophysical tests such as Doppler ultrasound monitoring. However, it is fetal heart rate monitoring (CTG) that remains the most common method for assessing the well-being of the fetus during the early stages of

---

[1]The NHS Maternity Stat.
[2]https://www.rcog.org.uk/.

delivery [6]. The clinical relevance of CTG is well understood; however, the main weakness with this approach is the poor standard of interpretation, demonstrated by high intra- and interobserver variability [7]. In general, the fetal heart rate (FHR) reflects the cardiac output, where a value between 120 and 160 beats per minute (bpm) indicates adequate blood delivery [8]. Random fluctuations around the baseline are normal (between 5 and 15 bpm, and is the FHR variability [HRV]) [9]. This usually means that the modulation influence provided by the central nervous system is healthy.

However, temporary decreases in FHR above 15 bpm that last between 15 seconds and several minutes are known as decelerations, which reflect events such as compression of the umbilical cord by uterine contractions, malfunction of the fetal heart muscle, or premature separation of the placenta [10]. Contractions reduce fetal oxygen supply by compressing the umbilical cord or by diminishing gas exchange in the utero-placental unit, which can have severe consequences if the placenta is already impaired. There is a general consensus among clinicians that the correlation between the depth of decelerations, including their frequency and timing depth, are indicators of the strength of the insult and the ability of the fetus to withstand it [11]. In contrast, temporary increases in FHR (>15 s, >15 bpm), called accelerations, accompany fetal movement and are generally thought to indicate a healthy state [12].

Clinical decisions are derived from CTG using visual pattern recognition; however, differences in the interpretation of these signals often leads to poor assessment. Although significant hypoxia is rare, false alarms are common, which can lead to serious abnormalities being overlooked [13]. Consequently, there is a need to explore better methods that can discriminate between healthy and hypoxic conditions. In this chapter, we present some background work in the area and evaluate the requirements for an ambulatory classification system that discriminates between healthy and pathological fetuses. The goal is to detect early in labor the signs of pathological conditions. From a clinical perspective, this capability provides a useful tool for assisting clinicians in their intrapartum decision making.

MONITORING INTRAPARTUM FETAL HYPOXIA
HYPOXIA

Intrapartum hypoxia is described as the impairment of the delivery of oxygen to the fetal brain and vital tissues during the progress of labor. It is estimated that between 1 and 7 in every 1000 fetuses experience oxygen deprivation during labor that is severe enough to cause the death of the fetus or severe brain injury [14]. This may exist in a pregnancy already impaired by maternal or fetal disease, or a rise in labor. However, in many cases true intrapartum hypoxia is not that common. The hallmark indications are metabolic acidosis and neurological signs, such as altered levels of consciousness or seizures [14]. Detecting its occurrence can be confirmed by cord blood (umbilical artery) metabolic acidosis with a base deficit of more than 15 [15].

Fetal hypoxia can be a slow-evolving process, if the uteroplacental unit is impaired (i.e., caused by placental disease and infections), or it can happen acutely during labor in situations where the umbilical cord is blocked or the uterine wall is ruptured [16]. If any of these conditions are present, hypoxia is likely, followed by hypoxemia and metabolic acidosis.

CARDIOTOCOGRAPHY

Preventing fetal hypoxia has been a significant challenge in medical science. Noninvasive methods to measure directly the fetal acid—base status and cerebral oxygenation during labor do not exist. Consequently, indirect observations are made, and the current standard approach for achieving this is to use cardiotocography (CTG) which measures the correlation between uterine contractions (UC) and the FHR [17].

Cardiotocography records are obtained using two transducers placed on the maternal abdomen. The first transducer is an ultrasound probe that records the FHR (cardio) and the second is a pressure transducer that measures the UC (Toco). The FHR and UC are printed on a strip known as a CTG trace [18].

The clinical relevance of some FHR characteristics is well understood [19]. The International Federation of Gynaecology and Obstetrics (FIGO)[3] and the UK NICE[4] guidelines are commonly used in the UK to interpret CTG traces. Table 6.1 highlights information provided by NICE and the classification of trace features.

The average FHR level, or baseline range between 110 and 160 bpm, in general reflects adequate cardiac output; when the fetal cardiovascular system is operating efficiently. Small random fluctuations around the baseline (between 5 and 15 bpm) is allowed and described as FHR variability. This usually indicates that the central nervous system of the fetus is intact and that the modulation influence is healthy. A temporary decrease in FHR (between 15 seconds and several minutes) and with amplitudes bigger than 15 bpm means that there is a deceleration in the FHR and often reflects events such as compression of the umbilical cord by UC, malfunction of the fetal heart muscle, or a separation of the placenta. Generally, larger insults are indicated by recurring episodes of deep, long decelerations whose onsets occur late with respect to the uterine contraction. Temporary increases in FHR (>15 seconds and >15 bpm) are referred to as accelerations and often accompany fetal movement and generally indicate that the fetus is healthy [14,20].

The purpose of monitoring a fetus during labor is to detect changes in the FHR that might indicate hypoxia and metabolic acidosis, so that timely action can be taken to prevent adverse outcomes [19]. Standard interpretation patterns are defined that include early and late deceleration, which are useful in the assessment of utero-placental and fetal well-being. Inappropriate FHR rises can be a surrogate marker for bad fetal progression and can be an indicator for urgent delivery.

---

[3]http://www.figo.org/.
[4]http://www.nice.org.uk/.

Table 6.1 Classification of FHR Trace Features (NICE)

Feature	Baseline (bpm)	Variability (bpm)	Decelerations	Accelerations
Reassuring	110–160	≥5	None	Present
Non-Reassuring	100–109 161–180	<5 for 40–90 minutes	Typical variable decelerations, with >50% of contractions occurring for >90 minutes Single prolonged deceleration for up to 3 minutes	The absence of accelerations with otherwise normal trace is of uncertain significance
Abnormal	<100 >180 Sinusoidal pattern ≥10 minutes	<5 for 90 minutes	Either a typical variable deceleration with >50% of contractions or late deceleration, both for >30 minutes Single prolonged deceleration for >3 minutes	

Visual pattern recognition and interference are the basis of clinical interpretation of CTG. However, these are inconsistently applied. Furthermore, CTG classical patterns have low specificity. Because significant hypoxia is rare, false alarms are common, leading physicians to disregard truly abnormal signals [14,20]. Consequently, it is generally believed that 50% of birth-related brain injuries are deemed preventable, with incorrect CTG interpretation leading the list of causes [14]. However, overinterpretation of CTG is also common and this has led to an increase in unnecessary cesarean sections. In the case where operative delivery is carried out based on CTG traces alone, between 40% and 60% of these babies will have been born without any evidence of significant hypoxia or metabolic acidosis [21].

The need for accurate monitoring and decision making during labor and delivery is critical to minimize suboptimal decisions and outcomes. The social costs of such errors are significant. Not only is cesarean birth typically twice the cost of vaginal birth [22], but also, particularly in a nulliparous women, it may initiate a legacy of increased health costs [18] as a result of higher risk of subsequent cesarean birth and medical complications [23]. This is further exacerbated by the fact that intrapartum care generates the most frequent malpractice claims and the greatest liability costs of all medical specialties [24].

AMBULATORY CTG MONITORING
AMBULATORY CTG MONITORING

The most common interpretation of CTG is performed by trained medical professionals and is mostly subjective. The challenge in recent years has been to develop systems that provide better objective measures [2]. From systematic reviews, appropriate use of computerized CTG (automated CTG trace interpretation techniques) show a significantly reduced perinatal mortality rate compared to traditional CTG methods when used both routinely and in women at increased risk of pregnancy complications [25]. However, this method is not widely utilized. Although the exact figures are not known, there is little evidence of utility or testing; a Cochrane review contained only two studies comparing computerized and manual CTG analysis, with no studies comparing computerized CTG to controls [17]. Consequently, there is a need to explore better methods that can discriminate between healthy and pathological deliveries [26].

More specifically, there is a need for robust scientific evidence to demonstrate their utility in global health organizations [27]. In one such study, Warrick et al. developed a system for the classification of normal and hypoxic fetuses from systems modeling of intrapartum CTG [14]. Their proposed solution models the FHR and UC signal pairs as an input—output system and estimates their dynamic relation in terms of an impulse response function. The authors claim that their system could detect almost half of the pathological cases 1 hour 40 minutes prior to delivery with a 7.5% false positive rate. Although Kessler et al. combined CTG with ST waveform analysis and concluded that by monitoring 6010 high-risk deliveries using their system, they were able to apply timely intervention for cesarean or vaginal delivery, thus reducing fetal morbidity and mortality [15].

CTG PREDICTION USING MACHINE LEARNING

Computer algorithms, and visualization techniques, are fundamental in supporting the analysis of data sets. More recently, the medical domain has been using such techniques, extensively.

Artificial neural networks have been used in a large number of studies to classify normal and pathological deliveries [28-30]. They have also been useful for distinguishing between nonlabor and labor events [31]. In [32], the authors argue that they have been particularly useful in helping to identify important risk factors associated with preterm birth. The global accuracy of these studies varied from 73% to 97%. With reference to fetal state, Hakan and Abdulhamit [33] discuss the use of an ANN and simple logistic-based algorithms to classify normal and pathological cases with reported accuracies between 98.5% and 98.7%.

Warrick et al. used a perinatal database or normal and pathological cases to train a support vector machine (SVM) classifier [14]. The results show that their system was able to detect half of the pathological cases, with very few false positives (7.5%), 1 hour 40 minutes before delivery. Although a study, carried out by Peterek et al. [34], utilized a Random Forest classifer to distinguish between physiological, suspicious and pathological fetus states represented in cardiotocography recordings. The authors report an overall classification accuracy of 94.69%. An SVM was used in [35] to predict normal and pathological fetal observations. A genetic algorithm (GA) was used to determine the critical features to train machine learning models. The authors argue that using the GA increased classification accuracy from 99.3% to 100%. Other studies have reported similar findings—for more information, the reader is referred to [36] and [37].

In [38], an adaptive neuro-fuzzy inference system was used to predict the fetal state using FHR and UC obtained from CTG recordings. The system was designed to predict normal and pathological cases using 1,831 CTG recordings (1,655 were classed as normal and the remainder pathological). Using the trained classifier, the authors reported accuracies for normal and pathological states between 97.2 and 96.6, respectively.

PROPOSED METHODOLOGY
THE CTG-UHB INTRAPARTUM DATA SET

The CTG-UHB intrapartum data set contains CTG recordings for singleton pregnancies with a gestational age less than 36 weeks [6]. The data set contains 552 CTG recordings (observations) selected from 9164 recordings collected between 2010 and 2012. The collection of data was performed by clinicians at the University Hospital in Brno (UHB) in conjunction with the Czech Technical University in

Prague using the STAN S21/S31 and Avalon FM40/50 fetal monitors to acquire the CTG records.

The data set contains no prior known development defects; the duration of stage two labor is less than or equal to 30 minutes; FHR signal quality is greater than 50% in each 30-minute window; biochemical parameters of umbilical arterial blood sample is available (i.e. pH); and the majority of deliveries are vaginal (only 46 cesarean section deliveries included).

Each recording begins no more than 90 minutes before actual delivery. For each CTG record, the FHR time series (measured in beats per minute) and UC signal (measured in millimeters of mercury) are provided—each sampled at 4 Hz. The FHR was obtained from an ultrasound transducer attached to the abdominal wall. Similarly, UP is extracted from a tocograph transducer, again, fitted to the abdominal wall.

DATA PREPROCESSING

CTG recordings more often than not contain noise mixed in with UC and FHR electrical activity. This noise, referred to as artifacts, can originate from various sources such as the subject themselves, the equipment, or the environment [39]. Consequently, raw signals need to be preprocessed. The preprocessing stage consists of three main steps: artifact removal, interpolation, and segment selection [40].

Preprocessing is a fundamental process within signal processing to ensure that artifacts that distort the CTG signal are removed and only the FHR and UC information remains. This significantly improves the detection of normal and pathological records. Therefore, it is important to remove as many of these artifacts as possible from the CTG signal before features are extracted. Certain artifacts reside at particular frequencies and can be removed by filtering the signal. This is normally achieved using high-pass, low-pass, and bandpass filtering [28].

Uterine Contraction Signal Filtering

Uterine activity has been found to comprise both "fast" and "slow" waves of high- and low-frequency signals [41]. The fast waves represent the individual electrical signals firing, whereas the slow waves correspond to the resulting mechanical contractions. Slow waves exist between 0.03 and 0.3 Hz, and the fast waves exist between 0.3 and 3.0 Hz. Buhimschi and Garfield [42] found in a study of 99 pregnant patients that 98% of uterine electrical activity occurred in frequencies less than 1 Hz, and that the maternal heart rate (electrocardiogram [ECG]) was always higher than 1 Hz. Furthermore, 95% of the patients, measured had respiration rates of 0.33 Hz or less. Therefore, Fergus et al. [41] considered that a 0.34−1 Hz bandpass filter removed most of the unwanted artifacts. Several other studies have adopted the same filtering scheme [43-45]. Focusing on the detection of preterm deliveries, Fele-Zorz et al. [46] showed that the 0.3−3 Hz filtered signals was the best filter for discriminating between preterm and term delivery records. The results show that sensitivities (true positives, in this instance preterm records), produced by several of the classifiers, was higher than those produced when other filters were used [46]. However, there was no appropriate filter to remove unwanted artifacts, such as the maternal heart rate.

FHR Signal Processing

Based on the findings in [47] and [48], the UC and FHR interaction manifests itself predominantly at lower frequencies, with many other studies focusing on low frequencies. For example, the following frequency bands were considered in [49-51] and [52]: very low frequency (VLF) at 0–0.03 Hz, low frequency (LF) at 0.03–0.15 Hz, movement frequency (MF) at 0.15–0.50 Hz, and high frequency (HF) 0.50–1 Hz. LF is mainly associated with the activity of the sympathetic system, HF with the activity of the parasympathetic system, and the MF band pertains to fetal movement and maternal breathing. Both LF and HF frequencies were used in [53], with LF between 0.05 and 0.2 Hz and HF between 0.2 and 1 Hz.

In [48], the authors describe the dynamic relationship between UP (as an input) and FHR (as an output) and posit an approach to analyze FHR. A nonparametric system-identification method was used to estimate system dynamics in terms of an impulse response function (IRF), that describes the linear, dynamic relation between very LF FHR energy (i.e., <30 mHz) and UP. This approach provided robust parameter estimates from noisy CTG collected under clinical conditions.

According to [47], FHR variability at frequencies greater than 0.03 Hz will act as noise for the identification procedure because there is no power in the uterine contraction signal above this frequency. Furthermore, based on their system identification model, the VLF FHR energy, which is <0.3 Hz, linearly related to uterine pressure.

According to Warrick et al., the FHR is influenced by a number of other (unobserved) physiological factors besides UP, to reduce the impact of these other factors, the raw signals were de-trended by a high-pass filter that would pass a reasonably long contraction or deceleration (cut-off frequency $fHP = 1/220 \text{ s} = 4.5 \times 10^{-3} \text{ Hz}$) [47,48].

To filter heart rate variability, Warrick et al. [50] used a high-pass filter with a cut-off frequency of 30 mHz corresponding to the lower limit of the LF band of the FHR, and increased the signal to 2 Hz to include the 1 Hz upper limit of the HF band of the fetal HRV. In contrast, in [47], a low-pass filter was used with a cut-off frequency of 4.5 mHz to remove power due to decelerations, which was increased to a sampling rate of 0.5 Hz.

Interpolation

Loss of sensor contact and interference from maternal heart rate often causes sharp drops in the signal well below the amplitude of interest. This is followed by a sharp restoration of the signal. These kinds of interruptions can be bridged using linear interoperation, when it lasts for periods less than 15 seconds—any longer interruptions are removed [47,48,51,54]. Several studies have shown the effectiveness of interpolation and varying signal quality. For more information, the interested reader is referred to [55-57].

FEATURE EXTRACTION
FHR Feature Extraction
The collection of raw CTG signals is always temporal. However, for analysis and feature extraction purposes, translation, into other domains, is possible and often required, such frequency representations via Fourier Transform [58,59] and wavelet transform [60]. The advantage of frequency-related parameters is that they are less susceptible to signal quality variations, because of electrode placement or the physical characteristics of the subjects [61]. In order to calculate these parameters, a transform from the time domain is required, that is, using a Fourier transform of the signal. Frequency features have been used in [62] and [63] and more recently in [64]. In [65], an overview of works related to spectrum analysis of FHR for both antepartum and intrapartum is provided.

A number of approaches exist to estimate baseline FHR, which is a key concept in the analysis of CTG. In [66], the authors proposed an algorithm for baseline estimation, including the extraction of accelerations and decelerations. In other works, it was found that common approaches, such as stable segment [67,68], filtering [69,70], and FHR density produced useful features for classification between normal and pathological cases. However, it was in [66] that a complete set of FIGO features was proposed and later extended in [71]. FIGO features are morphological features that are used by obstetricians in the ward to describe the visible properties of the FHR. In [72], the means of the FHR baseline were explored, including the number of accelerations, representing the transient increase in heart rate above the baseline by 15 bpm or more and lasting 15 seconds or more. The number of decelerations was also considered, which is defined as the transient episode of slowing FHR below the baseline level of more than 15 bpm and lasting 10 seconds or more.

Time and frequency domain features have been widely considered in the literature, the most common being the median of the FHR baseline, standard deviation, long-term irregularity, short-term variability, interval index, and delta and delta total values [73]. Nonlinear features have also been used extensively in adult heart rate variability analysis. In particular, a fractal dimension was used in [74] and [75], whereas waveform fractal dimension was examined in [76]. The most successful nonlinear methods, however, are approximate entropy and sample entropy [77-79]. Other approaches include de-trend fluctuation analysis [80], Lempel Ziv complexity [81], multifractal analysis [82], and multiscale analysis [83].

Uterine Contraction Feature Extraction
In several of the studies reviewed, in order to obtain frequency parameters, the use of power spectral density (PSD) features widely. Most studies focus on the peak frequency of the burst, in both human and animal studies, and is said to be one of the most useful parameters for predicting true labor [84]. On the other hand, one study [85] found medium frequency to be a more helpful feature for detecting uterine activity.

Several studies have shown that peak frequency increases as the time to delivery decreases; generally, this occurs within 1−7 days of delivery [86-91]. In particular, the results in [92] show that there are statistically significant differences in the mean values of peak frequency and the standard deviations in UC recordings taken during term labor (TL) and term non-labor (TN).

Amplitude-related UC parameters represent the uterine signal power, or signal energy. However, a major limitation is that the differences in patients can easily affect these parameters. Patients may differ in the amount of fatty tissue they have, and the conductivity of the skin−electrode interface, which leads to differences in the attenuation of uterine signals [84,89,93]. Examples of amplitude-related parameters include root-mean-square, peak amplitude and median amplitude.

Using the Student t test, [85] found that root mean square might be useful in distinguishing between information recorded early (before 26 weeks of gestation) and late (after 26 weeks). The results obtained are in agreement with [87], [86], and [94], which found that the amplitude of the power spectrum increased just prior to delivery. This was despite only analyzing the root-mean-square values, per burst, rather than the whole signal.

Meanwhile, [85] could not find any significant difference in root mean squares between preterm and term records. However, [95] did find that the root mean squares, in preterm contractions, were higher (17.5 mv $\pm$ 7.78), compared to term contractions (12.2 mV $\pm$ 6.25; $p < 0.05$). The latter study [95] could not find a correlation between root mean squares and the weeks left to delivery. Nevertheless, they do suggest that a greater root-mean-square value was, for the most part, a static symptom that indicated a woman's dispensation to give birth prematurely. They also found that the root-mean-square values, within each pregnancy, did increase within a few days of birth.

Sample entropy measures the irregularity of a time series, of finite lengths. This method was introduced by [96] to measure complexity in cardiovascular and biological signals. The more unpredictable the time series is within a signal recording, the higher its sample entropy. The process is based on calculating the number of matches of a sequence, which lasts for m points, within a given margin r. The disadvantage of this technique is the requirement to select two parameters, m and r. However, sample entropy did show a statistical difference between term and preterm delivery information, recorded either before or after the 26th week of gestation, when using any of the filters, but only using the signal from Channel 3 [85].

SYNTHETIC MINORITY OVERSAMPLING

In a two-class balanced data set, the prior probabilities will be equal for each. This is not the case for the CTG-UHB data set because it is not balanced. There are 552 observations in the data set, of which 506 represent women who delivered vaginally (majority class) and 46 (minority class) delivered by cesarean Section (16 with known pathological or abnormal outcomes and 30 with normal outcome). Classifiers are more sensitive to detecting the majority class and less sensitive to the minority class, and this leads to bias in classification [97]. Therefore, given a random sample taken from the data set, the probability of a classifier classifying a normal delivery will be much higher (92.6%, 511/552) than the probability of it classifying a delivery as pathological (0.08%, 46/552). This imposes a higher cost for misclassifying the minority (predicting that a pregnant woman is likely to have a normal vaginal delivery, only to deliver with a pathological abnormality) than the majority class (predicting that a pregnant woman will deliver with a pathological abnormality only to have a normal vaginal delivery).

In order to address this problem, it is necessary to resample the data set. Various resampling techniques are available, and these include undersampling and oversampling [98]. Undersampling reduces the number of records from the majority class to make it equal to the minor class—in this instance, it would mean removing 462 records, leaving us with a small data set. Data in the minority class is generated using oversampling. Given that the sample data set is small, it would be more sensible to oversample the minority class. One way of achieving this is through the synthetic minority oversampling technique (SMOTE) [99].

Several studies have shown that the SMOTE technique effectively solves the class skew problem [100-105]. Using SMOTE, the minority class (pathological) can be oversampled using each minority class record, in order to generate new synthetic records along line segments joining the k minority class nearest neighbors. This forces the decision region of the minority class to become more general and ensures that the classifier creates larger and less specific decision regions, rather than smaller specific regions. In [99], the authors indicated that this approach is an accepted technique for solving the problems related to unbalanced data sets.

MACHINE LEARNING ALGORITHMS

In this chapter, six advanced artificial neural network classifiers are considered as suitable classifiers for predicting normal and pathological cases. These classifiers include the back-propagation trained feed-forward neural network classifier (BPXNC), Levenberg–Marquardt trained feed-forward neural network classifier (LMNC), automatic neural network classifier (NEURC), radial basis function neural network classifier (RBNC), random neural network classifier (RNNC), and the perceptron linear classifier (PERLC) [106].

In the BPXNC, the network is trained to map a set of input data by iterative adjustment of the weights. The information from inputs is fed forward through the network to optimize the weights between neurons. Moreover, the optimization of the weights is made by backward propagation of the error during the training or learning stage. The BPXNC then reads the input and output values in the training data set and changes the value of the weighted links to reduce the differentiation between the predicted and observed values. The error in prediction is reduced across several training cycles (epoch 50) until the network reaches the best level of classification accuracy while avoiding overfitting [107].

The LMNC is similar to the BPXNC and has similar functionality; however, it is much more memory intensive. Furthermore, during the training stage, training is stopped when the performance on an artificially generated tuning set of 1000 samples per class is reached (based on k-nearest neighbor interpolation) and thereafter does not improve any more [106].

A NEURC has a single hidden layer. This classifier tries three random initializations, with fixed random seeds, and returns the best result according to the tuning set. This is done in order to obtain a reproducible result but is more demanding computationally [106].

The RBNC is mostly used in complicated pattern recognition and classification problems, such as a biomedical data set that is nonlinear. The classifier has one hidden layer with unit radial basis units. The mapping properties of the RBNC can be modified through the weights in the output layer.

The RNNC is a feed-forward neural net with one hidden layer of N sigmoid neurons. The input layer rescales the input features to unit variance; the hidden layer has normally distributed weights and biases with zero mean and standard deviation [106].

The PERLC is the simplest type of neural network classifier and is trained with a supervised training algorithm. This classifier assumes that the true classes of the training data are available and incorporated in the training process. The input weights in this classifier can be adjusted iteratively by the training algorithm so as to produce the correct class mapping for the output. However, the problem with this classifier is that it does not have a hidden layer; therefore, this leads to bias in result accuracy.

VALIDATION METHODS

The Holdout Cross-Validation techniques could be used to evaluate the performance of the classifiers used [108]. A common splitting of the data set is to use 80% for training and 20% for testing. For main generalization, the training and test sets must comprise randomly selected instances from the CTG-UHB data set. Because the exact selection of instances for the training is random, it is necessary to repeat the learning and testing stages. The average performance obtained from 100 simulations can be utilized. This number is considered, by statisticians, to be an adequate number of interactions to obtain an average [109]. After each repetition, the error rate for each classifier is stored and the learning experience of the algorithm wiped so that it does not influence the next test. Producing several repetitions provides average error rates, standard deviations, and performance values for each classifier.

The k-fold cross-validation is a validation technique used to estimate the accuracy of the classifiers. The results from k-fold cross-validation are often compared with the holdout technique. Sensitivity (true positives) and specificity (true negatives) measure the predictive capabilities of classifiers in binary classification tests. Sensitivities refer to the true positive rate or recall rate (pathological records). Specificities measure the proportion of true negatives (normal records). Sensitivities are considered a higher priority than specificities as it is important to predict a pathological delivery rather than miss classifying a normal delivery.

The area under the curve (AUC) is an accepted performance metric that provides a value equal to the probability that a classifier will rank a randomly chosen positive instance higher than a randomly chosen negative one (this obviously assumes that positive ranges higher than negative) [110]. The AUC is a good evaluation metric for classifiers that produce binary output (pathological or normal).

FUTURE RESEARCH DIRECTIONS

There are three future research directions to those discussed previously in this chapter: exploratory data analysis, feature selection, and evaluation.

EXPLORATORY DATA ANALYSIS

When working with data, it can be useful to make a distinction between two separate parts of the analysis workflow: data exploration and hypothesis confirmation. This distinction was championed by Tukey as a means of promoting a broader, more complete understanding of data analysis [111]. At the time, the distinction was primarily in response to a hypothesis-confirmation paradigm in statistical analysis. However, the utility of data exploration techniques has seen widespread use as a visualization technique within statistical contexts.

Exploratory data analysis (EDA) proposes the exploration of data for patterns and relationships without requiring a prior hypothesis. EDA's influence on data analysis practice has been substantial; it pioneered the development of many analytic techniques, including stem-and-leaf plots and boxplots, and has proven to be hugely influential to data analysis practice [112,113].

As an analysis strategy, EDA should be considered complementary to confirmatory data analysis (CDA). In contrast to the hypothesis-verification paradigm of CDA, EDA is characterized by processes including domain knowledge leverage, data visualization, statistical analysis, and data transformation.

Exploratory analysis should be informed by an understanding of the subject area from which the data was gathered. It is therefore important for the analyst to have an understanding of the subject area under analysis, including the current knowledge and theories in the area, together with an appreciation of those verifying studies and proofs that support that expertise. Such an understanding often enables a direct link between empirical results and preexisting theory and may greatly enhance the insights gathered from the data set.

Although some statistical examinations such as correlation analysis might give insight into the fitness of a set of features for use in subsequent machine learning analysis, a more thorough data exploration process involves the inspection of individual features, the verification of feature validity and data quality, and the identification of data preparation needs, all in conjunction with preliminary ANN testing. However, first there is a need to inspect the data set for variance, overlap, differing value magnitudes, null values, and other properties that might hinder classification, to act on the findings of this inspection and remove or alter values and features that classify poorly. Furthermore, it is useful to investigate and determine the effects of data transformations such as dimensionality reduction.

FEATURE SELECTION

From the study of features used in related work, there is a large number, and these will differ in the discriminant capabilities that they have. It is useful to perform some analysis to select the ones that are likely to provide a clear separation between normal and pathological cases. As well as using exploratory data analysis, particularly correlation, boxplots can highlight features that describe data in the same way. Using sets of faceted kernel density estimation [112] it is possible to see which of the features used overlap in values between normal and pathological cases. This will provide some insight about what features will classify with greater accuracy. Having carried out some exploratory data analysis of individual features, studies should proceed to develop a cross-feature, comparative analysis. This will make it possible to identify both features and feature combinations that potentially display relationships, which may be modeled by a machine-learning algorithm with less or greater difficultly.

There are other techniques that are equally as useful for feature selection. One such technique is principal components analysis (PCA), which is a statistical method that uses orthogonal transformation to convert a set of observations of possibly correlated variables into a set of values of linearly uncorrelated variable called principal components. [114]. Gram Schmidt has also been used extensively to select features using an orthogonalization procedure that permits the performance of forward variable selection by adding at each step the variable that most decreases the mean square error [115].

EVALUATION

A viable evaluation needs to build on the findings discussed in this chapter. Signal processing is a key requirement to separate noise and required information entwined in the signal being studied. An optimal set of features that best discriminates between normal and pathological cases is important. Using the machine learning algorithms discussed in this chapter, a full analysis of their capabilities needs to be performed. This will incorporate many of the most common artificial neural networking models currently available. The performance for each of the classifiers will be evaluated, using the sensitivity, specificity, mean error, standard deviation, and AUC values with 100 simulations and randomly selected training and testing sets for each simulation. Based on the findings, a recommendation for the ANN that is best suited for intrapartum hypoxia, along with their associated parameter settings, needs to be presented and justified.

CONCLUSIONS

Uterine contractions have the potential to damage an unborn fetus by diminishing the maternal blood flow to the placenta. Obstetricians interpret cardiotocography monitors to make a diagnosis of fetal hypoxia. However, this is a time consuming and subjective process that often leads to misclassification that causes damage to the fetus and can result in unnecessary cesarean sections.

Within a supervised-learning paradigm, this chapter presented an approach to classify normal and pathological records. A rigorous, methodological approach to data preprocessing was presented using best practices found in the literature. Possible features, supported by findings in the research domain, were highlighted and ways of selecting the most discriminant of features discussed. There were concerns that the number of minority observations (pathological) was small. To address this issue, the SMOTE oversampling technique was presented as a possible solution that creates new synthetic observations from known pathological observations. This is a technique commonly used to address imbalanced medical data sets.

The primary aim of this chapter was to provide a comprehensive discussion of intrapartum hypoxia and present some relevant literature in the area. It is a work in progress that we hope has mapped out a possible work plan for dealing with CTG data and how it might be used in a machine learning environment to predict normal and pathological records in the CTG-UHB data set.

REFERENCES

[1] Devane D, Lalor JG, Daly S, McGuire W, Smith V. Cardiotocography versus intermittent auscultation of fetal heart on admission to labour ward for assessment of fetal wellbeing. Cochrane Database Syst Rev 2012;2:CD005122.
[2] Brown R, Wijekoon JHB, Fernando A, Johnstone ED, Heazell AEP. Continuous objective recording of fetal heart rate and fetal movements could reliably identify fetal compromise. Med Hypotheses 2014;83(3):410−7.
[3] Rees S, Inder T. Fetal and neonatal origins of altered brain development. Early Hum Dev 2005;81(9):753−61.
[4] Rees S, Harding R, Walker D. An adverse intrauterine environment: implications for injury and altered development of the brain. Int J Dev Neurosci 2008;26(1):3−11.
[5] Warren JB, Lambert WE, Fu R, Anderson JM, Edelman AB. Global neonatal and perinatal mortality: a review and case study for the Loreto Province of Peru. Res Rep Neonatol 2012;2:103−13.

[6] Chudacek B, Spilka J, Bursa M, Janku P, Hruban L, Huptych M, Lhotska L. Open access intrapartum CTG database. BMC Pregnancy Childbirth 2014;14(16):1−12.

[7] Ugwumadu A. Are we (mis)guided by current guidelines on intrapartum fetal heart rate monitoring? Case for a more physiological approach to interpretation. Int J Obstet Gynaecol 2014;121(9):1063−70.

[8] Bogdanovic G, Babovic A, Rizvanovic M, Ljuca D, Grgic G, Djuranovic-Milicic J. Cardiotocography in the Prognosis of Perinatal Outcome. Med Arch 2014;68(2):102−5.

[9] Costa MD, Schnettler WT, Amorim-Costa C, Bernardes J, Costa A, Goldberger AL, et al. Complexity-loss in fetal heart rate dynamics during labor as a potential biomarker of acidemia. Early Hum Dev 2014;90(1):67−71.

[10] Pinto P, Bernardes J, Costa-Santos C, Amorim-Costa C, Silva M, Ayres-de-Campos D. Development and evaluation of an algorithm for computer analysis of maternal heart rate during labor. Comput Biol Med 2014;49(1):30−5.

[11] Warrick PA, Hamilton EF, Kearney RE, Precup D. A Machine-Learning Approach to the Detection of Fetal Hypoxiaduring Labor and Delivery. Assoc Adv Artif Intell 2012;33(2):79−90.

[12] Clark SL, Meyers J, Frye DK, Garthwaite T, Alan J, Lee BS, Perlin JB. Recognition and response to electronic fetal heart rate patterns: impact on newborn outcomes and primary cesarean delivery rate in women undergoing induction of labor. Am J Obstet Gynecol 2015;212(4):494.e1-6.

[13] Sola A, Golombek SG, Bueno MTM, Lemus-Varela L, Auluaga C, Dominquez F, et al. Safe oxygen saturation targeting and monitoring in preterm infants: can we avoid hypoxia and hyperoxia? Acat Paediatr 2014;103(10):1009−18.

[14] Warrick PA, Hamilton EF, Precup D, Kearney RE. Classification of Normal and Hypoxic Fetuses From Systems Modeling of Intrapartum Cardiotocography. IEEE Trans Biomed Eng 2010;57(4):771−9.

[15] Kessler J, Moster D, Albrechfsen S. Delay in intervention increases neonatal morbidity in births monitored with cardiotocography and ST-waveform analysis. Acta Obs Gynecol Scand 2014;93(2):175−81.

[16] Meloni A, Cofelice V, Deiana SF, Mereu R, Palmas G, Fanos V, et al. Asphyxia from the eyes of the obstetrician. J Pediatr Neonatal Individ Med 2014;3(2):1−7.

[17] Alfirevic Z, Devane D, Gyte GML. Continuous cardiotocography (CTG) as a form of electronic fetal monitoring (EFM) for fetal assessment during labour (Review). Cochrane Libr 2013;31(5):CD006066.

[18] Lutomski JE, Meaney S, Greene RA, Ryan AC, Devane D. Expert systems for fetal assessment in labour. Cochrane Libr 2013;(8):1−10.

[19] Talaulikar VS, Lowe V, Arulkumaran S. Intrapartum fetal surveillance. Obstet Gynaecol Reprod Med 2014;24(2):45−55.

[20] Freeman RK. Fetal Heart Rate Monitoring. 2012. p. 288.

[21] Spilka J, Georgoulas G, Karvelis P, Chudacek V. Discriminating Normal from 'Abnormal' Pregnancy Cases Using an Automated FHR Evaluation Method. Artif Intell Methods Appl 2014;8445:521−31.

[22] Simpson KR. Labor Management Evidence Update: Potential to Minimize Risk of Cesarean Birth in Healthy Women. J Perinat Neonatal Nurs 2014;28(2):108−16.

[23] Kok N, Ruiter L, Hof M, Ravelli A, Mol BW, Pajkrt E, et al. Risk for Maternal and Neonatal Complications in a Subsequent Pregnancy After Planned Cesarean Delivery in a First Birth, Compared with Emergency Cesarean Delivery: A Nationwide Comparative Cohort Study. Obstet Gynecol Surv 2014;69(5):237−9.

[24] Donn SM, Chiswick ML, Fanaroff JM. Medico-legal implications of hypoxic-ischemic birth injury. Semin Fetal Neonat Med 2014;19(6):317−21.

[25] Brown R, Wijekoon JHB, Fernando A, Johnstone ED, Heazell AEP. Continuous objective recording of fetal heart rate and fetal movements could reliably identify fetal compromise, which could reduce stillbirth rates by facilitating timely management. Med Hypotheses 2014;83(3):410−7.

[26] Chudacek V, Anden J, Mallat S, Abry P. Scattering Transform for Intrapartum Fetal Heart Rate Variability Fractal Analysis: A Case-Control Study. IEEE Trans Biomed Eng 2014;61(4):1100−8.

[27] Sacco A, Muglu J, Navaratnarajah R, Hogg M. ST analysis for intrapartum fetal monitoring. Obstet Gynaecol 2015;17(1):5−12.

[28] Rotariu C, Pasarica A, Andruseac G, Costin H, Nemescu D. Automatic analysis of the fetal heart rate variability and uterine contractions. IEEE Electrical and Power Engineering 2014:553−6.

[29] Rotariu C, Pasarica A, Costin H, Nemescu D. Spectral analysis of fetal heart rate variability associated with fetal acidosis and base deficit values. In: International Conference on Development and Application Systems; 2014. p. 210−3.

[30] Maeda K. Modalities of fetal evaluation to detect fetal compromise prior to the development of significant neurological damage. J Obstet Gynaecol Res 2014; 40(10):2089−94.

[31] Doret M. Uterine Electromyograpy Characteristics for early Diagnosis of Mifepristone-induced Preterm Labour. Obstet Gynecol 2005;105(4):822−30.

[32] Moslem B, Khalil M, Diab M. Combining multiple support vector machines for boosting the classification accuracy of uterine EMG signals. In: 18th IEEE International Conference on Electronics, Circuits and Systems; 2011. p. 631−4.

[33] Hakan S, Abdulhamit S. Classification of Fetal State from the Cardiotocogram Recordings using ANN and Simple Logistic. In: 3rd International Symposium on Sustainable Development; 2012.

[34] Peterek T, Gajdos P, Dohnalek P, Krohova J. Human Fetus Health Classification on Cardiotocographic Data Using Random Forests. In: Intelligent Data Analysis and its Applications; 2014. p. 189−98.

[35] Ocak H. A Medical Decision Support System Based on Support Vector Machines and the Genetic Algorithm for the Evaluation of Fetal Well-Being. J Med Syst 2013; 37(2):9913.

[36] Krupa N, Ma MA, Zahedi E, Ahmed S, Hassan FM. Antepartum fetal heart rate feature extraction and classification using empirical mode decomposition and support vector machine. Biomed Eng Online 2011;10(6):1−15.

[37] Czabanski R, Jezewski J, Matonia A, Jezewski M. Computerized analysis of fetal heart rate signals as the predictor of neonatal acidemia. Expert Syst Appl 2012;39(15): 11846−60.

[38] Ocak H, Ertunc HM. Prediction of fetal state from the cardiotocogram recordings using adaptive neuro-fuzzy inference systems. Neural Comput Appl 2013;23(6):1583−9.

[39] Romano M, Faiella G, Bifulco P, Addio D, Clemente F, Cesarelli M. Outliers Detection and Processing in CTG Monitoring. In: Mediterranean Conference on Medical and Biological Engineering and Computing; 2013. p. 651−4.

[40] Spilka J, Chudacek V, Koucky M, Lhotska L, Huptych M, Janku P, et al. Using nonlinear features for fetal heart rate classification. Biomed Signal Process Control 2012;7(4):350−7.

[41] Fergus P, Cheung P, Hussain P, Al-Jumeily D, Dobbins C, Iram S. Prediction of Preterm Deliveries from EHG Signals Using Machine Learning. PLoS One 2013; 8(10):e77154.

[42] Buhimschi C, Garfield RE. Uterine contractility as assessed by abdominal surface recording of electromyographic activity in rats during pregnancy. Am J Obstet Gynecol 1996;174(2):744—53.

[43] Moslem B, Diab MO, Marque C, Khalil M. Classification of multichannel uterine EMG signals. In: IEEE Annual International Conference on Engineering in Medicine and Biology Socity; 2011. p. 2602—5.

[44] Tong L, Change Y, Lin S. Determining the optimal re-sampling strategy for a classification model with imbalanced data using design of experiments and response surface methodologies. Expert Syst Appl 2011;38(4):4222—7.

[45] Moslem B, Khalil M, Diab MO, Chkeir A, Marque C. A Multisensor Data Fusion Approach for Improving the Classification Accuracy of Uterine EMG Signals. In: 18th IEEE International Conference on Electronics, Circuits and Systems; 2011. p. 93—6.

[46] Fele-Žorž G, Kavsek G, Novak-Antolic Z, Jager F. A comparison of various linear and non-linear signal processing techniques to separate uterine EMG records of term and pre-term delivery groups. Med Biol Eng Comput 2008; 46(9):911—22.

[47] Warrick PA, Hamilton EF, Precup D, Kearney RE. Identification of the dynamic relationship between intra-partum uterine pressure and fetal heart rate for normal and hypoxic fetuses. IEEE Trans Biomed Eng 2009;56(6):1587—97.

[48] Warrick PA, Hamilton EF, Precup D, Kearney RE. Classification of normal and hypoxic fetuses from systems modeling of intrapartum cardiotocography. IEEE Trans Biomed Eng 2010;57(4):771—9.

[49] Goncalves H, Costa A, Ayres-de-Campos D, Costa-Santos C, Rocha AP, Benardes J. Comparison of real beat-to-beat signals with commercially available 4 Hz sampling on the evaluation of foetal heart rate variability. Med Biol Eng Comput 2013;51(6).

[50] Signorini MG, Fanelli A, Magenes G. Monitoring fetal heart rate during pregnancy: contributions from advanced signal processing and wearable technology. Comput Math Methods Med 2014;2014(707581):1—10.

[51] Warrick PA, Hamilton EF. Subspace detection of the impulse response function from intrapartum uterine pressure and fetal heart rate variability. In: IEEE Computing in Cardiology Conference; 2013. p. 85—8.

[52] Warrick PA, Hamilton EF. Discrimination of Normal and At-Risk Populations from Fetal Heart Rate Variability. Comput Cardiol 2014;41:1001—4.

[53] Improta G, Romano M, Ponsiglione A, Bifulco P, Faiella G, Cesarelli M. Computerized Cardiotocography: A Software to Generate Synthetic Signals. J Health Med Informatics 2014;5(4):1—6.

[54] Krupa BN, Mohd Ali MA, Zahedi E. The application of empirical mode decomposition for the enhancement of cardiotocograph signals. Physiol Meas 2009;30(8): 729—43.

[55] Dong S, Boashash B, Azemi G, Lingwood BE, Colditz PB. Automated detection of perinatal hypoxia using time-frequency-based heart rate variability features. Med Biol Eng Comput 2014;52(2):183—91.

[56] Cesarelli M, Romano M, Ruffo M, Bifulco P, Pasquariello G, Frantini A. PSD modifications of FHRV due to interpolation and CTG storage rate. Biomed Signal Process Control 2011;6(3):225–30.

[57] Wei S, Lu Y, Liu X. Fetal heart rate analysis using a non-linear baseline and variability estimation method. In: 5th IEEE international Conference on Biomedical Engineering and Informatics; 2012. p. 532–6.

[58] Romano M, Cesarelli M, Bifulco P, Ruffo M, Frantini A, Pasquariello G. Time-frequency analysis of CTG signals. Curr Dev Theory Appl Wavelets 2009;3(2): 169–92.

[59] Cesarelli M, Romano M, Ruffo M, Bifulco P, Title No. IEEE Information Technology and Applications in Biomedicine; 2009. p.1–4.

[60] Warmerdam GJJ, Vullings R, Bergmans JWM, Oei SG. Reliability of spectral analysis of fetal heart rate variability. In: IEEE 36th Annual International Conference on the IEEE Engineering in Medicine and Biology Society; 2014. p. 2817–20.

[61] Rooijakkers MJ, Song S, Rabotti C, Oei G, Bergmans JWM, Cantatore E, et al. Influence of Electrode Placement on Signal Quality for Ambulatory Pregnancy Monitoring. Comput Math Methods Med 2014;2014:960980.

[62] Sibony J, Fouillot M, Benaudia A, Benhalla P, Blot P, Sureau C. Spectral analysis: a method for quantitating fetal heart rate variability. New York: Excerpta Medical Foundation; 1994. p. 325–32.

[63] Signorini MG, Magenes G, Cerutti S, Arduini D. Linear and nonlinear parameters for the analysis of fetal heart rate signal from cardiotocographic recordings. IEEE Trans Biomed Eng 2003;50(3):365–74.

[64] Siira S, Ojala T, Ekholm E, Vahlberg T, Blad S, Rosen KG. Change in heart rate variability in relation to a significant ST-event associates with newborn metabolic acidosis. BJOG 2007;114(7):819–23.

[65] Laar VJ, Porath MM, Peters CHL, Oei SG. Spectral analysis of fetal heart rate variability for fetal surveillance: review of the literature. Acta Obs Gynecol Scand 2008;87(3):300–6.

[66] Dawes GS, Houghton CR, Redman CW. Baseline in human fetal heart-rate records. Br J Obs Gynaecol 1982;89(4):270–5.

[67] de CAmpos DA, Bernardes J, Marsal K, Nickelsen C, Makarainen L, Banfield P, et al. Can the reproducibility of fetal heart rate baseline estimation be improved? Eur J Obs Gynecol Reprod Biol 2004;112(1):49–54.

[68] de CAmpos DA, Bernardes J. Comparison of fetal heart rate baseline estimation by SisPorto 2.01 and a consensus of clinicians. Eur J Obs Gynecol Reprod Biol 2004; 117(2):174–8.

[69] Pardey J, Moulden M, Redman CWG. A computer system for the numerical analysis of nonstress tests. Am J Obs Gynecol 2002;186(5):1095–103.

[70] Taylor GM, Mires GJ, Abel EW, Tsantis S, Farrell T, Chien PF, et al. The development and validation of an algorithm for real-time computerised fetal heart rate monitoring in labour. BJOG 2000;107(9):1130–7.

[71] Mantel R, van Geijn HP, Caron FJ, Swartjies JM, van Woerden EE, Jongsma HW. Computer analysis of antepartum fetal heart rate: 2. Detection of accelerations and decelerations. Int J Biomed Comput 1990;25(4):273–86.

[72] Bernades J, Moura C, de Sa JP, Leite LP. The Porto system for automated cardiotocographic signal analysis. J Perinat Med 1991;19(1–2):61–5.

[73] Camm J. Heart rate variability: standards of measurement, physiological interpreta-tion and clinical use. Task Force of the European Society of Cardiology and the North American Society of Pacing and Electrophysiology. Circulation 1996;93(5): 1043−65.

[74] Chaffin DG, Goldberg CC, Reed KL. The dimension of chaos in the fetal heart rate. Am J Obs Gynecol 1991;165(5):1425−9.

[75] Kikuchi T, Shimizu T, Hayashi T, Horikoshi N, Unno S, Taketani Y. Nonlinear ana-lyses of heart rate variability in normal and growth-restricted fetuses. Early Hum Dev 2006;82(4):217−26.

[76] Felgueiras CS, de Sa JP, Bernardes J, Gama S. Classification of foetal heart rate sequences based on fractal features. Med Biol Eng Comput 1998;36(2): 197−201.

[77] Georgoulas G, Stylios CD, Groumpos PP. Predicting the risk of metabolic acidosis for newborns based on fetal heart rate signal classification using support vector machines. IEEE Trans Biomed Eng 2006;53(5):875−84.

[78] Goncalves H, Rocha AP, de Campos DA, Bernardes J. Linear and nonlinear fetal heart rate analysis of normal and acidemic fetuses in the minutes preceding delivery. Med Biol Eng Comput 2006;44(10):847−55.

[79] Lake DE, Richman JS, Griffin MP, Moorman JR. Sample entropy analysis of neonatal heart rate variability. Am J Physio Regul Integr Comp Physiol 2002;283(3):789−97.

[80] Echeverria JC, Hayes-Gill BR, Crowe JA, Woolfson MS, Croaker GDH. Detrended fluctuation analysis: a suitable method for studying fetal heart rate variability? Physiol Meas 2004;25(3):763−74.

[81] Ferrario M, Signorini MG, Magenes G. Complexity analysis of the fetal heart rate for the identification of pathology in fetuses. Computers and Cariology; 2005. p. 989−92.

[82] Doret M, Helgason H, Abry P, Goncalves P, Gharib C, Gaucherand P. Multifractal analysis of fetal heart rate variability in fetuses with and without severe acidosis during labor. Am J Perinatol 2011;28(4):259−66.

[83] Helgason H, Abry P, Goncalves P, Gharib C, Gaucherand P, Doret M. Adaptive Multi-scale Complexity Analysis of Fetal Heart Rate. IEEE Trans Biomed Eng 2011;58: 2186−93.

[84] Vinken MP, Rabotti C, Mischi M, Oei SG. Accuracy of frequency-related parameters of the electrohysterogram for predicting preterm delivery. Obstet Gynecol Surv 2009; 64(8):529.

[85] Fele-Žorž G, Kavšek G, Novak-Antolič Z, Jager F. A comparison of various linear and non-linear signal processing techniques to separate uterine EMG records of term and pre-term delivery groups. Med Biol Eng Comput 2008;46(9):911−22.

[86] Buhimschi C, Boyle MB, Garfield RE. Electrical activity of the human uterus during pregnancy as recorded from the abdominal surface. Obstet Gynecol 1997;90(1):102−11.

[87] Buhimschi C, Boyle MB, Saade GR, Garfield RE. Uterine activity during pregnancy and labor assessed by simultaneous recordings from the myometrium and abdominal surface in the rat. Am J Obstet Gynecol 1998;178(4):811−22.

[88] Leman H, Marque C, Gondry J. Use of the electrohysterogram signal for characteriza-tion of contractions during pregnancy. IEEE Trans Biomed Eng 1999;46(10):1222−9.

[89] Maner WL, Garfield RE, Maul H, Olson G, Saade G. Predicting term and preterm delivery with transabdominal uterine electromyography. Obstet Gynecol 2003; 101(6):1254−60.

[90] Doret M. Uterine Electromyograpy Characteristics for early Diagnosis of Mifepristone-induced Preterm Labour. Obstet Gynecol 2005;105(4):822–30.

[91] Garfiled RE, Maner WL, Maul H, Saade GR. Use of Uterine EMG and cerical LIF in Monitoring Pregnant Patients. BJOG 2005;112:103–8.

[92] Maner WL, Garfield RE. Identification of human term and preterm labor using artificial neural networks on uterine electromyography data. Ann Biomed Eng 2007; 35(3):465–73.

[93] Lucovnik M, Kuon RJ, Chambliss LR, Maner WL, Shi S-Q, Shi L, et al. Use of uterine electromyography to diagnose term and preterm labor. Acta Obstet Gynecol Scand 2011;90(2):150–7.

[94] Buhimschi C, Garfield RE. Uterine contractility as assessed by abdominal surface recording of electromyographic activity in rats during pregnancy. Am J Obstet Gynecol 1996;174(2):744–53.

[95] Verdenik I, Pajntar M, Leskosek B. Uterine electrical activity as predictor of preterm birth in women with preterm contractions. Eur J Obstet Gynecol Reprod Biol 2001; 95(2):149–53.

[96] Richman JS, Moorman JR. Physiological time-series analysis using approximate entropy and sample entropy. Am J Physiol Heart Circ Physiol 2000;278(6):H2039–49.

[97] Spilka J, Georgoulas G, Karvelis P, Vangelis P, Oikonomou P, Chudacek V, et al. Automatic evaluation of FHR recordings from CTU-UHB CTG database. Inf Technol Bio Med Informatics 2013;8060:47–61.

[98] Loyola-Gonzalez O, Garcia-Borroto M, Medina-Perez MA, Marinez-Trinidad JF, Carrasco-Ochoa JA, Ita GD. An Empirical Study of Oversampling and Undersampling Methods for LCMine an Emerging Pattern Based Classifier. Pattern Recogn 2013; 7914:264–73.

[99] Chawla NV, Bowyer KW, Hall LO, Kegelmeyer WP. SMOTE: Synthetic Minority Over-sampling Technique. J Artif Intell Res 2002;16:321–57.

[100] Taft LM, Evans RS, Shyu CR, Eggar MJ, Chawla N. Countering imbalanced datasets to improve adverse drug event predictive models in labor and delivery. J Biomed Inform 2009;42(2):356–64.

[101] Wang Y, Simon M, Bonde P, Harris BU, Teuteberg JJ. Prognosis of Right Ventricular Failure in Patients with Left Ventricular Assist Device Based on Decision Tree with SMOTE. Trans Inf Technol Biomed 2012;16(3):383–90.

[102] Sun T, Zhang R, Wang J, Li X, Guo X. Computer-Aided Diagnosis for Early-Stage Lung Cancer Based on Longitudinal and Balanced Data. PLoS One 2013;8(5): 63559.

[103] Lin W, Chen JJ. Class-imbalanced classifiers for high-dimensional data. Brief Bioinform 2013;14(1):13–26.

[104] Nahar J, Imam T, Tickle KS, Shawkat Ali ABM, Chen YP. Computational Intelligence for Microarray Data and Biomedical Image Analysis for the Early Diagnosis of Breast Cancer. Expert Syst Appl 2012;39(16):12371–7.

[105] Blagus R, Lusa L. SMOTE for High-Dimensional Class-Imbalanced Data. BMC Bioinformatics 2013;14(106):1–16.

[106] 37steps. Pattern Recognition Tools 2013. Version 5.

[107] Ghaffari A, Abdollahi H, Khoshayand MR, Bozchalooi IS, Dadgar A, Rafiee-Tehrani M. Performance comparison of neural network training algorithms in modeling of bimodal drug delivery. Int J Pharm 2006;327(1–2):126–38.

[108] Russel S, Norvig P. Artificial Intelligence: A Modern Approach. 3rd ed. Harlow, Essex: Pearson; 2014. p. 1152.

[109] Salkind NJ. Statistics for People Who (Think They) Hate Statistics. Thousand Oaks, CA: Sage; 2014. p. 512.

[110] Fawcett T. An Introduction to ROC Analysis. Pattern Recogn Lett 2006;27(8): 861−74.

[111] Tukey JW. The future of Data Analysis. Ann Math Stat 1962;33(1):1−67.

[112] Tukey JW. Exploratory Data Analysis. Reading, MA: Addison-Wesley; 1977. p. 688.

[113] Velleman PF, Hoaglin DC. Exploratory Data Analysis. Washington, DC: American Psychological Association; 2012. p. 629.

[114] Abdi H, Williams LJ. Principle Component Analysis. Wiley Interdiscip Rev Comput Stat 2010;2(4):433−59.

[115] Guyon I, Elisseeff A. An Introduction to Variable and Feature Selection. J Mach Learn Res 2003;3:1157−82.

Recurrent Neural Networks in Medical Data Analysis and Classifications

7

Haya Al-Askar[1], Naeem Radi[2], Áine MacDermott[3]

Salman Bin Abdulaziz University, Department of Computer Science, Saudi Arabia, KSA[1];
Al Khawarizmi International College, Abu Dhabi, UAE[2]; Al Dar University College, Dubai, UAE[3]
E-mail: sun_2258@hotmail.com, n.radi@khawarizmi.com, ainemacdermott4@googlemail.com

INTRODUCTION

The development of medical information systems has played an important role in medical science. The aim of these developments is to improve the utilization of technology in medical applications [62]. Expert systems and different artificial intelligence methods and techniques have been used and developed to improve decision support tools for medical purposes. One of the most widely used classification tools for medical application is artificial neural networks (ANNs). ANNs have the ability to identify differences between groups of signals, which were utilized to identify different types of diseases and illnesses. This is related to their characteristics of self-learning, self-organization, nonlinearity, and parallel processing compared with linear traditional classifiers [43]. Feedforward neural networks suffer from some limitations when dealing with temporal pattern. Recurrent neural networks (RNNs) have advantages over feedforward neural networks, as they have the ability to discover the hidden structure of the medical time signal. Existing studies have indicated that RNNs have the ability to perform pattern recognition in medical time-series data and have obtained high accuracies in the classification of medical signals [35,57,68,69,71]. Additionally, it has been shown that RNNs have the ability to provide an insight into the feature used to represent biological signals [68]. Therefore, the employment of a dynamic tool to deal with time-series data classification is highly recommended [34]. This type of neural network has a memory that is capable of storing information from past behaviors [31]. One of the most important applications of RNNs is modeling or identifying temporal patterns, as Chung et al. have stated in their work [16]. They convey that "recurrent (artificial) neural network models are able to exhibit rich temporal dynamics, thus time becomes an essential factor in their operation." Different studies have indicated that RNNs can be applied to nonlinear decision boundaries [28]. The main advantages of RNNs is their ability to deal with static and dynamical situations [42,47,69]. One of their powerful properties are finite state machine approximation, which makes RNNs learn both temporal and spatial patterns [23]. This type of network is very useful for real-time applications like biomedical signal recording and analysis.

In this chapter, applications of RNNs for medical data classification will be discussed. There is a strong body of evidence emerging that suggests the analysis of uterine electrical signals, from the abdominal surface (electrohysterography [EHG]), could provide a viable way of diagnosing true labor and even predict preterm deliveries. Hence, the performance of three types of RNN architecture, including the Elman, Jordan, and Layer, in classification of uterine EHG signals for the prediction of term and preterm delivery for pregnant women will be presented and discussed as a case study.

MEDICAL DATA PREPROCESSING

Most of the recorded signals that represent time series in different applications contain noise. These noises may be due to measurement error or temporary incident, or may be related to problems with the recording tools [33]. For example, the biomedical signal of a patient may be interrupted by the patient's movements or breathing, or by the patient electrocardiogram (ECG) [15,33,44,61]. The signal characteristics are buried away in the noise [43]. Therefore, researchers need to filter these signals to remove or at least reduce these noises in order to measure the true propriety of the series [5]. The filter techniques play an important role in extracting the signal of interest and removing the unwanted effects of noise. The literature describes a number of filtering methods that have been designed, such as the band-pass filter, which allows specified frequencies to pass. For example, Balli et al. [6] have used a band-pass filter to remove high-frequency content and baseline noise on the ECG signals. It has been used on electronystagmography (EMG) signals to filter with different parameters [21,37,44,54,61,65] as well as electroencephalography (EEG) signals [3,54,68]. Each signal has its own optimal parameter to be used with the filter. For example, the most relevant information in EMG is contained in the range of 20–500 Hz [13,38], whereas heart rate effects can be eliminated at a low of 100 Hz. However, there are no perfect filters to remove unwanted artefacts [24]. Fele-Zorz et al. [22] showed that 0.3–3 Hz is the best range for classifying between preterm and term delivery. However, the frequency range of the motion noise is 1–10 Hz [15].

Some RNN models were designed in order to detect patterns in biological signals. In addition, some researches have proved that RNN is a very powerful tool for modeling EEG single [23]. Forney et al. [23] have shown that the Elman RNN (ERNN) is able to classify mental tasks. It has shown its ability to forecast the EEG signal. Their process was based on classification via forecasting (CVF). Each EEG signal is recorded from a person while he/she imagines mental tasks. ERNN has been trained to forecast the signals of each of these imagined mental tasks. The forecasting errors of ERNN are fed to the classifier as features; then the label of class is selected with the ERNN model that obtained the lowest forecasting error. This experiment has been performing very well and has achieved up to 93% classification accuracy. This is related to the dynamical link on the ERNN, which holds some of the temporal information from the EEG signal.

Furthermore, RNNs have been used to represent signals. Szkola et al. [66] applied RNNs to analyze speech signals in order to indicate the difference between healthy individuals and patients with larynx diseases. The proposed network was developed by combining the Elman and Jordan networks. The proposed network, called the Elman–Jordan network, aimed to improve the learning ability of the network. The features of patients' speech signals are extracted by the average mean squared errors obtained by the RNNs using the original signal. The task utilizes speech signals of patients from the control group and those with two types of laryngopathies, namely Reinke edema (RE) and laryngeal polyp (LP). Their experiment involved asking patients to separately pronounce different Polish vowels. Their proposed network has shown some improvement on the learning ability of the neural network and time speed and can be utilized as an initial step to making decisions about normal and disease states [66].

Another application of Jordan network was presented by Silva et al. [63]. They used the Jordan network to reconstruct the missing data on medical time series signal. They used signal with a multivariate channel. The Jordan network was trained to predict the missing gap in order to recover the corrupted signal [63].

Another RNN-based approach was established in 1996 by Cheron et al. [14]. Their main objectives of using dynamic RNNs were to find the relationship between muscle EMG activity and arm kinematics. The neural network used in that study consisted of fully interconnected neurons, and their experiments show that this RNN is perfectly able to identify muscle activity EMG signals. It can identify the complex mapping between muscle activity EMG and upper-limb kinematics during complex movements. Additionally, Mougiakakou et al. [55] investigated the ability of RNNs using a real-time learning algorithm. They used an RNN to model the glucose–insulin level of children with type 1 diabetes, and their results proved that RNNs are able to predict the glucose level for children with type 1 diabetes.

CLASSIFICATION

The importance of classification techniques in the medical community, especially for diagnostic purposes, has gradually increased. The important reason for improving medical diagnosis is to enhance the human ability to find better treatments, and to help with the prognoses of diseases to make the diagnoses more efficient [1], even with rare conditions [46]. The classification task involves the following: each object in a data set is represented by a number of attributes or features, and each of these objects can be determined according to a number of classes to which it belongs. The features can be assembled into an input vector x. The classifier will be provided by a number of previous objects (training set), each involving vectors of feature values and the label of the correct class. The aim of the classifier is to learn how to extract useful information from the labeled data in order to classify unlabeled data. Various methods have been employed for the classification task. They are categorized into two groups: linear and nonlinear classifiers. The linear classifiers are represented as a linear function of input feature x.

$$g(x) = wTx + b$$

where w is a set of weight values and b is a bias. For two classes, problems c_1 and c_2, the input vector x is assigned to class c_1 if $g(x) >= 0$ and to class c_2 otherwise. The decision boundary between class c_1 and c_2 is simply linear. In the previous studies, several traditional linear classifiers were designed and applied to perform classification in different areas such as linear discriminant analysis.

Nonlinear classifiers involve finding the class of a feature vector x using a nonlinear mapping function (f), where f is learnt from a training set T, from which the model builds the mapping in order to predict the right class of the new data. The most popular nonlinear classifier is the neural network. As a classifier, the ANN has a number of output units, one of each probable class. Nonlinear neural networks are able to create nonlinear decision boundaries between dissimilar classes in a nonparametric approach [13,31]. Chen et al. [13] asserted that neural networks have the power to determine the posterior probabilities, which can be used as the basis for establishing the classification rule.

ANN achievements have covered different types of medical applications such as the analysis of EEG signals [28]. Diab et al. [18] have used the ANN to classify uterine EMG signals for preterm deliveries and deliveries at term according to their frequency domain.

RNNs FOR CLASSIFICATION

Various medical applications based on RNNs have been developed over the last few years. One of the most prominent applications of RNNs is pattern recognition, such as automated diagnostic systems [69]. RNNs can utilize nonlinear decision boundaries and process memory of the state, which is crucial for the classification task [28,57,58]. A number of studies have confirmed that RNNs have the ability to distinguish linear and nonlinear relations in the signals. In addition, they have proven that RNNs possess signal recognition abilities [57]. Researchers are attempting to investigate the ability of RNNs to classify biological signals (e.g., EEG, ECG, and EMG). The procedure for signals classification is performed in two stages. The first step is extracting the features. These features will be used as an input to RNN classifier. This will be followed by the classifier techniques.

Currently, most research work is based on using RNNs for EEG signals classification. Koskela et al. [39] have been addressing the utilization of recurrent self-organizing map (RSOM) to EEG signals for epilepsy. It has been applied to detect the activity of epileptic neurons on EEG signals. The EEG sample was 200 Hz. The features been used in this experiment are spectral features and they were extracted with a 256 size window. The authors used wavelet transform to extract signals from each window, and 16 energy features from the wavelet domain have been computed for each window. The data is divided into training and testing sets; the training set contained 150,987 × 16 dimension vectors, and epileptic activity comprised 5430 patterns on the training set. The RSOM network has been run to classify the EEG signal as normal or epileptic activity. The results showed that RSOM achieved a better clustering result than a self-organizing map (SOM). The authors concluded that using context memory for detecting the EEG epileptic activity has enhanced the classification performance on SOM [39].

Another study was presented using the Elman network to classify the mental diseases on EEG signals combined with wavelet preprocessing. Petrosian et al. [57,58] investigated the ability of RNNs employed with wavelet preprocessing methods for diagnosis of epileptic seizures in EEG signals [58] and for the early detection of Alzheimer disease (AD) in EEG signals [57]. For diagnosis of epileptic seizures in EEG signals analysis, Petrosian et al. [58] examined the ability of RNNs combined with wavelet transformation methods to predict the onset of epileptic seizures. The signals were collected from EEG channel. The RNN was trained based on a decoupled extended Kalmen filter (DEKF) algorithm. In Alzheimer disease, for EEG signals detection task, the RNN has been used to distinguish between AD and healthy groups. In that study, the authors have used network training algorithm based on an extended Kalman filter (EKF). The signals were obtained from 10 healthy persons and 10 early AD patients. The EEG signals were recorded using 9 channels with 2 minutes length and with a 512 Hz sampling rate. EEG has been recorded to monitor the subject during the eyes closed resting state. The Fourier power spectra methods have been used to analyze the row EEG signals. The band-pass FIR filter has been used to screen each EEG signal into four subgroups (delta, theta, alpha, and beta). Furthermore, the fourth levels wavelets filter has been used on raw EEG signals. In the study, the inputs of the RNN were the original channel signals and the derived delta, theta, alpha, and beta for each signals as well as their wavelet-filtered subbands at levels 1−6. From their experiments, the best RNN result was achieved using parietal channel P3 raw signals as well as wavelet-decomposed subbands at level 4 as inputs. RNN achieved high performance in classifying AD, with 80% sensitivity and 100% specificity. Petrosian et al. [57] suggested that the combination of RNN and wavelet approach can analyze EEG signals for early AD detection.

Guler et al. [28] have also improved the diagnostic ability of the RNNs to detect EEG signals of epileptic seizures. The EEG signals that have been used in that experiment are recorded from five healthy volunteers with their eyes open, five epilepsy patients in the epileptogenic zone during seizure-free interval, and epilepsy patients during seizures. Lyapunov exponent methods have been applied to extract features, and 128 Lyapunov exponents' features have been calculated for each EEG segment. Statistical steps were used to reduce the dimensionality of the features. This is normally done by computing the maximum, minimum, mean, and standard deviation of the Lyapunov exponents for each EEG signals. The results achieved in this study confirmed that RNNs are better able to classify EEG signals than MLPs. The classification accuracy percentages of the RNNs were approximately 97% for the healthy subjects, 96.88% for seizure-free epileptogenic zone subjects, and 96% for epileptic seizure subjects, whereas MLPs classify the healthy subjects, seizure-free epileptogenic zone subjects, and epileptic seizure subjects with 92%, 91%, and 90.63%, respectively.

Another study has attempted to evaluate the diagnostic accuracy of RNNs by utilizing eigenvector methods to extract features of EEG signals of epileptic seizures [68]. The EEG signals that have been used on that study were obtained using surface EEG electrodes. The signals were recorded from five healthy volunteers with eyes open and eyes closed and from epilepsy patients during seizure-free intervals as well as during seizures activity. Consequently, the data involve five groups, two being healthy and three with an epilepsy diagnosis. Each set contains 100 single-channel EEG signals of 23.6 period. The signals were filtered using band-pass filter with 0.53–40 Hz. This research used three eigenvector methods (Pisarenko, multiple signal classification [MUSIC], and minimum-norm) to calculate the power spectral density (PSD) of signals. Frequencies and power levels of signals have been obtained by these eigenvector methods. After extracting the features using the eigenvectors methods, the features selections are proposed by finding the logarithm of the PSD values of each eigenvectors methods. Then two types of neural networks have been used to classify the signals, the MLP and the ERNN. The result indicates that ERNN has succeeded in classifying EEG signals. RNN networks provided the best classification performance, with an accuracy of 98%. This network outperformed MLP, which had an accuracy of 92% [68]. From these experiments, it has been concluded that the margin between eigenvector methods and RNN approaches can be applied to discriminate between the other biomedical signals.

Another biomedical signal that has been used to investigate RNNs' ability for classification is ECG signals. Ubeyli et al. [69] has also used RNNs to diagnose ECG signals of partial epileptic patients. The RNN has been applied to classify non-arrhythmic ECG waveforms as normal or partial epileptic. The ECG signals involve two types of beats, normal and partial epilepsy, and they were collected from the MIT-BIH Database created by the Massachusetts Institute of Technology [4]. The features were extracted by using wavelet coefficient and Lyapunov exponents. Also, in the ECG experiment, the authors have used statistical methods to reduce the dimensions of the extracted features. The trained ERNN obtained a high classification accuracy of 98% compared to MLP, which achieved 93%.

In addition, Ubeyli et al. [17] used ERNNs to distinguish the differences of beats on electrocardiogram (ECG) signals. An ECG signal involves four beats (normal beat, congestive heart failure beat, ventricular tachyarrhythmia beat, atrial fibrillation beat). The ECG signals contain 48 signals with 30 minutes length. The electrode was replaced on the subject's chest. The band-pass filter has been used to digitize signals at 360 Hz. The features have been extracted using a nonlinear dynamic method, that is, Lyapunov exponents. The ERNN with Levenberg–Marquardt leaning algorithm has been applied in order to classify the ECG signals. The findings of that study have confirmed the ability of ERNN to classify ECG signals with 94.72% accuracy [17].

Another biomedical signal that was used to examine the RNN capacity for classification is EMG signals [2]. This study focused on the automated detection of Parkinson diseases (PD) by using RNNs to classify EMG signals. The ERNN has been used to classify healthy and PD states. The EMG signals are recorded from the extensor carpi radialis muscle during rest and activated motion. The resting motion signals are obtained from abnormal PD patients, and muscular contraction signals are obtained from healthy individuals. The signal's duration was 30 minutes, with a sampling frequency of 100 Hz. In order to distinguish the EMG signals, the authors used the PSD features. The statistical measures such as mean and maximum PSD are computed as features. The results of their experiments show that ERNNs can classify EMG signals with 95% classification accuracy [2].

In addition, their study attempted to classify different types of conditions related to human muscles. For example, Ilbay et al. [35] used ERNNs for automated diagnoses of carpal tunnel syndrome (CTS). It has been applied on patients suffering from various CTS symptoms such as right, left, and bilateral CTS. In this experiment, the study collected EMG signals from 350 patients who suffer from CTS (left, right, and bilateral) symptoms and signs. Nerve conduction study (NCS) was applied by using surface electrode to record the EMG signals on both hands for each patient. NCS measures how fast electrical signals can be sent through nerves. Thus, they are able to diagnose CTS, and the results of this test are used to evaluate the degree of any nerve damage. During the NCS test, surface electrodes are located on the patient's hand and wrist, and then electrical signals are created to stimulate the nerves in the wrist, forearm, and fingers. Sensory responses are collected from the index finger (median nerve) or little finger (ulnar nerve), with ring electrodes. The following features, which have been used as RNN inputs, were extracted from these signals: right median motor latency, left median motor latency, right median sensory latency, left median sensory latency. RNNs are trained with the Levenberg-Marquardt algorithm. The results from this research showed that RNNs obtain 94% classification accuracy, which is higher than MLPNN with 88%.

The RNN has also been used to classify the signals recorded from the Doppler system. For example, Ubeyli et al. [69] evaluated the diagnostic ability of the ERNN employing Lyapunov exponents trained with Levenberg—Marquardt algorithm to classify arterial disease. In this study, signals have been collected from Doppler ultrasound. The Doppler ultrasound method has been used to evaluate blood flow in both the central and peripheral circulation. The main motivation of that study is to obtain nonlinear dynamic features from the ophthalmic arterial (OA) and internal carotid arterial (ICA) Doppler ultrasound signals. Overall, 128 Lyapunov exponent features were calculated from each OA and ICA Doppler signals segment (256 discrete data). However, these features have been reduced using statistical methods to represent signals for classification. The trained ERNN in this feature obtained high classification accuracy, with 97% for OA Doppler signals and ICA Doppler signals.

Table 7.1 Application of RNN in Classification

Paper Authors	Signal	Neural Network Name	Features
Koskela et al. [39]	EEG for epileptic	RSOM	16 energy features from the wavelet domain
Petrosian et al. [58]	EEG of epileptic seizures	Elman	The wavelet transformation methods
Petrosian et al. [57]	EEG of Alzheimer	Elamn	Delta, theta, alpha, and beta for each signals as well as a wavelet transformation method
Guler et al. [28]	EEG	Elman	128 Lyapunov exponents features
Ubeyli [68]	EEG	Elman	used three eigenvector methods (Pisarenko, multiple signal classification [MUSIC], and minimum-norm) to calculate the power spectral density (PSD)
Ubeyli [17]	ECG	Elman	Lyapunov exponent features
Arvind et al. [2]	EMG	Elman	The power spectral densities features
Ilbay et al. [35]	EMG	Elman	Right median motor latency, left median motor latency, right median sensory latency, left median sensory latency
Ubeyli et al. [69]	Doppler system	Elman	128 Lyapunov exponent features
Kumar et al. [40]	EEG	Elman	Wavelet, sample, and spectral entropy features

Kumar et al. [40] used an ERNN for epileptic diagnosis. They extract three features from EEG signals, including wavelet, sample, and spectral entropy features. Their results demonstrated that RNNs achieved high accuracy, with 99.75% to classify normal and epileptic seizures. Table 7.1 summarizes the various RNN architectures and their applications.

INTRODUCTION TO PRETERM

One of the most challenging tasks currently facing the healthcare community is the identification of premature labor [49]. Premature birth occurs when the baby is born before 37 weeks of pregnancy. A term birth occurs when the baby is born after the

37-week gestation period. The number of preterm births is increasing gradually; it badly affects healthcare development. The increase in preterm labor contributes to rising morbidity. It has been recorded that, in 2011, the percentage of babies born as preterm was 7.1% in England and Wales, according to the Office for National Statistics (2013). Approximately 50% of all perinatal deaths are caused by preterm delivery [7], with those surviving often suffers from health problem caused during birth.

Preterm birth has a great impact on new babies' lives, including health problems or increased risk of death. One million preterm babies die each year according to the World Health Organization (WHO). An earlier delivery has a significantly negative impact on babies' later lives. Preterm infants are usually born at low weights of less than 2500 grams compared with full-term babies [25]. In their future lives, they might suffer from more neurologic, mental, and behavioral problems compared with full-term infants [49]. In other cases, preterm birth leads to increased probability of asthma, hearing, and vision problems; some preterm infants may have difficulty with fine-motor and hand–eye coordination [72]. An early delivery affects the development of the kidneys and their function in later life [70]. Furthermore, 40% of survivors of extreme preterm births may be affected by chronic lung disease [29].

On the other hand, preterm births also have a negative effect on families, the economy, and community [24,30]. According to the WHO, more than three-quarters of premature babies can only be saved with very high-level effective care, which results in more infant hospitalizations and a lot of health care expenditure. Preterm infant needs intensive care, which will raise the cost of hospital care to around $1500 a day [25]. Furthermore, the reduced gestation duration increases the number of days spent in hospital. As a result, preterm births have a negative economic effect [64]. According to Mangham et al. [51], in 2009, in England and Wales the total cost to the public sector of preterm births was valued at £2.95 billion. However, attempting to have a better understanding of preterm deliveries can help to create the right decision and adopt prevention strategies to reduce the negative effects of preterm deliveries on infants, families, societies, and healthcare services [23,36,52].

Significant progress has been made in understanding the process of labor, and research on premature labor has attempted to discover the risk factors [13,22]. A number of researchers have found many factors leading to preterm delivery. According to Baker and Kenny [7], approximately one-third of preterm deliveries occurred because of membranes rupturing prior to labor. Another third might happen due to increasing spontaneous contractions (termed preterm labor [PTL]) [24,29]. Lastly, preterm birth can occur because of medical indication toward the best interests of the mother or baby. There are still doubts about which of these factors can increase the risk of preterm birth. However, there are some reasons preterm labor ultimately may or may not end in preterm birth [7]. These reasons may relate to the mother's illnesses, congenital defects of the uterus, and cervical weakness [26,59].

Other factors of preterm labor could be related to health and lifestyle of the mothers; these factors include uterine abnormalities, short cervix, recurrent antepartum hemorrhage, illnesses and infections, any surgery, underweight or obese mother, diabetes, stress, smoking, social deprivation, long working hours/late nights, alcohol and drug use, and folic acid deficiency. In some situations, the cause of preterm delivery is undetectable [18].

ELECTROHYSTEROGRAM

It has been recorded that electrical activity of the uterus muscle has been known for a long time, since at least the late 1930s [8]. However, it is only in the last 20 years that formal techniques have been available to record these activities [12]. The activity is recorded as signals. The method that has been used to record such signals in a time domain is called electrohysterography (EHG). EHG is a technique for measuring electrical activity of the uterus muscle during pregnancy, through uterine contractions [25,50]. EHG is a form of electromyography (EMG), the measurement of activity in muscular tissue.

The uterine muscle is like skeletal muscles. In smooth muscles, as Rabotti et al. [60] asserted, the way the contraction occurs is by the process of propagation of electrical activity over the muscle cells in the appearance of an action potential. The spreading of electrical activity in the action potential through the myometrium cells causes uterine contractions. Therefore, EHG is the measurement of the action potential propagating through the myometrial cells. Figure 7.1 represents the contraction that happens on muscle. The woman's body will slightly increase the number of electrical connections (gap junctions) between uterine cells [24].

From a medical point of view, the strengthening and increasing of uterine contractions over time is a sign of imminent labor and birth [73] and shoots up particularly in the last four days before delivery [45]. During parturition, the increasing of

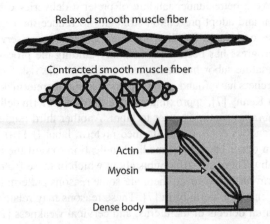

FIGURE 7.1

Schematic Representation of Smooth Cell Contraction.

the contractions will help the body to prepare for the final stage of labor and parturition [12,24]. They will help to shorten the cervix and force the fetus to descend into the birth canal. Therefore, the main function of uterine contractions is to generate the force and synchronicity that are necessary for true labor.

Over the last few decades, EMG has been used in two ways: the older method is an invasive one involving the insertion of needle electrodes into the uterus; however, this method is painful and uncomfortable for patients. Hence, it is unwanted. The second method is a noninvasive one that places electrodes on the woman's abdominal surface. Many experiments have used noninvasive EHG signals in order to study the pregnancy process and predict labor in both humans [22,49] and animals [26,59].

EHG signals have been recorded by placing bipolar electrodes on the abdominal surface. These electrodes are spaced out at a horizontal, or vertical, distance of 2.5−7 cm. The numbers of electrodes that have been used for recording EHG have been chosen differently in various studies. One study used 2 [19] whereas a few other studies used 4 electrodes [12,22,24]. Other studies used 16 electrodes to obtain EHG signals [18,53,54], and a high-density grid of 64 small electrodes was used in Rabonetti et al. [61].

The results of these different studies have confirmed that EHG records are different from woman to woman, depending if she is in true or false labor and whether she will deliver term or preterm [32]. Therefore, EHG can be used to predict and diagnose preterm birth [10]. In the literature, a number of research studies have confirmed the importance of EHG recordings in analyzing uterine contraction during pregnancy and parturition [9,48,60]. Analysis of the EHG provides a strong basis for understanding and identifying the progress of labor [20,22,27,49]. Furthermore, Gondry et al. [27] recognized uterine contractions from EHG records as early as 19 weeks of the pregnancy period.

UTERINE EHG SIGNAL PROCESSING

In the field of biomedical science, the analysis of EHG signals with powerful and advanced methodologies is becoming necessary. EHG is a technique for measuring electrical activity of the uterus muscle during pregnancy, through uterine contractions [25,50]. EMG is considered to be a helpful and effective method to detect preterm labor. EHG is a very sufficient measurement for recording electrical activity because it measures the contraction directly, rather than the physical response of contractions, which may get lost among other physical noise and disturbance [41]. In this section, the ability of RNNs to forecast EHG signals will be investigated. The analysis and characterization of uterine EHG signals is very challenging, which is related to their low signal-to-noise ratio (SNR) [67]. The ability of RNNs to forecast EHG signals can be used for preprocessing EHG signals. The signal preprocessing aims to improve the SNR [11]. The main objective of this experiment is to explore the possibility of applying RNNs as a filtering method to increase uterine EHG SNR value.

The data used in this research were recorded at the Department of Obstetrics and Gynaecology, Medical Centre, Ljubljana, between 1997 and 2006 [56]. In the TPEHG database, there are 300 patient records. These records are freely available, via the TPEHG data set, in the Physionet website [56]. The signals in this study were already collected by Fele-Žorž et al. [22]. Each record was collected by regular examinations at the 22nd week of gestation or around the 32nd week of gestation. The signal in records was 30 minutes long, had a sampling frequency (f_s) of 20 Hz, and had a 16-bit resolution over a range of ±2.5 mV.

Prior to sampling, the signals were sent through an analog three-pole Butterworth filter, in the range of 1 to 5Hz. Figure 7.2 shows four electrodes placed on the abdominal surface, with the navel at the symmetrical center. The black circles represent the electrodes. Each record is obtained from three channels: channel 1, channel 2, and channel 3. Channel 1 signal was measured between E2 and E1, channel 2 was recorded between E2 and E3, and channel 3 signal was recorded between E4 and E3.

The recording time shows the gestational age. Each recording was classified as a full-term or preterm delivery, after birth. Figures 7.3 and 7.4 show two examples of EHG signals taken from different records. The recordings were categorized as four types as follows:

- Early term: recordings made early, signed as a term delivery
- Early preterm: recordings made early, signed as a preterm delivery
- Late term: recordings made late, signed as a term delivery
- Late preterm: recordings made late, signed as a preterm delivery

Two experiments have taken place on 76 EHG signals with 38 preterm and 38 term values. The model was trained over channel 3 following the recommendation

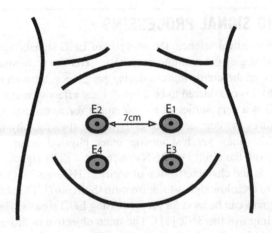

FIGURE 7.2

Placement of Electrodes on the Mother's Abdomen.

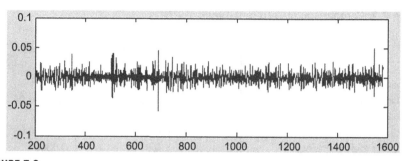

FIGURE 7.3

Row Data Plot for the Uterine EHG Signals, Term Subject.

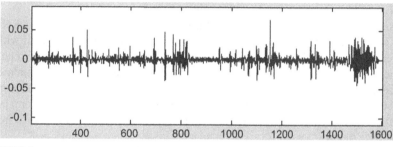

FIGURE 7.4

Row Data Plot for the uterine EHG signals, Preterm subject.

of Fele-Žorž et al. [22]. The first experiment used RNNs to model EHG signals before filtering, whereas the second experiment modeled the EMG signals with RNNs after using a band-pass filter configured between 0.3 and 4 Hz.

MODELING RNN FOR FORECASTING

In this section, the steps that have been used to build the RNNs to model EHG signals are presented. The maximization of the quality of uterine EHG signal produced by RNNs can be achieved by evaluating the SNR. These measurements have been designed to hold the highest amount of information from EHG signal as possible and the smallest amount of noise.

An experiment was undertaken to examine the performance of the network. The performance was evaluated using the mean squared error (MSE) and SNR. Table 7.2 shows the average results for the mean squared error, correlation coefficient (r), and signal-noise-ratio (SNR) using 76 uterine EHG signals. The best forecasting performance is measured by the SNR, which is a key measure of predictability, with higher values for SNR indicating better predictability. Table 7.2 shows the performance

Table 7.2 Comparison of Different Types of RNNs

	SNR	Correlation coefficient r	Mean standard error
Elman (before filtering)	7.9256	0.4506	0.0033
Elman (after filtering 0.3–4 Hz)	13.7702	0.2363	1.4504e-04
Jordan (before filtering)	16.138	0.856	0.0011
Jordan (after filtering 0.3–4 Hz)	16.7627	0.8550	4.0464e-04
layrecnet (before filtering)	21.1003	0.8445	0.0066
layrecnet (after filtering 0.3–4 Hz)	33.0693	0.9642	5.1178e-05

comparison of different types of RNNs for EHG noise reduction. These different RNN models were used to reduce the noises in the uterine EHG signals.

Among these models, it compared Elman, Jordan network, and Layer RNNs, with each layer having a recurrent connection with a tap delay associated with it (layrecnet). The results show that RNNs are able to model the nonlinear relation on the EHG signals. The layrecnet model provides the highest SNR measurement. Furthermore, the MSE and correlation coefficient values on this result indicated that layrecnet neural network is a better predictor than other RNNs. Therefore, layrecnet is considered the best model among the benchmark RNNs to remove noise from EHG signals.

In this experiment, the ability of using RNN architectures to forecast EHG signals to obtain high SNR has been presented. In the experiments, the results demonstrated that RNNs are capable of filtering the uterine EHG signals, achieving very high SNRs. In order to assess the performance of the various neural networks for processing EHG signals, the MSE and the correlation coefficient (r) have also been calculated. The results demonstrated that recurrent models are able to capture the temporal behavior of the signals.

CONCLUSION

This chapter has introduced different applications of RNNs for the purpose of analyzing medical time series. Previous studies have demonstrated that RNNs had considerable achievement in discriminating biological signals. Some of these studies had compared the RNN result with MLP's, and their results confirmed that RNNs obtained higher classification accuracies than MLPs. RNNs have a better ability to analyze and classify different types of biomedical signals. This chapter has also presented the application of RNNS for filtering EHG signals, which is one of the diagnostic approaches for detecting labor. Various RNNs are applied for the prediction of EHG and filtering. Results showed that the RNNs can successfully filter EHG signals with high SNR.

REFERENCES

[1] Akay MF. Support vector machines combined with feature selection for breast cancer diagnosis. Expert Syst Appl 2009;36(2):3240–7.

[2] Arvind R, Karthik B, Sriraam N, Kannan JK. Automated Detection of PD Resting Tremor Using PSD with Recurrent Neural Network Classifier. In: International Conference on Advances in Recent Technologies in Communication and Computing; 2010. p. 414–7.

[3] Akrami A, Solhjoo S, Nasrabad A. EEG-Based Mental Task Classification: Linear and Nonlinear Classification of Movement Imagery. In: Engineering in Medicine and Biology 27th Annual Conference. Shanghai, China; 2005. p. 4626–9.

[4] Al-Aweel IC, Krishnamurthy KB, Hausdorff JM, Mietus JE, Ives JR, Blum AS, et al. Postictal heart rate oscillations in partial epilepsy. Neurology 1999;53(7).

[5] Baghamoradi S, Naji M, Aryadoost H. Evaluation of cepstral analysis of EHG signals to prediction of preterm labor. In: 18th Iranian Conference on Biomedical Engineering. Tehran, Iran; 2011. p. 1–3.

[6] Balli T, Palaniappan R. Classification of biological signals using linear and nonlinear features. Physiol Meas 2010;31(7):903–20. Available at: http://www.ncbi.nlm.nih. gov/pubmed/20505216 (accessed November 20, 2013).

[7] Baker PN, Kenny L. Obstetrics by Ten Teachers. 19th ed. London: Hodder Arnold; 2011.

[8] Bozler E. Electrical Stimulation and Conduction in Smooth Muscle. Am J Physiol 1938; 122(3):614–23.

[9] Buhimschi C, Garfield RE. Uterine contractility as assessed by abdominal surface recording of electromyographic activity in rats during pregnancy. Am J Obstet Gynecol 1996;174(2):744–53.

[10] Chen H-Y, Chuang C-H, Yang Y-J, Wu T-P. Exploring the risk factors of preterm birth using data mining. Expert Syst Appl 2011;38(5):5384–7. Available at: http:// linkinghub.elsevier.com/retrieve/pii/S0957417410011619 (accessed December 23, 2012).

[11] Chendeb M, Khalil M, Hewson D, Duchêne J. Classification of non stationary signals using multiscale decomposition. J Biomed Sci Eng 2010;3(2):193–9.

[12] Cheung P. Evaluating the Effect of Data Preprocessing on the Prediction of Preterm Deliveries from EHG using Machine Learning Algorithms (MSc thesis). Liverpool, UK: John Moores Univ.; 2012.

[13] Chen X, Zhu X, Zhang D. A discriminant bispectrum feature for surface electromyogram signal classification. Med Eng Phys 2010;32(2):126–35. Available at: http:// www.ncbi.nlm.nih.gov/pubmed/19955011 (accessed November 4, 2013).

[14] Cheron G, Draye J-P, Bourgeios M, Libert G. A Dynamic Neural Network Identification of Electromyograph and Arm Trajectory Relationship during Complex Movements. IEEE Trans Biomed Eng 1996;43(5):552–8.

[15] Chowdhury RH, Reaz MBI, Ali M, Bakar A, Chellappan K, Chang TG. Surface electromyography signal processing and classification techniques. Sensors (Basel, Switzerland) 2013;13(9):12431–66. Available at: http://www.ncbi.nlm.nih.gov/ pubmed/24048337 (accessed October 31, 2013).

[16] Chung JR, Kwon J, Choe Y. Evolution of recollection and prediction in neural networks. In: 2009 International Joint Conference on Neural Networks; 2009. p. 571–7.

[17] Derya Übeyli E. Recurrent neural networks employing Lyapunov exponents for analysis of ECG signals. Expert Syst Appl 2010;37(2):1192—9.

[18] Diab MO, El-Merhie A, El-Halabi LKN. Classification of uterine EMG signals using supervised classification method. J Biomed Sci Eng 2010;3(9):837—42. Available at: http://www.scirp.org/journal/PaperDownload.aspx?DOI=10.4236/jbise.2010.39113 (accessed April 2, 2013).

[19] Doret M. Uterine Electromyograpy Characteristics for early Diagnosis of Mifepristone-induced Preterm Labour. Obstet Gynecol 2005;105(4):822—30.

[20] Devedeux D, Marque C, Mansour S, Germain G, Duchene J. Uterine electromyography: a critical reviewe. Am J Obstet Gynecol 1993;169(6):1636—53.

[21] Eswaran H, Wilson JD, Murphy P, Preissl H, Lowery CL. Application of wavelet transform to uterine electromyographic signals recorded using abdominal surface electrodes. J Matern-Fetal Neonat Me 2002;11(3):158—66. Available at: http://www.ncbi.nlm.nih.gov/pubmed/12380670 (accessed 5th August 2013).

[22] Fele-Žorž G, Kavšek G, Novak-Antolič Z, Jager F. A comparison of various linear and non-linear signal processing techniques to separate uterine EMG records of term and pre-term delivery groups. Med Biol Eng Comput 2008;46(9):911—22.

[23] Forney EM, Anderson CW. Classification of EEG during imagined mental tasks by forecasting with Elman Recurrent Neural Networks. In: The 2011 International Joint Conference on Neural Networks; 2011. p. 2749—55.

[24] Fergus P, Cheung P, Hussain A, Al-Jumeily D, Dobbins C, Iram S. Prediction of Pre-term Deliveries from EHG Signals Using Machine Learning. PLoS One 2013;8(10): e77154.

[25] Garfield RE, Maner WL, MacKay LB, Schlembach D, Saade GR. Comparing uterine electromyography activity of antepartum patients versus term labor patients. Am J Obstet Gynecol 2005;193(1):23—9.

[26] Goldenberg RL, Culhane JF, Iams JD, Romero R. Epidemiology and causes of preterm birth. Lancet 2008;371(9606):75—84.

[27] Gondry J, Marque C, Duchene J. Electrohysterography during pregnancy: preliminary report. Biomed Instrum Technol 1993;27(4):318—24.

[28] Guler N, Ubeyli E, Guler I. Recurrent neural networks employing Lyapunov exponents for EEG signals classification. Expert Syst Appl 2005;29(3):506—14.

[29] Greenough A. Long term respiratory outcomes of very premature birth (<32 weeks). Semin Fetal Neonatal Med 2012;17(2):73—6.

[30] Garfield RE, Maner WL. Uterine Electromyography in Humans — Contractions, Labor, and Delivery. In: Jarm T, Kramar P, Zupanic A, editors. 11th Mediterranean Conference on Medical and Biomedical Engineering and Computing. Heidelberg, Berlin: Springer; 2007. p. 128—30.

[31] Haykin S. Neural Networks: A comprehensive Foundation. Upper Saddle River, NJ: Prentice Hall PTR; 1998.

[32] Hassan M, Terrien J, Alexandersson A, Marque C, Karlsson B. Nonlinearity of EHG signals used to distinguish active labor from normal pregnancy contractions. In: 32nd Annual International Conference of the IEEE EMBS; 2010. p. 2387—90.

[33] Herrera JL. Time Series Prediction Using Inductive Reasoning Techniques. Instituto de Organizacion y Control de Sistemas Industriales; 1999.

[34] Hüsken M, Stagge P. Recurrent neural networks for time series classification. Neuro-computing 2003;50(C):223—35.

[35]   Ilbay K, Übeyli ED, Ilbay G, Budak F. A New Application of Recurrent Neural Networks for EMG-Based Diagnosis of Carpal Tunnel Syndrome. In: Cardot H, editor. Recurrent Neural Network for Temporal Data Processing. Croatia: InTech; 2011.

[36]   Iams JD. Prediction and early detection of preterm labor. Obstet Gynecol 2003;101(2): 402–12. Available at: http://www.ncbi.nlm.nih.gov/pubmed/12576267 (accessed May 2013).

[37]   Kavsek G, Pajntar M, Leskosek B. Electromyographic activity of the uterus above the placental implantation site. Gynecol Obstet Invest 1999;48(2).

[38]   Konrad P. The ABC of EMG: A Practical Introduction to Kinesiological Electromyography. Noraxon INC, USA, 1.0; 2005.

[39]   Koskela T, Varsta M, Heikkonen J, Kaski K. Temporal Sequence Processing using Recurrent SOM. In: Proceedings of the Second International Conference Knowledge-Based Intelligent Electronic Systems. Adelaide, SA: IEEE; 1998. p. 21–3. Retrieved from: http://ieeexplore.ieee.org/xpls/abs_all.jsp?arnumber=725861&tag=1.

[40]   Kumar SP, Sriraam N, Benakop PG. Automated detection of epileptic seizures using wavelet entropy feature with recurrent neural network classifier. In: TENCON 2008-2008 IEEE Region 10 Conference. Hyderabad: IEEE; 2008. p. 1–5.

[41]   Leman H, Marque C, Gondry J. Use of the electrohysterogram signal for characterization of contractions during pregnancy. IEEE Trans Biomed Eng 1999;46(10):1222–9.

[42]   Ling SH, Leung FHF, Leung KF, Lam HK, Iu HHC. An Improved GA Based Modified Dynamic Neural Network for Cantonese-Digit Speech Recognition. In: Grimm M, Korschel K, editors. Robust Speech Recognition and Understanding. Vienna, Austria: I-Tech; 2007. p. 460.

[43]   Liu B, Wang M, Yu H, Yu L, Liu Z. Study of Feature Classification Methods in BCI Based on Neural Networks. In: Conference proceedings: … Annual International Conference of the IEEE Engineering in Medicine and Biology Society. IEEE Engineering in Medicine and Biology Society. Conference (Vol.3: 2932–5). China.

[44]   La Rosa PS, Nehorai A, Eswaran H, Lowery CL, Preiss H. Detection of uterine MMG contractions using a multiple change-point estimator and K-means cluster algorithm. International Congress Series 2007;1300:745–8. Available at: http://linkinghub. elsevier.com/retrieve/pii/S0531513107001094 (accessed January 15, 2013).

[45]   Lucovnik M, Maner WL, Chambliss LR, Blumrick R, Balducci J, Novak-Antolic Z, Garfield RE. Noninvasive uterine electromyography for prediction of preterm delivery. Am J Obstet Gynecol 2011;204(3):228. e1-10.

[46]   Machado LO. No Title Medical Application Of Artificial Neural Networks: Connectionist Models of Survival. 1996, March.

[47]   Makarov VA, Song Y, Velarde MG, Hübner D, Cruse H. Elements for a general memory structure: properties of recurrent neural networks used to form situation models. Biol Cybern 2008;98(5):371–95.

[48]   Marque CK, Terrien J, Rihana S, Germai G. Preterm labour detection by use of a biophysical marker: the uterine electrical activity. BMC Pregnancy Childbirth 2007;7(Suppl 1):S5. Available at: http://www.pubmedcentral.nih.gov/articlerender. fcgi?artid=1892062&tool=pmcentrez&rendertype=abstract (accessed January 15, 2013).

[49]   Maner WL, Garfield RE, Maul H, Olson G, Saade G. Predicting term and preterm delivery with transabdominal uterine electromyography. Obstet Gynecol 2003;101(6): 1254–60.

[50] Marshall J. Regulation of activity in uterine smooth muscle. Physiol Rev Suppl 1962;5: 213—7.

[51] Mangham LJ, Petrou S, Doyle LW, Draper ES, Marlow N. The Cost of Preterm Birth Throughout Childhood in England and Wales. Pediatrics 2009;123:312—27.

[52] Muglia LJ, Katz M. The Enigma of Spontaneous Preterm Birth. N Engl J Med 2010; 362(6):529—35.

[53] Moslem B, Khalil M, Diab M, Chkeir A, Marque C. A Multisensor Data Fusion Approach for Improving the Classification Accuracy of Uterine EMG Signals. In: Electronics, Circuits and Systems (ICECS), 2011 18th IEEE International Conference on 11th-14th Dec. Beirut, Lebanon: IEEE; 2011. p. 93—6.

[54] Moslem B, Khalil M, Diab M, Chkeir A, Marque C. Classification of multichannel uterine EMG signals by using a weighted majority voting decision fusion rule. 2012 16th IEEE Mediterranean Electrotechnical Conference 2011:331—4. Available at: http://ieeexplore.ieee.org/lpdocs/epic03/wrapper.htm?arnumber=6196442 (accessed March 2013).

[55] Mougiakakou SG, Prountzou A, Iliopoulou D, Nikita KS, Vazeou A, Bartsocas CS. Neural network based glucose - insulin metabolism models for children with Type 1 diabetes. In: Conference proceedings: Annual International Conference of the IEEE Engineering in Medicine and Biology Society. IEEE Engineering in Medicine and Biology Society; 2006. p. 3545—8. Conference, 1(Mm).

[56] Physionet.org. The Term-Preterm EHG Database (TPEHG DB); 2010. Retrieved from: http://www.physionet.org/pn6/tpehgdb/.

[57] Petrosian AA, Prokhorov DV, Schiffer RB, Petrosian AA. Recurrent Neural Network based Approach for Early Recognition of Alzheimer's Disease in EEG. Recurrent Neural Network based Approach for Early Recognition of Alzheimer's Disease in EEG. Clin Neurophysiol 2001;112(8):1378—87.

[58] Petrosian A, Prokhorov DV, Homan R, Dashei R, Ii DW. Recurrent neural network based prediction of epileptic seizures in intra- and extracranial EEG. Neurocomputing 2000;30:201—18.

[59] Rattihalli R, Smith L, Field D. Prevention of preterm births: are we looking in the wrong place? Edition, Archives of disease in childhood. Fetal an dneonatal 2012;97(3):160—1.

[60] Rabotti C, Mischi M, van Laar J, Oei G, Bergmans J. Estimation of internal uterine pressure by joint amplitude and frequency analysis of Electrohysterographic signals. Physiol Meas 2008;29(7):829—41. Available at: http://www.ncbi.nlm.nih.gov/pubmed/ 18583724 (accessed January 13, 2014).

[61] Rabotti C. Characterization of uterine activity by electrohysterography (PhD thesis). Technische Universteit Eindhoven; 2010.

[62] Shortliffe EH, Perreault LE, Fagan LM, Wiederhold G. Medical Informatics: Computer Applications in Medicine. Reading: Addison-Wesley; 1990.

[63] Silva LEV, Duque JJ, Guzo MG, Soares I, Tin R. Medical Multivariate Signal Reconstruction Using Recurrent Neural Network. In: Computing in Cardiology. Piscataway, NJ: IEEE; 2010. p. 445—7.

[64] Shi SQ, Maner WL, Mackay LB, Garfield RE. Identification of Term and Pre-Term Labor in Rats using Artificial Neural Networks on Uterine EMG Signals. Am J Obstet Gynecol 2008;198(2):1—10.

[65] Shaker MM. EEG Waves Classifier using Wavelet Transform and Fourier Transform. Int J Biol Life Sci 2005;1(2):85—90.

[66] Szkoła J, Pancerz K, Warchoł J. Recurrent neural networks in computer-based clinical decision support for laryngopathies: an experimental study. Computational Intell Neurosci 2011 2011:289398.

[67] Terrien J, Marque C, Steingrimsdottir T, Karlsson B. Evaluation of adaptive filtering methods on a 16 electrode electrohysterogram recorded externally in labor. In: 11th Mediterranean Conference on Medical and Biomedical Engineering and Computing. Berlin: Springer; 2007. p. 2−5.

[68] Übeyli ED. Analysis of EEG signals by implementing eigenvector methods/recurrent neural networks. Digital Signal Proc 2009;19(1):134−43.

[69] Übeyli ED, Übeyli M. Case Studies for Applications of Elman Recurrent Neural Networks. In: Hu X, Balasubramaniam P, editors. Recurrent Neural Networks. Vienna, Austria: I-Tech; 2008. p. 440.

[70] Van der Heijden AJ, Keijzer-Veen MG. The Effect of Preterm Birth on Kidney Development and Kidney Function over Time. In: Morrison JC, editor. Preterm Birth - Mother and Child. Vienna, Austria: InTech; 2012. p. 341−56.

[71] Verplancke T, Van Looy S, Steurbaut K, Benoit D, De Turck F, De Moor G, et al. A novel time series analysis approach for prediction of dialysis in critically ill patients using echo-state networks. BMC Med Inform Decis Mak 2010;10:4.

[72] WebMd. Premature Labor. 2012. Available at: http://www.webmd.com/baby/premature-labor.

[73] WelcomeBabyHome. The Birth Process. 2006. Available at: http://www.welcomebabyhome.com/pregnancy/pregnancy_birth_process.htm (accessed January 11, 2013).

Assured Decision and Meta-Governance for Mobile Medical Support Systems

8

Martin Randles[1], Princy Johnson[2], Naeem Radi[3]

School of Computer Science, Liverpool John Moores University, Liverpool, UK[1];
School of Engineering, Liverpool John Moores University, Liverpool, UK[2];
Al Khawarizmi International College, Abu Dhabi, UAE[3]
E-mail: m.j.randles@ljmu.ac.uk, p.johnson@ljmu.ac.uk, n.radi@khawarizmi.com

INTRODUCTION

The use of electronic decision support systems continues to grow through the rise of the Internet with web-based applications capable of being used in a mobile setting. Following this phenomenon, there is an emerging interest in mobile computing and the additional opportunities for decision support, in situ, offered through wireless technologies. Mobile decision support may be defined as the set of activities performed through the process of a decision support model or implementation conducted through communications networks that interface with wireless or mobile devices [1]. These mobile devices may take a number of forms, including mobile/cellular phones, wireless-enabled handheld computers, laptop computers, in-vehicular devices, and paging devices. Additionally, decision support systems may be made mobile through the use of portable nonwireless devices such as computer laptops and personal digital assistants (PDAs). This presents a new set of issues, which are specifically related to mobile decision support.

In this chapter, some of the issues for ensuring that the system can benefit from the provision of autonomic type self-governance [2] are examined, in an environment that permits both code and user/device mobility for assured decision process and system operation. The difficulties with decision support governance on the Web are not created directly by mobility; rather, the problems lie in the crossing of domains and the entering of distinct isolated Internet partitions through rigorously controlled paths that are enforced by firewall constraints, for example. Policies are generally set regarding what is allowed through firewalls and by what means the mobility can occur. In moving a decision process, for example, it is necessary to ensure that all the supporting services and applications required for the transaction to complete also move with, or are available to, the decision process executing on a new host device. The decision process must also tailor its operation to the new host devices environment. It is proposed to use an established layered observation system [3] with a formal logical model in Situation Calculus to handle mobility, decision assurance, and process assurance [4]. The Situation Calculus offers a flexible formalism in which to reason about dynamic systems. The formalism used here, however, will be a calculus of situations extending the original Situation Calculus of McCarthy and Hayes [5].

In this instance, Situation Calculus is, in effect, presented as an executable modeling language, for mobility, meta-system, and decision system assurance, uniquely able to handle counterfactual reasoning, for deliberation on context to produce a deployable decision model that can be modified and updated at run time. For example, the location of a clinician in a work place directly affects the decision, mobility, and process models and the associated cognitive attributes of the context (the intentions or goals of a decision or governance process will vary according to context or location). In this instance, a logical representation of the domain permits intention reconsideration based on a clinician's location and deliberation, using counterfactual reasoning, on the decision/governance/mobility models and subsequent available options.

In this chapter, the background topics and related works are detailed in the next section. The third section provides a more thorough account of the Situation Calculus and its applicability, whereas the fourth section gives an overview of the implementation strategy and its workings. The fifth section reports on the application of these techniques to a real-world clinic—based case study, where decision models are adapted according to the context (situation) of the doctor (or other authenticated system user). The chapter finishes with a conclusion in the final section.

RELATED WORK AND LITERATURE REVIEW

In terms of decision and process assurance for a mobile decision application, context is crucial: This ought to include all contexts in which the decision is being made. Despite established definitions offering a wide scope for the context [6], very few approaches account for both the physical and cognitive context of the users [7]. Either the users' physical locations are considered, for mobility, giving proximity to resources, etc. [8] or the users' preferences or goals are used to give a context [9]; very rarely is a more complete account presented encompassing both the physical and mental states of the user: currently, there is greater emphasis on seeking to establish opportunities and potential applications for mobile decision support systems [10], rather than producing the systems with the previously documented inherent problems in mind. Research tends to focus on making decisions relevant to decisions in specific scenarios, for example, Parkinson disease [11], cardiovascular disease [12], kidney disease [13], or chronic headaches [14]. The modeling solution presented here allows the adaptation of decision process models based on a more complete user environmental and cognitive context. This is achieved through a logical representation of the decision model and a meta-process model for deliberation on the process itself. In this way, the decision context can be deduced using, for example, user preference in line with domain constraints, handling the trade-off between clinician autonomy and systems governance. Currently, design models for decision support do not employ deliberative behavior to support self-adaptation of the decision process, but rather use explicitly managed autonomy via policies and rule sets that predefine and try to predict all possible behavior specified at design time often using event condition action (ECA) constructs [15]. Although this is the traditional way of tackling such problems, it can be argued that often it is not possible to accomplish self-adaptation of decision process and governance, for mobility in open, ad hoc, and evolving decision support systems. Thus, in this chapter a decision process, governance, and mobility modeling approach is outlined for adjustable deliberation and autonomy, which accounts for cognitive aspects, such as intention revision and belief updates, based on ongoing (run-time) analysis. This is underpinned by the formal deliberative reasoning logic, extending the more usual belief—desire—intention (BDI) [16] framework, where the Situation Calculus specification is proposed to enable the necessary deliberation and logical deduction to cope with the dynamic nature of the behavior.

DECISION SUPPORT SYSTEM

A medical decision support system can be viewed as a multiagent system consisting of human and artificial (software) agents [17]. The medical decision process comprises an information field that includes all the agents and objects involved in the decision with a shared ontology to describe the environment. The information field is defined by the common ontology in the form of a normative structure where the human and artificial agents, involved in the decision process, abide by the norms. However, some autonomy must also be allowed within the decision processes so that an agent can "choose" not to follow a norm in certain circumstances. In order to ensure that the processes are robust and agent autonomy is bounded, an observer system is required. The observer system takes the form of a single (governance) meta-system, separate from the decision support process yet governing the operation of the decision support component. The meta-system is required to maintain quality of service through the monitoring of system performance measures, such as response time and quality of process, through the assessment of compliance to any guideline model, adjusting to mobility, and the inference of new rules based on the feedback from previous decision instances.

So the medical decision process is a goal-governed collection of individual agents, concerned with both the decision process itself and the management of the context in which the decision is taking place. The agents may be autonomous, heterogeneous, rational, and social. Norms arise from the social situation in that they involve providing rules for an agent community [18]. The norms can be associated with the decision-making process, as a practical application, or with the separate meta-system for governance of the system and mobile clinical processes. The provision of adjustable autonomous agent behavior is necessary to deliver the system services in a way where the majority of the administrative tasks are handled within the software itself. However, this autonomy must be reconciled with the governance of the system process.

Typically, a medical decision support system consists of a set of patient data inputs that are matched against a range of treatment options resulting in the best treatment option being output as a decision. The PROforma system [19] advanced this notion to consider the medical decision support system in an object-oriented manner. Here a decision task may have subclasses of plans, decisions, actions, and interrogations. Although this approach allows adaptation of the decision-making process with feedback of outcome into the knowledge base, the governance process is very difficult to achieve as there is no provision for run-time adaptation of the system itself: messages need to be passed before classes or aspects can become active in the system. This work thus provides the formal setting of a separated observer-type system to handle the run-time deliberation encompassing quality of service and quality of process concerns for the system, while also providing a formal means to address the mobile decision-making processes that are the system's core functionality.

A CALCULUS OF SITUATIONS FOR MOBILE DECISION SUPPORT SYSTEMS ASSURANCE

The intention in this work is to provide clinical decision support systems that have assured behavior of decision process and self-adaptive operation in a mobile setting. To this end, it is proposed to use a logical formalism to model the systems. Recent continuing advances in the representational power of the Situation Calculus language [20] have given a more modular representational style. This has led to applications of the Situation Calculus to many real problems. The original appeal was in applications to cognitive robotics and agent programming [21]. More recently, works have appeared addressing the specification and reasoning associated with dynamic and adaptable systems in general such as modeling ubiquitous information services [22] or solving logistics problems with Markov decision problems [23]. There are also works progressing on the meta-theory of Situation Calculus, improving representational and reasoning techniques. For instance, the ramification problem and complex temporal phenomena are addressed in the Inductive Situation Calculus [24].

Informally, in Situation Calculus, the basic concepts are actions and situations. It provides a quite natural way to represent commonsense-type formulations. A situation provides a snapshot of the world that may be changed by an action occurrence that then gives the successor situation: Actions are the cause of situation transitions. Each of the situations has a set of fluent values dictated by the initial situation, termed S_0, and the action history. Thus, the sequence of actions or action history fully specifies or comprises a situation. There is a primitive binary operation do; $do(a,s)$ denoting the successor situation to s resulting from performing the action a in situation s. Actions are generally denoted by functions, with arguments from the domain, and situations (action histories) are first-order terms. In seeking to accurately represent a domain, actions must have preconditions that must be true before the action can execute; necessary conditions that must hold before the action can be performed. The predicate *poss* is used with *poss(a,s)*, meaning that it is possible to perform the action *a* in a world resulting from the execution of the sequence of actions *s*. In order to address the frame problem, effect and frame axioms are combined into one Successor State Axiom [25]. These form the simple, yet highly expressive, primitives of the Situation Calculus. More commonly used formalisms, such as Event Calculus [26], lack the expressive power of the Situation Calculus because of the requirement for a linear time order [27]; counterfactual reasoning is possible in the Situation Calculus yet specifically excluded in the Event Calculus. Furthermore, exhaustive specification of the domain is not required, as behavior stems from the domain state and the logical rules in place for that domain: the main difference, in using Situation Calculus, from alternative approaches, where all eventualities must be defined at design time, is the concentration on cognition as the driver for system behavior and observer system function.

THE SITUATION CALCULUS LANGUAGE: FOUNDATIONAL AXIOMS

More formally, the Situation Calculus [4] is a language of three disjoint sorts: actions or tasks, situations and objects (a catch-all for anything that is not a task, action, or situation, depending on the domain). Generally, *s* and *a*, with suitable subscripts, will be used for situations and actions, respectively. Additionally, primarily using the constructs from [4], the language consists of

- Two function symbols of the sort situation;
- The constant symbol S_0 denoting the initial situation
- A binary function, *do*, mapping from the cartesian product of the set of actions with the set of situations to the set of situations (*do:action×situation → situation*). Situations are sequences of actions; *do(a,s)* is the result of adding the action *a* to the end of the sequence *s*.
- A binary predicate symbol, *poss*, which is a member of the cartesian product of the set of actions with the set of situations (*poss:action×situation*): *poss(a,s)* means it is possible to perform action *a* in situation *s*.
- Predicate symbols:
  - Of the sort (*action ∪ object*)^n for each $n \geq 0$ denoting situation-independent relations.
  - Of the sort (*action ∪ object*)^n×*situation* for each $n \geq 0$ denoting relational fluents: Situation-dependent relations.
- Function symbols:
  - Of the sort (*action ∪ object*)^n → *object* for each $n \geq 0$ denoting situation-independent functions.
  - Of the sort (*action ∪ object*)^n×*situation* → *object ∪ action* for each $n \geq 0$ denoting functional fluents: situation-dependent functions.

- Action functions to denote actions of the form $(action \cup object)^n \rightarrow action$ for each $n \geq 0$.
- An ordering relation $\subset$ *situation* $\times$ *situation* denoting a subsequence of actions: $s_1 \subset s_2$ means s_1 is a proper subsequence of s_2. Alternatively, the situation s_1 occurs before s_2.

The functional and relational fluents take one argument of the sort situation; by convention, this is usually the final argument. There are four immediate, domain-independent, axioms of the Situation Calculus, which detail the fundamental properties of situations in any domain-specific representation of actions and fluents:

1. Two sucessor situations are equal if and only if the preceeding situations were equal and the actions that changed each situation are equal. $(do(a_1,s_1) = do(a_2,s_2) \Leftrightarrow (a_1 = a_2) \wedge (s_1 = s_2))$
2. If a property holds in the initial situation and if for every action and situation that property holds in all successor situations, then the property holds for all situations (induction) $((\forall P)[P(S_0) \wedge \forall (a,s) \ (P(s) \Rightarrow P(do(a,s)))] \Rightarrow \forall s \ P(s)))$
3. There are no situations before the initial situation $((\neg \exists \ s)(s \subset S_0))$
4. If a situation is contained in a successor situation, then either the situation is contained in the predeeding situation or the situation is equal to the preceeding situation. $(s_1 \subset do(a,s_2) \equiv (s_1 \subset s_2) \vee (s_1 = s_2))$

MEDICAL DECISION SUPPORT SYSTEM CONTEXT IN SITUATION CALCULUS: AN EXAMPLE

In order to show how Situation Calculus may be used for Medical Decision Support Systems in a mobile setting, it is necessary to consider real-time concerns such as timing constraints (i.e., concurrency) for relevant clinical decision support; an example is shown here. Actions (i.e., diagnosis requests) or tasks occur in time, for certain durations or at the same time (concurrently) as other requests; it is necessary to consider the ways in which time for a clinical decision support task may be represented within the axioms of the Situation Calculus, as stated up to this point. The formalization described so far only conceives of actions occurring sequentially and without timing constraints. Decision support tasks, in a clinical system, may occur at the same time and have the same duration; one may occur completely within the time frame of another or their durations may just overlap. The representational device used within the Situation Calculus to address these problems is to consider instantaneous tasks, which initiate and terminate the task durations, with a relational fluent denoting the extent of the task. For instance, instead of the single task, *move(A,l_1,l_2)*, to represent moving some decision process, *A*, running at a clinician's location l_1 to an alternative location l_2, the instantaneous tasks *startMove* and *endMove* may be used and the procedure of moving represented by the relational fluent *moving(A,l_1,l_2,s)*: the *startMove* action causing the *moving* fluent to become true with the *endMove* action making it false. Similarly, the *communicate* task can be represented by the pair of instantaneous tasks *startCommunicate* and *endCommunicate* with the relational fluent *communicating(s)*. It is then quite simple to represent these actions and fluents in the Situation Calculus, to allow mobility in the clinical decision process, as defined:

poss(startMove(A,l_1,l_2),s) $\Leftrightarrow \neg \exists$($l_3$,$l_4$)moving(A, l_3,l_4,s)$\wedge$location(A,s)=l_1
[Moving a process creates a new unique situation and it's possible to move a process only if it is executing at a particular location in the situation]

poss(endMove(A,l_1,l_2),s) $\Leftrightarrow$moving(A, l_1,l_2,s)
[The move can only be terminated if the process is being moved]

moving(A, l_1,l_2,do(a,s)) $\Leftrightarrow$ a=startMove(A,l_1,l_2) $\vee$ [moving(A, l_1,l_2,s)$\wedge$

$$a \neq endMove(A,l_1,l_2)]$$

[Process movement is either ongoing or was initiated by a startMove action]

location(A,do(a,s))=$l_2 \Leftrightarrow \exists\ l_1$ a=endMove(A,l_1,l_2) $\vee$ [location(A,s)=$l_2 \wedge$

$$\neg(\exists\ l,l') \ a \neq endMove(A,l,l')]$$

[A process executes at a particular location if and only if it has moved to that location or it was executing at that location and there was no endMove action]

With this representation, complex concurrency can be handled. For example, for a particular decision process that requires the clinical context to be moved at the same time as a broadcast system update, followed by the update broadcast ending at the same time as replicating the decision process at a location l_3, followed by ending the movement of the clinical context, while replication at l_3 is ongoing:

{startMove(l_1,l_2), startBroadcast},{endBroadcast, startReplication(l_3)}, {endMove(l_1,l_2)}

represents the sequence of tasks commencing with simultaneously starting to move from l_1 to l_2 and broadcast, followed by simultaneously ending the broadcast and starting to replicate at location l_3, followed by ending the move at l_2 while the replication is still proceeding.

This gives rise to a concise representation for interleaved concurrency: two tasks are interleaved if one is the next action to occur after the other. Thus, an interleaved concurrent representation can be given for moving and broadcasting, for instance:

do([startMove(l_1,l_2),startBroadcast,endBroadcast, endMove(l_1,l_2)],S_0)

where broadcasting is initiated after a move is started and terminated before the end of the move. Alternatively, it might be the case that

do([startBroadcast, startMove(l_1,l_2), endBroadcast, endMove(l_1,l_2)],S_0)

Thus, any overlapping occurrences of moving and broadcasting, except for exact co-occurrences of the initiating or terminating actions, may be realized in the formalism. This is achieved without having to extend the formalism in any way.

The introduction of time into a Situation Calculus representation of clinical decision support does involve a new axiom and two new functions. The representational device for denoting time, in this case, is simply to add a temporal argument to actions. Thus *startBroadcast(t)* is the instantaneous action of the broadcast starting at time *t*. Thus, the function maps an action to a real number (*time: actions* $\rightarrow \Re$, where $\Re$ is the set of real numbers), *time(a)*. So, for example, *time (startBroadcast(t))=t*. The second new function likewise maps a situation to the real numbers (times) (*start:situation* $\rightarrow \Re$.); *start(s)* denotes the start time of

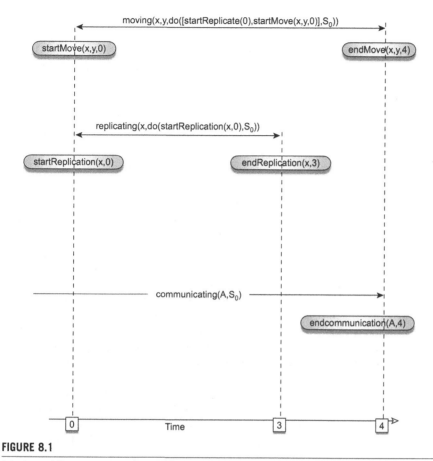

FIGURE 8.1

Interleaved time processes for mobility in situation calculus.

situation s. Thus, $start(do(a,s))=time(a)$. This facility to express time allows for the representation of complex interleaving processes. In Figure 8.1, the time line is illustrated where there are three overlapping processes concerned with movement of clinical context, replication of a service (where that service has become unavailable, for example), and communication between components (patient records and decision process, for example) [28]: the movement of a decision process from a location x to a location y, denoted ($moving(x,y,s)$); the replication of the service at location x ($replicating(x,s)$) and the communication with another process A ($communicating(A,s)$). The *moving* and *replicating* procedures begin together at $t = 0$ with the *replicating* finishing at $t = 3$ and the *moving* at $t = 4$. The *communicating* procedure is already occurring in the initial situation ($t = 0$) and finishes at the same time as the *moving* procedure ($t = 4$).

It is also possible to handle true concurrency, when one or more actions happen at the same time. This is achieved by simply considering concurrent actions as sets of simple actions:

The notation $a \in \Gamma$ denotes that the simple task action a is one of the tasks of the set of concurrent actions Γ. The *do* function symbol can be extended to accept concurrent actions as arguments: *do({startMove(x,y),openPatientFile(f)},S₀)*, (*i.e* Γ=*{startMove(x,y),openPatientFile(f)}*) for example. The successor state axioms can also be adapted to take account of concurrent actions, for instance:

```
moving(x,y,do(Γ,s))⇔startMove(x,y)∈Γ ᵛmoving(x,y,s) ^ endMove(x,y)∉Γ
```

IMPLEMENTATION STRATEGY

The strategy to handle decision process and decision assurance as well as incorporating mobility requires process meta-models to reason on the three cognate aspects of performance of application, decision process, and context/location, respectively. The control service ought to incorporate three core modules, for system governance: a service manager, the distributed shared system tuple space, for communication, and the system controller incorporating an observation system. The implementation then involves the control service model to continuously monitor services for nonoptimal behavior, to identify conflicts and errors, prescribing repair plans and performing reconfiguration. This is the case whether the reasoning is being performed over the operation of the system itself or the actual clinical decision process.

The clinical decision support system governance is then about specifying the system intentions based on individual and system deliberation on roles, responsibility, reward, and regulatory strictures through a formal representation of the beliefs, roles, the situated intentions, the normative intentions, and the reward intentions:

- Beliefs correspond to service information derived from a range of sources, including domain, environment, or the communicated beliefs of components via the shared space. Example: clinician location.
- Roles represent the state of affairs in an ideal world that maximize the service's own goals in terms of fulfilling a desire. By comparing the system belief set (observed system states) against its stated role, the system may detect a mismatch and instantiate a set of intentions to improve the system's performance, refine the decision process, or update the system's context. So the system high-level desires are propagated throughout the system to lower-level management systems in a form that sets desires local to the services. For instance, the high-level goal of medical decision system availability manifests itself in the goal of setting a repair strategy for services the agent believes to be damaged. Component roles provide action triggers to specify the requisite resources.
- Situated intentions represent action sets for the system to undertake in a given situation to achieve its specified desires and/or to address the mismatch between the system environment (beliefs) and the system's desires (goals), including

acting as a resource for other components and maintaining system norms. Example: updating clinician location.

- Normative intentions represent constraints on the process from external factors (e.g., legal or ethical). These form a set of actions to be undertaken to ensure a specified set of rules and regulations, including obligation and responsibility; rules are observed prior to a given intention being enacted. Example: maintaining patient confidentiality.

- Reward intention represents a set of system actions to optimize goal-oriented intentions such as minimizing costs or optimizing quality of service. For example, choosing the lower priced of two equivalent treatment options.

Thus, a clinical decision support system, in this context, can be specified as beliefs, desires, goals, and intentions viewed as a collection of constraints, each of which represents distinct beliefs, desires or goals, and so on. For example, beliefs are a run-time service's states, such as a service is available for decision support or not. Intentions are the system actions (execution), for instance, replicating a service triggered because of a mismatch between the systems beliefs (service unavailable) and system desires (service available).

The deliberation required for intention setting in the Situation Calculus is then possible. For instance, a report of an unavailable decision service, communicated in the system space, triggers a situation whereby the role of decision service reconnect is activated in the system controller. When the system detects a failure to connect to a particular medical service used in a decision process (e.g., patient records), it automatically retries as a responsibility to the connecting clinician/component/ agent. On failing a predetermined number of times, it attempts to connect to an alternative service and/or starts a diagnostic process assembled from its available resources, resulting in a repair strategy committed intention. The Situation Calculus representation of the entire deliberation process, for a session ID, can be specified, for instance:

```
retrial(id, do(a,s)) ⇔ retrial(id, s) ∧

                    ¬∃ t(a=read(space)→decision(id, t))∧¬retried(id,s) ∨ a=retry(id)
with poss(retry(id), s) ⇒ ¬available(service, s) ∧ ¬ retried(id,s)
giving rise to additional successor state axioms:
retried(id, do(a,s)) ⇔ retried(id, s) ∨ [(a=read(space)→ ¬available(service, s))∧

                                                    retrial(id,s)]
available(service, do(a,s)) ⇔ available(service,s) ∧

                        ¬ (a=read(space)→ ¬connected(service,s))
connected(service, do(a,s)) ⇔ ( connected(service,s) ∧

            a≠ f_connect(service)) ∨a= s_connect(service)
with poss(f_connect(service),s) ⇒ remote_service_exception(s)

poss(s_connect(service),s) ⇒ request(id, s)
```

If the system remains unavailable after retrying a specified number of times, then a diagnostic state would be entered, leading to repair strategies based in the implemented scripts.

```
diagnosing(service, do(a,s)) ⇔ [diagnosing(service,s) ∧
                                        ¬∃fault(a=service(fault))]∨ (a=findfault(service))
with poss(findfault(service),s) ⇒∃ id (retried(id,s))∧¬connected(service,s)
leading to
repairing(service, do(a,s))⇔[repairing(service,s) ∧
                                    ¬∃ r(a=repaired(service)]∨(a=repair(service))
with poss(repaired(service),s)⇒available(service,s)
poss(repair(service),s)⇒diagnosed(service,fault,s)
```

Although full details of the implementation are outside the scope of this chapter, the specification can be coded and executed in a range of suitable scripting languages. To handle the mobile aspects, the implementation is executed through cloud-type architectures, with the cloud being considered as a federation of services and resources controlled by the system controller and discovered through the system space.

The system controller with an associated observation system controls access to and from the individual decision processes within the cloud. It brokers requests to the system based on system status and governance rules, in objects programmed in the chosen scripting language, derived from the deliberative process, stated above, either as an abstraction that inspects calls between the system space and decision support system or as a monitor that analyzes the state information stored within the system space.

Each decision support application and associated meta-control model, when it first registers itself to the cloud, sends a meta-object, which may be serialized from an XML definition file, for example. This meta-object contains the properties of the decision process or governance construct it is describing and is stored within the system space. Each decision support service maintains its own meta-object and updates the system space as and when its state changes. The meta-object contains all information required for the cloud to discover the most relevant process. This allows the querying of the decision process status through the published state properties (fluents from situation calculus).

In addition, the meta-objects also describe actions that can be executed either as specific tasks or as events. The action/event model consists of the decision support service informing the system controller when an event occurs. For example, an event occurrence can be serialized as an XML document containing the data that is new to the service. The scripting language should specifically be structured in terms of rules, conditional statements, and variable assignments that are translated from the normative specification to software system objects, encapsulating all the logical inference processes and variable instantiations, thus allowing the scripted object to be inspected, modified, recompiled, and reevaluated at run time, through the specification. In this way, the base rules for deliberation to control the cloud architecture have been transcribed, from the Situation Calculus reasoned representation, into scripted objects that can be modified as a result of observation system deliberation on system events.

For example, it may be the case that a service is required to fulfill a clinician's requirements to deliver a diagnostic decision or access a patient's records: In the given Situation Calculus representation, an availability rule is defined together with resolution strategies in the case of a decision support service being unavailable.

This specifies that if the medical service is not available for calling, then the cloud status is queried to see if a medical service instance alternative is available. If no instance is found, the repair strategy is regeneration of the medical decision support application. Calls are then rerouted to the newly generated application, or the alternative instance if located. This is shown in a pseudo-code script:

```
define service s
if (service.availableServices.likeMe.count=0)
        service.s = regenerate(me.machineID)
else
        service.s = services.availableServices.likeMe()
end if
rerouteCalls(s)
```

Thus, a set of normative positions can be specified for the control system giving decision process self-governance, as required.

CASE STUDY

The following section outlines how the techniques were used to produce an adaptable, distributed guideline model for a breast-cancer decision support system [29]. In this chapter, one goal of the system was that it should adapt its classification of patient treatment based on historical evidence to improve the level of care given to patients. A guideline decision process published by the National Institute of Clinical Excellence (NICE), United Kingdom [30], was subjected to run-time analysis using a Situation Calculus representation and was used as a base on which to decide on treatment for a patient.

Theoretical management requirements were introduced so that certain treatments were no longer available and that given a choice between treatments, the cheaper would be preferable. Although the NICE guidelines remained static, these new requirements were added, as new decisions, to supplement the original model, thereby adapting its behavior. The decision support system, considered in this case study, was required to output treatment options based on rule sets with patient data as inputs as shown in Figure 8.2 [28].

In addition, as the Situation Calculus assurance process provides a formal model for the decision support system, associated performance metrics, and context, when

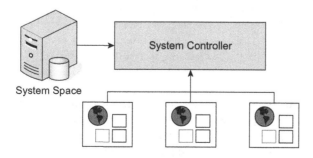

FIGURE 8.2

Treatment Options.

a patient profile is executed against the NICE guidelines, historical data is preserved for later analysis. Thus, as part of the assurance process, any deviations from guidelines by clinicians can be audited, used for system training or annotated accordingly. Another consequence of the process of auditing the patients' progress through the decision model was that for any return to the hospital at a later date, the clinicians would be presented with the exact context appertaining to both the patient details and the exact reasoning behind the decision outcomes. A clinician using this system has a normative position of acceptable behavior and preferred methods of interacting with the system. Thus, the clinician, when using the system from any access point in a mobile setting, will be granted the exact resources required based on their previous context. For example, if the clinician uses a particular decision model, and often applies a range of particular strictures upon the model, the system will adapt the model to the clinician's concerns: Thus, when a clinician logs into the system, their local decision model is obtained with its specializations applied.

The rule base for a particular decision model can be easily produced in the formalism: For example, a simple treatment rule for using the drug tamoxifen, which is recommended in the guidelines for postmenopausal patients with positive oestrogen receptors, can be formally stated as:

```
NICEtreatment(patient, tamoxifen,do(a,s))⇔[ NICEtreatment(patient, tamoxifen,s)∧
                    ¬∃treatment( a=nice_treament_decision(patient, treatment)∧
                                    (treatment≠tamoxifen))]∨
                        [a=nice_treatment_decision(patient,tamoxifen)]
with
poss(nice_treatment_decision(patient,tamoxifen),s)⇒(oesreceptor(patient,s)=pos)∧
                                    (menostatus(patient,s)=post)
```

All necessary rules can, similarly, be generated for the other options, within NICE or any other set of guidelines. The main concerns of the meta-system are assurance for the decision support outcome and the process together with handling context and mobility for the application.

QUALITY OF PROCESS

The rules governing the meta-system are required to reason over the operation of the system. A quality of process concern may involve assessing the clinician's adherence to a specified guideline treatment:

```
compliance(patient, treatment,service_decision, do(a, s)) ⇔
                [compliance(patient,treatment,service_decision,s)∧
                a≠treament_decision(patient,treatment1)]∨
            [a=treatment_decision(patient,treatment) ∧
                service-decision(patient, s)=treatment]
```

In order to express the efficacy of the treatment decisions for the quality of process, it is obviously appropriate to consider the outcomes of courses of treatment. These courses of treatment occur over a period of time, and it is thus necessary to employ the Situation Calculus technique that deals with the duration of actions.

Therefore, the treatment duration is covered by two instantaneous actions *startTreatment* and *endTreatment* with a fluent *treating* through the duration of the treatment. So, for a patient *p,* continuing with the example of tamoxifen treatment given above, there may be a reward function such as:

```
reward(treatment(p,tamoxifen), do(a,s))=r ⇔
a=endTreatment(p,tamoxifen)∧ reward(treatment(p,tamoxifen), do(a,s))=r ∨
                  a=endTreatment(p,tamoxifen) ^ [(r=100 ^living(p,s)) ∨
                                               (r=-500 ^¬living(p,s))]
with
fitness((treatment(tamoxifen)∧menostatus(p,s)=post∧oesreceptor(p,s)=pos),do(a,s))=
      fitness((treatment(tamoxifen)∧menostatus(p,s)=post∧oesreceptor(p,s)=pos),s)+
                          reward(treatment(p,tamoxifen), do(a,s))
```

In this way, the success of each rule occurrence can be assessed, including previously untried treatments instigated by the clinician and flagged for noncompliance. Thus, less successful treatments will be deleted from the decision options whereas the decisions that lead to more favourable results will be chosen, improving the quality of process.

QUALITY OF SERVICE AND MOBILITY

Quality of service concerns can be dealt with by the meta-system through monitoring demand against system capacity. If response time is too slow, for instance, it may be necessary to regenerate the service at a location closer to areas of higher demand. The service location may be specified as

```
at(location, service, do(a,s)) ⇔ (at(location, service, s)∧(a≠move(service,location1)∨
                  a≠delete(service, location)))∨(a=regenerate(service, location))
```

Facilitating the regeneration of a service due to high demand requires the specification of a procedure to detect the behavior and prescribe the action to take to rectify the potential failure. The CPU load can be monitored:

```
cpuload(do(a, s)) =n ⇔[cpuload(s) =n ∧ a≠ sense_CPULOAD] ∨ [a =sense_CPULOAD ∧
                                    SR(sense_CPULOAD, s)=n]
heavyload(do(a, s)) ⇔ [heavyload(s) ∧(( a≠ sense_CPULOAD) ∨
                  ¬(a= sense_CPULOAD ∧SR(sense_CPULOAD, s) <60)) ] ∨
                  [ a = sense_CPULOAD ∧ SR(sense_CPULOAD, s) >60]
with response time given as
roundtriptime(do(a, s)) =n ⇔[ roundtriptime(s) =n ∧ a≠ sense_ROUNDTRIPTIME] ∨
                  [a=sense_ROUNDTRIPTIME∧SR(sense_ROUNDTRIPTIME, s)=n]
unresponsive(do(a,s)) ⇔ [unresponsive(s) ∧(( a≠ sense_ROUNDTRIPTIME)∨
                  ¬(a= sense_ROUNDTRIPTIME ∧SR(sense_ROUNDTRIPTIME, s) <1000)) ] ∨
                  [ a = sense_ROUNDTRIPTIME ∧ SR(sense_ROUNDTRIPTIME, s) >1000]
regenerated(service, location, do(a,s)) ⇔ regenerated(service,location, s)∨
                  a=regenerate(service, location)
with
poss(regenerate(service, location), s) ⇒ heavyload(s) ∨ unresponsive(s)
```

This shows the specification from an immediate observer's perspective. The representation describes a centralized control structure, where the observer acts as the system controller. The actors, within the system, are mandated to act within the normative position of the system as monitored by the observer system.

CONCLUSIONS AND FUTURE WORK

This work is concerned with the governance of assured medical decision support for decision process, system performance, and mobility. It is proposed that the formal setting of Situation Calculus is a flexible and valuable notation for implementing such systems. The formal modeling is implemented through any suitable scripting language to take as input the formally stated decision model and associated meta-model, checking consistency, and output the code for the meta-model allowing variation and adaptation of the context to the observed circumstance. In establishing a decision model and an observer-based meta-model in the Situation Calculus, it is possible to specify reasoning and deliberation on the tasks through the logic, without an exhaustive enumeration of the entire state space.

The approach involved the handling of location and temporal aspects within the Situation Calculus, as well as dealing with the decision process itself and its governance: In relation to the requirements, of modeling self-governance and the automatic run-time maintenance and tuning of large-scale, complex, distributed systems, the major weak point of most approaches is the necessary enumeration of all possible states in advance. Such enumeration is impossible for this work as the evolution of large-scale complex systems is, in general, not predictable. Even if enumeration were possible changes in state compositions would result in an exponential increase in the number of system states. Furthermore any practical utilization, including the facility for deliberation on the system by itself, requires the additional provision of modeling and verification methods to sit above the primitive constructs of the formalism. Thus, the need for a formalism giving a "propositional account" has been established. This naturally leads to the adoption of mathematical logic: Instead of enumerating states and their transition functions, a sentence describing what is true in the system and its environment and the causal laws in effect for that environment are favored. This means that decision models and their associated governance are determined by the logical consequences of the systems description, through entailment; a nonprocedural specification is provided, where properties may be verified and logical deduction used to establish correctness of the process is obtained that is executable, giving a formal system simulator. Throughout this work, the formalism used is required not only to model the systems' tasks but also to provide the deliberative functions for meta-task analysis.

REFERENCES

[1] Tarasewich P, Nickerson RC, Warkentin M. Issues in Mobile E-Commerce. Commun Assoc Inform Syst 2002;8:41−64.
[2] Randles M, Taleb-Bendiab A, Miseldine P, Laws A. Adjustable Deliberation of Self-Managing Systems. In: Proceedings of IEEE International Conference on the Engineering of Computer Based Systems (ECBS 2005) Maryland, USA; 2005. p. 449−56.

[3] Randles M, Taleb-Bendiab A, Miseldine P. Addressing the Signal Grounding Problem for Autonomic Systems. In: Proceedings of International Conference on Autonomic and Autonomous Systems; 2006 (ICAS06), pp. 21, Santa Clara, USA, July 19-21.

[4] Levesque HJ, Pirri F, Reiter R. Foundations for the Situation Calculus. Linköping Electronic Articles in Computer and Information Science; 1998. http://www.ep.liu.se/ea/cis/1998/018/.

[5] McCarthy J, Hayes P. Some Philosophical Problems from the Standpoint of Artificial Intelligence. Machine Intell 1968;4(1):463−502.

[6] Dey A. Providing Architectural Support for Building Context-Aware Applications (PhD thesis). College of Computing, Georgia Institute of Technology, Atlanta, GA, USA, 2000, 170 p.

[7] Ni Hi, Zhou X X, Yu Z, Miao K. OWL-Based Context-Dependent Task Modeling and Deducing. In: proceeding of the 21st International conference on Advanced Information Networking and Applications Workshops; 2007. p. 846−51. AINAW'07.

[8] Castro P, Muntz R. Managing Context Data for Smart Spaces. IEEE Pers Commun 2000;7:44−6.

[9] Prekop P, Burnett M. Activities, Context and Ubiquitous Computing. Comput Commun 2003;26(11):1168−76.

[10] Chignell M, Yesha Y, Lo J. New methods for clinical decision support in hospitals. In: Proceedings of the 2010 Conference of the Center for Advanced Studies on Collaborative Research (CASCON '10). Toronto, ON: Canada; November, 2010.

[11] Klucken J, Barth J, Kugler P, Schlachetzki J, Henze T. Unbiased and mobile gait analysis detects motor impairment in Parkinson's disease. PLoS One 2013;8(2):e56956.

[12] Hervás R, Fontecha J, Ausín D, Castanedo F, Bravo J. Mobile monitoring and reasoning methods to prevent cardiovascular diseases. Sensors (Basel) 2013;13(5):6524−41.

[13] Di Noia T, Ostuni VC, Pesce F, Binetti G, Naso N. An end stage kidney disease predictor based on an artificial neural networks ensemble. Expert Syst Appl 2013;40(11): 4438−45.

[14] Abdel-Aziz K, et al. EHMTI-0276. A novel mobile health application for patients with chronic headache. J Headache Pain 2014;15(1):1.

[15] Moore P. Intelligent Context: the realization of decision support under uncertainty. Inter-cooperative Collective Intelligence: Techniques and Applications. Berlin: Springer; 2014. p. 111−39.

[16] Shehory O, Arnon S. A Brief Introduction to Agents. Agent-Oriented Software Engineering. Berlin: Springer; 2014.

[17] Moreno A. Agents Applied in Healthcare. AI Communications 2003;16(3):135−7.

[18] Itaiwi, Al-Mutazbellah Khamees, et al. Norm's Benefit Awareness in Open Normative Multi-agent Communities: A Conceptual Framework. Distributed Computing and Artificial Intelligence, 11th International Conference. Springer International Publishing; 2014.

[19] Sutton DR, Fox J. The syntax and semantics of the PROforma guideline modeling language. J Am Med Inform Assoc 2003;10(5):433−43.

[20] Vassos S, Levesque HJ. On the Progression of Situation Calculus Basic Action Theories: Resolving a 10-year-old Conjecture. AAAI 2008:8.

[21] Lesperance Y, Levesque H, Reiter R. A Situation Calculus Approach to Modeling and Programming Agents. In: Rao A, Wooldridge M, editors. Foundations and Theories of Rational Agency. New York, USA: Kluwer Academic Press; 1997.

[22] Kelly RF, Pearce AR. Asynchronous knowledge with hidden actions in the situation calculus. Artificial Intell 2015;221:1–35.

[23] Gianni M, Kruijff GJM, Pirri F. A stimulus-response framework for robot control. ACM Trans Interactive Intell Syst 2015;4(4):21.

[24] Denecker M, Ternovska E. Inductive situation calculus. Artificial Intell 2007;171(5): 332–60.

[25] Reiter R. The frame problem in the situation calculus: a simple solution (sometimes) and a completeness result for goal regression. Artificial Intell Mathematical Theory Comput 1991;27:359–80.

[26] Kowalski RA, Sergot M. A Logic Based Calculus of Events. New Generation Comput 1986;4(4):319–40.

[27] Belleghem K, Denecker M, De Schreye D. On the Relation between Situation Calculus and Event Calculus. J Logic Program 1997;31(1–3):3–37.

[28] Randles M, England D, Taleb-Bendiab A. Task modelling using situation calculus. Task Models and Diagrams for User Interface Design. Berlin: Springer; 2010. p. 103–16.

[29] The 2nrich Project: http://www.cms.livjm.ac.uk/2nrich.

[30] NICE. National Institute for Clinical Excellence; 2015. www.nice.org.uk.

Identifying Preferences and Developing an Interactive Data Model and Assessment for an Intelligent Mobile Application to Manage Young Patients Diagnosed with Hydrocephalus

Anthony Farrugia[1], Stephen Attard[2], Mohammed Al-Jumaily[3,6], Sandra C. Buttigieg[4], Vincent Cassar[1], Ali Ghuname[5]

Department of Management, University of Malta, Malta[1]; Paediatrics (Neurology) at Mater Dei Hospital, Malta[2]; Dr Sulaiman Al Habib Hospital, Dubai, UAE[3]; Department of Health Services Management, University of Malta, Malta[4]; Al Dar University College, Dubai, UAE[5]; Liverpool John Moores University, Liverpool, UK[6]
E-mail: anthony.farrugia@um.edu.mt, stephen.e.attard@gmail.com, maljumaily@yahoo.fr, sandra.buttigieg@um.edu.mt, vincent.cassar@um.edu.mt, ghuname@gmail.com

INTRODUCTION

In today's modern world, a new trend in mobile applications development can be seen with the increase in the number of mobile applications being developed for many specific domains, especially in health care. These mobile applications, better known as "apps," are sophisticated systems specially designed for smart devices to reach a wider audience that wants to stay connected on the Internet or use software on the move. Although this trend of mobile applications development is still in its infancy, a huge increase in the number of apps being developed over a short period of time from the conception of smartphones is evident in the number of diverse applications being made available on a daily basis on Apple's iPhone, Blackberry, Windows mobile, and Google's Android—from the first smartphone, called Simon, designed by IBM in 1992 and released in 1993 [1] till today. According to the International Data Corporation on Worldwide Quarterly Mobile Phone Tracker, vendors shipped a total of 287.8 million smartphones worldwide during the first quarter of this year [2]. It is evident that smart devices have become the main technological pocket-sized tool for anyone who wants to stay connected with e-mails, social networking, web browsing, mobile banking, instant messaging, and e-commerce.

This chapter proposes a new application called iNAS (intelligent NeuroDiary Application System). It is a web-based mHealth software that provides management support, administration, communication, and follow-up treatments of young patients with hydrocephalus. It will support smartphone and tablet computing versions of the app, including a web-based interface for clinicians. The smartphone app, which is a user-centered remote patient-monitoring system, will be designed to be used by patients so as to allow them to enter information about their headaches, such as pain level, duration, nausea, and other symptoms related to hydrocephalus. The tablet version of the app will provide an alternative input method that offers user-patients the flexibility to enter information related to hydrocephalus. The web front end is restricted to clinicians and provides a central control, including the facility to check a user's status, to input and complete other medical information, and to include recommendations by health professionals to attend an appointment with a clinician.

As part of the development process, we have carried out intensive interviews with expert panels specializing in hydrocephalus at the Neurology Department, Liverpool Walton Centre, Liverpool, United Kingdom, and at the Paediatric Department at Mater Dei Hospital in Malta. We have identified the necessary data items needed for the proposed system. The interviews were vital in depicting the main specific requirements and preferences for structuring the data and the designs for the proposed mobile user interface (MUI). We present the data needed for the proposed solution to be able to effectively manage patients diagnosed with hydrocephalus. The data selected will also allow the proposed system to scale well for future analysis and research to assist clinicians understand better how to manage their patients diagnosed with hydrocephalus.

MOBILE COMPUTING AND CURRENT TRENDS

Pen-computing technology was the main motivator in the 1980s and early 1990s that has driven and pushed the limits of technology to invent innovative tablet and mobile computing as we know it today [3]. With all the benefits mobile computing brings about together with embedded robust platform and wireless connectivity, these mobile devices, especially smartphones, are becoming preferred for various tasks and applications, especially in clinical medicine [4]. The increasing use of smart devices for mobile communication, web browsing, social networking, and emails made them the preferred choice among users because of the wide selection of different apps available for download at anytime from anywhere. Smart devices apps can be downloaded for free or at a cost (typically in the range of US$0.99–4.99) from the respective online stores [4].

When users purchase smart devices apps, a percentage of the profit is returned to the developers, and this incentive is urging more developers to produce higher-quality and better apps. Apps operate on specific smartphones, which include the leading Android, with just half (51.7%) of phones sold during the first quarter of last year (2014) in the United States alone, followed by iPhone, 41.4%, Windows Phone 8 with just 5.6%, and Blackberry 0.7% of the smartphone market share [5]. Each smartphone brand has an associated app distribution store where individual users can choose and download an app according to their tastes and needs. In 2012, the Apple store saw 40 billion downloads of apps from more than 500 million active accounts [6]. In addition, Apple's developer community has created more than 775,000 apps for iPhone, iPad and iPod touch worldwide, and developers have been paid more than seven billion dollars by Apple [6]. On the other hand, Google Android has an estimated 800,000 apps, Windows Phone has up to 125,000, and Blackberry World has now around 70,000 apps [7].

Smart Devices are the second widely used technology after traditional computing devices, and this trend is likely to continue in the coming years [8]. Today, users want portability and personalized information. This requirement and the computing sales revolution embraced by the continual evolution of technology are presenting new and innovative opportunities in the medical field [9].

MOBILE TECHNOLOGIES IN HEALTH CARE

Recent developments in mobile computing and wireless technology have generated new technological dimensions in the field of medical science [4,9,11-13]. Mobile health, shortened as "mHealth," is reshaping and transforming various aspects in the field of medicine, including medical education distribution, remote access of patients' data, point-of-care applications, medical encyclopedias, and diagnosis and treatment of various medical conditions [13-15]. According to the National Institutes of Health in a statement released during the first mHealth Summer Institute in 2011, mobile technologies in health care "allow providers to help patients improve their health in real time, enabling them to personalise healthcare options and monitor progress" [10].

Various studies have been carried out to analyze the implications when integrating and using mobile technologies and tools in medical health [9,11]. One particular study revealed that participants on questionnaires related to the use of smartphones among clinicians and trainees showed that a large majority of 85% from the total number of participants used a smartphone, of which the iPhone was the most favorite, with a total of 56% [11]. In a separate study carried out to investigate the acceptability and the use of smartphone also indicated that 84% of the total number of medical students believe that smartphone apps will be very useful in their future medical needs [9]. Specific studies were also conducted to reveal mobile technology use in specific domains in health care. These showed that 79% of the respondents use drug guide apps, 18% use medical calculators, 4% use apps for coding and billing, and 4% of the respondents, namely, pediatricians, use pregnancy wheels apps [11]. Their study also revealed that the most frequently requested apps were as follows: 55% to obtain reference materials, 46% request apps for the classification and treatment algorithms, and 43% use apps for general medical knowledge [11]. Moreover, studies in mobile health are showing a noticeable shift and a higher desire to use smartphones and tablet computing as diagnostic devices, decision support, and treatment tools [11-15]. In this vast field, various mobile applications are emerging rapidly, providing efficient and effective sources of health information, patient self-management, and self-supporting tools.

Despite the fact that the clinical use of smartphones and mobile applications will likely continue to increase and there is a strong desire for these applications among clinicians and trainees, there is still an absence of high-quality and popular mobile applications [11]. Research shows that many of these mobile applications are being developed as a result of enthusiasm in new technologies, with the majority lacking research and ethical background and provide insufficient and unreliable information about the health issue concerned [11].

CURRENT PRACTICES IN MANAGING PATIENTS WITH HYDROCEPHALUS
HYDROCEPHALUS

The term *hydrocephalus* relates to an imbalance between the production and absorption of cerebrospinal fluid (CSF) that may cause an increase in intracranial pressure. Figure 9.1 shows swollen ventricles caused by excessive cerebrospinal fluid (CSF) causing a hydrocephalus brain. Hydrocephalus is not a single disease entity but a

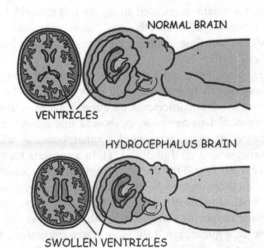

FIGURE 9.1

Normal and hydrocephalic brain.

result of a variety of conditions that may be congenital or acquired. The following are types of different processes that may produce hydrocephalus [16]:

1. Obstructive hydrocephalus (also known as noncommunicating hydrocephalus): occurs when CSF flow is obstructed within the ventricular system or in its outlets to the arachnoid space, resulting in impairment of the CSF from the ventricular to the subarachnoid space. The most common form of noncommunicating hydrocephalus is obstructive and is caused by intraventricular or extraventricular space-occupying lesions that disrupt the ventricular anatomy (Figure 9.1).
2. Communicating hydrocephalus: occurs when full communication occurs between the ventricles and subarachnoid space. It is caused by defective absorption of CSF (most often), venous drainage insufficiency (occasionally), or overproduction of CSF (rarely).
3. Benign external hydrocephalus: a self-limiting deficiency of absorption in infancy and early childhood with raised intracranial pressure (ICP) and enlarged subarachnoid spaces. The ventricles usually are not enlarged significantly, and resolution within 1 year is the rule.
4. Arrested hydrocephalus: A form of hydrocephalus with incomplete obstruction or lack of absorption, which stabilizes. It may decompensate especially after minor head injury.

CAUSES OF HYDROCEPHALUS

There are different causes of hydrocephalus. Table 9.1 lists these causes with some descriptions on each of them.

Table 9.1 Causes of Hydrocephalus

Congenital causes of hydrocephalus in childhood	Genetic conditions: X-linked Aqueductal stenosis Brain malformations: myelomeningocele, Dandy-Walker malformation, neuronal migration defects; vascular malformations Prenatal infection Prenatal hemorrhage
Acquired causes in infancy and childhood	Late manifestation of congenital causes Intraventricular hemorrhage in preterm infants Vascular lesions: vein of Galen malformation Infection: meningitis Brain tumors Head injury Idiopathic (unknown cause)
Causes in adolescents and adults	Idiopathic Subarachnoid hemorrhage that blocks CSF absorption Head injury Brain tumors As a complication of brain surgery Brain infections: meningitis Manifestation of congenital causes like aqueductal stenosis

CHILDREN WITH HYDROCEPHALUS

The clinical symptoms and signs are fundamentally related to an increase in intracranial pressure, but the manifestations depend on the age of the child. Infants and young children usually present with the following symptoms and signs: Irritability, poor feeding, impaired level of consciousness, vomiting, failure to thrive, developmental delay, increasing head circumference crossing centiles, or macrocephaly, poor head control. As further pressure builds up, these infants manifest a tense anterior fontanelle, dilated scalp veins, "Setting sun" sign (combination of upper eyelid retraction and failure of upgaze), and when the pressure is critically high they will manifest Cushing triad (bradycardia, abnormal respiratory contro/apneic spells, hypertension), impaired consciousness, and/or seizures. Older children and adolescents present with headache that tends to be posterior and worse on lying flat and coughing, visual disturbance, diplopia, papilledema, impaired concentration, vomiting, and in later stages drowsiness or impaired consciousness, seizures, and coma [16].

TREATMENT OPTIONS FOR PEDIATRIC HYDROCEPHALUS

The treatment of hydrocephalus should always start with the stabilization of the child's airway, breathing, and circulation followed by medical treatment of raised intracranial pressure. In a number of situations, children have a mild degree of hydrocephalus as manifested by macrocephaly and ventriculomegaly on brain imaging that does not progress and the child remains well and without any other symptoms. This situation requires careful clinical follow-up.

However, in children with suggestive symptoms, definitive treatment of hydrocephalus requires surgical insertion of a shunting device to divert cerebrospinal fluid out of the ventricular system of the brain. A shunt is a narrow tube to drain out excess cerebrospinal fluid that has built up inside the brain to another part of the body such as the heart or abdomen. Shunts are named according to where they are inserted in the brain and where they are inserted to let the excess CSF drains out. The CSF may be diverted into a few body sites, most commonly into the peritoneal cavity, hence the name ventriculoperitoneal shunting. The latter drains CSF by means of a tube inserted into the lateral ventricle through a burr hole in the skull and tunneled subcutaneously into the peritoneum. Thus, a ventriculoperitoneal (VP) shunt, which is the most common type of shunt, as shown in Figure 9.2, drains CSF into the abdomen; a ventriculopleural shunt drains into the space surrounding the lung and a ventriculoatrial (VA) shunt drains into the atria of the heart. Children with ventriculoperitoneal (VP) shunts are prone to a number of complications that may require emergency treatment.

Endoscopic third ventriculostomy is an alternative surgical procedure that involves making a hole in the floor of the third ventricle, thus allowing CSF to drain into the basal cisterns, and therefore out of the ventricles, relieving the hydrocephalus. This procedure has been shown to be very effective in the children with obstruction between the third ventricle and the cortical subarachnoid spaces and can obviate the need for a permanent VP shunt.

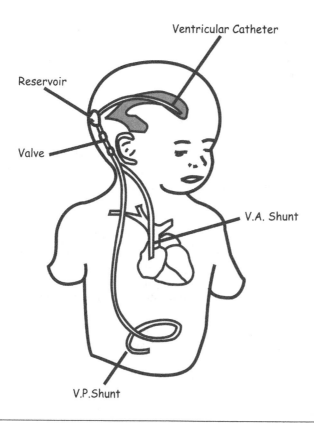

FIGURE 9.2

Child showing the two different types of shunt systems (VP and VA shunts).

In children with VP shunts, a number of complications can arise, most commonly from shunt blockage or infection and less commonly overdrainage. Apart from being an important consideration in the original decision to insert a shunt, repeated shunt complications can lead to impaired cognitive development, visual impairment, repeated surgery as well as a risk of long-term disability and death. The two-year shunt failure rate is around 50% [16].

ASSESSMENT AND INFORMATION REQUIRED IN THE PROPER MANAGEMENT OF A CHILD WITH HYDROCEPHALUS

During the first consultation and subsequent follow-up visits, a number of information sources need to be considered by the neuropediatric team, the most important of which is the clinical state of the infant or child. This information translates into the input data that our intelligent mobile application will use, process, and access, as described in the later section of this chapter.

DEVELOPMENT METHODOLOGY

Various software development methodologies exist to support software engineers to develop their software products. For our proposed system, we will be using the spiral model to actively involve the different stakeholders and engage them in every stage of the software development life cycle until a satisfactory operational prototype is produced [18]. The information obtained from a panel of experts comprising pediatric neurology specialists and neurosurgeons was used to elicit the data parameters and preferences needed for the new intelligent application. As part of the systems analysis exercise, we have used a qualitative approach. A series of one-to-one interviews with a resident pediatric neurologist at Mater Dei Hospital in Malta were carried out using a mixture of close- and open-ended questions. The former were used to elicit the different types of users, the main data items, the visualization of input required, the interpretation of results, the required outputs, and the alert messages to be sent to the clinicians, whereas the latter were used to identify further desirable system requirements and preferences, which include ease of use, data protection, and system scalability.

Our main aim of this chapter is to identify the appropriate data parameters and system preferences to be able to develop an intelligent mobile application, thus we are presenting a finalized set of data parameters and preferences which are critical to the proposed mobile intelligent system to manage patients diagnosed with hydrocephalus.

FINDINGS

With reference to the information gathered from the systems analysis exercise, we have elicited all the required data items needed for our intelligent mobile system. We have characterized the main data items into two main categories (a) patients' history and general information and (b) new clinical problems. Regarding the user interface, three main options will be presented: (a) new users, (b) existing users, and (c) the headache diary. New users (patients) will need to input basic medical information to be able to start using the application. For registered and existing users, we will allow them to update their profile and some medical information as shown in Table 9.2. Patients, remotely, can perform a checkup anytime they want and can also record a headache event. According to the data parameters conveyed in Table 9.3, the new intelligent system will help users verify whether their problem is an emergency or not. We have also taken into consideration our patients' age, which is vital for the data collection and processing. Finally, existing users will have a diary of headache events and will be allowed to record their pain events and any other related information about the particular headache as displayed in Table 9.4.

Table 9.2 Patients' History and Information

Data Parameters	Units	
Age	Years and months (note: <2 or >2 years)	
Weight and centiles	Kilograms	
Head circumference and crossing centiles up	Centimeters; Yes/No	
Does the child suffer from any particular condition of the nervous system?	Yes/No If yes, what is it?	
Neuro-imaging findings and date		
Cause of hydrocephalus		
Shunt or not		
Name of child's consultant neurosurgeon		
Details of shunt operations (date and procedures)		
Shunt complications (Date, type)		
Details of current shunt: Site, Side, Type.	Yes/No B/I/U	
Latest visual acuity	**Right**	**Left**
	6/6	6/6
	6/9	6/9
	6/18	6/18
	6/24	6/24
	6/36	6/36
	6/60	6/60
	Counting fingers	Counting fingers
IQ test or not, and date	Normal Mild impairment Moderate Severe Profound	
Epilepsy	Yes/No Controlled with medication, Yes/No	
Mobility in terms of the Gross Motor Function Classification System	Level I: Walks without limitations Level II: Walks with limitations Level III: Walks using a hand-held mobility device Level IV: Self-mobility with limitations; may use powered mobility Level V: Transported in a manual wheelchair	
Hand function in terms of the Bimanual Fine Motor Function Classification System (BFMFCS)	Level 1: One hand manipulates without restriction; other hand manipulates without limitation OR has limitations in more advanced fine motor skills. Level 2: One hand manipulates without restriction; other hand has ability only to grasp or hold OR both hands have limitations in more advanced fine motor skills.	

Continued

Table 9.2 Patients' History and Information—cont'd

Data Parameters	Units
	Level 3: One hand manipulates without restriction; other hand has no functional ability OR One hand has limitations in more advanced fine motor skills; other hand has ability only to grasp or worse. Child needs help with tasks. Level 4: Both hands have ability only to grasp; OR one hand has ability only to grasp; other hand has ability only to hold or worse. Child needs support and/or adapted equipment. Level 5: Both hands have ability only to hold or worse. Child requires total assistance, even with adaptations.

With the decisive data parameters identified and the way the mobile intelligent system will be developed, we will be able to:

- Manage patients diagnosed with hydrocephalus efficiently;
- Provide researchers with up-to-date repository of information about patients diagnosed with hydrocephalus;
- Establish room for future data analysis using proper data-mining tools and artificial intelligence techniques;
- Incorporate user-friendly mobile and web user interface screens, which are easy to use and difficult to misuse;
- Create medical records that clinicians and medical staff need about their patients;
- Review data-mining tools and artificial intelligence literature in the field of neurology with specific focus on hydrocephalus.

The mobile user interface screens will be developed with a subset of the above-mentioned data items as in Table 9.3. The data conveyed in Tables 9.2 and 9.5 will be used and accessed by authorized clinicians and neurosurgeons through an authorized web user interface to update their assigned patients' medical history and other related medical information. The web user interface will allow clinicians to input the full medical details of their patients as in Tables 9.2 and 9.5 from a standard web application screen. As a result, clinicians will be able to make more effective use of the system while working from their clinic.

THE INTELLIGENT NEURODIARY APPLICATION SYSTEM (iNAS)

Currently, limited applications exist to store, process, and disseminate patients' data diagnosed with hydrocephalus. A main section of our intelligent system will be a NeuroDiary. The NeuroDiary is primarily designed to allow patients to

Table 9.3 The Mobile User Interface Data Elements and the Interactive Data Model

Already registered?	**Interactive Data Input Model for the MUIs**
	New patient details
	(Patient ID, name, surname, address, country, nationality, e-mail, mobile number)
	Basic history and information details
	(Age, weight, cause of hydrocephalus, shunted or not?, total number of shunted operations, date of last shunt operation, ….)
Already registered?	**Interactive Data Input Model for the MUIs**
	Identification Details
	Username & Password
	Sub Menu
	Choice 1: Update your clinical profile info
	Choice 2: Problem check up
	1. Update Your Clinical Profile Info
	To update the clinical profile, users are listed with their clinical history and information fields and are asked to complete any missing details and information.
	2. Problem Check Up
	To check whether a sudden problem that has occurred is an emergency or not, users are asked if they would like to perform an emergency checkup. This depends on the user's age so the first data input parameter will be the user's age.
Already registered?	**Case 1: Child Less Than 2 Years Old**
	• If the child is less than 2 years old (details provided by parents) we are asking for the following important data parameters:
	• Shunted, Yes/No?
	• Age when shunted
	• Irritable? Yes/No
	• Lethargic? Yes/No
	• Not waking up? Yes/No
	• Squint? Yes/No
	• Date
Already registered?	**Case 2: Child Is Older Than 2 Years**
	• If the child is older than 2 years, we are asking for the following data parameters in this logical order:
	• Headache location (rotating head to point to a specific headache location)
	• Is the pain gradual or sudden?
	• How severe is the pain? (0 to 10)
	• Is the pain worse sitting, worse lying, or neither?
	• Has the child got any (a) nausea, (b) vomiting, (c) blurred vision, (d) flashing lights, (e) floaters?
	• Acute deterioration in level of consciousness
	• Eye Opening (E4 spontaneous, E3 to verbal stimulus, E2 to pain, E1 no response to pain)
	• Verbal (V5 orientated, V4 confused, V3 inappropriate words, V2 incomprehensible sounds, V1 no sounds)
	• Motor (M6 obeys commands, M5 localizes to pain stimulus, M4 withdraws from pain, M3 abnormal flexion to pain, M2 abnormal extension to pain, M1 no response to pain)
	• Date and time of day

Table 9.4 The Mobile User Interface to Record a Headache Event

My headache diary	**Recording a Headache Event**
	• Where is the pain located? (Rotating head to point to a specific headache location)
	• How severe was the pain? (0 to 10)
	• Is the pain worse sitting, worse lying, or neither?
	• Did the pain wake you up at night?
	• Did the light bother you?
	• Did you feel better after you sleep?
	• Did you experience (a) nausea, (b) vomiting, (c) blurred vision, (d) flashing lights, (e) floaters?
	• Did you take medication?
	• Is there anything else that you would like to add?
	• Date and time of day

Table 9.5 Patient Presenting a Problem

Headache Characteristics	Units
Intensity?	x/10 or WHO pain ladder
Which part of the head?	Diagram of the head
Time of day	
Associated vomiting	Yes/No
Wakes child up or early morning?	Yes/No
Visual disturbance	Yes/No
New eye symptom?	Yes/No, type
Deterioration in motor function.	Yes/No
Deterioration in hand function.	Yes/No
Deterioration of epileptic control	Yes/No
Deterioration in cognitive function	Yes/No
Fever >38°C	Yes/No

ACUTE DETERIORATION IN LEVEL OF CONSCIOUSNESS [17]
Score out of 15

Eye Opening
E4 spontaneous
E3 to verbal stimulus
E2 to pain
E1 no response to pain

Verbal
V5 orientated
V4 confused
V3 inappropriate words
V2 incomprehensible sounds
V1 no sounds

Table 9.5 Patient Presenting a Problem—cont'd

Motor	
M6 obeys commands	
M5 localizes to pain stimulus	
M4 withdraws from pain	
M3 abnormal flexion to pain	
M2 abnormal extension to pain	
M1 no response to pain	
Pupil Information	
Right pupil size	Millimeters
Right pupil reaction	Brisk/sluggish
Left pupil size	Millimeters
Left pupil reaction	Brisk/sluggish

use the system as an electronic diary to record information on headache events occurrences. The system provides a direct link between patients and clinicians, allowing data to be collected from young patients diagnosed with hydrocephalus and to show the severity of pain and its associated symptoms over time. Using user profiles, it is possible to monitor a patient's headache information via the web front end after a clinician has added the patient to their caseload. NeuroDiary provides an efficient way to manage caseloads through search facilities and real-time alerts. NeuroDiary is the first of its kind that provides an end-to-end solution that allows information to flow freely between patients and clinicians. This places NeuroDiary in a unique position to build on and extend exiting treatment mechanisms currently used to manage outpatients and provide treatments for patients suffering with hydrocephalus.

THE AIM OF THE PROPOSED INTELLIGENT NEURODIARY APPLICATION SYSTEM

The iNAS is a complete information system primarily designed for patients diagnosed with hydrocephalus. The system will store medical information related to hydrocephalus patients and allow patients remotely to have their condition logged into the system and processed by trained clinicians without the need for regular visits to a clinic or a hospital. This does not mean that infants and children will never see a doctor again, but we are aiming to minimize clinical and hospital operational costs and at the same time save clinicians' and patients' valuable time on nonurgent and unnecessary one-to-one visits. The iNAS will also provide the clinicians with a central reference point of information that will allow them to analyze their patients' data and view how their patients' current condition is progressing. Additionally the system allows patients to monitor carefully any risky progressions of their condition while having easy access to consultations when they feel it is necessary. By implementing a central database, clinicians will be able to monitor their patients while also monitoring and suggesting appropriate treatments plans. However, if an urgent situation occurs, it will alert both the patient and clinician, and will ensure that an efficient and effective alert is created and a physical contact has been made.

Thus, we are developing an intelligent system to manage hydrocephalus and make it easier for all parties involved to submit, communicate, and disseminate the correct information at the right time to all individuals concerned. To achieve this level of system functionality and supervision, the software will require constant administration to configure and update the various symptoms that the patients may be dealing with, creating new pain locations, properties, and symptoms, and it may require adding entirely new hydrocephalus-related data items to the database. The administrators will also be responsible for adding new patients and clinicians to the user list and ensure that all users' details concerned are sufficiently protected. Despite the implementation of high level on-the-fly client-side validation embraced by reliable server-side validation scripting, iNAS will ensure that data input from an external environment (user input) is accurate, complete, private, secured, authentic, nonfabricated, and nonrepudiated. These approaches prevent rogue machines from generating unrealistic data items and online users from falsifying clinician accounts and have unauthorized access to medical information from the knowledge and repository database.

REQUIREMENTS

The successful implementation of iNAS requires a variety of important and useful components and robust infrastructure [26]. Despite the requirements of the physical components like hosting iNAS services on particular server machines to hold the central database, iNAS will also require additional software components. We require a main database that will store patients' medical information, user profile information, headache events records, patient details, and treatment plans. The database will also contain a knowledge base that processes data from the main data repository and use it to store any findings or hidden patterns among data sets. The iNAS will also require web services to manage and execute data requests coming in and out from the server, and the use of mobile frameworks like jQuery Mobile or Android for the implementation of the mobile user interfaces. The application also requires multiple management services that are simultaneously running and functionally interlinked. The list of the management services will be the following: the state manager, the registrant and user manager, the patient manager, and the medical event manager. These management services will be used by specific user roles.

The iNAS will mainly constitute four distinct user roles: the *super-admin*, *admin*, *clinician*, and *patient*. Each role has a predefined permission level that allows it perform the necessary business processes and functions. Each user role is part of a collective hierarchy, with the highest role having all the permissions of the lesser roles. For the intelligent system, in logical sequence order by higher hierarchy, the roles are the Executive-admin, the Admin, the Clinician, and the Patient. Each user role assigned will have accessible functions per management service as mentioned earlier.

- **State Manager**—used only by Executive-admins to
  - create new Executive-admins,
  - view all condition preset values and their corresponding details,
  - modify the medical condition details,
  - add, remove, or update all the properties related with hydrocephalus and headache pain management (such as drop-down lists medical information, pain locations, pain properties and associated symptoms, alert configurations), and
  - access all medical-related data, including drop-down lists medical information, pain locations, pain properties and associated symptoms, alert configurations.
- **Registrants and User Manager**—used by Admins and Executive-admins roles to
  - create new registrant details (patients, clinicians, and admins),
  - modify and update existing registrant information (patients, clinicians, and admins),
  - delete unwanted registrants (patients, clinicians, and admins),
  - assign registrants to user-specific roles,
  - grant and revoke permission access to existing roles,
  - view all users by registrant mode or user role mode,
  - can lock and unlock a user's access to the server, and
  - monitor log in information.
- **Patient Manager**—used by Clinicians, Admins, and Executive-admins to
  - create new patients and complete the necessary details,
  - add and update medical information and patients history about the current condition (hydrocephalus-related),
  - continue and discontinue the monitoring of patients assigned,
  - assign patients to new clinicians (in case an existing clinician discontinues her or his medical career),
  - view patients (according to the assigned clinician; i.e., clinicians cannot see each other's patient details although they may have access to generalized data from data sets),
  - view processed generalized data from patients' data sets (how many patients have a VP shunt or a VA shunt as in Figure 9.2),
  - receive alerts (mobile alert or a short message service) from assigned patients (The system will generate three types of alerts; these are graded from 1 to 3, 1 being the least to worry about whereas level 3 is a high-alert message: 1, Make an appointment but not urgent; 2, Call your clinician now; 3, Emergency, you must visit the hospital now),
  - access all alerts generated by the system and list unattended or unread alerts,
  - mark alerts as viewed and view who has triggered the alert (according to headache events inserted), and
  - only admins and super-admins can delete alerts generated by the system.

- **Medical Event Manager**—used by all users to
  - create a new headache event,
  - view past and current events by time stamp,
  - select and choose the necessary data items to complete an accurate headache event (pain location, associated symptoms, severity of pain, time of day, and other useful data items as described in Table 9.4),
  - delete and modify headache events,
  - discontinue headache events,
  - access and view total headache events history, and
  - view all triggered alerts.

The second important component of iNAS is the server side that hosts the main web-front ends and the business logic. This will be housed using a cloud-based framework as cloud computing offers high availability, security, on-demand usage, traffic monitoring, load-balancing, and scalability [27]. The entire system must be able to scale well with the increase of data that we expect to be generated over time. Using a RESTful (Representational State Transfer) API (application programming interface), which is architectural in style, unlike SOAP (service oriented application protocol), which is a protocol, will offer iNAS a cutting-edge advantage, especially in bandwidth consumption and reliability as RESTful API is the most popular building style for cloud-based APIs, such as those provided by Amazon, Microsoft, and Google. Through these APIs, iNAS will communicate with the users' devices to disseminate, control, and moderate the server database data that is provided to the users' devices.

A cloud-based infrastructure will provide the necessary manageable components to maintain the database, the API, and the Interfaces available 99.999% all year. Figure 9.3 shows how a web application scales well on the cloud. This is equivalent to less than 5 minutes' downtime per year [28]. For security issues, the cloud infrastructure will provide encryptions for all data traffic. In addition to this, we will enforce a preset number of failed login user attempts (three times). If users surpass this quota, they will be forced to verify their accounts and their credentials through the administrator to log in again. This approach will enhance user security issues and concerns. The cloud environment will also enhance database queries and transactional performance.

The iNAS user interface screen must be easy-to-use, difficult to misuse, reliable and easy on users' mistakes (robust). This will be achieved with clear and easily identifiable UI elements supported by the Bootstrap web technologies. This approach ensures that all user interfaces will be flexible enough and retain image quality according to the different screen sizes by the variety of devices that may be used to integrate and communicate with iNAS.

DESIGN OF THE PROPOSED SYSTEM

Using a modular approach embraced by the three-tier software architectural framework, we ensure that the different services offered by iNAS through multiple servers still reflect the main distinct tiers used in software development. The Presentation

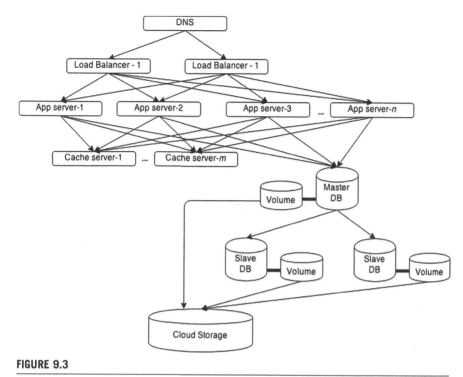

FIGURE 9.3

Architecture-scalable application in the cloud.

tier will manage the user interface and accept all user inputs. The Logic tier, which coordinates the main business logic and houses the main application, will transmit instructions and data to the Presentation tier, accepting input and sending data to the third tier (the data tier). The Data representation layer or data tier is responsible for storing and retrieving data from the database and pushing it to the Logic tier for the required processing. A simple overview of a three-tier architecture is shown in Figure 9.4.

The implementation of the patients' mobile user interfaces will be easy to use and navigate. Current literature shows that many patients have a learning curve, need training on how to use an electronic diary, and must have or acquire self-discipline skills to use an electronic dairy on a regular basis. The iNAS mobile interface screens will be implemented using the JQuery mobile framework. This will facilitate development since JQuery mobile contains a wide range of mobile user interface widgets and tools supported by HTML 5 technology [29].

IMPLEMENTATION

In this subsection, we provide a collection of images to provide a glimpse of what the new mobile version of the user interface might look like and to illustrate how the

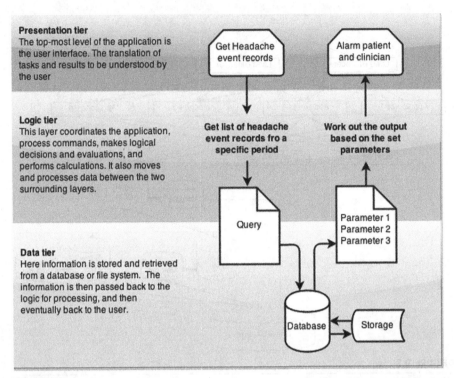

Presentation tier
The top-most level of the application is the user interface. The translation of tasks and results to be understood by the user

Logic tier
This layer coordinates the application, process commands, makes logical decisions and evaluations, and performs calculations. It also moves and processes data between the two surrounding layers.

Data tier
Here information is stored and retrieved from a database or file system. The information is then passed back to the logic for processing, and then eventually back to the user.

Get Headache event records

Alarm patient and clinician

Get list of headache event records fro a specific period

Work out the output based on the set parameters

Query

Parameter 1
Parameter 2
Parameter 3

Database

Storage

FIGURE 9.4

Simple overview of a three-tier application.

process of creating a new patient entry will be displayed to the user. The pages are organized as follows:

- **Pain location**, which provides a list of configured pain locations for the user to assign to the new entry, allows multiple pain locations to be selected. When patients log in, they are required to submit where the pain is located by choosing the appropriate head section as shown in Figure 9.5. However, we will replace this with a rotating head so that users may choose a particular head section and at the same time find it more interactive and appealing.
- **Pain details** allows patients to define when the pain was most painful and how it has progressed. They will be directed to submit more information about their pain; if it is either gradual or a sudden type of pain, the severity of pain and similarly shown in Figures 9.6 and 9.7. However, in the new proposed system, further symptoms related to hydrocephalus will be added.
- **Date and Time** allows the user to state when the event has started and when it has ended, or set it as still ongoing. In the new proposed system, the current date will be provided automatically but patients can also record past headache events

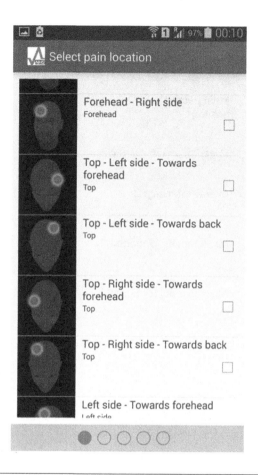

FIGURE 9.5

Inputting headache locations.

and can change date and time before submitting and add a headache event
record to their headache diary.

- **Symptoms**, which provides a list of configured pain symptoms associated with
  hydrocephalus. The user can select multiple symptoms from the provided list as
  shown in Figure 9.8. In the new proposed system, more symptoms related to
  hydrocephalus will be added.
- **Save Log Entry** provides a final summary page showing all the selected features
  and details provided from the previous pages. Here the user can do a final
  checkout before submitting the entry and saving the headache event. Figure 9.9
  presents the log-in details of the proposed system. In the new proposed system,
  this will also be featured, but it will reflect the new pain and symptoms submitted
  related to hydrocephalus.

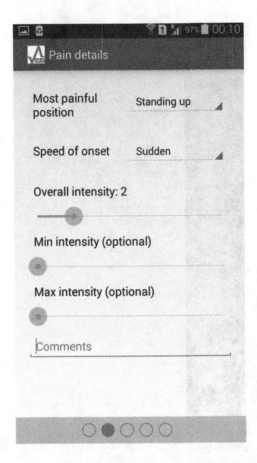

FIGURE 9.6

Inputting headache locations.

THE PROPOSED METHODS OF ANALYSIS

It is important to understand the underlying rationale of the framework embedded in the study. The purposes of the study are twofold: first, to develop an intelligent system to better manage patients with hydrocephalus; second, to assess this system in context in order to standardize the effective quality of the health care process by shaping and implementing a proper clinical pathway. In order to achieve these purposes, this research is grounded in the theory of integrated care pathway (also known as critical pathway, care map, or anticipated recovery pathway [19]). Because clinical pathways are used to systematically plan and follow up a patient-focused care program, it will be ideal for the study to use this framework as a pillar as the intention is to develop a better mechanism to support hydrocephalus patients throughout their lives.

As defined by the European Pathway Association in [20], a care pathway is a complex intervention for the mutual decision-making and organization of care

FIGURE 9.7

The start and end of the ongoing headache event.

processes for a well-defined group of patients during a well-defined period. Indeed, this study will analyze and devise a care pathway to manage a well-defined group of patients that has been diagnosed with hydrocephalus and are receiving continuous support and treatment for their condition. To successfully implement a clinical pathway as stated by the European Pathway Association in [20], it should include

- An explicit statement of the goals and key elements of care based on evidence, best practice, and patients' expectations and their characteristics.
- The facilitation of the communication among the team members and with patients and families.
- The coordination of the care process by coordinating the roles and sequencing the activities of the multidisciplinary care team, patients, and their relatives.
- The documentation, monitoring, and evaluation of variances and outcomes.
- The identification of the appropriate resources to support these patients efficiently and effectively.

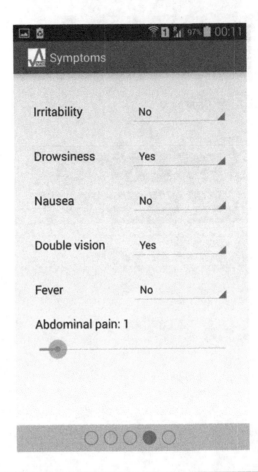

FIGURE 9.8

The selection screen of different symptoms.

In order to simplify the whole process and better understand how clinical pathways work, the Care Process Organization Triangle (CPOT) proposed by Vanhaecht in [21] will be used for this study. The CPOT has been adapted (Figure 9.10) to reflect the clinical pathway specifically designed for hydrocephalus patients. In summary, the CPOT is divided into three major categories, the structure, which is the neurology department within hospitals where the intervention will take place and the current procedures and practices to assess and treat patients diagnosed with hydrocephalus. The second category is the process, which includes the new mechanism, and the intervention used by the clinicians, neurologists, and neurosurgeons to deliver quality health care and to support their patients better. Because our proposed system will be patient centered (meaning that the patient is continuously involved in the monitoring and treatment process by the use of mobile app), the study will also involve the patient. The final and third category is the outcome.

FIGURE 9.9

The save log screen of the system.

This includes the actual results that show whether the intervention implemented helps clinicians with managing hydrocephalus patients better or not.

In view of the above, this research will be divided into three sequential substudies. These are as follows:

- Study one: The development of the intelligent system and the mobile app
- Study two: The usability and testing of the application by clinicians
- Study three: Patient satisfaction with the mobile app

Study One: Describe How the System Will Be Developed

The first study will involve current research on hydrocephalus and interviewing neurologists and neurosurgeons to elicit working procedures, patient assessment and monitoring procedures, valuable data items, user interface designs, and preferences to build the entire intelligent system.

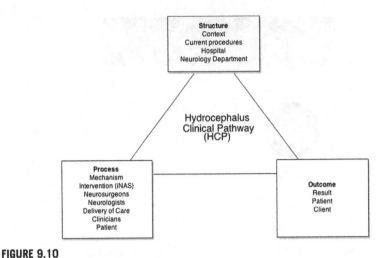

FIGURE 9.10

The hydrocephalus clinical pathway (HCP).

Study Two: The Usability and Testing of the Application by Clinicians

In order to test the usability of the application, a nonequivalent group quasi-experimental design will be used [22,23] and data collected through a quantitative daily diary technique [24]. A quasi-experimental design is preferred over a randomized control group design because the context features extensively. For this particular study, the whole population of pediatric neurologists and pediatric neurosurgeons who work at the Mater Dei general hospital in Malta will participate in the study. In addition, a further three pediatricians will also participate. Following a preexperimental questionnaire, the two neurologists, the one neurosurgeon, and the three pediatricians will be divided at random into two equivalent groups based on a measure of their current system knowledge, which will be taken to mark an equivalent baseline before being randomly assigned into two groups: the control group and the experimental group. This approach will reduce selection differences [22]. As Reichardt [22] stated, such initial differences between the groups of participants are a potentially serious threat to the internal validity of the design since the observed outcome difference between the treatment groups could be due not just to the effect of the treatment but to the effects of selection differences or prior learning. During study two, both groups will be given a questionnaire (pretest) to elicit current practices when managing their patients with hydrocephalus, knowledge of hospital system, and ease of use of patient management.

As shown in Figure 9.11, only the experimental group will then be given the software (intervention) to be used for 30 days and data will be collected every day. During this 30-day period, a time-based quantitative daily diary technique will be used to help us track the usability of the mobile application [24], while the control group will continue to use the manual system. Part of the 30-day

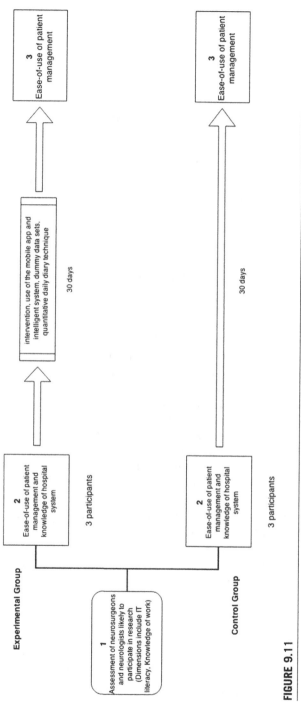

FIGURE 9.11

The iNAS nonequivalent quasi experimental design and assessment methodology.

measures will assess the effectiveness of the manual system (in the case of the control group) as opposed to the mobile app integration (in the case of the experimental group). These measures will be compared. At the end of the 30-day period, a posttest questionnaire (similar to the pretest) will be filled in by both groups. The results of this study may lead to refined improvements prior to study three.

Study Three: Patient Satisfaction with the Mobile App

In the final study, which treats patient satisfaction, a satisfaction with application qualitative and quantitative questionnaire will be distributed to a random sample of patients and/or their guardians about their satisfaction with usage. This questionnaire will measure (a) software user interaction, (b) learnability, (c) cognition facilitation, (d) user control and software flexibility, (e) system—real world match, (f) graphic design, and (g) navigation and editing/consistency. Using a 5-point Likert-type scale model, we will adapt our usability questionnaire as already used by Hollin et al. [25]. The in-depth interviews will be conducted 60 days after patients have been allowed to use the mobile app to integrate with the intelligent system. In addition, the results of study three will be shared with clinicians to assess patients' perception and understanding of the mobile app.

At all stages of the research study, prior to the experiment, the researcher will brief the respective participants and explain to them what the study is about, the consent form to fully participate in the study, and that we guarantee full confidentiality of the data and at no step will the researcher harm or deceive the participant.

In line with the above substudies, to establish and implement the integrated care pathway for patients with hydrocephalus, the study will describe health care systems, eHealth, mobile technologies in health care, the concept of evidence-based medicine, and evidence-based management. Furthermore, the study will define hydrocephalus and its main causes, the treatment options available, list the complications among hydrocephalus patients, and how young patients with hydrocephalus are assessed and supported within the neurology department. The study will also analyze the trends in the use and integration of artificial intelligence and data-mining techniques in health care and also show the design, implementation, and assessment process of the proposed system to support effectively and efficiently the management of hydrocephalus patients.

Our intelligent NeuroDiary Application System (iNAS) supports paraclinical evidence obtained from constant information from the patient, which enables clinicians to make a diagnosis of ongoing medical conditions and instigate treatment earlier. It overcomes the need to physically collect and interpret data from remote facilities, such as home, which can be a time-consuming process, expensive, and often impossible due to a clinician's existing work commitments. This has been one of the key motivating factors for the development of the intelligent NeuroDiary Application mobile platform and information system. Using the iNAS will provide benefits to both patients suffering with hydrocephalus and clinicians caring for them. It will allow patients to create a unique user profile that can be used to record all events and concerns that they may have as they live with their postoperative hydrocephalus treatments. It will inform patients and clinicians about concerns that arise, based on the clinical data recorded using the app as and when issues arise. This will help to elevate concerns about specific events that occur and to put the patient's mind at ease with regards to normal events that commonly occur after treatments, for example, after the installation of a shunt.

CONCLUSION

The main aim and objective of our study is implementing a proper integrated clinical pathway to better manage hydrocephalus patients, thus enhancing the quality of care across the continuum of the health care process by improving risk-adjusted patient outcomes, promoting patient safety, increasing patient satisfaction, increasing the efficiency in the caring and in the patient management process, and optimizing the use of resources. Our research supports the literature, which indicated that the development and use of mobile applications will continue to increase. Specifically in health care, mobile apps will become more sophisticated and will be increasingly integrated in the fields of medicine and health care. Currently, a trend is becoming evident in improving current health applications and developing new mobile systems using patient-centered approach (mHealth). Although research shows that many medical mobile applications are being developed bluntly as a result of heightened enthusiasm for technologies, mobile users, many of which may be patients and medical staff, need to rigorously verify the application by identifying its sources and analyzing its reliability. Only at this point will users trust and use the mobile application for medical purposes.

This chapter highlighted and presented the necessary data items needed to support the management of patients diagnosed with hydrocephalus. The data elements presented are the result of intensive interviews carried out with a team of experts from the neurology and pediatric departments. Full requirement specifications of the proposed system have been developed as a result of this investigation. This will be used to collect the required patients' details, information about their condition, and their headache events using the data elements that we have identified in this study as shown in Tables 9.2–9.4. With regard to the current managing practices of patients diagnosed with hydrocephalus within the pediatric neurology unit, it is clearly evident that there is a lack of digitized information and proper intelligent systems that are now becoming essential to manage patients better. From our findings, we have realized and established numerous data elements, which were produced and verified by a panel of experts within the neurology department. These data elements are needed by clinicians and neurologists so as to process their patients' medical records efficiently, as well as to be able to visualize future analytical reports that will be produced by our intelligent system. Thus, we are in the process of developing an intelligent system, which will be accessible on Android, Windows phones, and Apple devices to reach a wider audience of users while providing a reliable solution that addresses the needs of hydrocephalus patient management.

REFERENCES

[1] Handel MJ. mHealth (Mobile Health)—Using Apps for Health and Wellness. Explore 2011;7(4):256—61.

[2] Smartphone OS Market Share, Q1; 2014. Available at: http://www.idc.com/prodserv/ smartphone-os-market-share.jsp (accessed on July 1, 2014)

[3] Hormby T. The story behind Apple's Newton; 2006. Available at: http://lowendmac. com/orchard/06/john-sculley-newton-origin.html (accessed on June 29, 2014).

[4] Sclafani J, Tirrell TF, Franko OI. Mobile Tablet Use among Academic Physicians and Trainees. J Med Syst 2013;37(1):1—6.

[5] Kovach S. Android Is The Most Popular Smartphone Operating System In The US. Available at: http://www.businessinsider.com/kantar-smartphone-market-share-2013-6 (accessed on June 19, 2013).

[6] Apple. App Store Tops 40 Billion Downloads with Almost Half in 2012. Available at: http://www.apple.com/pr/library/2013/01/07App-Store-Tops-40-Billion-Downloads- with-Almost-Half-in-2012.html (accessed on June 20, 2013).

[7] Pure Oxygen Labs. How Many Apps Are in Each App Store? 2013. Available at: http:// www.pureoxygenmobile.com/how-many-apps-in-each-app-store/ (accessed on June 20, 2013).

[8] Bertolucci J. Smartphone Sales Boom — Who Needs A Laptop? 2012. Available at: http://www.techhive.com/article/249313/smartphone_sales_boom_who_needs_a_ laptop_.html (accessed on 20 June 2013).

[9] Robinson T, Cronin T, Ibrahim H, Jinks M, Molitor T, Newman J, Shapiro J. Smart- phone Use and Acceptability among Clinical Medical Students: A Questionnaire- Based Study. J Med Syst 2013;37(3):1—7.

[10] National Institute of Health. Available at: http://www.nih.gov/news/health/feb2011/od- 28.htm (accessed on July 1, 2014).

[11] Tirrell TF, Franko OI. Smartphone App Use among Medical Providers in ACGME Training Programs. J Med Syst 2013;36(5):3135—9.

[12] Paschou M, Sakkopoulos E, Tsakalidis A. easyHealthApps: e-Health Apps Dynamic Generation for Smartphones & Tablets. J Med Syst 2013;37(3):1—12.

[13] Payne FK, Wharrad H, Watts K. Smartphone and medical related App use among medical students and junior doctors in the United Kingdom (UK): a regional survey. J Med Inform Decis Mak 2012;12(1):121—32.

[14] Peck AD. App-solutely fabulous. Hundreds of new apps for iPAD and tablets make mHealth a reality and a lifestyle choice. Med Econ 2011;88(22). Available at: http:// medicaleconomics.modernmedicine.com/medical-economics/news/modernmedicine/ modern-medicine-feature-articles/app-solutely-fabulous-mobile-?id=&sk=&date=& %0A%09%09%09&pageID=1 (accessed on 2 July 2014).

[15] Bennett CC, Hauser K. Artificial intelligence framework for simulating clinical decision-making: A Markov decision process approach. Artificial intelligence in medicine 2013;57(1):9—19.

[16] Kandasamy J, Jenkins MD, Mallucci CL. Contemporary Management and recent advances in paediatric hydrocephalus. Br Med J 2011;343:d4191.

[17] Walker HK, Hall WD, Hurst JW. Clinical Methods: The History, Physical, and Laboratory Examinations. 3rd ed. Boston: Butterworths; 1990 Available at: http://www.ncbi.nlm.nih.gov/books/NBK380/ (accessed on 1 July 2014).

[18] Farrugia A, Al-Jumeily D, Al-Jumaily M, Hussain A, Lamb D. Medical Diagnosis: are Artificial Intelligence systems able to diagnose the underlying causes of specific headaches? In: Proceedings of 6th International Conference on Developments in eSystems Engineering. IEEE Computer Society; 2014. ISBN 978-1-4799-5263-2; 2014.

[19] Royal College of Nursing. Care Pathways. Retrieved from: www.rcn.org.uk. (accessed on 15 December 2014).

[20] European Pathway Association. Clinical Care Pathways. Retrieved from: www.e-p-a.org. (accessed on 15 December 2014).

[21] Vanhaecht K, De Witte K, Sermeus W. The impact of clinical pathways on the organisation of care processes (PhD dissertation). KULeuven, 154pp, Katholieke Universiteit Leuven; 2007.

[22] Reichardt CS. The SAGE Handbook of Quantitative Methods in Psychology: Quasi-Experimental Design. Thousand Oaks, CA: Sage.

[23] Osborn DR. Quasi-experimental designs. Salem Press Encyclopedia of Health; 2014.

[24] Iida M, Shrout PE, Laurenceau J-P, Bolger N. Using diary methods in psychological research. APA Handbook of Research Methods in Psychology, vol 1. Foundations, Planning, Measures and Psychometrics. Washington, DC: American Psychological Association; 2012.

[25] Hollin II, Griffin MM, Kachnowski SS. How will we know if it's working? A multifaceted approach to measuring usability of a specialty-specific electronic medical record. Health Inform J 2012;18(3):219–32.

[26] Farrugia A, Al-Jumeily D. The design and implementation and evaluation of a Web-based Student Teachers' ePortfolio (STeP). Int J Web Appl 2012;4(2):96–105.

[27] Laudon K, Laudon J. Management information systems: Managing the digital firm. 13th ed. Boston: Pearson; 2014.

[28] Chaffey D. E-business and e-commerce management: Strategy, implementation and practice. 4th ed. Harlow, Essex: FT Prentice Hall; 2009.

[29] JQuery Mobile. A Touch-Optimised Web Framework. Available at: http://jquerymobile.com/, (accessed on 3 March 2014).

Sociocultural and Technological Barriers Across all Phases of Implementation for Mobile Health in Developing Countries

10

Yvonne O' Connor[1], Siobhan O' Connor[2], Ciara Heavin[1], Joe Gallagher[3], John O' Donoghue[4]

Health Information Systems Research Centre, University College Cork, Ireland[1]; School of Nursing, Midwifery & Social Work, University of Manchester, UK[2]; Health Research Group, University College Dublin, Ireland[3]; Global eHealth Unit, Department of Primary Care and Public Health, Imperial College London, UK[4]

E-mail: Y.OConnor@ucc.ie, siobhan.oconnor@manchester.ac.uk, c.heavin@ucc.ie, joejgallagher@gmail.com, j.odonoghue@imperial.ac.uk

INTRODUCTION

The advent of mobile information technology (IT) has brought about profound opportunities in terms of their organizational application [1] by introducing new flexibility in terms of when, where, and how these technologies can be applied [2]. In the last decade, the application of mobile IT within health care, referred to as mobile Health or mHealth [3], has revolutionized the delivery of health care services [4]. The last decade witnessed a multitude of mHealth initiatives being deployed worldwide, with reports of more than 100,000 applications currently available to a variety of users [5]. mHealth offers a range of opportunities to its end users, from greater patient empowerment to improved clinical decision making, disease surveillance and monitoring, behavioral change and self-monitoring [5], to name but a few. With the documented evidence of numerous benefits and positive health-related outcomes associated with mHealth initiatives, many new mHealth projects are becoming ever more commonplace in developing regions [6]. mHealth is considered an appropriate avenue for delivering health care services, as the health care infrastructure and services are often insufficient in developing countries [7]. The unique characteristics of mHealth (e.g., ability of health workers and patients to communicate over vast distances) help improve the existing underresourced health infrastructures, ultimately translating into benefits for patients [8]. However, it is reported that some mHealth projects have failed (as depicted later in this chapter). Failure is defined as an infrequent, inappropriate, and ineffective long-term use of mHealth technologies [9]. As a result, this chapter's primary focus is on identifying barriers to mHealth technology implementation in an effort to understand why some mHealth initiatives fail. To understand this phenomenon, the IT implementation process is subsequently described.

MOBILE HEALTH IMPLEMENTATION

Implementation of IT is defined as "an organisational effort directed toward diffusing appropriate information technology within a user community" [10]. Prescott and Conger [11] argue that some studies embrace the concept of "adoption" to cover the entire process of implementation. However, research exists which demonstrates that implementing IT is performed over several phases. In 1990, Cooper and Zmud [12] presented a detailed overview of the implementation phases for IT. They proposed that IT implementation consisted of six phases, namely, (1) initiation, (2) adoption, (3) adaptation, (4) acceptance, (5) routinization, and (6) infusion. Each phase is described in Table 10.1 as per Cooper and Zmud [12].

Although numerous implementation models exist in the literature [13-14] the researchers employ the Cooper and Zmud model [12] of IT implementation for three reasons: (1) the model is one of the most comprehensive models in literature for exploring IT implementation; (2) each phase is clearly defined, making it easier for examination purposes; and (3) the definition of IT implementation adopted for this study coincides with the definition proposed by Cooper and Zmud [12]. Employing a theoretical lens following Cooper and Zmud's [12] technological diffusion model will enable the researchers to gain better insights into mHealth implementation processes within a developing world context. Implementation of any IT solution is usually a costly and difficult process [15]. In developing countries, the

Table 10.1 Description of Phases in Technological Diffusion Model

Phase	Description
Initiation	Scanning of organizational opportunities with mHealth technologies
Adoption	Negotiations to achieve organizational backing
Adaptation	Development, installation, and maintenance of new mHealth technology
Acceptance	Organizational members are induced to commit to using the new mHealth technology
Routinization	Organization's consideration of the new mHealth technology as a normal activity
Infusion	Integration of new mHealth technology with the organization's system to support higher levels of individual/organizational work

Adapted from Cooper and Zmud [12]

implementation process is often more challenging due to economic, demographic, and environmental factors [16]. Yet there exists a dearth of research that focuses on mHealth technology implementation in developing countries. Moreover, extant research is criticized for embracing the concept of adoption to cover the entire process of implementation although numerous phases exist. This chapter seeks to address this gap in extant literature by identifying key barriers to mHealth implementation, vis-à-vis a literature review, using the Cooper and Zmud [12] model as a baseline reference.

METHODOLOGY

A literature review across a number of domains was performed. The selection strategy employed to identify the primary, secondary, and tertiary literature is illustrated in Figure 10.1.

This nascent research area relies on a significant body of interdisciplinary scholarship [17] that encompasses IT/technology, health, developing countries, eHealth, and mHealth literature (Figure 10.1). In order to fully pursue the concept of mHealth implementation in developing countries, the authors had to move beyond the primary literature to provide comprehensive coverage of the topic under investigation. First, mHealth in developing countries research was reviewed and examples are provided in subsequent sections (Step 1a in Figure 10.1). When this search revealed no documented examples, as per Cooper and Zmud [12] implementation phase definition, the authors reviewed the eHealth literature in developing countries (Step 1b in Figure 10.1). In reviewing later implementation

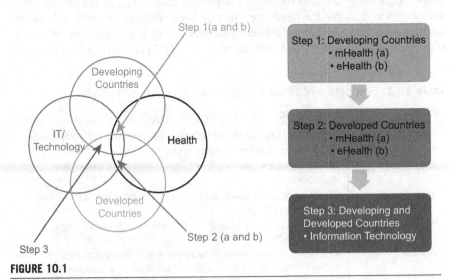

FIGURE 10.1

Literature Selection Strategy.

phases, it became apparent that little evidence on mHealth and eHealth research in developing countries exist, which required the authors to view potential barriers initially from a developed country (Step 2a and b in Figure 10.1) and a wider IT perspective (Step 3 in Figure 10.1). This is due to the fact that the vast majority of mHealth initiatives deployed in developing countries are pilot studies and have not yet reached large-scale nationwide implementation [8]. The authors acknowledge that it will take some time to reach a level of maturity of mHealth in developing countries.

POTENTIAL BARRIERS TO mHEALTH IMPLEMENTATION IN DEVELOPING COUNTRIES

This section identifies various barriers that could hinder individual phases of implementation. According to Norris et al. [18], "frequently, public health interventions and campaigns have limited success because they emphasise the need for change when none is apparent and they fail to raise personal awareness." This section comprises seven subsections, six of which are structured based on the Cooper and Zmud model presented in the second section of this chapter, while the seventh subsection summarizes the findings.

POTENTIAL BARRIERS TO mHEALTH INITIATION

As the name suggests, the initiation phase is the first phase of implementation according to the Cooper and Zmud model [12]. During this phase, active and/or passive scanning of organizational problems/opportunities and IT solutions are undertaken. That implies seeking new technological innovations to assist organizations in achieving their goals and/or address existing problems. From reviewing and synthesizing the literature, the following barriers have been identified that impact the initiation process of mobile IT, namely, lack of market competition, lack of awareness, and switching costs.

Market Uncertainty

It is deduced from the work of Mansfield et al [19] that market uncertainty can diminish the possible introduction of technological innovations into organizations. In 1986, Robertson and Gatignon [20] argued that the motivation to recognize new technology stems from the external market. This point is further reinforced by Funk and Methe [21], who found that market uncertainty can impact an organization's decision to employ technological innovations. However, because of economic hardship faced by organizations in developing countries, the introduction of mHealth onto the marketplace has been limited. Many of the mHealth projects explored in development countries are funded and transferred from western societies, primarily on a pilot study basis [22,23].

Lack of Awareness

One of the major obstacles faced by users in resource-poor settings is their unawareness of the opportunities mobile technologies may provide in their location. This unfamiliarity with potential mobile technological resources is a counterproductive factor when seeking new technological resources, as information is required to facilitate decision making and stimulate progress to ensure existing practices can be improved upon. This inexperience or unawareness of the benefits of using mobile IT to solve organizational problems and/or increase opportunities therefore goes unnoticed. As such, lack of awareness hinders mobile IT implementation at the initiation phase.

Switching Costs

With various competing priorities for a dwindling financial resource, organizations in developing countries are often compelled to examine the criticality of investing in potential products. When deciding to invest in mHealth, users may switch from using one technological innovation to another, or substituting vendors (commonly referred to as "switching costs"). Borrowing and adapting the work of Kim and Gupta [24], this study defines switching costs as an organization/individual's subjective perception of disutility (e.g., time, effort, economic resources, and emotional discomfort) associated with the process of switching from one vendor to another. In developing countries, the luxury and opportunities of switching technologies is not feasible because of economic constraints in such environments. In general, initial investments already devoted to existing technologies in the organization/individual's current situation may discourage customers from switching to new mobile IT [25]. As a result, switching costs are likely to play a substantive role as a barrier to mobile IT initiation.

Politics

It is reported that internal politics can also have a major influence on the direction and depth of technological advancements within a given context [26]. In his work, Ziaie identified a number of impediments to IT implementation in a developing country (Iran) based on political or ideological reasons, including, sanctions, lack of support from highest political bodies, and unfamiliarity of higher authorities with IT-related complications. Kalathil [27] argues that information transparency that can be facilitated by IT may threaten decision makers in developing countries where corruption is more prevalent. Without sufficient governmental support, mHealth initiatives are less likely to succeed.

POTENTIAL BARRIERS TO mHEALTH ADOPTION

The adoption phase of the Cooper and Zmud [12] model is the second stage of implementation, whereby the primary focus is on negotiations to achieve organizational backing. To achieve this, it is important that a decision is attained to invest resources necessary to accommodate the implementation effort. Indeed, Chib [28] contends that the nascent stage of mHealth adoption has resulted in an overstatement of its associated benefits. A review of the literature revealed that this process encounters a number of barriers, namely, insufficient readiness/resources, lack of supporting policy, and social influence/contextual barriers.

Insufficient Resources

It is reported that the majority of mHealth initiatives in developing countries are funded by external benefactors and are not self-sustaining, thereby affecting long-term sustainability of such projects [29]. It is imperative that resources and support are available when implementing IT applications. Without sufficient resources, mHealth solutions are destined to fail, as experienced by Medhi et al. [30] and Matheson et al. [31]. Both researcher groups witnessed drawbacks to using mHealth solutions due to insufficient technical support and funding difficulties, respectively.

Lack of Supporting Policy/Legal Issues

Policy pertaining to mHealth can be defined as "a set of statements, directives, regulations, laws, and judicial interpretations that direct and manage the life cycle of mHealth" [32]. The use of mHealth approaches within or between institutions involves several factors that require proper planning, supported by well-defined policies at the institutional, jurisdictional, and global levels. The absence and variety of these policies may lead to inadvertent widening of gaps in health status and knowledge levels between different sectors of the population, and increase rather than decrease health inequity. A systematic review of policy issues within the eHealth domain found 99 different policy issues, which could be grouped into nine categories [33]. Recent WHO analysis indicates a lack of knowledge about available mHealth applications and public health outcomes and absence of supportive policies at the country or regional level [34]. Low- and middle-income countries struggle to develop and implement policy and legal solutions in a rapidly changing field given their constrained resources.

Social Influence/Contextual Factors

Social influence is complex in nature and may be viewed from three perspectives: (1) compliance, (2) identification, and (3) internalization, all of which can be affected by a number of contextual factors, including limited resources and lack of expertise [35]. As outlined in O' Connor et al. [36], a person's intention to adopt a new mHealth technology is directly related to a number of contextual factors in association with the individual's value system, which is heavily influenced by social values among others. This is an important note, in that mHealth solutions that may be acceptable within a developed country setting may not directly translate successfully to a developing countries environment unless the individual's value system, which includes social influence, is correctly taken into account. Social influence should not be seen as an independent or standalone construct when looking at adoption [37,38]; therefore, a more holistic viewpoint should be considered to help ensure overall adoption.

POTENTIAL BARRIERS TO mHEALTH ADAPTATION

Adaptation is the third phase of IT implementation as outlined in Cooper and Zmud's model [12]. This encompasses the development, installation, and maintenance of the IT application in the organization. A review of the literature revealed that this process encounters a number of barriers that can impact the adaptation phase of mHealth implementation, namely, language barrier, lack of training, poor availability of mHealth technologies, poor technical infrastructure, and issues regarding security and privacy of data.

Language Barriers

Language barriers have been identified as another factor that can negatively impact how mHealth technologies can be used, especially in low-resource settings. Although web-based machine language translations continue to improve [39], there is a lack of tailored applications designed to meet the needs of developing counties. For instance, South Africa not only has 11 official languages but many more indigenous ones [40] that are rarely reflected in mHealth technologies. This can cause barriers when using mHealth technologies as it can be difficult to scale up the intervention to address each individual language.

Lack of Training

The education and training of frontline health care workers is also critical when implementing mHealth initiatives in low-resource settings [29]. Chib's [18] study of midwives in Indonesia showed that although they were comfortable using the basic text messaging and call functions on their mobile phones, they required additional support and training to use more advanced features. The brain drain of highly skilled workers from low-resource settings is another well-documented issue [41] that leaves a shortage of well-educated and technically competent health care professionals to roll out of mHealth programs. Hafkin and Taggart [42] highlight the gender inequalities that exist within developing countries, with women receiving less education than men, leaving them with limited IT knowledge and skills. In the context of developing countries, it is reported that 41% of the population are nonliterate [43], and even the literate among the poor are considered novice users of computer technologies [30]. This directly impacts the implementation of mHealth as many women are health care workers as well as community health care workers.

Poor Technical Infrastructure

The technical infrastructure underpinning any mobile IT system not only consists of mobile devices with appropriate software and operating systems but also reliable mobile networks and protocols for transmitting data [44]. Network connectivity and high bandwidth are important because a slow or regularly interrupted connection can affect the quality of information provided to users. Extant research identifies the reliability and coverage of the network infrastructure as key barriers to mHealth projects [19]. Although mobile phone coverage has skyrocketed in Africa over the last decade [45], it is still not accessible in many rural areas. Unfortunately, the availability of high-speed networks, especially in sub-Saharan Africa, continues to suppress organizations from participating in the economy by using mobile IT [46]. An example of this can be found in the work of Blaschke et al. [47], who reported that a mobile application to monitor childhood nutrition in Malawi was hampered by poor network coverage in some districts. This prevented local community health workers sending SMS messages at the point of care.

Security and Privacy Issues

The implementation of mHealth solutions can also be limited by data security and privacy concerns that arise from legal and ethical issues related to the confidentiality of patient information [48]. These concerns can range from unauthorized access or theft of mobile devices [49], to poor security standards and policies [50], and unregulated or malicious mobile applications [51]. Chang et al. [52] reported mobile devices being stolen during the implementation of an antiretroviral treatment program for HIV/AIDS among peer health workers in Uganda, thus endangering patient confidentiality.

Poor Change Management

Change management is a complex and dynamic process that requires a systematic approach to dealing with change both from the organizational and individual perspective [53]. Effective change management is pertinent throughout implementation, because if this process is poorly managed, it can mean the abandonment of mHealth systems [54]. Wijethilake et al. [55] highlighted that change management in the context of electronic health solutions in developing countries has not been well researched. Mars [56] reports that poor change management can derail mHealth implementation when a tele-rehabilitation system that was rolled out in South Africa failed due in part to poor change management, among other factors.

POTENTIAL BARRIERS TO mHEALTH ACCEPTANCE

The next phase of IT implementation in Cooper and Zmud's model of technological diffusion [12] is acceptance. During this stage, organizational staff are persuaded and encouraged to use the IT application so that it becomes part of organizational work. A review of the literature revealed that this process encounters a number of barriers that can impact the acceptance phase of mobile IT implementation, namely, user resistance, cultural value, practical technology issues, and lack of motivation.

User Resistance

User resistance is defined as "opposition of a user to change associated with a new IS implementation" [57]. Studies indicate that one of the challenges to mHealth remains the acceptability of the technologies to both patients and health care practitioners [19]. Skulimowski [58] posits that clinicians are typically more traditional when it comes to alternatives to face-to-face delivery of medicine. Hasvold and Scholl [59] found that a mobile application, introduced to digitize a whiteboard used to organize patients and surgeries, reduced nurses' coordination and communication with colleagues. The decreased personal interaction led to strong resistance from nursing staff to and ultimately abandonment of the mobile device as they valued regular professional contact for learning and day-to-day support managing a busy surgical unit.

Cultural Value

Cultural differences that exist in countries may affect behavior in the use and adoption of technology [60]. Culture diversity between developing and developed countries can be observed based on "individualism versus collectivism," "power distance," and "masculinity versus femininity" [61,62]. Bofu et al. [63] reports on gender disparity; women and even girls have been sidelined in development issues, and when they attempt to contribute, men have overshadowed them. This highlights, for instance, the cultural values which exist in some developing countries. According to Al Sukkar and Hasan [64], it is unlikely that cultural values can be easily changed or adjusted to conform to any changes introduced by new technology. This conformity, therefore, may have an impact on scanning of organizational opportunities and IT solutions in developing countries. Moreover, Braa and Nermunkh [65] found that because of the contextual constraints, the social system perspective is more critical in the third than in the first world. Any technological solutions that fail to capture local cultural factors in developing countries are often reported to fail [24].

Practical Technology Issues

Practical issues with mobile equipment can hamper the adaptation of mobile IT applications. Commonly cited, practical issues pertaining to mHealth technologies documented in the literature include battery power and screen size [19]. Battery issues are of particular importance in developing countries where electricity supply is unreliable because of insufficient generating capacity and a poor infrastructure [66]. Screen size is another practical issue that can affect the adaptation of mHealth technology. Chae and Kim [67] contend that a small screen combined with increasingly complex functionality can frustrate users of mobile devices. This is due to the fact that users can only view a small amount of information because of the size of the display, forcing them to waste time scrolling repeatedly or performing additional menu selections, which can often lead to navigation errors [68]. Zolfo et al. [69] demonstrate how these problems can be exacerbated in low-resources settings where there is limited access to modern mobile technology. They compared the use of a Nokia N95 to an iPhone among health care workers in Peru and found that the small screen and keyboard of the device limited the physicians' abilities to access educational material on HIV/AIDS treatment and management.

Lack of Motivation

One of the many challenges when implementing mHealth initiatives in developing countries is adequately motivating the many stakeholders involved at local, regional, and national levels [70]. Farrington et al. [71] cite inertia and the vested interests of different groups, such as health care workers, policy makers, and politicians, for poor progress of mHealth interventions for mental illness in poorer countries. They report this disinterest stems from a desire to maintain the status quo and prevent change, which could potentially revolutionize how the health system operates.

POTENTIAL BARRIERS TO mHEALTH ROUTINIZATION

Routinization is the second last phase of the Cooper and Zmud [12] model of implementation. At this stage of implementation, the mHealth technology has been utilized in practice for a long period of time, and often cannot be achieved if users face and do not overcome the previously documented barriers. As a result, the use of the technology is not perceived as novel but as a normal activity [72]. From synthesizing the literature pertaining to routinization, one key issue, that is, discontinued use, emerged.

Discontinued Use

Research has shown that the long-term sustainability of any technological solution depends on its continued use as opposed to initial usage [73]. The concept of "continuance" has proven to be instrumental for the success of mHealth initiatives in developing countries as shown by Akter and his colleagues [74,75]. Medhi et al. [31] found that rural health care workers using the CommCare application in India reverted to traditional paper-based data collection methods after a period of time using the mHealth solution. Discontinued use will have a profound negative impact on the implementation of mHealth initiatives in developing countries. That is, the benefits obtained from using mHealth will not translate to the patient and/ or clinician, which may not compensate for what is usually a costly and difficult implementation process [16]. In addition, negative perceptions around future mHealth projects may emerge as end users may consider that invested time, effort, and money into a project as wasted.

POTENTIAL BARRIERS TO mHEALTH INFUSION

Infusion is the last phase of implementation, where the mobile IT is used to its fullest potential [12]. That implies that the end user utilizes various features that the IT artifact has to offer, integrate the IT in their work, while seeking novel ways of using the IT outside of its intended use [76]. Infusion of mHealth technologies in developing countries is not well documented. The authors therefore examine research surrounding IT infusion and apply it to mHealth. The following barriers have been identified from the literature that can impact the infusion of mobile IT, namely, habit, lack of personal innovativeness, and immaturity of the system.

Habit

The impact of habit on IT infusion has been explored in extant infusion literature [77-78] and found to have a significant effect on infusion. Habit refers to "the extent to which an individual tends to use mobile Health technology automatically (adapted from Limayem and Hirt [79]) often inferred from past experiences" [80]. Limayem and Hirt [82] found that habit plays an important role in explaining usage behavior. Subsequently, Limayem et al. [81] found that habitual routines are often established during the routinization phase, which can hinder infusion of technological solutions [73]. The underlying premise for this argument is that individuals who have made it customary to habitually utilize mHealth technologies in a restrictive manner, become less receptive to novel uses of the technology and, thus, maintain a level of current usage through established ways [78]. Therefore, preestablished methods of performing actions using mHealth solutions may prohibit the user from progressing beyond the routinization phase and not achieving infusion.

Lack of Personal Innovativeness

Another barrier to mHealth infusion pertains to the innovativeness levels of individual users. Personal innovativeness refers to the extent to which a person's predisposition or attitude reflecting his or her tendency to experiment with mHealth technologies independently of the communicated experience of others (adapted from Schillewaert et al. [82]). That implies individuals must be open to innovate with existing mHealth solutions. As part of their research, Jones et al. [26] found that personal innovativeness was positively related to infusion. The underlying rationale for the strong association between personal innovativeness and infusion is that users who infuse any technological solution are required to use all possible and appropriate applications for both intended and unintended purposes [80]. As a result, a lack of personal innovativeness may restrict the user from experimenting with the mHealth technology and gaining additional insights into how the mHealth technology can be fully applied, thus achieving maximum benefits.

Immaturity of the System

Maturation of technology refers to the degree to which a technology is mature for widespread implementation (adapted from Wu and Subramaniam [83]). Therefore, a technological solution would be considered immature when it has associated system restrictiveness and incompatibility with existing systems. Previous research has demonstrated that mobile IT with a high degree of system restrictiveness had negative impacts on utilization [84,88] as users have no freedom to restructure the system to their own preferences in order to maximize potential benefits. Mobile IT used in developing countries is based on older technologies that offer basic and limited functionality to the end user (i.e., little smartphone use exists). This limited functionality may not facilitate compatibility with existing systems. Nowadays, smartphones offer an array of functionality that integrates previously independent systems (e.g., GPS, camera, and voice/text communication). Yet, there is a paucity of smartphones usage in developing regions. In terms of its immature development status, mHealth in developing regions may not demonstrate the full potentials of mHealth for adopters as the perceived benefits in such regions are not well established. The underlying premise of this argument is that the basic mobile solutions employed by users in developing countries offer specific technological capabilities, which may potentially place constraints on the users.

POTENTIAL BARRIERS TO MOBILE IT IMPLEMENTATION

A summary of the barriers associated with individual implementation phases of the Cooper and Zmud [12] technological diffusion model are presented in Figure 10.2. From the literature analysis, it is evident that phases of the mHealth implementation process experience a collection of barriers or challenges that could have an impact on mHealth implementation. From Figure 10.2, the nature of the barriers provides an insight into the complexity associated with each phase. The following section will discuss this in greater depth.

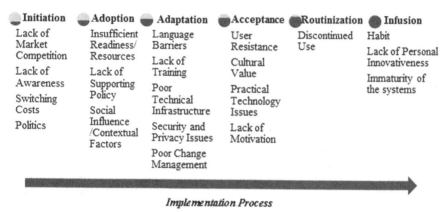

Implementation Process

FIGURE 10.2

Barriers that could impact mHealth Implementation.

DISCUSSION AND FINDINGS

The findings reveal that numerous barriers could potentially hinder the implementation of mHealth initiatives within developing countries. From reviewing and synthesizing the findings, it is evident that the barriers (a) can be categorized as sociocultural and technological barriers and (b) exist across multiple levels, namely, individual, organizational, and governmental.

The existing state of low-resource countries in terms of the health domain is heavily influenced by their sociocultural traditions. This organizational socioculture is deeply embedded within health processes and is very different to that in developed countries. That is, mHealth initiatives primarily adhere to western designs and fall short of recognizing the unique sociocultural factors associated with developing regions [24]. Sociocultural factors are described by Shier et al. [85] as "those aspects of the social environment that are a direct result of the intersection between the cultural underpinnings of a society (such as a collective system of values, beliefs, and thoughts) and its social processes and organisational mechanisms (such as, social interaction and relationships and institutional dynamics)." Neglecting such sociocultural factors when implementing mHealth could result in failure. When implementing IT (such as mHealth) it is imperative therefore to be aware of the sociocultural aspects involved [86]. Sociocultural barriers to mHealth implementation in developing countries identified in this chapter include lack of market competition, lack of awareness, switching costs, politics (initiation phase); lack of supporting policy, social influence, perceived threat/mismanagement expectations (adoption phase); language barriers, lack of training, poor change management (adaptation phase); user resistance, cultural value, lack of motivation (acceptance phase), and habit (infusion phase).

Addressing sociocultural barriers is only one stepping stone toward resolving issues associated with mHealth implementation in developing countries. Practitioners and academics should be aware of the technological barriers that could hinder the implementation process. Technological barriers are described as limited access to useful, relevant, and appropriate hardware and software, especially in "instances where the use of the technology is perceived as not being sufficient to perform the tasks or accomplish the objectives for which the technology was initially utilised" [87]. Technological barriers are often reported as a significant cause of poor implementation and diffusion rates in developing countries [88]. Technological barriers identified in this chapter that could potentially hinder the implementation of mHealth solutions in developing countries include lack of market competition (initiation phase); insufficient readiness/resources (adoption phase); poor technical infrastructure, security and privacy issues (adaptation phase); practical technology issues (acceptance phase); discontinued use (routinization phase); and immaturity of the system (infusion phase).

Our findings reinforce previous research that the sociocultural, in addition to the technological, dimensions associated with ICT initiatives are essential for successful implementation. Our findings also reveal that barriers to mHealth implementation exist across various stakeholders at different levels within the health system. That is, barriers to mHealth initiatives are observed at the individual, organizational, and national level. The majority of the barriers are identified at the organizational level. Despite this, all levels identified are interconnected and require effective communication and collaboration to facilitate the successful implementation of mHealth initiatives. At the national level, appropriate policies, procedures, and ethical and legal frameworks should be established to ensure that organizations and, subsequently, can implement mHealth initiatives. This finding argues that implementing mHealth initiatives requires multistakeholder input.

CONCLUSION

One approach to ensuring that mHealth initiatives can be successfully implemented and used is to identify barriers to implementation. For developing countries, to date a vast array of research exists that focuses on barriers to generic IT adoption; however, the majority of these papers embrace the concept of adoption to cover the entire process of implementation. As outlined earlier, implementation of IT artifacts occur over six phases (Table 10.1). This chapter makes a very clear contribution to both theory and practice. The barriers for mHealth deployment within a developing country setting are presented under each of the six implementation phases. This provides a high degree of granularity, which in turn enables the authors to classify the barriers from a sociocultural and technological barrier perspective. This degree of detail will greatly increase the chances for success when mHealth solutions are deployed within low-resource settings.

To our knowledge, Cooper and Zmud's model has not been utilized in this manner in other studies of mHealth in low-resource settings. Although this chapter has sought to identify barriers that occur at each phase of mHealth implementation, our approach has some limitations. First, the exploratory nature of the literature has meant that a rigorous or systematic search of the literature was not undertaken. This could result in the omission of additional barriers to mHealth implementation in extant literature that has not been included in our results. In addition, most case studies that were used did not explicitly state the phase of implementation being undertaken, so our interpretations were based on evaluating Cooper and Zmud's definitions against the description of the mHealth initiatives uncovered in the literature. Although every effort was made to identify the correct phase of implementation in line with the Cooper and Zmud model, the barriers outlined above are based on our interpretation and we would actively encourage future research in this area to describe in detail how mHealth programs are implemented. That being said, the taxonomy of barriers to mHealth implementation presented in this chapter underpins the key issues that occur when rolling out an mHealth program in a developing country.

This chapter provides for the first time a detailed step-by-step breakdown of the implementation process for mHealth in developing countries. Future research should focus on a qualitative systematic review to take into account the complex nature of mHealth implementations to provide a higher degree of rigor in the research findings. This will help to ensure that mHealth solutions will have a greater chance of success when implemented within low-resource settings.

REFERENCES

[1] Scheepers H, Scheepers R. The Implementation of Mobile Technology in Organizations: Expanding Individual Use Contexts. ICIS 2004.
[2] Varshney U. Mobile health: Four emerging themes of research. Decis Supp Syst 2014; 66:20–35.

[3] Istepanian RSH, Jovanov E, Zhang YT. Guest Editorial Introduction to the Special Section on M-Health: Beyond Seamless Mobility and Global Wireless Health-Care Connectivity. IEEE Trans Inform Technol Biomed 2004;8:405–14.

[4] Burley L, Scheepers H, Fisher J. Diffusion of Mobile Technology in Healthcare. In: Proceedings of the Euro mGOV First European Mobile Government Conference. Brighton, UK; 2005.

[5] XU W, LIU Y. mHealthApps: A Repository and Database of Mobile Health Apps. JMIR Mhealth Uhealth 2015;3:e28.

[6] Nhavoto JA, Grönlund A. Mobile Technologies and Geographic Information Systems to Improve Health Care Systems: A Literature Review. JMIR mhealth uhealth 2014;2:e21.

[7] Kahn JG, Yang JS, Kahn JS. "Mobile" Health Needs and Opportunities in Developing Countries. Health Aff 2010;29:252–8.

[8] Chib A, van Velthover MH, Car J. mHealth Adoption In Low-Resource Environments: A Review of the Use of Mobile Healthcare In Developing Countries. J Health Commun 2014:1–53.

[9] Lyytinen K, Hirschheim R. Information Systems Failures: A Survey and Classification of the Empirical Literature. Oxford: Oxford Surveys in Information Technology, Oxford University Press; 1987. p. 257–309.

[10] Kwon TH, Zmud R. Unifying the Fragmented Models of Information Systems Implementation. In: Boland RJ, Hirschheim R, editors. Critical Issues in Information Systems Research. New York: John Wiley and Sons; 1987. p. 227–51.

[11] Prescott MB, Conger SA. Information Technology Innovations: A Classification by IT Locus of Impact and Research Approach. ACM SIGMIS Database 1995;26:20–41.

[12] Cooper RB, Zmud R. Information Technology Implementation Research: A Technological Diffusion Approach. Manage Sci 1990;36:123–39.

[13] Thompson VA. Bureaucracy and Innovation. Alabama: University of Alabama Press University; 1969.

[14] McFarlan FW, McKenney JL. The Information Archipelago-Gaps and Bridges. Harvard Business Rev 1982;60:109–19.

[15] Sousa RD, Goodhue GL. Understanding Exploratory Use of ERP Systems. AMCIS 2003. Proceedings.

[16] Dewan S, Riggins FJ. The Digital Divide: Current and Future Research Directions. J Assoc Inform Syst 2005;6:13.

[17] Chib A. The Aceh Besar Midwives with Mobile Phones Project: Design and Evaluation Perspectives Using the Information and Communication Technologies for Healthcare Development Model. J Comput Med Commun 2010;15:500–25.

[18] Norris AC, Stockdale RS, Sharma S. A Strategic Approach to M-Health. Health Inform J 2009;15:244–53.

[19] Mansfield E, Rapoport J, Romeo A, Villani E, Wagner S, Husic F. The Production and Application of New Industrial Technology. New York: Norton; 1977.

[20] Robertson TS, Gatignon H. Competitive Effects on Technology Diffusion. J Marketing 1986;50:1–12.

[21] Funk JL, Methe DT. Market- and Committee-Based Mechanisms in the Creation and Diffusion of Global Industry Standards: The Case of Mobile Communication. Res Policy 2001;30:589–610.

[22] Heeks R. Health Information Systems: Failure, Success and Improvisation. Int J Med Inform 2006;75:125–37.

[23] Avgerou C. Information systems in developing countries: a critical research review. J Inform Technol 2008;23:133−46.

[24] Kim HW, Gupta S. Investigating Customer Resistance to Change in Transaction Relationship with an Internet Vendor. Psychol Market 2012;29:257−69.

[25] Jones E, Sundaram S, Chin W. Factors Leading to Sales Force Automation Use: A Longitudinal Analysis. J Pers Sell Sales Manage 2002;22:145−56.

[26] Ziaie P. Challenges and issues of ICT industry in developing countries based on a case study of the barriers and the potential solutions for ICT deployment in Iran. In: International Conference on Computer Applications Technology (ICCAT).IEEE; 2013.

[27] Kalathil S. Dot. Com for Dictators. Foreign Policy 2003:43−9.

[28] Chib A, Wilkin H, Hoefman B. Vulnerabilities in mHealth implementation: a Ugandan HIV/AIDS SMS campaign. Global Health Prom 2013;20:26−32.

[29] Goel S, Bhatnagar N, Sharma D, Singh A. Bridging the Human Resource Gap in Primary Health Care Delivery Systems of Developing Countries with mHealth: Narrative Literature Review. JMIR mhealth uhealth 2013;1:e25.

[30] Medhi I, Jain M, Tewari A, Bhavsar M, Matheke-Fischer M, Cutrell E. Combating rural child malnutrition through inexpensive mobile phones. In: Proceedings of the 7th Nordic Conference on Human-Computer Interaction: Making Sense Through Design; 2012. p. 635−44. ACM.

[31] Matheson AI, Baseman JG, Wagner SH, O'Malley GE, Puttkammer NH, Emmanuel E, et al. Implementation and Expansion of an Electronic Medical Record for HIV Care and Treatment in Haiti: An Assessment of System Use and the Impact of Large-Scale Disruptions. Int J Med Inform 2012;81:244−56.

[32] Scott RE, Chowdhury MF, Varghese S. Telehealth policy—looking for global complementarity. J Telemed Telecare 2002;8:55−7.

[33] Khoja S, Durrani H, Nayani P. Scope of Policy Issues in eHealth: Results from a Structured Literature Review. J Med Internet Res 2012;14:e34.

[34] Al-Shorbaji N. Panel discussion participation at World Bank Day @ mHealth Summit—Part 3. Washington, DC: Internet; 2009.

[35] Kelman HC. Compliance, identification, and internalization: Three processes of attitude change. J Conflict Resolution 1958:51−60.

[36] O' Connor Y, Treacy S, O'Donoghue J. Examining Contextual Factors and Individual Value Dimensions of Healthcare Providers Intention to Adopt Electronic Health Technologies in Developing Countries. In: IFIP 8.6 Creating Value for All Through IT. Berlin: Springer; 2014. p. 345−54.

[37] Fulk J, Schmitz J, Steinfield CW. A Social Influence Model of Technology Use. Org Commun Technol 2001:117.

[38] Gupta B, Dasgupta S, Gupta A. Adoption of ICT in a Government Organization in a Developing Country: An Empirical Study. J Strat Inform Syst 2008;17:140−54.

[39] McNab C. What social media offers to health professionals and citizens. Bull World Health Org 2009;87:566.

[40] Deglise C, Suggs S, Odermatt P. Short Message Service (SMS) Applications for Disease Prevention in Developing Countries. J Med Internet Res 2012;14:e3.

[41] Coloma J, Harris E. From Construction Workers to Architects: Developing Scientific Research Capacity in Low-Income Countries. PLoS Biol 2009;7:e1000156.

[42] Hafkin N, Taggart N, Gender. Information Technology, and Developing Countries: An Analytic Study. Academy for Educational Development LearnLink for the Office of

Women in Development. United States Agency for International Development; 2001. Retrieved July 29, 2014, from: http://pdf.usaid.gov/pdf_docs/PNACM871.pdf.

[43] United Nations Education, Scientific and Cultural Organisation. The Global Literacy Challenge. A profile of youth and adult literacy at the mid-point of the United Nations Literacy Debate; 2003—2012. Available at: http://unesdoc.unesco.org/images/0016/001631/163170e.pdf.

[44] Leung CH, Chan YY. Mobile learning: a new paradigm in electronic learning. In: The 3rd IEEE International Conference on Advanced Learning Technologies; 2003. p. 76—80.

[45] Aker JC, Mbiti IM. Mobile Phones and Economic Development in Africa. CGD Working Paper 211. Washington, D.C.: Center for Global Development; 2010. Available at: http://www.cgdev.org/content/publications/detail/1424175 (accessed March 1, 2014).

[46] International Telecommunications Union. Study on international Internet connectivity in sub-Saharan Africa. 2013. Available at: http://www.itu.int/en/ITU-D/Regulatory-Market/Documents/IIC_Africa_Final-en.pdf (accessed March 1, 2014).

[47] Blaschke S, Bokenkamp K, Cosmaciuc R, Denby M, Hailu B, Short R. Using mobile phones to improve child nutrition surveillance in Malawi. Brooklyn, NY: UNICEF Malawi, UNICEF Innovations, Mobile Development Solutions; 2009.

[48] Galpottage PAB, Norris A. Patient Consent Principles and Guidelines for E-Consent: A New Zealand Perspective. Health Inform J 2005;11:5—18.

[49] Fitch CJ, Adams C. Managing Mobile Provision for Community Healthcare Support: Issues and Challenges. Business Proc Manage J 2006;12:299—310.

[50] Luxton DD, Kayl RA, Mishkind MC. mHealth Data Security: The Need For HIPAA-Compliant Standardization. Telemed e-Health 2012;18:284—8.

[51] Tanzer O. mHealth Applications and Security. HIMSS Europe, World of Health IT Conference (WoHIT), Nice, France. Available at: http://85.236.157.21/~himss/presentations/0204/RISSO9%202%2003%20PDF/4%20Security%20of%20the%20data%20in%20mhealth/01%20Oguz%20Tanzer/Dr.OguzTanzer-WoHIT_2014_mHealth%20Applications-Security_v8.pdf.

[52] Chang LW, Kagaayi J, Arem H, Nakigozi G, Ssempijja V, Serwadda D, Quinn TC, Gray RH, Bollinger RC, Reynolds SJ. Impact of a mHealth intervention for peer health workers on AIDS care in rural Uganda: a mixed methods evaluation of a cluster-randomized trial. AIDS Behav 2011;15:1776—84.

[53] Paton RA, McCalman J. Change Management: A Guide To Effective Implementation. Thousand Oaks, CA: Sage; 2008.

[54] Marshall C, Lewis D, Whitter M. mHealth Technologies In Developing Countries: A Feasibility Assessment And A Proposed Framework. Working Paper Series 25; 2013. URL: http://www.uq.edu.au/hishub/docs/WP25/WP25%20mHealth_web.pdf.

[55] Wijethilake D, Vatsalan D, Senevirathne G, Chapman K, Thilakaratne K, Sudhahar S, Arunathilake D, Wickramasinghe Y. HealthChange: A Change Management Model for an eHealth Solution in Developing Countries. IST-Africa; 2010. Conference, Durban, South Africa.

[56] Mars M. Telerehabilitation in South Africa — Is there a way forward? Int J Telerehabil 2011;3:11—8.

[57] Kim HW, Kankanhalli A. Investigating User Resistance to Information Systems Implementation: A Status Quo Bias Perspective. Manage Inform Syst Q 2009;33:567—82.

[58] Skulimowski AM. The challenges to the medical decision making system posed by mhealth: the IPTS Report. Prog Business Found Eur Comm 2004;81:1—7.

[59] Hasvold PE, Scholl J. Disrupted Rhythms and Mobile ICT in a Surgical Department. Int J Med Inform 2011;80:e72−84.

[60] Straub D, Keil M, Brenner W. Testing the technology acceptance model across cultures: A three country study. Inform Manage 1997;33:1−11.

[61] Hofstede G. Culture's Consequences: International Differences in Work-Related Values. Beverly Hills, CA: Sage; 1980.

[62] Hofstede G, Hofstede GJ, Minkov M. Cultures and Organizations: Software of the Mind. London: McGraw-Hill; 1991.

[63] Bofu A, Norte G, Stafeev A, Chakravarthy J. Challenges to Achieve MDGs in the Developing Countries Led; 2014. https://novoed.com/mhealth/reports/48587.

[64] Al Sukkar A, Hasan H. Toward a model for the acceptance of internet banking in developing countries. Inform Technol Devel 2005;11:381−98.

[65] Braa J, Nermunkh C. Health information systems in Mongolia: A difficult process of change. In: Avgerou C, Walsham G, editors. Information Technology in Context: Studies from the Perspective of Developing Countries. Hampshire, UK: Ashgate Publishing; 2000. p. 113−33.

[66] Eberhard A, Foster V, Briceño-Garmendia C, Ouedraogo F, Camos D, Shkaratan M. Underpowered: The State of the Power Sector in Sub-Saharan Africa. Washington, DC: World Bank; 2008. Available at: https://openknowledge.worldbank.com/handle/10986/7833.

[67] Chae M, Kim J. Do size and structure matter to mobile users? An empirical study of the effects of screen size, information structure, and task complexity on user activities with standard web phones. Behav Inform Technol 2004;23:165−81.

[68] Albers MJ, Kim L. User Web browsing characteristics using palm handheld for Information Retrieval. In: the Proceedings of 2000 Joint IEEE International and 18th Annual Conference on Computer Documentation; 2000. p. 125−35.

[69] Zolfo M, Iglesias D, Kiyan C, Echevarria J, Fucay L, Llacsahuanga E, et al. Mobile learning for HIV/AIDS healthcare worker training in resource-limited settings. AIDS Res Ther 2010;7:35.

[70] Mechael P, Batavia H, Kaonga N, Searle S, Kwan A, Goldberger A, Fu L, Ossman J. Barriers and Gaps Affecting MHealth in Low and Middle Income Countries: Policy White Paper. Columbia University. Earth institute Center for Global Health and Economic Development (CGHED): with mHealth alliance; 2010.

[71] Farrington C, Aristidou A, Ruggeri K. Mhealth and Global Mental Health: Still Waiting For the Mh2 Wedding? Global Health 2014;10:17.

[72] Zmud RW, Apple LE. Measuring Technology Incorporation/Infusion. J Product Innov Manage 1992;9:148−55.

[73] Bhattacherjee A. Understanding information systems continuance. An expectation−confirmation model. MIS Q 2001;25:351−70.

[74] Akter S, D'Ambra J, Ray P. User Perceived Service Quality of mHealth Services in Developing Countries. ECIS; 2010. Proceedings.

[75] Akter S, Ray P, D'Ambra J. Continuance of mHealth services at the bottom of the pyramid: the roles of service quality and trust. Electronic Markets 2012;8:1−19.

[76] O'Connor Y, O'Reilly P, O' Donoghue J. M-health Infusion by Healthcare Practitioners in the National Health Services (NHS). Health Policy Technol 2013;2:26−35.

[77] Beaudry A, Pinsonneault A. Advancing the Theory of Infusion: An Appropriation Model of the Infusion Process. Montréal, Canada: Cahier du GreSI; 1999.

[78] Ng EH, Kim HW. Investigating Information Systems Infusion and the Moderating Role of Habit: A User Empowerment Perspective. In: Proceedings of International Conference of Information Systems, ICIS; 2009. Proceedings, Paper 13.

[79] Limayem M, Hirt SG. Force of Habit and Information Systems Usage: Theory and Initial Validation. J Assoc Inform Syst 2003;4:3.

[80] Bergeron F, Raymond L, Rivard S, Gara MF. Determinants of EIS Use: Testing a Behavioral Model. Decis Supp Syst 1995;14:31−146.

[81] Limayem M, Hirt SG, Cheung CMK. How Habit Limits the Predictive Power of Intention: The Case of Information Systems Continuance. MIS Q 2007;31:705−37.

[82] Schillewaert N, Ahearne MJ, Frambach RT, Moenaert R. The adoption of information technology in the sales force. Ind Market Manage 2005;34:323−36.

[83] Wu X, Subramaniam C. Understanding RFID Adoption in Supply Chain: An Empirical Study. In: Proceedings of Forty Second Hawaii International Conference on Systems Science; 2009.

[84] Ramamurthy K, Sen A, Sinha P. Data Warehousing Infusion and Organizational Effectiveness. IEEE Trans Syst Man Cybernet A 2008;38:976−94.

[85] Shier ML, Jones ME, Graham JT. Sociocultural Factors to Consider When Addressing the Vulnerability of Social Service Users: Insights from Women Experiencing Homelessness. Affilia 2011;26:367−81.

[86] Nambisan P, Kreps GL, Polit S. Understanding Electronic Medical Record Adoption in the United States: Communication and Sociocultural Perspectives. Interact J Med Res 2013;2:e5.

[87] Paul DL, Pearlson KE, McDaniel R. Assessing Technological Barriers to Telemedicine: Technology-Management Implications. IEEE Trans Eng Manage 1999;46:279−88.

[88] Mansoor Y, Kamba MA. Information Acceptance and ICT Resistance: Promoting the Role of Information in Rural Community Development. Library Phil Pract 2010:409.

Application of Real-Valued Negative Selection Algorithm to Improve Medical Diagnosis

11

Ayodele Lasisi[1], Rozaida Ghazali[1], Tutut Herawan[2]

Faculty of Computer Science and Information Technology, Universiti Tun Hussein Onn Malaysia, Johor, Malaysia[1]; Universitas Teknologi Yogyakarta & AMCS Research Center, Yogyakarta, Indonesia[2]

E-mail: lasisiayodele@yahoo.com, rozaida@uthm.edu.my, tutut@uty.ac.id

INTRODUCTION

The increase in size in the amount of data stored in medical databases has prompted the need for effective data-mining techniques. Medical data are processed and analyzed using different data-mining techniques to extract useful information. This extracted information is valuable for decision making and for diagnosis, risk analysis, and predictions. The most important data mining technique in solving problems related to areas like medical data mining, and others is classification [1]. Hence, the amount of medical data requires the need for a powerful data analysis tool in extracting useful knowledge. Disease diagnosis is one of the application areas where data-mining tools have proven successful. In the past 10 years, heart disease has been reported to be the leading cause of death all over the world [2]. Data mining is a crucial step in the discovery of knowledge from large data sets. In recent years, data mining has found its purpose in every field, including health care. The diagnosis of a particular disease can be assisted with medical history data comprising of a number of tests available [3]. Complete diagnosis at an early stage followed by adequate treatment can result in significant life-saving [4].

Attempts have been made by investigators to develop automated means for computer-aided diagnosis on varieties of diseases [5]. In computer-aided decision systems, computer algorithms provide reliable support to a physician in diagnosing a patient [6]. Some computer algorithms include but are not limited to support vector machine, artificial neural network, random forest, naïve Bayes, and k-nearest neighbor. This chapter focuses on algorithms within the artificial immune system (AIS) domain. These algorithms imitate the way the biological immune system (BIS) protect the body by fighting and eradicating bacteria, viruses, and molecules deemed harmful to the body system. Relying on the recognition qualities of the lymphocytes (also called white blood cells), namely, the B cells and T cells, alien

231

invaders known as pathogens are destroyed upon detection. The negative selection algorithm (NSA) with real-valued data representation called V-Detector, based on the proliferation of T cells from the thymus to maturation, is used for medical data analysis and disease detection accordingly. The battle against disease-causing organisms could prove to be a difficult task as the pathogens are adaptive in nature. With this in mind, it is proper to tackle such diseases with an adaptive mechanism. Most of the AIS algorithms are built on the adaptive immune system, and NSA falls into this category. The ability to store in memory activities of previously seen infections, learn from their molecular structures, and adapt effectively in combating the infectious disease makes NSA the appropriate algorithmic system for detecting such diseases.

The structure of the chapter is as follows: the related work is introduced in the next section. The constituents of biological immune systems are discussed in the third section. Discussed in the fourth section is the AIS, the proponents that linked immunology and computing, as well as the algorithms developed. The NSA is introduced in the fifth section, with further elaborations on how the real-valued NSAs function. The sixth section presents the experimental procedures, and the conclusions comprise the final section.

RELATED WORK

The movement of computer-developed algorithms (generally referred to as data-mining algorithms) for use in the medical field herald a new direction for exploring the data patterns and projecting useful insights that assist the medical practitioners in making correct diagnoses. A couple of the data-mining techniques as found in literature will be discussed in this section. In [7], the naïve Bayes classifier was used in the diagnosis of heart disease. Comparison with some other algorithms showed that the naïve Bayes produced better accuracy results. The implementation of C4.5 algorithm, ID3 algorithm, and CART algorithm for diagnosing medical data such as diabetes, hepatitis, and heart disease was reported in [8]. The CART algorithm generated a classification accuracy rate of 83.20%, whereas the ID3 and C4.5 algorithms accounted for 64.80% and 71.40% classification accuracy rates, respectively. Furthermore, an improved support vector machine algorithm termed multiple knot spline—smooth support vector machine (MKS-SSVM) proposed by Purnami et al. [9] was applied and tested on the diabetes disease and heart disease data. After experimentation, results reveal the effectiveness of the MKS-SSVM over the SSVM, climaxing at an accuracy of 96.62%. With the prospect of improving neonatal jaundice diagnosis, Ferreira et al. [10] adopted the following algorithms, namely, J48, simple CART, naïve Bayes, Multilayer Perceptron, SMO, and simple logistic algorithms. All the algorithms are able to diagnose the neonatal jaundice. A survey in [11] highlighted a number of data-mining techniques for breast cancer diagnosis. Listed among the techniques are decision trees, association rule base classifiers, artificial neural network, naïve Bayes classifiers, support vector machines, and logistic regression. From the survey, it was concluded that the decision tree at 93.62% accuracy proved to be the best with respect to the other algorithms.

BIOLOGICAL IMMUNE SYSTEM

The medical practitioners and scientists are loaded with the responsibility of proffering and inventing solutions in tackling diseases considered dangerous and harmful to the human body system. Most, if not all, of the solutions are directed at boosting the immune system so as to fight against the pathogenic carriers of such diseases. It should be noted that the biological immune system in its entirety is robust and powerful in keeping the body strong and healthy. As such, the biological immune system is a dynamic, powerful, intelligent, and interconnection of multiple layers of defenses in protecting and eradicating unwanted/lethal pathogens from the body. Several cells within the immune system are capable of eliminating numerous antigens (substances that induces an immune response). The white blood cells also called lymphocytes comprise two of these antigen-eliminating cells, which are the B cells and T cells. They both develop and originate from the bone marrow, with the B cells involved in humoral processes and T cells migrating to the thymus to become mature for protecting the body. In the family of T cells, there exist three prominent types, namely, the killer T cells, helper T cells, and suppressor T cells. The destruction of foreign invaders by the killer T cells is executed by binding and infusing toxic chemicals into them. Helper T cells activates the B cells, whereas the suppressor T cells avert allergic autoimmune diseases by inhibiting the actions of other immune cells.

The immune system utilizes two lines of defense known as the innate immune system and adaptive immune system [12,13]. As the first line of defense, the innate immune system is triggered, and it is nonspecific, in that it does not concentrate on a particular kind of pathogen. Upon the pathogen breaking and bypassing the innate immunity line of defense, the adaptive immunity comes to the rescue. It is specific as it targets, matches a particular pathogen, and stores in memory the structure of the pathogen for faster detection and elimination if encountered again [14]. The phagocyte, which internalizes and destroys invaders, represents the most important cell in the innate immune system. It becomes an antigen-presenting cell (APC) that processes and presents antigenic peptides (a kind of molecule called major histocompatibility complex) on its surface to the T cells and B cells via interpreting the antigen appendages and the extraction of features. The major histocompatibility complex molecules simply depicted as MHC are equipped with the function to distinguish between what is self from nonself.

Consequently, after the T cells and B cells receive the antigen peptides, they are activated as induced by the antigen's molecular structure. Earlier, it was stated that helper T cells activates B cells, and this activation is due to the release of cytokines.

Thus, the B cells become stimulated and secrete antibodies that bind to the antigen for recognition. The binding process is achieved when the antibody's paratope of the B cells unite with the antigen's epitope [15]. The innate immunity and adaptive immunity are interlinked and influence each other. The Helper T cells can act as medium of connection between the two immunity levels, resulting in a more efficient specific immune response.

ARTIFICIAL IMMUNE SYSTEM

AIS is a computational paradigm that has evolved from the interactions and collaborations between computer scientists and immunologists in the development of algorithms that draws inspiration from the vertebrate immune system. It connects and fosters the immunology, computer science, and engineering disciplines [16,17]. Detection, diversity, learning, and tolerance have been highlighted as the properties of the immune system [18], and channel AIS with the capacity to adapt to changing situations and effective for problem-solving tasks such as pattern recognition, learning and memory acquisition, distributed detection, optimization, etc. [19]. The definition of AIS given in [20] reveals that the AIS algorithms developed are adaptive in nature as reflected in adaptive immunological cells of B-cells, T-cells and dendritic cells.

The earliest work of AIS can be traced back to the work of Jerne in 1974 [21]. His work shows the philosophical aspect of the functioning of the immune network, which proposes that cells and molecules of the immune system can be able to perform the recognition of foreign substances, respond to foreign substances, and regulate one another. Simply put, he proposed that the immune system is a network of interacting cells and antibodies, and his perspective is referred to as immune network theory [21]. From the theoretical perspective of immunology, Farmer et al. [22] developed an immune system model with computer simulation functions based on the immune network hypothesis of Jerne [21]. They compared the immune networks with neural networks. The first attempt to use the immune network in problem solving is reported in the work of Ishida [23]. It focused on the development of distributed diagnosis systems based on the interactions within immune networks. Furthermore, Bersini and Varela also pioneered works abstracted from the way the natural immune network memorizes and functions, leading to models and algorithms [24,25]. Self—nonself discrimination as it applies to computer security was the intention of Stephanie Forrest and her colleagues [26]. They were inspired at how the immune system recognizes self (normal) from nonself (abnormal), and an NSA was proposed. The works in [24,26] actually announces the pathway from immunology to computing. With the great advantages that can be extracted from the immune-inspired algorithms in solving varieties of problems in different application areas, more AIS algorithms began to surface. The algorithms coupled with the proposition in [26] are the clonal selection algorithm (CLONAG) [27], artificial immune network algorithm (AINE) [23], danger theory inspired algorithms

[28], and dendritic cell algorithm (DCA) [29], thus constituting the five major AIS algorithms that have been constantly developed and popularized.

NEGATIVE SELECTION ALGORITHM

The biological negative selection traces its roots to the underlying principle of central tolerance, an immune mechanism to prevent reaction to self antigens [30]. The selection of T cells and their maturation form the basis of NSA. T cells are developed in the bone marrow, and they are made to undergo a censoring mechanism in the thymus. Their passage from the thymus depends greatly on their reaction to the self cells of the body. It simply means that only those cells that do not react to the self cells are eligible to migrate, whereas the ones reacting are eliminated [31]. The migration of T cells denotes maturation, and is equipped with the full functionality of protecting the body [32,17]. Forrest et al. [26] proposed and developed the NSA based on binary (strings) representation. Two principal stages of the NSA are the generation and detection stages. Set of detectors are produced at the generation stage and further used for change detection. Summarized below are the steps in NSA execution [33]:

Given a universe U which contains all unique bit-strings of length l, self set $S \subset U$ and nonself set $N \subset U$, where

$$U = S \subset U \quad \text{and} \quad S \cap N = \varnothing$$

1. Define self as a set S of bit-strings of length l in U.
2. Generate a set D of detectors, such that each fails to match any bit-string in S.
3. Monitor S for changes by continually matching the detectors in D against S.

Although the NSA based on binary (strings) representation shows to be effective for computer and network security, the binary representation falls short in dealing with real-world applications. This limitation gave rise to the proposition of Real-Valued NSA (RNSA) by González et al. [34], which implement real-valued data. The detectors of the RNSA is fixed and chosen beforehand, and in an effort to dynamically choose the detectors, Ji and Dasgupta [35] initiated an improved version of RNSA called Variable-Sized Detectors (V-Detectors). In aligning with the objective of this study, focus will be directed at the variations of NSA based on real-valued representation, the V-Detectors.

REAL-VALUED NSA

The introduction of real-valued NSA by González et al. [34] came to address the problems posed by the first implementation [26] as earlier mentioned. The real-valued NSA is based on the use of constant-sized detectors, where the detectors are generated randomly. It adopts n-dimensional vectors in real space $[0,1]^n$ to encode antigens and antibodies. Antigens denoting the elements $\{e_1, e_2, e_3, e_4, \ldots, e_n\} \in U$

to be detected in $[0,1]^n$, and antibodies representing the detectors. Common to both the detectors and the self elements are a center and a radius, which are denoted as $d = (c_d, r_{ns})$ and $s = (c_s, r_s)$ respectively. For a detector, the center $c \in [0,1]^n$ and a nonself recognition radius $r_{ns} \in \mathbb{R}$. The c_s and r_s for the self elements are the self center and self radius respectively. The self radius, which is the same as the detector radius ($r_s = r_d$), permits other elements to be considered as self elements that lie close to the self center [36]. An element e lies within a detector $d = (c_d, r_{ns})$, if (1) holds. Thus, this signals the classification of the element as nonself.

$$D(c, e) = \left(\sum\nolimits_{i=1}^{n} (c_i - e_i)^2 \right)^{1/2} < r_{ns} \tag{1}$$

where the $D(c, e)$ depicts the distance (Euclidean) between c and e.

VARIABLE-SIZED DETECTORS (V-DETECTORS)

Inspired by real-valued NSA with constant-sized detectors, Ji and Dasgupta [35] put forward a variable-sized detector algorithm termed V-Detector with the sole purpose of maximizing the coverage area of each detector. It differs from the RNSA with fixed detectors in that for every detector, there is assigned a radius ($r_s \neq r_d$) and is equal to its distance to the self region. The algorithm begins execution with the random generation of detectors. The center of each detector is determined and cannot be located within the hyper-sphere region of the self element. The radius of the detector is dynamically resized, if such a center is exposed and targeted, until the boundary of the region draws nearer to the closest self element. A detector set accommodates the detectors provided the above conditions are upheld, and the detector radius which was resized depicted r is greater than the radius of the self element r_s. The termination criteria of the algorithm is when a predefined number of detectors are generated that can adequately cover the nonself space.

EXPERIMENTAL INVESTIGATION AND CLASSIFICATION RESULTS

The goal of this investigation is to discover the performance potentials of real-valued NSA. Also, its adaptability to medical data sets and how that influences its overall effectiveness. The V-Detector is considered for experimentation, implementations are conducted using MATrix LABoratory (MATLAB), and the medical data sets retrieved from UCI Machine Learning Repository [37], which has been frequently used within the anomaly detection domain. Three of the selected data sets are Breast Cancer Wisconsin, Biomedical, and BUPA Liver Disorder data sets. Furthermore, three benchmarked algorithms, namely, the sequential minimal optimization (SMO) [38] from the family of support vector machine, the multi-layer perceptron (MLP) [39] from the neural network family, and nonnested generalized exemplars (NNGEs) [40] from the nearest neighbor category are incorporated for comparison.

The Biomedical data set contains 209 observations (134 for normal and 75 for carriers) of blood measurements to identify carriers of a rare genetic disorder. Each blood sample consists of four measurements and a label (normal or carrier). There exist missing values within the Biomedical data and constitute 15 vector points that were removed. After removal, a total of 194 observations (127 for normal and 67 for carriers) of blood measurement are left. The Breast Cancer Wisconsin data set is used to distinguish malignant from benign samples. It contains 699 instances with 10 attributes (including the classes). The removal of 16 missing values from the data set resulted in the construction of new data sets with 683 instances (444 benign and 239 malignant). The BUPA Liver Disorder data set is composed of 7 attributes in total, with 6 of the attributes having numerical values depicting blood tests that are thought to be sensitive to liver disorders that might have arisen from excessive alcohol consumption, and the last attribute representing the class distinguishing between a patient with liver disorder and those considered free of the disease. It has 345 patients, 200 of the patients labeled healthy, with the remaining 145 patients labeled as having a disorder.

EXPERIMENTAL PROCEDURE

The V-Detector algorithm comprises of a training stage and a testing stage. In order to pass the data sets as input for execution in MATLAB, for a two class data set, the normal class is employed as the training data (100%) and considered as *self* and the other class as *nonself*. In the case of data sets with three classes, one of the classes is selected as the *self* and the remaining as *nonself*. This procedure is repeated for all the classes, which simply means that each of the class is employed as self for training, with others as nonself. For testing, all the data elements are used in classifying either as *self* or *nonself*. In all the experiments, 100% of the training data is used and have an execution of 30 runs each, with the average values recorded. The Euclidean distance shown in equation (2) is integrated to measure the affinities between the detectors and real-valued elements. All the data sets are normalized with the *min-max normalization* process in range [0,1].

$$D(c, e) = \sqrt{\sum_{i=1}^{n} (c_i - e_i)^2} \tag{2}$$

where $c = \{c_1, c_2, \dots, c_n\}$ are the centers of the detectors, $e = \{e_1, e_2, \dots, e_n\}$ are the real-valued antigens' coordinates, and D is the distance.

In the selection of parameter values, the same radius values r_s as used in [1,3] have been utilized. The V-Detector radius values r_s equal 0.05 for all the medical data sets of Breast Cancer Wisconsin, Biomedical, and BUPA Liver Disorder, respectively. An important parameter is the number of detectors needed for the coverage of nonself space. The parameter settings for V-Detector as in [3] include estimated coverage $c_0 = 99.98\%$, and maximum number of detectors $T_{\max} = 1000$.

ASSESSMENT MEASURES

The performance metrics to assess the effectiveness of the algorithms are the detection rate (DR) and false alarm rate (FAR). Both terms are defined as follows and depicted in (3) and (4):

> **Definition 1.** Detection rate, DR, which represents the ratio of true positive and the total nonself samples identified by detector set, where TP and FN are the tallies of true positive and false negative.

$$DR = \frac{TP}{TP + FN} \tag{3}$$

> **Definition 2.** False alarm rate, FAR, which represents the ratio of false positive and the total self samples identified by detector set, where FP and TN are the tallies of false positive and true negative.

$$FAR = \frac{FP}{FP + TN} \tag{4}$$

SIMULATION RESULTS AND DISCUSSIONS

The simulation experiments are performed on a 3.40-GHz Intel Core i7 Processor with 4 GB of RAM. The results after series of experiments for each data set are tabulated and graphed.

The performance results in Table 11.1 reveal the experimentation performed on the Breast Cancer Wisconsin data. The V-Detector, SMO, MLP, and NNGE algorithms performed outstandingly by acquiring detection rates not lower than 95%. The difference between the highest and lowest detection rates is approximately 4% with V-Detector recording rates of 98.95%, followed closely by SMO with 97.00%. The NNGE is not far behind, with a detection rate of 96.00%, and MLP finishing up with a 95.30% detection rate. In terms of the false alarm rate, the V-Detector has no record of any false positives, generating 0.00% false rate. MLP algorithm produced the highest false alarm rate at 5.40%. The graph representation in Figure 11.1 embodies the above analysis.

Table 11.1 Results for Breast Cancer Wisconsin Data

Algorithms	Detection Rate (%)	False Alarm Rate (%)
V-Detector	98.95	0.00
SMO	97.00	3.40
MLP	95.30	5.40
NNGE	96.00	3.90

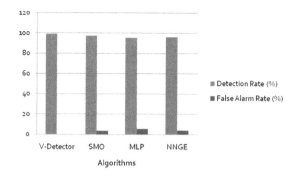

FIGURE 11.1

Graph plots for Breast Cancer Wisconsin.

Table 11.2 Results for Biomedical Data

Algorithms	Detection Rate (%)	False Alarm Rate (%)
V-Detector	71.64	0.00
SMO	87.60	17.50
MLP	90.90	13.30
NNGE	88.00	14.90

The Biomedical data result analysis is shown in Table 11.2 and diagrammatically depicted in Figure 11.2. The V-Detector was able to generate a detection rate of 71.64% but could not surpass the performance of the other algorithms based on its detection rate. SMO generated a detection rate of 87.60%, NNGE accounted for an 88.00% detection rate, and the MLP gave rise to the highest detection rate at 90.90%. With respect to the false alarm rate, there exist contrast differences when compared with the results produced for the detection rate. Although the

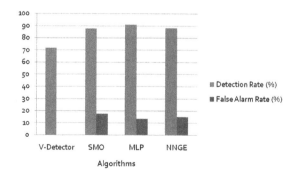

FIGURE 11.2

Graph plots for Biomedical.

Table 11.3 Results for BUPA Liver Disorder Data

Algorithms	Detection Rate (%)	False Alarm Rate (%)
V-Detector	74.44	0.00
SMO	58.30	57.60
MLP	71.60	32.40
NNGE	66.70	36.30

SMO, MLP, and NNGE generated good detection rates, their false alarm rates were consequently high as well at 17.50%, 13.30%, and 14.90%, respectively The V-Detector on the other hand produced a false rate of 0.00%, which supersedes the other algorithms.

The performance results for the BUPA Liver Disorder data are reflected in Table 11.3. The graphical plots of the detection rates and false alarm rates are shown in Figure 11.3. The values for detection rate and false alarm rate signifies that the algorithms' adaptability to the data vary significantly. With respect to the algorithms, the V-Detector produced the highest detection rate, thus proving superior to the other algorithms. The SMO could account for a 58.30% detection rate, which is the lowest of all. Both the MLP and NNGE generated rates at 71.60% and 66.70%, respectively. Also, the false alarm rates for the SMO, MLP, and NNGE algorithms were very high, climaxing at 57.60% for SMO. The MLP and NNGE produced false positive rates at 32.40% and 36.30%, whereas the V-Detector once again generated a 0.00% false rate, ultimately making it superior.

The number of detectors needed to cover the search space is an important parameter to determine the effectiveness of real-valued NSA. The detector number varies with the V-Detector, requiring less amount of detector in attaining good detection rates. Table 11.4 reveals the average detectors accounted by V-Detector algorithm for all data sets. The number of mean detectors aligns

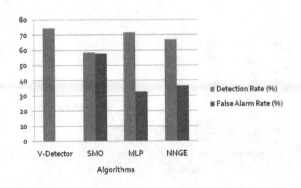

FIGURE 11.3

Graph plots for BUPA Liver Disorder.

Table 11.4 Generated Detectors for V-Detector

Data sets	Number of Mean Detectors
Breast Cancer Wisconsin	1000
Biomedical	184
BUPA Liver Disorder	914

with the rules stated in Ma et al. [41] for generating small amounts of detector to circulate the search space.

Overall, it can be noted that the V-Detectors' performances outweighs that of SMO, MLP, and NNGE for the Breast Cancer Wisconsin and BUPA Liver Disorder data. The performance with regard to Biomedical data for the V-Detector eclipsed the 70% range, but the other algorithms yielded better results in terms of detection rate. Thus, on a ratio of 2:1 for detection rate with respect to all the data sets, the V-Detector outperformed the SMO, MLP, and NNGE, respectively.

CONCLUSION

This chapter describes the use of NSA that incorporates real data termed V-Detector serves as inspiration in mining medical data. Its adaptive inherent functionalities proved decisive in the recognition and detection of disease causing organisms, and also breathe a new lease of life as alternatives for the computer algorithms that have already been applied to medical data for knowledge discovery and diagnosis. Experimental results on the Breast Cancer Wisconsin, Biomedical, and BUPA Liver Disorder data sets shows the superiority of the V-Detector in comparison to SMO, MLP, and NNGE. Higher performances are recorded with the Breast Cancer Wisconsin and BUPA Liver Disorder data sets for the V-Detector. However, for Biomedical data, the V-Detector performed considerably well when compared against the standard algorithms. On the whole, the V-Detector detection abilities cannot be pushed aside, though improvements could still be integrated with evolutionary and optimization algorithms so as to further enhance its detectors for greater efficiency.

ACKNOWLEDGEMENTS

As an expression of gratitude, the authors with the deepest appreciation would like to thank the Office for Research, Innovation, Commercialization and Consultancy Management (ORICC), Universiti Tun Hussein Onn Malaysia (UTHM) and Ministry of Higher Education (MOHE) for financially supporting this Research under the Fundamental Research Grant Scheme (FRGS), Vote No. 1235.

REFERENCES

[1] Jabbar MA, Deekshatulu BL, Chandra P. Heart disease prediction system using associative classification and genetic algorithm, arXiv Prepr 2013. arXiv1303.5919.

[2] Shouman M, Turner T, Stocker R. Using data mining techniques in heart disease diagnosis and treatment. Electron. Commun. Comput. (JEC-ECC), 2012 Japan-Egypt Conf 2012:173–7.

[3] Khemphila A, Boonjing V. Heart disease classification using neural network and feature selection. Syst. Eng. (ICSEng), 2011 21st Int. Conf 2011:406–9.

[4] Gudadhe M, Wankhade K, Dongre S. Decision support system for heart disease based on support vector machine and artificial neural network. Comput. Commun. Technol. (ICCCT), 2010 Int. Conf., 2010. p. 741–5.

[5] Tsai D-Y, Watanabe S, Tomita M. Computerized analysis for classification of heart diseases in echocardiographic images. Image Process. 1996. Proceedings., Int. Conf., 1996. p. 283–86.

[6] Mazurowski MA, Zurada JM, Tourassi GD. Selection of examples in case-based computer-aided decision systems. Phys Med Biol 2008;53:6079.

[7] Muhammed L-N. Using data mining technique to diagnosis heart disease. Stat. Sci. Business, Eng. (ICSSBE), 2012 Int. Conf., 2012. p. 1–3.

[8] Kumar DS, Sathyadevi G, Sivanesh S. Decision support system for medical diagnosis using data mining. Int J Comput Sci Issues 2011;8:147–53.

[9] Purnami SW, Zain JM, Embong A. Data mining technique for medical diagnosis using a new smooth support vector machine. Networked Digit. Technol., Springer; 2010. p. 15–27.

[10] Ferreira D, Oliveira A, Freitas A. Applying data mining techniques to improve diagnosis in neonatal jaundice. BMC Med Inform Decis Mak 2012;12:143.

[11] Kharya S. Using data mining techniques for diagnosis and prognosis of cancer disease. Int J Comput Sci Eng Inf Technol 2012;2:55–66.

[12] Janeway Jr CA. How the immune system recognizes invaders. Life, Death and the Immune System. Sci Am 1993;269:72.

[13] Ou C-M. Multiagent-based computer virus detection systems: abstraction from dendritic cell algorithm with danger theory. Telecommun Syst 2011:1–11.

[14] Lasisi A, Ghazali R, Herawan T. Negative Selection Algorithm: A Survey on the Epistemology of Generating Detectors. Proc. First Int. Conf. Adv. Data Inf. Eng. (DaEng-2013), Lect. Notes Electr. Eng., 2014. p. 167–76.

[15] Oprea ML. Antibody repertoires and pathogen recognition: the role of germline diversity and somatic hypermutation. Citeseer; 1996.

[16] Dasgupta D. An Overview of Artificial Immune Systems. Artif Immune Syst Their Appl 1998:3–19.

[17] Dasgupta D, Yu S, Nino F. Recent advances in artificial immune systems: models and applications. Appl Soft Comput 2011;11:1574–87.

[18] Boukerche A, Jucá KRL, Sobral JB, Notare MSMA. An artificial immune based intrusion detection model for computer and telecommunication systems. Parallel Comput 2004;30:629–46.

[19] De Castro LN, Von Zuben FJ. Artificial Immune Systems: Part I– Basic Theory and Applications. Tech. Rep. - RT DCA 01/99, Sch. Comput. Electr. Enginnering. Brazil: State Univ. Campinas; 1999.

[20] de Castro LN, Timmis J. Artificial immune systems: a new computational intelligence approach. New York: Springer Verlag; 2002.

[21] Jerne NK. Towards the network theory of the immune system. Ann. Immunol. (Inst. Pasteur) 1974;125C:373−89.

[22] Farmer JD, Packard NH, Perelson AS. The immune system, adaptation, and machine learning. Phys. D Nonlinear Phenom 1986;22:187−204.

[23] Ishida Y. Fully distributed diagnosis by PDP learning algorithm: towards immune network PDP model. Neural Networks 1990:777−82. 1990 IJCNN Int. Jt. Conf.; 1990.

[24] Bersini H, Varela FJ. Hints for adaptive problem solving gleaned from immune networks. Parallel Probl. Solving from Nat., Springer; 1991. p. 343−54.

[25] Bersini H, Varela FJ. The immune learning mechanisms: reinforcement, recruitment and their applications. Comput Biol Metaphor 1994;1:166−92.

[26] Forrest S, Perelson AS, Allen L, Cherukuri R. Self-nonself discrimination in a computer. Res. Secur. Privacy, 1994 1994:202−12. Proceedings., 1994 IEEE Comput. Soc. Symp.

[27] De Castro LN, Von Zuben FJ. The clonal selection algorithm with engineering applications. Proc. GECCO; 2000. p. 36−9.

[28] Aickelin U, Cayzer S. The Danger Theory and Its Application to Artificial Immune Systems. Proc. 1st Int. Conf. Artif. Immune Syst. (ICARIS 2002), Canterbury, UK; 2002. p. 141−8, http://www.cs.nott.ac.uk/~uxa/papers/icaris_danger.pdf.

[29] Greensmith J, Aickelin U, Cayzer S. Introducing dendritic cells as a novel immune-inspired algorithm for anomaly detection. Artif. Immune Syst., Springer; 2005. p. 153−67.

[30] Lederberg J. Genes and Antibodies Do antigens bear instructions for antibody specificity or do they select cell lines that arise by mutation? Science 1959;129:1649−53.

[31] Igawa K, Ohashi H. A negative selection algorithm for classification and reduction of the noise effect. Appl Soft Comput 2009;9:431−8.

[32] Greensmith J, Whitbrook A, Aickelin U. Artificial immune systems Handb. Metaheuristics, Springer; 2010. p. 421−448.

[33] Stibor T, Timmis J, Eckert C. The link between r-contiguous detectors and k-CNF satisfiability. Evol. Comput. 2006. CEC 2006. IEEE Congr; 2006. p. 491−8.

[34] Gonzalez F, Dasgupta D, Kozma R. Combining negative selection and classification techniques for anomaly detection. Evol. Comput. 2002. CEC'02. Proc. 2002 Congr; 2002. p. 705−10.

[35] Ji Z, Dasgupta D. Real-valued negative selection algorithm with variable-sized detectors. Genet Evol Comput 2004; 2004:287−98.

[36] González FA, Dasgupta D. Anomaly detection using real-valued negative selection. Genet Program Evolvable Mach 2003;4:383−403.

[37] Bache K, Lichman M. UCI machine learning repository; 2013. URL, Http//archive.Ics.Uci.Edu/ml. 901.

[38] Platt J. Sequential minimal optimization: A fast algorithm for training support vector machines; 1998.

[39] Fine TL. Feedforward neural network methodology. Springer Science & Business Media; 1999.

[40] Martin B. Instance-based learning: nearest neighbour with generalisation. New Zealand: University of Waikato Hamilton; 1995.

[41] Ma W, Tran D, Sharma D. A practical study on shape space and its occupancy in negative selection. In: Evol. Comput. (CEC), 2010 IEEE Congr; 2010. p. 1−7.

Development and Applications of Mobile Farming Information System for Food Traceability in Health Management

12

Yu-Chuan Liu[1], Hong-Mei Gao[2]

Assistant Professor, Department of Information Management, Tainan University of Technology, Tainan, Taiwan[1]; Professor, Department of Logistic Management and Engineering, Tianjin Agricultural University, Tianjin, China[2]

E-mail: t00258@mail.tut.edu.tw, gaohongmei@126.com

FOOD TRACEABILITY FOR SAFETY AND HEALTH
FOOD SAFETY AND TRACEABILITY

Foodborne disease incidents arising from natural, accidental, and deliberate contamination of food have become one of the major global public health threats of the 21st century. Issues for food safety, agro-processing, and the environmental and ecological impact of agriculture have been exacerbated by the incidences such as the human form of bovine spongiform encephalitis (BSE, or mad cow disease), genetically engineered foods, and contamination of fresh and processed agriculture. In addition to the foodborne illnesses, the globalization, consumer demand, and terrorism threats have also impelled the necessary of traceability systems in supply chains for food and agriculture. Costs for food safety include human, economic, and political issues that can be exacerbated by increasing the numbers of human pathogens, antibiotic-resistant bacteria, and zoonotic pathogens in meat and dairy products. Unsafe agricultural practices such as the use of manure, chemical fertilizer, pesticide, and contaminated water on fresh fruits and vegetables also cause food safety concerns.

Modern food production, processing, and distribution systems may integrate and commingle food from multiple sources, farms, regions, and countries. Food products covered by traceability standards include fresh produce such as fruit and vegetables, bulk foods such as milk and coffee, fish and seafood, and livestock for meat and dairy. The smallest traceable unit will be dependent on food product and industry practices. Good practices in traceability entail making the lot number and name of the production facility visible on each case of product and recording the quantity and shipping location. Some of the typical traceability data include the physical location that last handled the product, supply chain partner, amount of production, physical location product was shipped from, lot number of the product shipped to each location and date/time when the product was received, shipped, or harvested. Traceability requires each facility to record data when a product is moved between premises, transformed, and further processed or when data capture is necessary to trace the product. Such instances are known as critical tracking events and are vital to linking products across the supply chain. The heightened awareness of food-related safety issues among food consumers drives the demand for more information about the vertical food supply chain about the origin and handling of the basic commodities and food products generated and consumed throughout the world. The term of traceability, according to International Organization for Standardization (ISO), can be defined as the ability to trace the history, application, or location of an entity, by means of recorded identifications. Traceability is an essential subsystem of quality management and must be managed by setting up a traceability system, which keeps the tracking data of product routes and of selected attributes.

A traceability system can consist of two elements, the routes of the product, including the manufacturing, distribution, and retail procedures, and the extent of traceability wanted [1]. Food traceability system is aimed to provide information visibility through the farming, production, packing, distribution, transportation, and sales process and receiving enthusiastic research interests due to the food supply chain globalization. Accuracy and transparency of products and activities in the way food was grown and handled throughout the supply chain is becoming an important quality index in food and agribusiness [2]. Food traceability requires that all stakeholders within the food supply chain, including agriculture and feed producers, food manufacturers, retailers, etc., must be able to identify the source of all raw materials and ingredients and also to whom the products have been sold. The food companies must apply identification systems and data-handling procedures, and these must be integrated into their quality management system. The sector encompassing IT centers ought to find a reasonable compromise between the simple, step-by-step passing of traceable unit IDs for the neighboring actors, and the accumulated enormously huge databases of the actors. The traceability system is to provide services for the supply chain actors on a cooperative basis aimed at mutual interests [3]. In addition, the IT centers have to support the supply chain and value chain management, as well as the work of the authorities that are responsible for human health.

Opara [4] reviewed the concepts of supply chain management and traceability in agriculture and highlighted the technological challenges, including food product label and identification; activity/process characterization; information systems for data capture, analysis, storage, and communication; and the integration of the overall traceable supply chain in implementing traceable agricultural supply chains. Wang et al. [5] addressed that the values on traceability can be integrated with the supply chain management processes to manage the business process and improve its performance. By modeling the stylized marketing chain composed of farms, marketers, and consumer, Pouliot and Sumner [6] showed that exogenous increases in food traceability create incentives for farms and marketing firms to supply safer food by increasing liability costs. Golan et al. [7] summarized that there were three motives for food suppliers to establish product tracing systems: to improve the supply (production) management, to differentiate and market foods with subtle or undetectable quality attributes, and to facilitate trace-back for food safety and/or quality. The aim of a traceability system is to collect the product related information along the supply chain. This information is essential when facing food safety crisis, and provides efficient management for the corresponding product recall action. Although a recall action could be absolutely critical for a company, both in terms of incurred costs and of media impact, at present most companies do not possess reliable methods to precisely estimate the amount of product that would be discarded in the case of a recall. Dabbene and Gay [8] introduced novel criteria and methodologies for measuring the worst-case (or the average) quantity of product that should be recalled in the case of mixed batches of sausage production process. Considering the food traceability system as part of the logistics management, Bosona and Gebresenbet [9] summarized the literature review on the food traceability issues. The definition, driving forces, barriers, benefits, traceability technologies, improvements, and performances of food traceability system had been discussed. It was pointed out that the development of full-chain food traceability system is quite complex in nature, and a deeper understanding of real processes from different perspectives such as economic, legal, technological, and social issues are essential. Consequently, studies on the integration of traceability activities with food logistics activities, the linkage between traceability system and food manufacturer, standardization of data capturing and communication protocol for different drivers, and performance evaluation frameworks for food traceability system need to be focused.

CURRENT DEVELOPMENTS FOR FOOD TRACEABILITY

Consumers in Europe, Japan, the United States, and elsewhere are concerned about what is happening to their food supply, where is it from, how was it produced, and, most importantly of all, is it safe. Every company connected with the world's food supply chain has to embrace traceability or find it difficult to stay in business. This is uncompromising, and pressure continues to mount from consumers, the media, retailers, and government regulatory agencies. In 1985, a UN General Assembly resolution gave rise to the guidelines for consumer protection, and identified food as one of three priority areas of essential concern to consumer health. The CODEX Alimentarius (Food & agriculture organization of the United Nations, 1999) evolved from these UN guidelines for the FAO Codex Alimentarius guidelines regarding food. This codex also deals with quality issues on ensuring consumers received products that are safe and do not pose a threat to health [10]. Quality assurance is composed of three key elements, managing hygiene to ensure food safety, ensuring quality through grading and other measurements, and providing mechanisms for product recalls. The General Food Law, Regulation (EC) 178, of the European

Parliament and the Council referring to traceability is effective since January 1, 2005, and consists of five major concerns [11]:

1. The traceability of food, feed, food-producing animals, and any other substance intended to be, or expected to be, incorporated into a food or feed shall be established at all stages of production, processing, and distribution.
2. Food and feed business operators shall be able to identify any person from whom they have been supplied with a food, a feed, a food-producing animal, or any substance intended to be, or expected to be, incorporated into a food or feed. To this end, such operators shall have in place systems and procedures which allow for this information to be made available to the competent authorities on demand.
3. Food and feed business operators shall have in place systems and procedures to identify the other businesses to which their products have been supplied. This information shall be made available to the competent authorities on demand.
4. Food or feed which is placed on the market or is likely to be placed on the market in the Community shall be adequately labeled or identified to facilitate its traceability, through relevant documentation or information in accordance with the relevant requirements of more specific provisions.
5. Provisions for the purpose of applying the requirements of this Article in respect of specific sectors may be adopted in accordance with the procedure laid down in Article 58, paragraph 2, referring to Committee and Mediation Procedures.

The processes for ensuring hygiene in the EU red-meat system have focused on Hazard Analysis Critical Control Point (HACCP) systems beginning at the farm level. Food and feed business operators in European Union (EU) have to conform to the traceability directives demanded by their customers along the entire chain. Large retailers in Europe like Aldi, Lidl, Real, Metro, and Marks & Spencer are very rigorous in their criteria for traceability. The new EU regulations mandate that all food and feed business operators be legally bound to have traceability systems, even when their customers do not require it. The Italian Standards Institute (UNI) has enacted specific legislative measures in Italy. Two specific standards have been issued: UNI 10939 "Traceability system in agricultural food chain—General principles for design and development" in April 2001, and UNI 11020 "Traceability system in agro-food industries—Principles and requirements for development" in December 2002. The Canadian Cattle Identification Agency (CCIA) introduced mandatory identification of all Canadian cattle and bison in July 2002. Other legislative acts have been introduced in several European countries, such as France, Spain, and Greece, but they primarily relate to quality issues rather than food safety. Chrysochou et al. [12] concluded from a group study across 12 European countries that the amount of confidence in the information provided, perceived levels of convenience, impact on product quality and safety, impact on consumers' health and the environment, and potential consequences on ethical and privacy liberties constitute important factors influencing consumers' perceptions of traceability. Labeling and traceability of genetically modified organisms are current issues in trade and regulation. Currently, labeling of genetically modified foods containing detectable transgenic material is required by EU legislation. The regulatory issues of risk analysis and labeling are currently harmonized by Codex Alimentarius [13].

After a series of mad cow disease outbreaks, Japan made it mandatory to adopt an radio frequency identification (RFID)—enabled traceability system in 2004 and has also developed a food traceability system for other food products in the food chain via the Internet. Web-based food traceability systems have also been adopted in Australia and Korea [14]. Unfortunately, there is currently no general legal requirement for the establishment of traceability systems in food chains. Consequently, traceability is basically voluntarily, a small number of pioneer companies are developing their own systems. An early study revealed that the U.S. red-meat system is falling behind when compared against its major competitors, such as the United Kingdom (UK), Denmark, Canada, Japan, Australia, New Zealand, and many other trading partners in terms of traceability, transparency, and other quality assurances (TTA) [15]. They noted that the U.S. red-meat inspection system is designed principally to control pathogens, whereas some competitors' systems are designed also to trace meat back to its origin and provide information on other "extrinsic" characteristics. Golan et al. [16] investigated the traceability baseline in the United States and concluded that private sector food firms have developed a substantial capacity to trace. Firms balance the private costs and benefits of traceability to determine the efficient level of traceability.

The best targeted government policies for strengthening firms' incentives to invest in traceability are aimed at ensuring that unsafe or falsely advertised foods are quickly removed from the system, while allowing firms the flexibility to determine the manner. A system for tracking every input and process to satisfy every objective would be enormous and very costly. U.S. food producers have developed an enormous capacity to track the flow of food along the supply chain. Some traceability systems are deep, tracking food from the retailer back to the farm, whereas others only back to some key points in the production process. Some systems are very precise and can track food products to the minute of production or the exact area of a field where they were grown. Others are less precise, such as tracking product to farms in a large geographical area. Firms determine the necessary breadth, depth, and precision of their traceability systems depending on characteristics of their production process and their traceability objectives [17]. Domestically and internationally, it has now become essential that producers, packers, processors, wholesalers, exporters and retailers ensure that livestock, poultry, and meat are identified, which ensures traceability through all or parts of the complete life cycle. Smith et al. [18] summarized that the U.S. food industry is developing, implementing, and maintaining traceability systems designed so as to (1) ascertain origin and ownership, and deter theft and misrepresentation, of animals and meat; (2) monitor, control, and eradicate foreign animal diseases; (3) provide biosecurity protection for the national livestock population; (4) ensure compliance with requirements of international customers; (5) ensure compliance with country-of-origin labeling requirements; (6) aim at improvement of supply-side management, distribution and/or delivery systems and inventory controls; (7) facilitate value-based marketing; (8) isolate the source and extent of quality-control and food-safety problems; and (9) minimize product recalls and make crisis management protocols more effective.

OBJECTIVE AND OUTLINE OF THIS CHAPTER

In facing the global competition for agricultural market, implementation of traceability systems is essential for the famous agro-product of Taiwan to export overseas. The Taiwan government has set up the standards and authentication system of Taiwan Good Agriculture Practice (TGAP) and Traceable Agriculture Product (TAP) for agriculture in 2007. Traceability data include records of production flow control, risk management control, and operational checklist and must be provided according to the international standard guidelines such as CODEX, HACCP, ISO-9000, ISO-22000, GAP, and EurepGAP. The Chinese government started the 12th 5-year national development plan in 2012. The food safety and traceability—related projects and researches were hence becoming a key focus for public and private sectors. As the IT and automation applications for traceability information system increases, the e-business of farm management is becoming more and more practical. Documentation is a major component of the traceability system to trace the history, application, and location of what is under consideration. As some field data can be acquired by sensor networking, most activity information was input manually for the traceability information systems. The complicated traceability recording procedure causes an obstacle for the implementation of a traceability system in Taiwan and China.

Easy data collection to automatically record the activities information is necessary. The objective of this research is to develop a mobile farming system to enhance the efficiency of e-traceability data construction and collection. System architecture and operation scenarios for the mobile farming information system are analyzed. An end-to-end mobile application that traces the farming activities by using mobile handheld devices (smartphone and/or tablet) to capture information on farming operations is developed and implemented. The mobile system consists of a front-end application service with mobile devices and back-end web server. The farming information for every operation is coded in two-dimensional QR code labels. By scanning the proper operation labels, the corresponding traceability data can be uploaded simultaneously to the back-end web server. Applications of this mobile contract farming information management system for traceability data collection show that the complexity of traceability data construction can be significantly reduced and help to improve consumers' confidence for healthy food choices.

The basic concepts and current status of food traceability is conveyed in the Introduction. The next section shows the development of mobile contract farming information system. The detailed system analysis, modeling, and development of the mobile farming information system will be illustrated. Two application cases of the mobile farming information system are revealed in the third section. The prototype system is implemented in the traceability of mango exporting in Tainan. A collaborative research project for the agriculture traceability of white gourd in Tianjin is also performed. The fourth section presents the summary and conclusions of this research.

DEVELOPMENT OF MOBILE FARMING INFORMATION SYSTEM
INFORMATION TECHNOLOGY APPLICATIONS FOR THE AGRO-FOOD INDUSTRY

Developments of agro-food industries are facing global challenges that can only be supported by information technologies. The major IT development lines, the support potential of their integration, organizational requirements for the utilization, and possible consequences for the future organization of the agro-food sector were reviewed [19]. A new model and prototype of a new Farm Information Management System, which meets the changing requirements for advising managers with formal instructions, recommended guidelines and documentation requirements for various decision-making processes, was developed [20]. As achieving end-to-end traceability across the supply chain is quite a challenge from a technical, coordination, and cost perspective, Kelepouris et al. [21] suggested an RFID technology and outlined both information data model and system architecture that made traceability feasible and easily deployable across a supply chain. Based on an integration of alphanumerical codes and RFID technology, the traceability system for Parmigiano Reggiano (the famous Italian cheese) was developed [22]. Manthou et al. [23] provided empirical insights regarding the use of Internet-based applications in the agro-food supply chain by focusing on the Greek fruit canning sector. The companies' perceptions regarding perceived benefits, constrained factors, and motivation factors toward the use of Internet-based applications were studied. A personal digital assistant (PDA)—based record-keeping and decision-support system for traceability in cucumber production was developed on a Windows Mobile platform invoking a Geographic Information System (GIS) control [24]. Two agricultural production enterprises were chosen as case studies to evaluate the system, and the results show that the efficiency of production record keeping and decision support is greatly improved by the simple and friendly system. A state-of-the-art review in the recent advancements in the food processing and packaging industries in the fields of smart packaging and materials, automation and control technology, standards, and their application scenarios, production management principles, and their improvements was proposed [25]. An overview of recent developments in wireless sensors and sensor networks applied in agriculture and food production for environmental monitoring, precision agriculture, M2M-based machine and process control, building and facility automation, and RFID-based traceability systems was presented in [26]. A traceability system in the food (baking) industry was proposed by Pinto et al. [27] merging production management, food safety management, and systems with regulatory requirements to facilitate recall procedures with economic and safety benefits. The generated outputs are also important records in case of an audit.

A quick response (QR) code is a two-dimensional barcode introduced by the Japanese company Denso-Wave in 1994. Users photograph QR codes, and the software integrated into their phones decodes the messages and displays, manipulates, or stores the information on their mobile devices as shown in Figure 12.1. In Japan, QR codes are widely used to enter information such as addresses into mobile phones or even to purchase goods. They can be found in advertising, in the print media, on business cards, products, websites, and vending machines [28].

Current traceability systems based on RFID tags have problems of expensive price and weakness of reading if applied onto the surface of products containing much water. To provide a traceability system for fishery products that uses much inexpensive media and ensures high efficiency, a system based on a combination of printed 2D codes and the Internet was proposed by Seine et al. [29]. By adding digital encryption along with identification by weight information, the system was assured its usability by a series of experiments conducted for the distribution of cultured flounder in Hakodate, Japan. A viticulture service–oriented framework (VSOF) that turns context elements or QR codes decoded by mobile devices was developed in [30]. The QR codes are used to automatically associate a field location to the relevant database tables or records and also to access contextual information or services. The possibility of exchanging contextualized information and accessing contextualized services in the field, using well-known devices such as cell phones, may contribute to increase the rate of adoption of information technology in viticulture and contribute to more efficient and closer-to-the-crops practices.

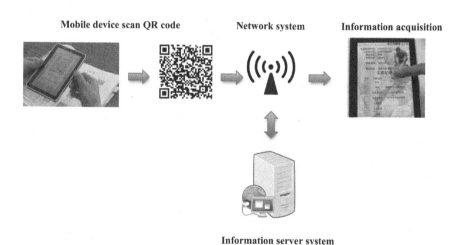

FIGURE 12.1

Application scenario for QR code with mobile devices.

INFORMATION TECHNOLOGY APPLICATIONS FOR AGRO-FOOD INDUSTRY

Food traceability can be accomplished mostly by attaching a two-dimensional label—QR code being the usual case—on the package of the food or agro-products. As mentioned earlier, the TAP system was launched in 2007 for the traceability of agriculture products. Like most implementation cases, the TAP system is voluntarily used rather than an obligation for farmers and agro-business. Some examples of traceability labels in Taiwan are shown in Figure 12.2. The products can range from rice, eggs, and vegetables to seafood such as shrimps and fishes. Consumers can use a mobile phone to scan the QR code of the label, attached on the package of the product, to get the traceability information of the product.

An example of egg traceability is shown in Figure 12.3. As the QR code is scanned by the mobile device, a cell phone or tablet, the basic producer information provided by the TAP system is firstly displayed as illustrated in Figure 12.3a. The upper picture on the right-hand side is the brief producer information, including the unique traceability ID number, the name and location of the producer, and the auditing organization. The lower picture on the right-hand side lists the brief production information, which in this case is the feed beginning date and feeding forage of

FIGURE 12.2

Traceability examples of different products in Taiwan.

FIGURE 12.3

(a) Brief product information from TAP system. (b) Detailed production information of the eggs from the TAP system.

the chicken and the date the egg was cleaned and packed. The reason for showing the auditing organization is to reveal that the production process has met the requirements and is qualified by an auditing organization defined by the legislation of the Taiwan government. Producers can apply for the auditing process of the TAP system. A unique traceability ID number will be authorized for the qualified product to be traced in the TAP system. The detailed production data can be found by clicking on the web link, which will lead to the corresponding web page (as shown in the lower images in Figure 12.3b). In this case, the area for feeding, the breed and quantity of chicken, feeding history, and logistic conditions are listed. Data of feeding forage, selection and packing processes, and quality inspection records can be downloaded. The production and quality data about the chicken and eggs can all be acquired from the TAP system.

The TAP system is established and maintained by the government. Only those producers who have applied and passed the auditing process can have their product traced by the TAP system. Contents provided for the producers and consumers are fixed and unified, without any flexibility. Another example of traceability provided by private business is also illustrated. Tea is one of the world-famous agro-products of Taiwan. Some companies provide their own traceability information, which is mainly focused on the marketing of the cultivated characteristics and e-commerce considerations. A QR code label is printed in the package of the tea, as shown in Figure 12.4. In addition to providing only the production date and type of tea as the traceability information, an attractive multimedia video is also available for the introduction of the tea when scanning the QR code. Instead of linking to the detailed production data, consumers can be led to the purchasing page of the company. As the TAP system is voluntarily accessible, companies can also choose to provide their own traceability information with proper broadness and depth of information.

Irrespective of whether the traceability system is provided by the public or private sector, the production data must be input into the traceability system for consumers' queries. For organized farm and/or firms, the collection of production data can be done more systematically with the application of IT tools. However, it is a big challenge for small farms or individual farmers to maintain detailed farming records and upload them to the public or private sector. A typical way of recording the farming information is to make notes of farming activities. An official notebook provided by the TAP system is a typical example of the way farmers keep records of their farming activities, as shown in Figure 12.5. Records of the farming data include date, activity, fertilizer, pesticides, diluting ratio, usage quantity, performer, and the auditing remark. Farmers usually make the note of farming data by handwriting and logging in to the user interface of the traceability system to input the farming data according to the notebook. Some pages of the notebook are full of deletion marks, which makes it difficult to judge whether it is a careless mistake or written over on purpose. It is obvious that most farmers are much more familiar with farming rather than handwriting and those IT tools of keyboard and mouse. Moreover, the records may not be real-time data; in some cases they probably write all the data just before

FIGURE 12.4

Private traceability system that focused on the marketing purpose.

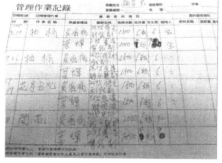

FIGURE 12.5

A typical notebook for farming data recording.

harvest, and in some worse cases can even be wrong data. Effective traceability information cannot be reached by unreliable farming records. Even if the data were correctly recorded, the minute recording procedure of manual handwriting and typing causes a lot of trouble for farmers and becomes an obstacle for the implementation of the traceability system. An efficient farming data collection tool is essential and crucial to enhance the efficiency of e-traceability.

SYSTEM ARCHITECTURE FOR THE MOBILE FARMING INFORMATION SYSTEM

The purpose of this research is to develop a mobile farming information system to collect the farming data by using cell phones instead of by handwriting before inputing them to the traceability system. System architecture of the proposed mobile traceability system is shown in Figure 12.6. The farming data are collected by the mobile devices that can provide data communication anytime and anywhere through the mobile 3G (4G) or Wi-Fi network. The data to be collected for traceability, including the farming activities messages such as seeding, weeding, fertilizing, disease prevention, harvesting and shipping, are designed to be stored in QR codes. By scanning the QR code with mobile device, the data stored in the QR code can be decoded, thus enabling a transaction with the application services to be uploaded to the traceability database. To design the mobile application system, the information relationship and operation scenarios for collecting the farming activities messages should be first analyzed.

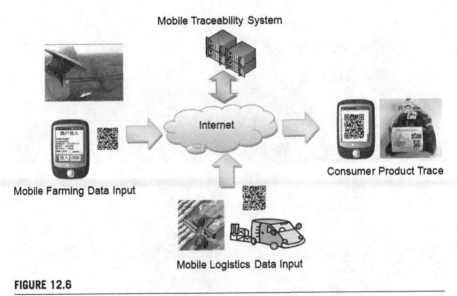

FIGURE 12.6

System architecture of the proposed mobile traceability system.

As analyzed in the previous section, the farming data is collected originally in the notebook shown in Figure 12.5. According to the items recorded in the notebook, the main information entities and their relationships are shown in Figure 12.7. The basic traceability information includes the farmer's identity information, cropland, and crop planted. All the farming activities are performed on the cropland. The farming activities can be divided into three categories: the farming operations for all kind of crops such as seeding and pruning without the need of further attribute records; the fertilizing operations, for which the fertilizer and amount used need to be recorded; and the disease prevention operations, with the use and records of pesticides. All the required operations are encoded into QR codes, and every farming operation is transformed into a distinct QR code label. Different fertilizers and pesticides are all encoded into distinct QR codes. By scanning the proper QR code, the farmer can

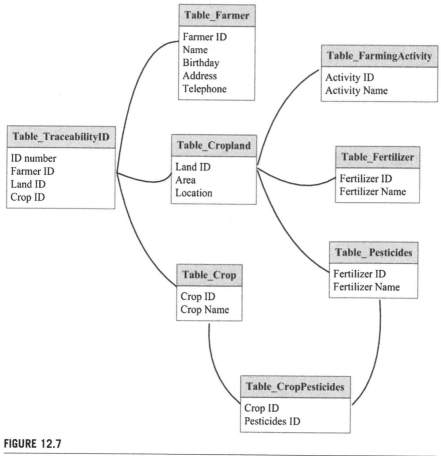

FIGURE 12.7

Main database relationship for the mobile traceability data collection system.

easily upload the operation messages into the data collection system. As the usage of pesticide is critical, for pesticide residues can be harmful to humans, the relationship of allowable pesticide levels for a crop is constructed to guarantee safety in terms of pesticide usage.

Operation scenarios for farming activity message collection are analyzed in Figure 12.8. The farming information collection is started by scanning the corresponding QR code label. The mobile device will decode and link to the application server and enable farmer authentication transaction by the application program (AP). The farmer should input the proper username and password and the mobile system will verify the validation. As the verification process is completed, the AP will show the decoded farming operation message and start the confirm request transaction. The farmer needs to confirm that the operation messages are identical with the one he performed. The operation messages will be uploaded to the database after the confirm signal is entered. In cases where more detailed attributes are required to be recorded, the detailed activity messages request transaction will be enabled after finishing the authentication as shown in Figure 12.9. The messages required include the amount used, the unit, and dilution ratio of fertilizer (or pesticide). Detailed operation scenarios for the pesticide usage recording process is shown in Figure 12.10. The process is started by (1) scanning the QR code for Cyhalothrin, (2) performing the username and password authentication, (3) enabling the message input transaction, (4) inputing the usage amount, unit, and dilution ratio

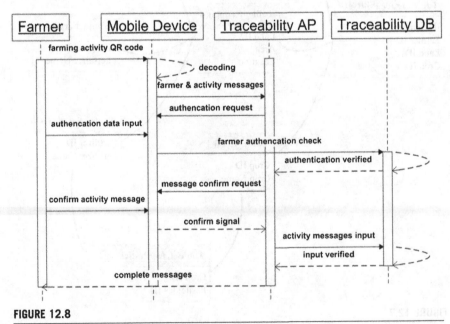

FIGURE 12.8

Sequential diagram for the farming operations without detailed records.

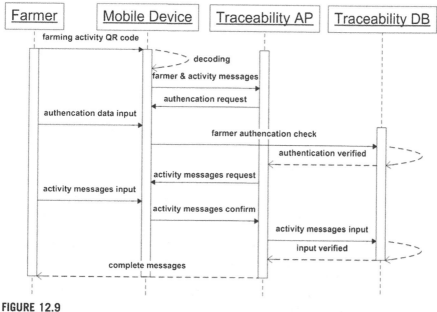

FIGURE 12.9

Sequential diagram for the farming operations with detailed records.

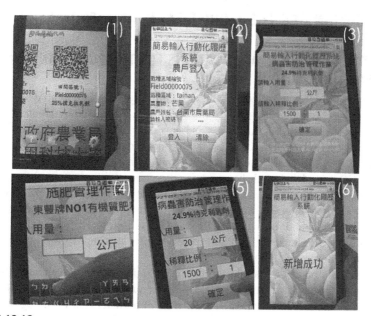

FIGURE 12.10

Detailed operation scenario for the pesticide usage recording process: (1) scanning the QR code for Cyhalothrin, (2) performing the username and password authentication, (3) enabling the message input transaction, (4) inputing the usage amount, unit, and dilution ratio of Cyhalothrin, (5) confirming the input, and (6) completing message upload.

of Cyhalothrin, (5) confirming the input, and (6) completing message upload. After the data is collected through the mobile device, the traceability data can be queried simultaneously. This system is suitable for the traceability management of subcontract supply farmers. Minimized interactive operations with the mobile devices are considered for the system. The farmer only needs to scan the QR code, input the amount used, and press the confirm button to finish the traceability data record and upload simultaneously.

By properly encoding the farming messages to the QR codes, the messages can be read by the mobile devices and uploaded simultaneously to the application server of the mobile farming system. The farming activity information can be captured by simply scanning the QR code labels and uploading in real time, instead of manual handwriting and inputing by batches to the traceability system. The miscellaneous traceability data construction can be significantly reduced. The mobile farming system can work for both the traceability systems of the public and private sectors. Data collected by the mobile farming information system is stored by the database system and can be output to the required file format of the electrical data exchange for TAP. The mobile farming system is itself also a traceability system to show the farming data and producer information when consumers scan the QR code label provided by the system. Two application examples for both the public and private traceability systems will be shown in the next section.

APPLICATIONS OF THE MOBILE FARMING INFORMATION SYSTEM

INTRODUCTION OF THE APPLICATIONS FOR THE PUBLIC AND PRIVATE TRACEABILITY SECTORS

Documentation or data collection in traceability systems is essential to provide traceable data. Most farming activity information was recorded by manually handwriting that is often making mistakes and becoming unreliable. The mobile traceability information system collects the farming data by simply scanning the farming activity QR code. The unreliable handwriting is replaced by simply scanning the QR code label, and the corresponding traceability data can be uploaded simultaneously to the back-end web server without any other input operation. The manual operations are significantly reduced, and hence, the mistake can be minimized. The threshold or obstacle of IT-related operations that were usually repelled by farmers are minimized, and that will be helpful to simplify the farming data collection for farmers.

Implementation of the mobile farming information system is validated through two projects. One is the traceability data collection for mango exporting in Taiwan. The mango export to Japan every summer is an important event for mango farmers as the price is much higher than the domestic market. Tainan, which possesses the largest agricultural area in Taiwan, is the main farmland for mango export to Japan.

Farmers of mango who export must join the TAP system to provide traceability information as the Japan government requested. Department of agriculture of Tainan City started the project of applying the mobile farming information system in 2011–2012, with the Tainan University of Technology in Taiwan, to replace the manual and unreliable handwriting of traceability data. The mobile farming information system plays as a tool of traceability data collection with the following functions: collect traceability data by simply scanning the QR code label, store the data in database system, and import to the TAP system through electrical data exchange protocol.

Another application for the mobile farming information system demonstrates that it can also play as a private traceability system. A collaborative project, jointed by Tainan University of Technology (Taiwan), Tianjin University of Agriculture (China), and Tianjin Shunzi Vegetable Cooperative (China), for the traceability of white gourd planting in Tianjin was also performed in 2014. The mobile farming information system also served as the traceability system to provide mobile farming data collection and detail producer information with multimedia videos for marketing purpose. These two cases show that the mobile farming information system can be applied either for traceability system as an effective farming data collection and importing tools for the public or as a private sector.

MANGO TRACEABILITY DATA CONSTRUCTION FOR TAP SYSTEM IN TAIWAN

Mango exportation is one of the important and high-valued agro-businesses in Taiwan. In addition to the epidemic prevention, the traceability information is also essential to meet Japanese legislation. Realizing that manual handwriting and computer operations are very difficult for individual and mostly elder farmers, the agriculture bureau of Tainan city government planned to build a simplified traceability system for those who cannot apply the auditing process of the formal TAP system. The pilot project was initiated from the end of 2011 to test the implementation of the mobile farming information system and farmers' acceptance of the mobile device solutions. The development process took place from the end of 2011 to the July 2012. The activities of the pilot project can be summarized as follows:

1. Kickoff meeting

    The pilot project began by the kickoff meeting held by mango farmers, government employees, and the technical team form Tainan University of Technology. Five mango farmers joined the pilot project voluntarily.
2. Farming data and QR code definition

    The system analysis for the production activities and related information required for mango farming was firstly reviewed. The farming data definition from TAP system, including farming activities, fertilizer, and pesticides, were applied to the pilot system, to ensure the data exchange when importing to the TAP system will be consistent. The QR code for every farming activity was encoded after the data definition was decided.

3. Database and brief traceability system development

As analyzed in the previous section, the database architecture and the mobile data collection, storage, and query system is developed. All the function can be operated via the mobile devices. The normal farming activities, such as irrigation, weeding, branch trimming, etc., can be recorded by scanning and confirming the corresponding QR code label as shown in Figure 12.11(a). Activities for fertilizing and pesticides application that needed further input of the usage quantity are shown in Figure 12.11(b). The operations for farmers to click the confirm button and for inputing numbers are minimized.

4. Mobile farming SOP and training

To provide effective training for the mobile farming information system, standard operation procedure was established, including the brief operation instructions of the hardware device, the QR code scanning process, and the usual questions and answers for the usage.

5. Field testing and auditing

As the mobile system mostly operated in the mango farmland that is usually located on the hills far away from the urban area, the field test for the mobile communication at the farmland is necessary to guarantee the effectiveness of the system. The field testing and auditing were performed at the site of the farmland, as shown in Figure 12.12. The data communication through mobile 3G network worked effectively for the mobile system at the farmland hill.

The pilot project ended at the harvest of mango exporting, which is usually during the first two weeks of July. The field test results revealed that mobile farming data collection could be operated in the farmland hill under the current telecommunication facilities in Taiwan. The operation scenarios with the use of mobile device scanning

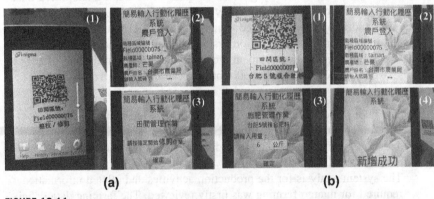

(a) **(b)**

FIGURE 12.11

(a) Mobile farming data collection by (1) scan the QR code, (2) farmer authentication, and (3) confirm the activity. (b) Farming data with quantity input by (1) scan the QR code, (2) farmer authentication, (3) input the usage quantity, and (4) confirm the activity.

FIGURE 12.12

Farmland site testing of the mobile system: (1) the farming data, (2)—(3) operation on farmland hill site, (4) the QR code label, and (5)—(8) the technical team and the 2012 National Invention and Creation Award in Taiwan.

were acceptable to the farmers. The proposed mobile farming information system was shown to be efficient for the farming data collection and, hence, effective for the traceability system to replace the unreliable manual handwriting. The technology and corresponding implementation results had won the 2012 National Invention and Creation Award in Taiwan. Another project for the water chestnut and rice farming were stared since 2013 to spread the application of mobile farming information for individual farmers in Tainan. The aim is to provide safety with traceable information on agro-products for consumers and to enhance the development of agro-business in Tainan.

PRIVATE TRACEABILITY SYSTEM FOR WHITE GOURD IN TIANJIN, CHINA

Traceability systems in China are attracting increasing research and industrial interests. The food safety and traceability-related projects were one of the focus issues in the 12th 5-year national development plan started since 2012 by the China government. The academic cooperation between Tainan University of Technology (TUT) and Tianjin University of Agriculture (TUA) has been started since 2012. Research about the food and agro-product traceability in TUA have got financial support from the Spark Program 2013 of the Ministry of Science and Technology of PRC, and science and technology developing program form the Tianjin Municipal Science and Technology Commission. The Tianjin Shunzi Vegetable Cooperative (TSVC) is one of the famous farms in Tianjin whose white gourd has won the 2012 "One Village One Product" paradigm of ministry of agriculture in China and became one of the distinguished agro-products in Tianjin. In addition to the farming production, TSVC also developed the agro-touring business to provide urban citizens a weekend agricultural tourism opportunity with vegetables and fruits plucking, country scenery, and country meals with local characteristics. They joined the TUA project in 2014 to implement the mobile farming information system to build their own traceability system for the white gourd. The aim of the traceability system is not only to improve the safety traceability but also to promote the value of the brand "Qinmei" for TSVC.

The implementation of mobile farming data collection is similar to the mango case in Tainan. The difference is to build a platform for traceability information query with the purpose of product brand marketing. The home page of the back-end server of the mobile platform is shown in Figure 12.13. As a private traceability service platform, the home page of the service platform shows the organizations

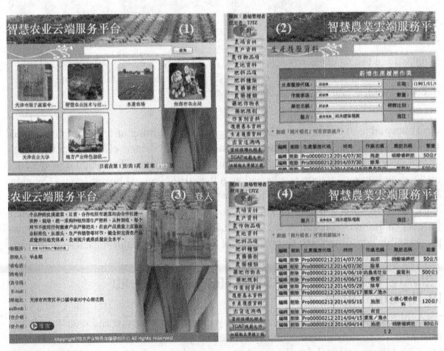

FIGURE 12.13

Mobile server platform user interfaces: (1) home page, (2) main function screen, (3) farm information editing screen, and (4) farming data editing screen.

registered in this sector. After being logged in to the system by the administrator of the organization, the production data of farm information, farmer, product, fertilizer, pesticides, harvesting, and packing information can all be maintained in the platform. The farm information includes name of the contact farmer, telephone and fax numbers, e-mail, address, and the multimedia video provided in accordance with the text information and pictures. The farming data uploaded can be queried, and only the administrator can delete or edit the farming data to ensure the correctness and reliability. By scanning the traceability label, the brief traceability information, including name of the organization and producer, traceability ID number, telephone number, and location of the farmland, is displayed on the mobile device (as shown in Figure 12.14). The detailed farm and traceability information can be obtained by further clicking the corresponding linkage. As the traceability system implemented, the white gourd of TSVC was becoming more famous and won the golden prize of the 2014 excellent agricultural products of Tianjin. The traceability system can improve not only the transparency of the farming procedure but also the brand image of social responsibility.

FIGURE 12.14

Traceability system user interfaces: (1) first page of brief traceability information, (2) farm information, (3) traceability data, (4) the farmland, (5) traceability label, (6)–(7) technical team and the farmers, and (8) the golden prize of 2014 excellent agricultural products of Tianjin.

SUMMARY AND CONCLUSIONS

The global burden of foodborne illness caused by bacteria, viruses, parasitic micro-organisms, pesticides, contaminants, and other food safety problems is thought to be considerable. Traceability is becoming an common element of public (both regulatory and voluntary) interventions and of private systems. Food contamination may occur at the farm, during processing or distribution, in transit, at retail, or in food service establishments. Unsafe food can be recalled because information on all possible sources and supplies of contaminated food can be traced. Many developing countries lag in developing and implementing food safety and traceability standards, but some have selectively met demands in high-income export markets dues to regulatory, technical, and administrative investments. Traceability data involves miscellaneous records that is mostly kept by manual handwriting. To reduce the complicated and unreliable traceability data recording procedure, the mobile farming information system is developed to enhance the efficiency of e-traceability. The operation scenarios for the mobile traceability data construction and collection are studied, the architecture for the system and database are schemed, and the application examples are proposed in this research. By properly encoding the farming activity messages to the QR code labels, the farming data can be read by the mobile devices and uploaded simultaneously to the mobile platform server. The farming activity information can be captured by simply scanning the QR code labels and uploaded in real time. The miscellaneous traceability data collection can be significantly reduced. The mobile farming information proposed can be implemented either as the mobile data collection tool for public traceability or a private traceability system. These two applications are verified through implementation projects in Tainan and Tianjin. The results showed that the mobile farming information can be successfully implemented. Food traceability can be more credible when the farming data is collected more reliably.

ACKNOWLEDGEMENTS

This work was supported by 2013 Industrial Park Industry-Academia Cooperation Project from Ministry of Education of ROC (102B-26-006), the 2013 Spark Program of the Ministry of Science and Technology of PRC, and 2013 program of the Tianjin Municipal Science and Technology Commission (13ZLZLZF04400).

REFERENCES

[1] Moe T. Perspectives on traceability in food manufacture. Trends Food Sci Technol 1998;9:211–4.
[2] Opara LU, Mazaud F. Food traceability from field to plate. Outlook Agric 2001;30(4): 239–47.

[3] Varga M, Csukas B. On the way toward the sector spanning agrifood process traceability. Agric Inform 2010;1(1):8−18.

[4] Opara LU. Traceability in agriculture and food supply chain: a review of basic concepts, technological implications, and future prospects. J Food Agric Environ 2003;1(1): 101−6.

[5] Wang X, Li D, Li L. Adding value of food traceability to the business: a supply chain management approach. Int J Serv Oper Inform 2009;4(3):232−57.

[6] Pouliot S, Sumner DA. Traceability, Liability, and Incentives for Food Safety and Quality. Am J Agric Econ 2008;90(1):15−27.

[7] Golan E, Krissoff B, Kuchler F, Nelson K, Price G, Calvin L. Traceability in the US Food Supply: Dead End or Superhighway. Choices-The Magazine of Food, Farm, and Resources Issues, second quarter 2003:17−20.

[8] Dabbenea F, Gay P. Food traceability systems: Performance evaluation and optimization. Comput Electron Agric 2011:75139−46.

[9] Bosona T, Gebresenbet G. Food traceability as an integral part of logistics management in food and agricultural supply chain. Food Control 2013;33:32−48.

[10] Regattieri A, Gamberi M, Manzini R. Traceability of food products: General framework and experimental evidence. Journal of Food Engineering 2007;81:347−56.

[11] Schwagele F. Traceability from a European perspective. Meat Sci 2005;71:164−73.

[12] Chrysochou P, Chryssochoidis G, Kehagia O. Traceability information carriers. The technology backgrounds and consumer's perceptions of the technological solutions. Appetite 2009;53(3):322−31.

[13] Miraglia M, Berdal KG, Brera C, Corbisier P, Holst-Jensen A, Kok EJ, et al. Detection and traceability of genetically modified organisms in the food production chain. Food Chem Toxicol 2004;42:1157−80.

[14] Choe YC, Park J, Chung M, Moon J. Effect of the food traceability system for building trust: Price premium and buying behavior. Inform Syst Front 2009;11(2):167−79.

[15] Dickinson DL, Bailey DV. Meat Traceability: Are U.S. Consumers Willing to Pay for It? J Agric Resource Econ 2002;27(2):348−64.

[16] Golan E, Krissoff B, Kuchler F, Calvin L, Nelson K, Price G. Traceability in the U.S. food supply: economic theory and industry studies, Economic Research Service, U.S. Department of Agriculture, Agricultural economic report no. 830, March 2004.

[17] Golan E, Krissof B, Kuchler F. Food raceability: One ingredient in a safe and efficient food supply. Amber Waves 2004;2(2):14−21.

[18] Smith GC, Tatum JD, Belk KE, Scanga JA, Grandin T, Sofos JN. Traceability from a US perspective. Meat Sci 2005;71:174−93.

[19] Schiefer G. New technologies and their impact on the agri-food sector: an economists view. Comput Electron Agric 2004;43(2):163−72.

[20] Sørensena CG, Fountasb S, Nashf E, Pesonend L, Bochtisa D, Pedersene SM, et al. Conceptual model of a future farm management information system. Comput Electron Agric 2010;72(1):37−47.

[21] Kelepouris T, Pramatari K, Doukidis G. RFID-enabled traceability in the food supply chain. Ind Mana Data Syst 2007;107(2):183−200.

[22] Regattieri A, Gamberi M, Manzini R. Traceability of food products: General framework and experimental evidence. J Food Eng 2007;81(2):347−56.

[23] Manthou V, Matopoulos A, Vlachopoulou M. Internet-based applications in the agri-food supply chain: a survey on the Greek canning sector. J Food Eng 2005; 70(3):447−54.

[24] Li M, Qian JP, Yang XT, Sun CH, Ji ZT. A PDA-based record-keeping and decision-support system for traceability in cucumber production. Comput Electron Agric 2010;70(1):69−77.

[25] Mahalik NP, Nambiar AN. Trends in food packaging and manufacturing systems and technology. Trends Food Sci Technol 2010;21(3):117−28.

[26] Wang N, Zhang N, Wang M. Wireless sensors in agriculture and food industry—Recent development and future perspective. Comput Electron Agric 2006;50(1):1−14.

[27] Pinto DB, Castro I, Vicente AA. The use of TIC's as a managing tool for traceability in the food industry. Food Res Int 2006;39:772−81.

[28] Gao HM, Liu YC. Conceptual Design of Mobile Data Collection System for Traceability in Agriculture. Appl Mech Materials 2014;513−7:1131−4.

[29] Seine K, Kuwabara S, Mikami S, Takahashi Y, Yoshikawa M, Narumi H, et al. Development of the traceability system which secures the safety of fishery products using the QR code and a digital signature. Proc IEEE TECHNO-OCEAN '04 2004. Nov. 9-12, Kobe, Japan.

[30] Cunha CR, Peres E, Morais R, Oliveira AA, Matos SG, Fernandes MA, et al. The use of mobile devices with multi-tag technologies for an overall contextualized vineyard management. Comput Electron Agric 2010;73(2):154−64.

Telehealth in Primary Health Care: Analysis of Liverpool NHS Experience

13

Nonso Nnamoko[1], Farath Arshad[1], Lisa Hammond[2], Sam Mcpartland[3], Pat Patterson[2]

Centre for Health and Social Care Informatics — CHaSCI, Liverpool John Moores University, Liverpool, UK[1]; NHS Liverpool Community Health, Wavertree Technology Park, Liverpool, UK[2]; Primary Care Commissioning IM&T Team, Informatics Merseyside, Liverpool, UK[3]
E-mail: N.A.Nnamoko@2011.ljmu.ac.uk, F.N.Arshad@ljmu.ac.uk, Lisa.Hammond@liverpoolCH.nhs.uk, Sam.mcpartland@imerseyside.nhs.uk, Patricia.Patterson@LiverpoolCH.nhs.uk

INTRODUCTION

Increasing health care cost and managing patient expectations has called for a rethink in the way health care is provided in the United Kingdom. Current service transformations are relying significantly on harnessing the advantages that may be possible through greater use of the information and communication technology (ICT) infrastructure already in place within the UK National Health Service (NHS). Certainly, the drive to deliver out-of-hospital care, which promotes immediate and tailored support to patients in a cost-effective manner, is receiving much attention, especially now that health service providers struggle to cope with the rising numbers of elderly people, particularly those with long-term conditions (LTCs) [1]. Telehealth is receiving increasing interest within the NHS as a means to deliver health care from a distance. This is partly because improvements in technology is making the medium faster, cheaper, and easy to use, but even more encouraging has been its use to engage with hard-to-reach groups [2]. This effort to move services closer to patients is believed to help the NHS achieve good-quality health care delivery, at a time and place suitable to patients while remaining within the financial envelope. However, with interest on telehealth technologies now widespread, academics fear that local health communities are being left without the information they need to effectively roll out the technology [3]. Whereas the impact of telehealth technologies in health care has received huge coverage, the area of user experience is still underresearched [4].

This chapter describes and analyzes the process of incorporating a telehealth system (Motiva) on a 6-month pilot project within the Liverpool local NHS, United Kingdom. The Motiva system was developed by Philips, and offers remote management facility to patients with LTC [5]. The implementation relied on clinicians who otherwise operate a conventional care delivery method that is more hospital based. The Centre for Health and Social Care Informatics (CHaSCI) at Liverpool John Moores University (LJMU) conducted a feasibility study after the pilot. The study reflects the aim of the pilot, which sought to strengthen the quality of primary care delivered to patients and also to educate clinicians on the use of telehealth systems. In addition, the study provides detailed insight into user experience of the telehealth system. For both patients (including carers) and clinicians involved in the pilot project, a quantitative and qualitative exercise was carried out through paper-based questionnaire and one-to-one semistructured interviews, respectively. The sources for this analysis include information from related research and documents from the funding institutions that worked closely with both Philips and CHaSCI to structure and deliver the overall project. The study procedure and key findings forms the core of this chapter but first, we describe the components of the telehealth project. The Conclusion and Recommendation sections highlight areas that may be influential in deciding on the direction of travel for the telehealth work stream within the local health economy.

CHARACTERISTICS OF THE MOTIVA PILOT PROJECT

In 2010, Liverpool Primary Care Trust (PCT) was approached by Philips with the opportunity to run a proof of concept using assistive telehealth in the local area for a limited time period. The key objectives were to evaluate the use of assistive telehealth technology to

- identify if the perceived benefits in the use of telehealth technology can be demonstrated, including associated cost savings and patient experience;
- evaluate how telehealth can support the clinical pathways developed as part of the Quality, Innovation, Productivity and Prevention (QIPP) agenda [6];
- identify key lessons learnt from the proof of concept that can support and facilitate any future rollout of telehealth locally, including the identification of any dis-benefits associated with assisted telehealth; and
- identify opportunities to change the way that local health care is delivered to patients suffering with long-term conditions.

The motivation for this study came from Liverpool PCT's need to understand patients' perception of the system, the impact of the system on patient welfare, and on clinician workload. In addition, because an earlier preliminary study (with five patients) was not successful, Liverpool PCT and the system manufacturer (Philips) both wanted an up-to-date report of the system usage to assess if there is need for further modification(s).

COHORT RECRUITMENT AND TIME SCALES

The proof of concept pilot was undertaken in three phases, each spanning a period of 3 months. Phase 1 was conducted with patients diagnosed with heart failure (HF) only. Phase 1 did not work as anticipated because the daily monitoring was done by lower-qualified clinical staff and there were issues regarding the cohort (i.e., involved HF patients only from one health center). Therefore phase 1b was considered with a different approach; recruiting patients with chronic obstructive pulmonary disease (COPD) and diabetes in addition to those with HF. Patients were also recruited from other health care providers managed by Liverpool Community Health in the Anfield area of Liverpool. This time, the telehealth monitoring exercise was undertaken by highly qualified clinical staff (community matrons). This model was successful and enabled the phase 2 pilot in which patient recruitment was extended to another team of community matrons based in the Edge Hill area of Liverpool. New patients were recruited during phase 2 but patients enrolled onto phase 1b were kept on the system as part of phase 2.

The recruiting community matron(s) were responsible for obtaining patient consent and ensuring that the patients' general practitioners (GPs) were informed. The community matrons at Everton Road Health Centre monitored the patients on a daily basis (Monday–Friday) during phase 1b. For phase 2, the matrons at Edge Hill Health Centre were also involved in the monitoring process. Figure 13.1 shows the selection method used to identify patients potentially suitable for inclusion in the pilot study. The analysis reported in this chapter was deemed to be of an audit nature, and so ethical approval was not considered necessary by the NHS provider.

Once patients commenced on the telehealth program, they began to send their vital signs for review. Patient data was recorded automatically using compatible monitoring devices supplied with the system (Figure 13.2) and transmitted to the system's back end. Patients must complete the monitoring exercise every day of the week (Monday–Sunday) before 11:00 AM. Generally patients recorded their blood pressure and weight as a standard. In addition, diabetic patients would record their blood glucose levels whereas patients with COPD would record their saturation levels. Clinicians must access and review captured data after 11:00 AM each working day (Monday–Friday).

The matrons would use their own clinical judgement to assess the patient's results on a daily basis and treat accordingly. Patients also received educational videos on the chronic disease area they were being monitored for on the telehealth program. The analysis and results provided in this chapter covers phases 1b and 2 only and provides answers to the objectives outlined in the previous section.

METHOD

The study was conducted among two user groups (i.e., patients and clinicians) using two survey approaches—a simple questionnaire focused on the system use, followed by a second more general one-to-one discussion about telehealth and its impact on user roles/duties. The questionnaire consists of a range of multiple-choice questions about user experience/satisfaction of the telehealth system, and spaces for free text comments.

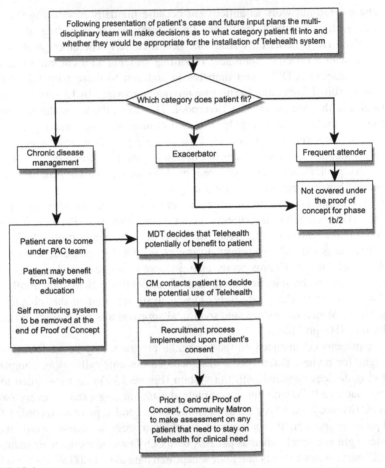

Following presentation of patient's case and future input plans the multi-disciplinary team will make decisions as to what category patient fit into and whether they would be appropriate for the installation of Telehealth system

Which category does patient fit?

Chronic disease management

Exacerbator

Frequent attender

Not covered under the proof of concept for phase 1b/2

Patient care to come under PAC team

Patient may benefit from Telehealth education

Self monitoring system to be removed at the end of Proof of Concept

MDT decides that Telehealth potentially of benefit to patient

CM contacts patient to decide the potential use of Telehealth

Recruitment process implemented upon patient's consent

Prior to end of Proof of Concept, Community Matron to make assessment on any patient that need to stay on Telehealth for clinical need

FIGURE 13.1

Telehealth patient identification processes.

An earlier test study had been conducted by Philips, and some of their questions were adapted and incorporated into the version reported here. (Note: Philips had only tested the system with five patients, and the NHS provider required an objective view of the patient experience with the proof of concept telehealth work, hence the commissioning of the study undertaken and reported in this chapter.) Key lines of inquiry are shown in Tables 13.1 and 13.2.

Paper-based questionnaires were distributed to patients (n = 45; 24 of 45 = 53% response rate) who took part in the system pilot, along with a self-addressed stamped envelope to receive replies. Nonresponders were not followed up because of time limitations. All 24 respondents had already completed the clinical trial when they answered the questionnaire, although some used the system more than others because of a series of changes made during the pilot as detailed in the previous

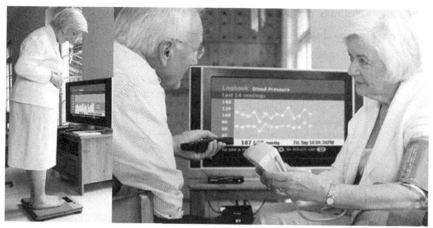

FIGURE 13.2

Patients using specially adapted equipment for measuring vital signs.

section. A follow-on interview was arranged with a small sample of patients, selected based on mobility ($n = 6$; 4 of 6 = 67% response rate). Patient attrition rate was attributed to three factors: despondency, delay in return (note: we had limited time scale to undertake the study and produce a report), and withdrawal from scheduled appointments. The clinician survey took a similar approach, complementing targeted questionnaire study with semistructured interviews. However, both study phases for clinicians were conducted consecutively per subject so they were first asked to complete a prevalidated questionnaire, followed by a semistructured interview. In total, 12 clinicians including 7 matrons, 3 nurses, and 2 GPs were considered. However, as only the matrons and nurses had direct involvement with the telehealth system, we conducted the full study (questionnaire and interview) with them, and approached the GPs for general opinions on telehealth. The nurses' opinions were sampled via telephone as face-to-face interviews could not be arranged in time.

In view of the heterogeneous nature of the questionnaire content and its administration method (paper-based), the data available did not permit the use of formal

Table 13.1 Key Lines of Inquiry Covered in the Quantitative (Paper) Study

Section No.	Patients' Questionnaire	Clinicians' Questionnaire
Section 1	First impressions about Motiva (4 embedded questions)	First impressions about Motiva (4 embedded questions)
Section 2	Effects of Motiva on care pathway (12 embedded questions)	User satisfaction/performance (4 embedded questions)
Section 3	User perception (15 embedded questions)	

Table 13.2 Key Lines of Inquiry Covered in the Qualitative (Oral) Study

Question	Semistructured Interview with Patient(s)
1.	Highlight the most negative/positive aspect(s) of the Motiva system from your point of view
2.	Did you learn anything new from the process?
3.	Is there anything else about being involved in the telehealth project that you wish had been different?
4.	Is there anything else you think we have not covered on the questionnaire with regards to your experience?
	Semistructured interview with clinician(s)
1.	Highlight the most positive/negative aspects of the project?
2.	Did you learn anything new about telehealth technology in general?
3.	How has the use of telehealth affected the tasks you would normally undertake? That is, has the load increased or decreased?
4.	Do you feel more confident about new technology now?
5.	Is there anything else about being involved in the project you wish had been different—including those not covered in the questionnaire?

statistical techniques for analysis. Instead, we report a broad qualitative and quantitative analysis of the findings (similar to narrative synthesis). Although several published methodologies exist for analyzing heterogeneous data [7,8], they are often domain or subject specific, time consuming and mostly used in large-scale analysis. The method used in this chapter is suitable for analyzing studies with diverse outcomes [9] and indeed a standard practice within the health care domain for analyzing heterogeneous data sets [10,11]. We gauged patient experience using their individual and collective responses to the questions. We did not use a formal scoring method as no well-validated generic instrument for automatic review of such a questionnaire with diverse content exists yet for end users [9].

ANALYSIS AND RESULT
PATIENTS

As background, 24 and 4 patients were considered for the quantitative (questionnaire) and qualitative (interview) studies respectively. We first asked users to indicate the condition for which they were enrolled on the pilot project, before completing the different sections of the questionnaire (see Table 13.1). Of the 24 respondents, 18 were identified as having COPD, 5 were HF patients, and only 2 have diabetes.

QUESTIONNAIRE SECTION 1: FIRST IMPRESSIONS (EMBEDDED QUESTIONS 1—4)

All respondents (100%) indicated they received adequate information/instructions about the pilot (telehealth proof of concept) project and the system usage prior to

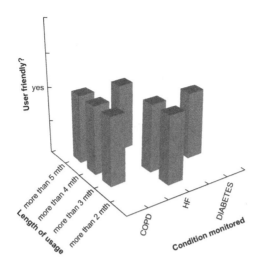

FIGURE 13.3

A 3-way response correlation chart.

installation. We also asked users to rate their first experience using the system with five options (i.e., outstanding, satisfactory, neutral, poor, or very poor). There was strong indication from the response that their experience was average at the least. Majority (54%) said it was outstanding, 37.5% said it was satisfactory, and the remaining ($n = 2$) answered "neutral." When asked if the system was user friendly and how long they had used it, all 24 patients, regardless of length of usage, indicated that the system was easy to use. Majority (92%) used the system for at least 3 months, and the other 2 patients used it for a little under 3 months (Figure 13.3). This result is very important as it eliminates bias in subsequent findings.

QUESTIONNAIRE SECTION 2: EFFECTS OF MOTIVA ON CARE PATHWAY (EMBEDDED QUESTIONS 5–16)

To gauge the impact on care pathway, we asked users 12 questions (mostly yes or no type) with space for further comments (optional). For simplicity, we arranged user responses to the yes or no type questions ($n = 6$) into Table 13.3. The other 6 questions are explained in a question/response format.

In line with recent findings on telehealth outcomes [12], the monitoring of vital signs via the telehealth system reassured patients (95.83%), empowered patients (91.67%), improved care at home (87.50%), and reduced hospital/GP visits (70.83). Additional comments supplied by respondents suggest that patients and their family felt reassured knowing that monitoring and help were available. Also, the cumulative trend visualization of measured signs along with other on-screen help led to better understanding of the condition. Most respondents who experienced improved home care stated that communication with clinical staff was improved,

Table 13.3 System Effects of Motiva on Patients' Care Pathway

Questions	Yes	No	No Response
Facilitate lifestyle change(s)	12 (50%)	11 (45.83%)	1 (4.16)
Reduced visits to GP/hospital	17 (70.83%)	8 (29.16%)	—
Facilitate change in medication regime	5 (20.83%)	19 (79.17%)	—
Led to better understanding of condition	22 (91.67%)	2 (8.33%)	—
Led to a more efficient home care	21 (87.50%)	3 (12.50%)	—
Provide re-assurance/security	23 (95.83%)	1 (4.17%)	—

discussions were tailored, and visits (GP or hospital) were only arranged when necessary. Basically, patients monitored from their own homes, received help from clinicians at any occurrence of abnormality in measurements observed. This is important as research suggests that older patients prefer care at home through self-management rather than institutional [13]. However, care must be taken to ensure adequate contact is maintained because some patients, particularly the elderly who often live alone, value the social contact with clinicians [14]. Some researchers argue that home care through telehealth reduces close contact [15,16], and data/information integrity may be undermined [2], resulting in poor clinical decisions and distrust between patients and clinicians. In contrast, this project enhanced the clinical care and immediacy of response to accommodate patient needs, perhaps because of the implementation strategy and/or the organizational structure of the local NHS provider.

The community matron's role was introduced into the United Kingdom in 2005 in order to reduce unplanned hospital admissions of patients living with long-term conditions, and their services largely involves visits to patients' homes [17]. This service level was maintained during the pilot period, and consequently GP/hospital visits were reported to have reduced. This result shows a positive effect of the matrons' job role and echoes research findings that telehealth reduces hospital visits [18] and associated cost [2], by enabling individuals to perform certain tasks at home. Most respondents who reduced the number of visits to their GP wrote that complications were detected early and dealt with promptly via telephone discussion(s) and/or in some cases, a matron visiting them at home. In addition, some of those who did not reduce GP/hospital visits revealed that this was in fact a positive outcome. One respondent was placed under intensive care because the system revealed some potentially dangerous fluctuations in their measurement. Another wrote that visits remained the same because they "had to attend regardless."

Half of the respondents agreed to have made lifestyle changes particularly in improving exercise regime and diet control. The other half (less one patient who did not respond) did not make lifestyle changes, but additional comments suggest their response had more to do with their health and/or physical status levels. For instance, one respondent wrote "No reason to"; others wrote "breathing problems," "difficulty walking, painful legs," "I find it difficult to get weighed without the scales supplied with the system." We also noticed that majority (79.17%) had not made changes to their medication regime as a result of using the system. Examination of the additional comments indicates they had no need to make changes. Of those who did (20.83%), some added it was in response to rapid changes in measurements observed through trend visualizations. Basically, some patients had all or part of their medication(s) altered to reflect changes in their measurements, and others became more aware of therapeutic solutions to changes in their measurements. For instance, one respondent wrote, "Just better understanding of when to use medicines"; a comment among others which echoes that the system led to better understanding of condition according to results (see Table 13.3).

In other questions (not shown in Table 13.3), we asked users to identify in one of three options (increased, the same, reduced) their observations regarding clinical support since the introduction of Motiva. (Recall: study was conducted after the project, so this includes the period after the pilot.) Of the 23 patients who responded to this question, 30.43% ($n = 7$) said support increased and 65.22% ($n = 15$) said it stayed the same; another indication that the local NHS organizational setup played a part in the success of the pilot as explained earlier. The only respondent who experienced reduced clinical support added, "Have not needed to see my Matron as much." In addition to on-screen visualizations of measurement trends, the system provided patients with educational videos to explain their condition, so we asked respondents if they watched the regular educational video clips presented daily through the system. Those who answered "Yes" had five other related questions to complete (Table 13.4) and those who answered "No" were asked to explain why before they continue with the last section of the questionnaire.

Overall, 16.67% ($n = 4$) of the respondents neither watched the videos nor provided comments to explain why. However, the rest ($n = 20$) watched the videos and attempted all or part of the follow-on questions.

QUESTIONNAIRE SECTION 3: USER PERCEPTION (EMBEDDED QUESTIONS 17–31)

Respondents were asked to rate their perception of Motiva services toward better understanding of their condition. As expected, the majority of respondents were either extremely satisfied ($n = 13$) or very satisfied ($n = 8$). The remaining 3 were not sure (neutral). Respondents were also asked specific questions about elements of the system they liked or disliked (Table 13.5), and other questions regarding their experience with the system and telehealth in general (Table 13.6).

Almost two-thirds of the respondents (62.5%) liked the educational information supplied, and the rest did not answer the question. As expected, a large percentage of respondents liked the fact that their measurements were being tracked (95.83%) and help was always available (78.26%). Majority (95.83) also liked monitoring

Table 13.4 Abstract of User Responses to the Relevance of Educational Videos

Q	Was enough effort made to encourage you? (20 responded)
A	They all agreed that enough effort was made.
Q	What encouraged you? (13 responded)
A	Most respondents agreed that the videos came-up automatically and were easy to follow. One patient added, "….understanding my condition and how I could try to ease my breathing." Another wrote, "felt less isolated knowing other people unfortunately have similar problems."
Q	What did you find most useful about the videos? (15 responded)
A	Most respondents agreed they were informative, providing clear explanation of their condition. Some wrote that the videos helped them make lifestyle changes.
Q	What was not so useful about the videos? (7 responded)
A	Of the 7 respondents, 6 found everything useful, with one adding, "Was on a course so I knew some of the information." However, one respondent found the videos frightening, adding that "it revealed the dangers associated with bad management."
Q	What additional videos would you like in the future? (7 responded)
A	Respondents were mostly satisfied with available videos but one of them added that they would like to see statistics showing how they compared to others with similar condition, in terms of management.

Table 13.5 Patients' View of Liked and Disliked Elements of Motiva (Quantitative)

Questions	Like	Dislike	No Response
Educational information to manage condition better	15	—	9
Knowing measurements are being tracked	23	—	1
Knowing I can always contact clinicians if I have concerns	18	—	6
Having to monitor regularly	23	—	1
Having to monitor within set times (regimented)	19	4	1

regularly but unsurprisingly a high percentage (79.16%) felt it was regimented (i.e., on or before 11:00 AM each day). Because the matrons owe the same duty of care, which largely involves visits to patients' homes [17], and the conventional method has been proven to improve patient's quality of life [19][20], the set time for telehealth monitoring exercise is inevitable. This means that patients' measurements must be transmitted in time for clinicians (matrons and nurses), who have to review them and still carry out other duties such as home visits as required.

Table 13.6 Patients' Experience/Perception of Motiva and Telehealth in General

Questions	Yes	No	No Response
Would you like telehealth in other aspects of your health	16	8	—
Did you experience any kind of system failure with Motiva	12	12	—
Would you recommend Motiva	23	—	1
Would you consider telehealth in the future	21	2	1
Would you like to continue using Motiva	20	3	1
Would you like to see changes to enhance Motiva service(s)	4	19	1

As expected, majority of the respondents (66.66%) would like telehealth in other aspects of health care. Overall, 83.33% want to carry on using the system, 95.83% would recommend it, and 87.5% would consider telehealth in the future. Half of the respondents experienced system failure, and a small percentage (16.66%) would like to see some changes made to the system. We also asked what follow-on support they would like to see after the pilot, and only 50% responded. Among their suggestions were regular contact and/or educational health care information via phone (50%), e-mail (25%), or post (12.5%). One respondent added they would like a dedicated discussion forum guided by experienced clinical staff members. We observed that this section of the questionnaire was sparsely completed, and there was little evidence to explain the responses supplied, perhaps because of the survey length. According to Frede [21], the longer the survey, "the fewer respondents complete it and the more drop out." We knew this could adversely affect quality, so we included some of the questions (with low response rate) in the semistructured interview to obtain more information.

SEMISTRUCTURED INTERVIEW (FOUR EMBEDDED QUESTIONS)

Because all 24 respondents agreed the system was user friendly regardless of the length of usage and/or condition monitored (Figure 13.3), we focused on functionality of the system and impact on patient health, especially areas of the questionnaire that lacked evidence (additional comment) or those with low response count. We asked if they learnt anything new about their condition through the period they used the system. All 4 respondents agreed they had learnt one or more facts about their condition, particularly around "breathing technique." We then asked them to highlight the most negative/positive aspect(s) of the system from their experience (Table 13.7). The most disliked element centered on the frequency of measurements required. Of the respondents, 3 (of 4) reported that the frequency at which some of the variables (e.g., weight and blood pressure) were requested was inappropriate.

Table 13.7 Patients' View of Positive and Negative Aspects of Motiva (Qualitative)

Positive(s)	Negative(s)
Ability to visualize and track measurements Easy to use Boosts confidence Reassured knowing that measurements are being tracked by clinicians Educative and effected lifestyle changes	Frequency of measurement, especially weight. System failure/Internet connectivity issues

For instance, one respondent said that daily prompts to measure weight for a well-managed diabetes case would be unnecessary, hence the need for a personalization option within the system. Another added that "blood pressure varies at different times of the day but the test was only conducted once daily." The intention was to use Motiva to drive service improvement that would see patient self-management and education as an integral part of the care offered; resulting in longer-term goals of reducing hospital outpatient referrals and admissions.

As expected, many users experienced system failure at some point during the process but explained that these were often minor technical issues and were promptly managed by the technical support team. Despite the negatives highlighted, patient satisfaction with the system was high. All respondents ($n = 4$) expressed their dissatisfaction with the project ending. This result was captured when we asked respondents to highlight anything they wish had been different about the pilot system, including items not covered within the questionnaire. One respondent added that "confidence level has dropped since the termination." Further comments suggest they would in fact like to see something else put in place after the termination, particularly to help maintain the same level of communication with clinicians.

CLINICIANS

This cohort comprised 12 clinicians, made up of 7 matrons, 3 nurses and 2 GPs. The feasibility study was conducted in two parts eliciting quantitative (Table 13.1) and qualitative (Table 13.2) data. GPs were only approached to sample their opinions on telehealth, as they had no direct contact with Motiva. The results reported in the questionnaire section consists of 10 clinicians only (i.e., excluding GPs). We included GPs' opinions within the semistructured interview section.

QUESTIONNAIRE SECTION 1: FIRST IMPRESSIONS (FOUR EMBEDDED QUESTIONS)

Majority of the clinicians (80%) used the system at least 3 months before the pilot ended. The other 20% used it a little over 2 months. We asked if users were provided with adequate information and training prior to use with three options (yes, no, not sure). Majority (80%) answered "yes," and the rest (20%) were not sure. One respondent who was not sure added, "Training was brief and I have poor computer background," suggesting this could be due to poor computer literacy, and some clinicians are less receptive to the use of new technologies [22]. We then asked users to rate their first experience using the system with five options (i.e., outstanding, satisfactory, neutral, poor, very poor). Majority (70%) had either an outstanding ($n = 2$) or satisfactory ($n = 5$) experience. Those who had either poor ($n = 2$) or very poor ($n = 1$) experience agreed (in additional comment) that they struggled at the beginning because the system was imposed on them and they have poor computer background. One added, "it was time consuming and took a huge amount of time out of daily schedules." Unsurprisingly, two of the three users who had either poor or very poor first experience answered "no" when we asked if the system was user friendly. However, majority (80%) found it easy to use.

QUESTIONNAIRE SECTION 2: PERFORMANCE AND SATISFACTION (FOUR EMBEDDED QUESTIONS)

We asked users to rate their satisfaction level with Motiva services in understanding their patients. Five options were provided (i.e., extremely satisfied, very satisfied, neutral, very dissatisfied or extremely dissatisfied). Only eight users responded to this question, of which three were neutral, four were very satisfied, and one was extremely satisfied. We were unable to establish the reasons behind their choices because there were no additional comments to explain these choices even though we had included related questions in the semistructured interview as detailed in the following section. Other questions revealed that the system was fit for purpose but could benefit from further modifications (Table 13.8). Majority (90%) were satisfied with available features and would in fact recommend Motiva, although a good number of users (70%) would like to see some changes to further enhance the system.

SEMISTRUCTURED INTERVIEW (FIVE EMBEDDED QUESTIONS)

To establish the underlying reasons behind some of the user responses in the questionnaire, we asked respondents to highlight the most positive/negative aspects of the project and to explain how telehealth affected the tasks they would normally undertake. (i.e., has the load increased or decreased?). We discuss their responses to both questions in parallel and explain results of other queries posed.

Table 13.8 Clinicians' View of Motiva Performance

Questions	Yes	No	Not Sure
Satisfied with features offered by Motiva?	90%	—	10%
Would you recommend Motiva?	90%	—	10%
Would you like to see enhancements made?	70%	10%	20%

Respondents were particularly happy with Motiva services in facilitating quick assessment and timely intervention. In fact, all respondents agreed they responded quickly to patients during the pilot, solely based on the wealth of patient information received on a daily basis. Respondents added that patients had expressed to them feeling safer, independent, and understood their condition better (70%); interventions were tailored to patient needs (80%), and they reported that unnecessary hospital visits were reduced as a result (100%). In contrast to suggestions that home care through telehealth reduces contact with clinicians [9], the study results show that home visits to patients either increased (70%) or stayed the same (30%) during the pilot. The matrons attributed this to organizational setup and the Motiva operational model. Prior to the pilot project, matrons had a caseload of patients with whom they agreed individualized care plans, along with GPs and other staff. The plans, along with agreed patient's data sets, are then shared in confidence among clinicians through a central system called EMIS Web [23]. The Motiva clinical interface however generalized the client (patient) base by displaying the entire cohort, with masked patient biodata and risk alerts sorted by priority. Remote monitoring has been shown to be an efficient use of resources [2], [18] because clinicians were able to monitor and analyze the data at the office, thereby freeing time for conducting other examinations or for seeing more patients. However, clinicians were forced to monitor any patient, with or without prior knowledge of their health status, which resulted in other issues as follows.

Integration

Majority (90%) agreed that lack of integration with the current system (EMIS Web) caused delay in intervention. When faced with unfamiliar patients, clinicians would refer to EMIS Web for assessment before intervening. Majority (90%) agreed there was increased time loss because of this unfamiliarity. One respondent said, "I spent huge amount of time each day reading unfamiliar patients' history."

Flexibility

The system was designed to run a full 7-day week rather than the 5-day week arrangement within the participating NHS service provider, so clinicians experienced huge time loss on Mondays in dealing with backlogs. That is, measuring data captured over the weekend was accessed on Mondays. In addition, users highlighted that default the setting of the system does not allow for personalized care. For instance, baseline (upper and lower limits) and monitoring frequency of variables (e.g., weight) are rigid and could not be tailored to patients' individual needs. One respondent added that "some patients do not need to monitor their weight daily." Others said "the default settings automatically override any changes made," "I often rang patients who did not require attention because the system raised false alarm," "safe blood pressure limits differ among individuals," etc. There were also concerns regarding the set monitoring time (on or before 11:00 AM each day), as a small percentage (30%) found it regimented. The system raised a false alarm whenever a patient failed to monitor within the cut-off period each day.

Speed

Respondents experienced low transfer speed at times perhaps because of firewall setting and general web traffic issues. Majority explained (70%) that this happened around the same time each day, thus reducing time for field work (i.e., home visits).

Other areas that raised some concern were centered on the appropriateness of the patient cohort. The majority (60%) agreed that some of the patients did not need telehealth, and a majority of those who would benefit from it were left out of the pilot. Some (50%) said the system was imposed on them and hence they struggled at the beginning. A small percentage (20%) argued that the system caused anxiety among patients. Despite the negatives, majority (80%) said they learnt new things about telehealth and almost two-thirds feel more confident now about new technology. When asked if there are other things about being involved in the project they wished had been different, including those not covered in the questionnaire, most of them echoed some of the negative aspects outlined above. There was also a debate about who should be in charge of the system. Half the respondents (50%) said it is a waste of expertise asking highly qualified staff (matrons and nurses) to be in charge, 20% said some part should be handled by junior staff members (i.e., health care assistants [HCAs]), 10% believed it should be completely handled by HCAs, and the rest were indifferent.

The one-to-one interviews with the GPs showed support for benefits telehealth can bring for patients by focusing on remotely reviewing trend data to decide on follow on action, i.e. arrange visits or appointments with GPs or hospitals without patient/ carers explicitly having to do so. There was recognition that such technology will enable patients to remain independent and safe allowing prioritizing of patient needs much more effectively. The two GPs interviewed did both point out that such technological interventions as telehealth needs careful planning, resourcing and training.

LIMITATIONS

The sample size reported in this study was small due to a number of reasons. As with similar pilot projects [24], only a small number of patients ($n = 45$) were enrolled. Although all patients had the opportunity to provide feedback on their experience, only 24 took the opportunity. We were unable to follow-up nonresponders because of time constraints. Also, more input from other GPs within the locality would have been useful to back up the general support identified.

CONCLUSION AND RECOMMENDATIONS

Our findings show overwhelming support for the telehealth project from both user groups. Telehealth holds great promises for improving clinical management and health care services delivery by enhancing access, quality, efficiency, and cost-effectiveness [25,26]. In particular, telehealth can help reach out to patients generally underserved traditionally because of the nature of their illness or age, for example, those with LTC who require constant monitoring and the elderly, especially those technically incapable of moving [25]. Further, evidence points to important socioeconomic benefits to patients, carers, clinicians, and the health care providers, including educational opportunities and enhancements to patient—clinician communication [27]. In order of number of responses and comments received, some of the strongest outcomes of this study were centered on reassurance, education, effective home care, and reduced GP/hospital visits. Our result shows that patients felt reassured, and this was echoed by clinicians during their interview sessions. The ability to take specific measures every day and to see the results fostered a sense of well-being for patients. This also applied to those patients who sometimes forgot to take their readings—leading to the clinician calling to check that all was well. Patients also became more knowledgeable about their illness. In contrast to some research findings [15], we observed some improvements in communication (physical or via telephone) between patients and clinicians. GP/hospital visits were also reduced.

Clinicians considered in this study have wholeheartedly supported telehealth, commending its many features to enable patients to remain independent and safe. This according to most clinicians is largely due to the security offered through real-time monitoring at a distance and scheduling tailored follow-on care quickly. Particularly, it was recognized that telehealth technology brings huge advantages in terms of the speed with which decisions could be made, and extension beyond the pilot period would be considered of benefit. Clinicians reported of patients' disappointment at the telehealth pilot coming to an end, and this was echoed by patients themselves during the one-to-one interview session. Although support for telehealth is strong, it would have been useful to have conducted the feasibility study over a longer period. More patient feedback would have been captured if time had been allocated to follow up on patients who had not returned their questionnaires. Studies of this nature needs adequate time and scheduling within the overall program of work.

ACKNOWLEDGMENTS

Funders: Liverpool Community Health (LCH); Informatics Merseyside (IM); Liverpool Primary Care Trust and Philips (especially for the discussion and images provided by S. Douglas). Our thanks also go to all the matrons, GPs, and patients who gave up time to provide valuable input for the study.

REFERENCES

[1] Steventon A, Bardsley M, Billings J, Dixon J, Doll H, Hirani S, Cartwright M, Rixon L, Knapp M, Henderson C, Rogers A, Fitzpatrick R, Hendy J, Newman S. Effect of telehealth on use of secondary care and mortality: findings from the Whole System Demonstrator cluster randomised trial. BMJ Jun. 2012;344(jun21 3). e3874—e3874.
[2] Loane M, Wootton R. A Review of Telehealth. Med Princ Pract 2001;10(4):163—70.

[3] Sade L. Telehealth hindered by lack of clinical evidence, says academic. Guardian Professional 04-Jul-2012.

[4] Whitten P, Love B. Patient and provider satisfaction with the use of telemedicine: Overview and rationale for cautious enthusias. J Postgrad Med 2005;51(4):294−300.

[5] Philips. Remote patient management delivered through a patient's home television [Online]. Available: http://www.healthcare.philips.com/gb_en/products/telehealth/products/motiva.wpd; 2012.

[6] Brocklehurst P, Jones C, Tickle M. QIPP: cutting budgets or working smarter? Br Dent J 2011;210(8):369−73.

[7] Tsamardinos I, Lagani V, Triantafillou S. Towards Integrative Causal Analysis of Heterogeneous Data Sets and Studies. J Mach Learn Res 2012;13:1097−157.

[8] Troyanskaya OG, Dolinski K, Owen AB, Altman RB, Botstein D. A Bayesian framework for combining heterogeneous data sources for gene function prediction (in Saccharomyces cerevisiae). Proc Natl Acad Sci U S A 2003;100(14):8348−53.

[9] Boaz A, Ashby D, Young K. Systematic Reviews : What have they got to offer evidence based policy and practice? ESRC UK Centre for Evidence Based Policy and Practice: Working paper 2002;2 [Online]. Available: http://kcl.ac.uk/content/1/c6/03/45/85/wp2.pdf (accessed: 07-Nov-2013).

[10] Taylor A, Agamanolis S. Evaluation of the User Experience of a Standard Telecare Product - The Personal Trigger, 2010 Second Int Conf eHealth. Telemedicine Soc Med Feb. 2010:51−6.

[11] Mair F, Whitten P. Systematic Review of studies of patients' satisfaction with telemedicine. BMJ 2000;320(June):1517−20.

[12] Darkins A, Ryan P, Kobb R, Foster L, Edmonson E, Wakefield B, Lancaster AE. Care Coordination/Home Telehealth: the systematic implementation of health informatics, home telehealth, and disease management to support the care of veteran patients with chronic conditions. Telemed J E Health 2008;14(10):1118−26.

[13] Koch S. Home telehealth—current state and future trends. Int J Med Inform 2006;75(8):565−76.

[14] Rahimpour M, Lovell NH, Celler BG, McCormick J. Patients' perceptions of a home telecare system. Int J Med Inform 2008;77(7):486−98.

[15] Chan M, Estève D, Escriba C, Campo E. A review of smart homes- present state and future challenges. Comput Methods Programs Biomed 2008;91(1):55−81.

[16] Dishman E. Inventing wellness systems for aging in place. Computer (Long Beach Calif) 2004;37(5):34−41.

[17] Lillyman S, Saxon A, Treml H. An evaluation of the role of the community matron: a literature review. J Health Soc Care Improv November 2009.

[18] Johnston B, Wheeler L, Deuser J, Sousa KH. Outcomes of the Kaiser Permanente Tele-Home Health Research Project. Arch Fam Med 2000;9(1):40−5.

[19] Leighton Y, Clegg A, Bee A. Evaluation of community matron services in a large metropolitan city in England. Qual Prim Care 2008;16(2):83−9 (7).

[20] Wright K, Ryder S, Gousy M. Community matrons improve health: patients' perspectives. Br J Commun Nurs 2007;12(10):453−9.

[21] Frede S. Survey length can impact concept measures, data quality. Lightspeed Ahead Newsletter. Q4 edition 2010: 5−8.

[22] Field MJ. Telemedicine and Remote Patient Monitoring. JAMA 2002;288(4):423.

[23] emis-online, EMIS Web. [Online]. Available: http://www.emis-online.com/emis-web#. (accessed: 28-Oct-2013).

[24] Bentley CL, a Mountain G, Thompson J, a Fitzsimmons D, Lowrie K, Parker SG, Hawley MS. A pilot randomised controlled trial of a Telehealth intervention in patients with chronic obstructive pulmonary disease: challenges of clinician-led data collection. Trials 2014;15(1):313.

[25] Craig J, Patterson V. Introduction to the practice of telemedicine. J Telemed Telecare 2005;11(1):3—9.

[26] Heinzelmann P, Lugn N, Kvedar J. Telemedicine in the future. J Telemed Telecare 2005;11(8):384—90.

[27] House AM, Roberts JM. Telemedicine in Canada. Can Med Assoc 1977;117(4):386—8.

Swarm Based-Artificial Neural System for Human Health Data Classification

14

Habib Shah[1], Rozaida Ghazali[2], Tutut Herawan[3], Sami Ur Rahman[4], Nawsher Khan[5]

Faculty of Computer and Information Systems, Islamic University Madina, KSA[1]; Faculty of Computer Science and Information Technology, Universiti Tun Hussein Onn Malaysia, Johor, Malaysia[2]; Universitas Teknologi Yogyakarta & AMCS Research Center, Yogyakarta, Indonesia[3]; Department of Computer Science and Information Technology, University of Malakand, Pakistan[4]; Department of Computer Science, Abdul Wali Khan University, Mardan, Pakistan[5]
E-mail: habibshah.uthm@gmail.com, rozaida@uthm.edu.my, tutut@uty.ac.id, softrays@hotmail.com, nawsherkhan@gmail.com

INTRODUCTION

Human serious disease prediction methods are vital, as they provide important data for practitioners and health authorities to manage the risk factors of the critical diseases [1]. The prediction of epidemiology can lead to better prerequisite managements to save human beings, swarms, and animal lives. Use of artificial soft computing techniques to detect, predict, diagnose, cluster, and classify different diseases for human beings is not new [2]. The most common diseases in the human body are musculoskeletal, hormonal, neurologic dementia, Parkinson, stroke, poor vision, hearing impairment, balance problem, visual macular degeneration, cataract, cardiovascular, lung, kidney, skin, and hair (hair loss, dry skin, itching) [3,4], infections, bone marrow and immune system, gastrointestinal, psychiatric (depression, anxiety, sleep disturbance, insomnia), and so on [5-8]. According to the World Health Organization (WHO), ischemic heart disease, stroke, lower respiratory infections and chronic obstructive lung disease have remained the top major killers during the past decade [9]. HIV deaths decreased slightly from 1.7 million (3.2%) deaths in 2000 to 1.5 million (2.7%) deaths in 2012. Lung cancers (along with trachea and bronchus cancers) caused 1.6 million (2.9%) deaths in 2012, up from 1.2 million (2.2%) deaths in 2000. Similarly, diabetes caused 1.5 million (2.7%) deaths in 2012, up from 1.0 million (2.0%) deaths in 2000 [9].

Cancer is an important serious medical disorder, which is not a single disease but a cluster of more than 200 different serious medical complications [10]. Commonly, cancer can be defined as any disease that is characterized by the uncontrolled expansion and spread of abnormal and infected cells. In other words, cancer refers to any one of a large number of diseases characterized by the development of abnormal cells that divide uncontrollably and have the ability to infiltrate and destroy normal body tissue. Cancer refers to any malignant tumor [11]. The pattern of growth of cancer cells often resembles a twisted and distorted version of the tissue that is arising [12,13].

Furthermore, cancer (the most serious disease) is a class of diseases characterized by out-of-control cell growth. There are more than 100 types of cancer, and each is classified by the type of cell that is initially affected. Cancer can spread throughout the body. The abnormal cells lead to disability and death [14] if the spreading of abnormal cells is not properly controlled [15]. The external risk factors for the propagation of cancer are chemicals, tobacco, and infectious organisms; internal factors are inherited mutations, hormones, and immune conditions. These factors may act together or in a sequence to initiate or promote the development of cancer. Common types of cancer affect the breast, skin, lungs, blood, and the gastrointestinal system [1].

Breast cancer has been identified as the most predominant cancer among women and also leads as the main cause of cancer death among women [16]. Three most common cancers among men are prostate, lung, and colorectal. Lung cancer is the leading cause of death among men of all races, and mainly Hispanics. In contrast, among Asian/Pacific Islander men, liver cancer is the second most common. The number of men getting cancer is rising in the world. This is partly because men are living longer than ever before, age being the biggest risk factor. However, the number of men surviving is also increasing. Overall, men are 14% more likely to get cancer than women [13].

The important issue in addressing breast cancer is the effectiveness of the treatment, which in turn is influenced by the accuracy of prediction [16]. Hence, accurate prediction in patients with early-stage breast cancer is of significant importance to reduce the mortality rate of those patients [17,18]. The prediction, classification, and diagnosis of cancers are of high priority for medical researchers [19]. Different techniques are used to diagnose, detect, cluster, classify, and predict cancer early on. The most well-known techniques used to detect and diagnose cancer diseases are mammography [20], fine-needle aspiration cytology (FNAC) [21], isotonic separation, and fuzzy artificial immune system. Furthermore, several researchers have used statistical and artificial intelligence techniques to predict cancer [18].

In artificial intelligence (AI), accuracies of different classifiers, namely, artificial neural network (ANN), multilayer perceptron [22], backpropagation neural network, probabilistic neural network, recurrent neural network (RNN) [23], and support vector machine, were compared to determine an optimum classification and prediction scheme with a high diagnostic accuracy for cancer detection [24,25]. Recently, the ANN has become a common tool because of its ability to represent the behavior of linear or nonlinear functions that are multidimensional and complex in the classification, prediction, detection, and diagnosis of breast cancer data set [3,26]. ANN has been confirmed as a robust method for cancer prognosis [27]. Various learning algorithms are used to train ANN for breast cancer classification, such as BP and LM; however, the bio-inspired training algorithms are more robust than standard algorithms. To get high accuracy in breast cancer classification task, the five swarm intelligence algorithms are used.

The rest of this chapter is organized as follows. The next two sections express the different issues on human health and related works on human health, respectively. The fourth section presents a brief overview of optimization learning algorithms for training ANN. The fifth and sixth sections describe the two proposed bio-inspired learning algorithms and present the experimental setup and results for cancer prediction. Conclusions are given in the final section.

ISSUES ON HUMAN HEALTH

Over the last three decades, there has been increasing global concern over the public health impacts attributed to environmental pollution, in particular, the global burden of disease. Many factors influence human health, including food, improper management of solid waste, cleanliness, economic status, literacy, air quality, social activities, heat waves, chemical hazards, climate change, natural hazards, geographical and environmental factors, wars, biological hazards, disease types, pollution, and lifestyle [28,29]. Public health problems caused by environmental contamination and emerging infectious diseases are a growing concern in both the developed and the developing world. The effects on health from exposure to chemicals and air pollutants vary from allergies to cancer [30,31].

A significant quantity of diseases could be prevented, for example, cancers caused by cigarette smoking and heavy use of alcohol [32]. The World Cancer Research Fund (WCRF) has estimated that up to one-third of the cancer cases that occur in economically developed countries like the United States are related to overweight or obesity, physical inactivity, and/or poor nutrition and thus could also be prevented. Certain cancers are related to infectious agents, such as human papillomavirus (HPV), hepatitis B virus (HBV), hepatitis C virus (HCV), human immunodeficiency virus (HIV), and *Helicobacter pylori* [33,34]. Many of these cancers could be prevented through behavioral changes or the use of protective vaccinations or antibiotic treatments. Screening offers the ability for secondary prevention by detecting cancer early, before symptoms appear. Early detection usually results in less extensive treatment and better outcomes [35]. Screening is known to reduce mortality for cancers of the breast, colon, rectum, cervix, and lung (among heavy smokers) [36]. A heightened awareness of changes in the breast, skin, or testicles may also result in detection of tumors at earlier stages [10,11,13,26,30,35]. Screening for colorectal and cervical cancers can actually prevent cancer by allowing for the detection and removal of precancerous lesions [37]. There were an estimated 14.1 million cancer cases around the world in 2012; of these, 7.4 million cases were in men and 6.7 million in women. This number is expected to increase to 24 million by 2035.

Lung cancer was the most common cancer worldwide in men and women, contributing to 13% and 17%, respectively, of the total number of new cases diagnosed in 2012. Breast cancer (women only) was the second most common cancer, with nearly 1.7 million new cases in 2012. Among women, the colorectal cancer was the third most common cancer, with nearly 1.4 million new cases in 2012. The top three, lung, prostate, and colorectal cancers, contributed nearly 42% of all cancers (excluding nonmelanoma skin cancer) [32]. Other common cancers contributing more than 5% were stomach and liver, as given in Table 14.1 [38].

Table 14.1 The Top Common Cancers Types for Men and Women Worldwide

	Men			Women		
Rank	Cancer	New Cases Diagnosed	%	Cancer	New Cases Diagnosed	%
1	Lung	1,242	16.7	Lung	1,677	25.2
2	Prostate	1,112	15	Breast	614	9.2
3	Colorectum	746	10	Colorectum	583	8.8
4	Stomach	631	8.5	Prostate	528	7.9
5	Liver	554	7.5	Stomach	320	4.8
6	Bladder	330	4.4	Liver	320	4.8
7	Oesophagus	323	4.3	Cervix uteri	239	3.6
8	Non-Hodgkin lymphoma	218	2.9	Oesophagus	230	3.5
9	Kidney	214	2.9	Bladder	228	3.4
10	Leukemia	201	2.7	Non-Hodgkin lymphoma	168	2.5
11	Lip, oral cavity	199	2.7	Leukemia	160	2.4
12	Pancreas	178	2.4	Pancreas	151	2.3
13	Brain, nervous sys	140	1.9	Kidney	133	2
14	Larynx	138	1.9	Corpus uteri	124	1.9
15	Melanoma of skin	121	1.6	Lip, oral cavity	117	1.8
16	Other pharynx	115	1.6	Thyroid	111	1.7
17	Gallbladder	77	1	Brain, nervous	101	1.5
18	Thyroid	68	0.9	Ovary	101	1.5
19	Multiple myeloma	62	0.8	Melanoma of skin	99	1.5
20	Nasopharynx	61	0.8	Gallbladder	52	0.8
21	Testis	55	0.7	Larynx	27	0.4
22	Hodgkin lymphoma	39	0.5	Other pharynx	27	0.4
23	Kaposi sarcoma	1,242	0.4	Multiple myeloma	26	0.4

RELATED WORKS ON HUMAN HEALTH

Different types of ANN are being used in a wide range of health applications, ranging from cancer detecting, diagnosis, MRI, and classifying tumors via X-ray and CRT images [8,45] to the classification of malignancies from proteomic and genomic (microarray) assays for nearly 23 years. Thousands of research papers have been published on the area of computational intelligence for the prediction and classification of cancer and other risky diseases. However, the majority of published research papers are concerned with using computational intelligence to identify, classify, detect, or distinguish tumors and other malignancies [10,11,13,26,30,35]. In other words, computational intelligence has been used primarily as an aid to cancer diagnosis and detection. Only relatively recently have cancer researchers attempted to apply soft computing toward cancer prediction and prognosis.

SWARM-BASED ARTIFICIAL NEURAL SYSTEM

Before beginning with a detailed analysis of what swarm-based intelligence learning algorithms work best for which kinds of problems, it is significant to have a good understanding of what ANN learning is and what it isn't. ANN is a branch of computer science research that is used for a variety of statistical, probabilistic, and optimization problems to learn from past patterns and to then use that prior training to classify new data, identify new patterns, or predict novel trends. An artificial neural network (ANN) is a structure that is based on iterative actions of biological neural networks (BNN), also called the simulation process of BNN. ANNs are at the key base of computational systems designed to produce, or mimic, intelligent behavior. In 1943, a set of simplified neurons was introduced by McCulloc and Pitts [39]. These neurons were illustrated as models of biological systems and were transformed into theoretical components for circuits that could perform computational tasks [40].

ANN has been developed for the fields of science and engineering such as pattern recognition, classification, scheduling, business intelligence, robotics, or even for some form of mathematical problem solving. In computer science, ANN gained a lot of steam over the last few years in areas such as forecasting, data analytics, as well as data mining. ANN systems can be categorized as Feed Forward Neural Network (FFNN), Self-Organizing Map (SOM), Hopfield Neural Network (HNN), Simple Recurrent Network (SRN), Feed forward Radial Basis Function (RBF) Network, Ridge Polynomial Neural Networks (RPNN), and Pi-Sigma Neural Network (PNN) [41-43].

ANNs can be used to solve linear, as well as nonlinear, programming tasks through the learning process of supervised and unsupervised algorithms. As its biological predecessor, an ANN is considered an adaptive system; in other words, each parameter is changed during its operation and is deployed for solving the problem at hand (called the ANN training phase). Back-propagation (BP) is a well-known supervised learning algorithm for training ANN for solving different tasks. It has a long history of achievements; however, trapping in local minima and slow convergence make it deficient for solving science and engineering problems.

In the last two decades, researchers have developed efficient training algorithms for ANN, based on swarm intelligence behaviors. Swarm intelligence (SI) can be defined as "the emergent collective intelligence of groups of simple agents inspired by the collective behavior of social insect colonies and other animal societies" [44]. Also, SI algorithms are the systems that allow arrangement with natural social insect and artificial swarms for a specific mission using its decentralized nature and self-organization technique. The self-organization involves a set of dynamical mechanisms whereby structures appear at the global level of a system from interactions of its lower-level components [19]. The four bases of self-organization make SI attractive, and its positive feedback (amplification), negative feedback (for counter -balance and stabilization), amplification of fluctuations (randomness, errors, random walks), and multiple interactions are robust features. SI agents collect information from local searching of either direct or indirect resources.

Examples of SI include group foraging of social insects such as ant, birds, fishes, bat, and termites; cooperative transportation; division of labor as flocks of birds; nest-building of social insects; and collective sorting and clustering [45,46]. Some human artifacts also fall into the domain of swarm intelligence, notably some multirobot systems, and also certain computer programs that are written to tackle optimization and data analysis problems. Scientists favor SI techniques because of SI's distributed system of interacting autonomous agents, the properties of best performance optimization and robustness, self-organized control and cooperation (decentralized), division of workers, distributed task allocation, and indirect interactions. Ants are individual agents of ant colony optimization (ACO) [47]. All SI techniques use the social insect behaviors of moving, flying, searching, birthing, population, growing, housing, and schooling, and the flocking of birds, fish, bees, and ants.

One motivating alternative to designing the topology, training, and exploiting the capabilities of an ANN is to adopt an efficient learning strategy based on computational, evolutionary, mathematical, and swarm intelligence algorithms. It is well known that designing and training tasks can be stated as optimization problems; for that reason, it is possible to apply different types of SI algorithms, such as particle swarm optimization (PSO), Ant Colony Optimization, ABC, Cuckoo Search (CS), Bat Algorithm, Bees Algorithm, and so on. ABC is the most attractive algorithm based on honey bee swarm, and is focused on the dance and communication [48], task allocation, collective decision, nest site selection, mating, marriage, reproduction, foraging, floral and pheromone laying, and navigation behaviors of the swarm [49-51]. ABC is a new stochastic algorithm that tries to simulate the behavior of the bees in nature, which tasks consist in exploring their environment to find a food source. The exploring and exploiting are the properties that make the ABC famous and attractive for researchers.

ABC algorithm has been used in a wide range of science and engineering problems, because of its simple implementation and enough exploration and exploitation of straightforward processes for solving tough problems. From the literature, the performance of ABC algorithm is outstanding compared with other algorithms, such as a genetic algorithm (GA), differential evolution (DE), PSO, ant colony optimization, and their improved versions [48-50]. In particular, the ABC has a high efficiency in classification, clustering, forecasting, and constrained and unconstrained optimization problems. Although the ABC algorithm is more powerful than standard learning algorithms, the slow convergence, poor exploration, and unbalance exploitation are the weaknesses that attract researchers for innovations of new learning algorithms. Different researchers have used various strategies and variants for creating strong and balanced exploration and exploitation processes of ABC algorithms. For example, Modified Artificial Bee Colony (MABC) [52], an Improved Artificial Bee Colony (IABC) [53], PSO-ABC [54], a Combinatorial Artificial Bee Colony(CABC) [50], the parallel Artificial Bee Colony (PABC) [55], the Novel Artificial Bee Colony (NABC), an Application Artificial Bee Colony (AABC), and many other types are some recent improvements for different mathematical, statistical, and engineering problems. Here, two hybrid algorithms proposed for the classification of cancer diseases are detailed.

THE PROPOSED LEARNING ALGORITHMS

Although the ABC algorithm has outstanding performance in some optimization problems compared to other standard computational learning algorithms, there is still an insufficiency in typical ABC algorithms regarding its solution search equation, which is good at exploration but poor in exploitation [56]. The ABC algorithm requires the user to fiddle with several parametric settings, such as swarm size and limit. If those settings are not chosen appropriately to the particular application, the algorithm may converge prematurely or never converge at all. The fitness function can decrease the training error with low magnitude. Furthermore, ABC has technical weaknesses such as slow convergence, trapping in local solution, and poor exploration and exploitation properties [57]. Here, two new swarm-based learning algorithms are proposed for guiding ANN with efficient amounts of exploration and exploitation processes for the classification of cancer disease in the human body. These are Global Guided Artificial Bee Colony (GGABC) and Hybrid Guided Artificial Bee Colony (HGABC) algorithms. The proposed GGABC and HGGABC are detailed in the following subsections.

GLOBAL GUIDED ARTIFICIAL BEE COLONY (GGABC) ALGORITHM

The ABC algorithm was developed by Dervish Karaboga in 2005 for solving optimization problems [49]. The success story of ABC algorithms is quite lengthy; however, the high efficiency, robustness, and attractive tools have made it very well known among researchers since then. Furthermore, Karaboga used natural social insects' behaviors for solving science and engineering problems. The ABC algorithm became famous through its exploration and exploitation processes [49,58]. Although ABC algorithm has overcome some shortcomings of previous learning algorithms, slow convergence and trapping in local minima make it a focus for researchers. Different researchers used various improved techniques to make ABC algorithms most efficient and robust through the proper quantity and quality of exploration and exploitation processes [59]. Some improved ABC versions are Global ABC, Gbest Guided ABC, Improved ABC, Hybrid ABC, Guided ABC, and so on [56,60-62]. The Global ABC algorithm used for training ANN became smart because of their efficient finding ability through the gbest honey bee information [57].

Usually, the exploration and exploitation are strategies that can be improved with the best movement of neighbor agent information in the standard bee algorithm. The performance of ABC algorithm depends on agent dancing and strong power of intelligence [49], so if the agent has enough intelligence, it can provide strong exploration and exploitation processes in the particular area for given problems. In bee algorithm, the employed and onlooker bees have the duty of exploitation procedures, whereas the scout bees are used for getting sufficient amounts of exploration. The Global ABC has successfully improved the exploitation through global best bee methods. Furthermore, the guided ABC has outstanding performance, with strong exploration due to the guided scout bees [61].

Combining the best agent strategies of global ABC and guided ABC algorithms for getting sufficient amounts of exploration and exploitation with balance quantity [57,61], the new hybrid algorithm is called the Global Guided Artificial Bee Colony (GGABC) algorithm. The GGABC agents used global employed/onlooker and guided scout bees to find the best food source. The GGABC will merge their best finding approaches with original ABC by the following steps. The exploitation procedure will increase through equation (1) using global ABC strategy, and exploration with equation (2), through guided scout bees. The pseudo-code of the proposed GGABC algorithm is detailed as:

GLOBAL GUIDED ABC ALGORITHM

1: Initialize the population of solutions X_i where $i = 1, ..., SN$
2: Evaluate the population
3: Cycle = 1
4: Repeat from step 2 to step 13
5: Produce new solutions (food source positions) $V_{i,j}$ in the neighborhood of x_{ij} for the Global employed bees phase as:

$$v_{ij} = x_{ij} + \phi_{ij}\left(x_{ij} - x_{kj}\right) + c_1 \operatorname{rand}(0,1)\left(x_j^{best} - x_{ij}\right)$$
$$+ c_2 \operatorname{rand}(0,1)\left(y_j^{best} - x_{ij}\right) \tag{1}$$

Where x_{ij} shows best food source, c1 and c2 are two constant values, x_j^{best} is the jth element of the global best solution found so far, y_j^{best} is the jth element of the best solution in the current iteration, ϕ_{ij} is a uniformly distributed real random number in the range [-1, 1].

7: Calculate the probability value P_i for the solutions x_i by means of their fitness values by using the equation as:

$$p_i = \frac{fit_i}{\sum_{k=1}^{SN} fit_n} \tag{2}$$

The calculation of fitness values of solutions is defined by the equation as

$$fit_i = \begin{cases} \dfrac{1}{1 + fit_i} & f_i \ >= 0 \\ 1 + abs(f_i) & f_i \ < 0 \end{cases} \tag{3}$$

Normalize P_i values into [0, 1]

8: Produce the new solutions (new positions) v_i for the global onlookers from the solutions x_i, selected depending on P_i, and evaluate them as

$$v_{ij} = x_{ij} + \phi_{ij}\left(x_{ij} - x_{kj}\right) + c_1 \text{rand}\,(0,1)\left(x_j^{best} - x_{ij}\right) \\ + c_2\text{rand}\,(0,1)\left(y_j^{best} - x_{ij}\right) \tag{4}$$

9: Apply the Greedy Selection process for the onlookers between x_{ij} and v_{ij}.

10: Determine the abandoned solution (source), if exists, and replace it with a new randomly produced solution x_i for the scout using the following equation (5) as

Guided Scout Bee Phase

$$v_{ij} = x_{ij} + \phi^*\left(x_{i,j} - x_{k,j}\right) + (1 - \phi)^*\left(x_{i,j} - x_{best,j}\right) \tag{5}$$

11: Memorize the best food source position (solution) achieved so far

12: Cycle = cycle + 1

13: Until cycle = Maximum Cycle Number (MCN)

Figure 14.1 shows the flow chart for proposed GGABC algorithm.

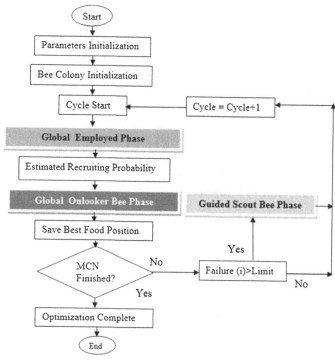

FIGURE 14.1

Flow chart of the proposed GGABC algorithm.

HYBRID GUIDED ARTIFICIAL BEE COLONY (HGABC) ALGORITHM

Backpropagation is one of the most attractive and unique supervised-learning algorithm proposed by Rumelhart et al. for training ANN [63,64]. Because of its great rate of flexibility and learning competences, it has been efficiently used in a wide range of science and engineering applications. It can be proved that BP can reach the extreme within a limited number of epochs for a given task. The merits of BP are that the adjustment of weights is always toward the descending direction of the error function and that only some local information is needed. The forward phase is where the activations propagate from the input layer to the output layer. The backward phase is where the the observed actual value and the requested nominal value in the output layer are propagated backwards so it can modify the weights and bias values. Each node is composed of two sections. The first section generates a sum of the products of the weight multipliers and input signals. The second takes the result of the first section and puts it through its activation function, with scales the input to a value between 0 and 1. Signal e is the output of the first section, and $y = f(e)$ is the output of the second section. Signal y is also the output signal of an artificial neuron. In the feed-forward phase, the input signals are propagated through the input and hidden layers of processing elements, generating an output pattern in response to the input pattern presented.

The Guided ABC algorithm has a global ability to find global optimistic result, and the BP algorithm is a standard method, relatively with simple implementation, and works very well [61]. Combining the step of GABC with BP, a new hybrid (HGABC) algorithm is proposed in this article for training MLP [65,66]. The key point of this hybrid GABC-BP algorithm is that the GABC is used at the initial stage of searching for the optimum using global best methods. Then the training process is continued with the BP learning algorithm. The flow diagram of the GABC-BP model is shown in Figure 14.2. In the initial stage, the GABC algorithm finishes its training procedures, and then the BP algorithm starts training with the optimal weights of the Guided ABC algorithm, following which BP trains the network for an additional 500 epochs.

HGABC ALGORITHM APPROACH

```
1: Initialization Phase
2: repeat
3: Employed Bee Phase
4: Onlooker Bee Phase
5: Guided Scout Bee Phase
6: Memorize the best solution achieved so far
7: Until (Cycle = Maximum Cycle Number)
7: Save best solution
8: Assign all network inputs and output to BP
9: Initialize all weights from step 7
10: repeat
11: Present the pattern to the network
// Propagated the input forward through the network
   12:  for each layer in the network
   13:   for every node in the layer
```

```
14:    Calculate the weight sum of the inputs to the node
15:    Add the threshold to the sum
16:    Calculate the activation for the node
17:  end
18: end
// Propagate the errors backward through the network
19:   for every node in the output layer
20:   calculate the error signal
21: end
22: for all hidden layers
23:   for every node in the layer
24:    Calculate the node's signal error
25:    Update each node's weight in the network
26:  end
27: end
// Calculate Global Error
28:   Calculate the Error Function
29: end
30:  While ((maximum number of iterations < than specified))
```

Figure 14.2 shows the flow chart for proposed HGABC algorithm.

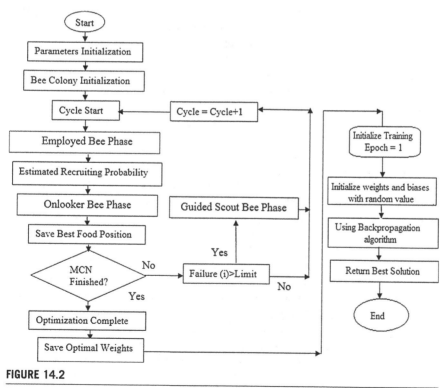

FIGURE 14.2

Flow chart of the proposed HGABC algorithm.

CLASSIFICATION OF HEALTH DATA USING THE PROPOSED APPROACH

One of the most challenging problems for researchers is to use metaheuristic learning algorithms for classification tasks. ANN techniques can be used for cancer classification, which are still challenging problems in mathematical, medical, and statistical areas in the shape of nonlinearity. The medical time-series task is the most popular challenge for researchers for getting health and economic stability. Nevertheless, when using standard learning techniques for MLP training classification and prediction tasks, the efficiency is limited [67-69]. ANN needs to be used for classification of time series with the swarm-based learning algorithm. Prediction of cancer types such as breast, lung, and heart is a technical challenge for ANN researchers.

EXPERIMENTAL DESIGN

ANN achievement in classification and prediction tasks depend on different issues, such as a network's topology choice, selection of suitable input—output variables, activation function, initial and range of weight values, bias, stopping criteria, and learning technique. In addition, the proper number of input, hidden, and output nodes and a learning parameter have an important role in ANN performance. Consequently, if the earlier issues adjusted properly, ANN can offer good accuracy for classification and prediction assignment. For solving the above issues, this section explains the experimental design that included demonstration of the data set, variable selection, data preprocessing, data partitioning, network model topology, proposed and standard training techniques of the networks, model selection, and performance metrics for this research work. Here, standard ABC, Global ABC, Guided ABC, proposed Global Guided ABC, and HGABC learning algorithms are detailed with their parameters to train MLP for cancer classification tasks.

In this article, three types of breast cancer data from UCI have been used for classification purpose. The breast cancer Wisconsin (original) of 1992, breast cancer Wisconsin (prognostic) of 1995, and breast cancer Wisconsin (diagnostic) of 1995; these breast cancer databases were obtained from the University of Wisconsin Hospitals, Madison. The data sets have been collected by Dr. William at the University of Wisconsin Madison Hospitals [70]. There are 400 records selected for prediction [70]. Each record in the database has nine attributes: clump thickness, uniformity of cell size, single epithelial cell shape, marginal adhesion, single epithelial cell size, bare nuclei, bland chromatin, normal nucleoli, and mitoses. Each instance has one of two possible classes: two for benign and four for malignant. The nine attributes detailed in Table 14.2 are graded on an interval scale from a normal state of 1—10, with 10 being the most critical position. The network was trained and evaluated using standard 70%—30% deviation for training and testing purposes, respectively. To improve the performance of MLP with bio-inspired learning algorithms, the breast cancer data has been normalized for classification in the interval of [0 1].

Table 14.2 Breast Cancer Data Description of Attributes

No.	Attribute Description	Domain	Breast Cancer (Original) 1992		Breast Cancer (Prognostic) 1995		Breast Cancer (Diagnostic) 1995	
			Mean	SD	Mean	SD	Mean	SD
1	Clump thickness	1–10	4.59	3.07	4.65	3.07	4.65	3.08
2	Uniformity of cell size	1–10	3.39	3.04	3.33	2.98	3.41	3.05
3	Single epithelial cell shape	1–10	3.53	2.98	3.45	2.95	3.53	2.98
4	Marginal adhesion	1–10	2.97	2.91	2.97	2.92	2.97	2.92
5	Single epithelial cell size	1–10	3.58	2.47	3.56	2.45	3.56	2.45
6	Bare nuclei	1–10	4.21	3.84	4.23	3.91	4.21	3.87
7	Bland chromatin	1–10	3.72	2.16	3.75	2.16	3.75	2.17
8	Normal nucleoli	1–10	3.30	3.20	3.32	3.20	3.32	3.21
9	Mitoses	1–10	1.82	1.97	1.79	1.93	1.89	1.97

In this research, an MLP model is trained and tested through ABC, Global ABC, Guided ABC, HGABC, and GGABC algorithms for classification of breast cancer task. The analysis of simulation results for breast cancer for classification task is needed to measure the performance of proposed ANN learning techniques with standard algorithms. An accuracy measure is often defined by the forecasting error, which is the difference between the actual and classified signals. Some objective functions like mean square error and normalized mean square error are the most frequently used. Therefore, to calculate the performance of the above-mentioned algorithms, simulation experiments were performed by Matlab 2012a software, and the mean square error (MSE), root mean square error (RMSE), mean absolute error (MAE), accuracy, and convergence rates were calculated. The stopping criteria for all algorithms mentioned above were 3000 maximum cycle number (MCN) with 10 trials performed, of which the average was taken and recorded. To analyze the best performance for breast cancer classification, various MLP topologies were used as given in Table 14.3. The training data set was used to find the best MLP neuron and bias weight values. Training and testing processes were repeated by changing the number of hidden nodes in order to obtain the

Table 14.3 Parameter Setting for Bio-Inspired Learning Algorithms

Parameters	ABC	Global ABC	Guided ABC	GGABC	HG ABC
Number of Food Sources	20	20	20	20	20
MCN	3000	3000	3000	3000	3000
Upper Bound UB	10	10	10	10	10
Lower Bound LB	−10	−10	−10	−10	−10
C_1	—	1.5	—	1.3	—
C_2	—	1.6	—	1.2	—
Dimension (D)	13, 17, 21, 23, 27, 29, 37, 41				

smallest classification error values. After training the MLP with the above algorithms, an output is generated that represents the classification (malignant or benign) of the prediction.

SIMULATION RESULTS ON HEALTH DATA CLASSIFICATION

For simulation comparison, the evaluation of each of the above-mentioned learning algorithm is used for the breast cancer classification task. Experimental results for cancer classification using the MLP model with the experimentally identified best parameter values are shown in Table 14.3. The average simulation results of the above five bio-inspired algorithms for breast cancer classification are given in Tables 14.4 to 14.7. The best average simulation results with different network topologies; initial weight values and various numbers of hidden nodes were used to train MLPs for the breast cancer classification task. Every topology were run with 10 trails, and the average of each topology is calculated with MSE, RMSE, and the accuracy for finding the efficiency of two proposed bio-inspired learning algorithms.

In the following Table 14.4, the best average simulation results for breast cancer classification are discussed. From Table 14.4, the MSE through proposed GGABC and HGABC are less than the MSE from other learning algorithms. Also, the proposed HGABC algorithm has also outstanding MSE than the other four learning algorithms. The above five learning algorithms were tested after training the network, with optimal weight values on the breast cancer data set for the classification task. Again, the proposed bio-inspired GGABC and HGABC were successful in getting less MSE out of the sample data. Table 14.5 shows that the proposed HGABC algorithm has excellent MSE as compared to ABC, GABC, and GGABC. One may notice that with the same number of iterations and ANN topology, HGABC can get better MSE.

The RMSE values for the breast cancer classification task are given in Table 14.6, where the proposed GGABC and HGABC learning algorithms reach the success

Table 14.4 Average MSE (Training) on Out-of-Sample Data for Breast Cancer Classification

Data set	NN Structure	ABC	Global ABC	Guided ABC	GGABC	HGABC
Breast Cancer (Original) 1992	9-3-2	0.0085231	0.0009334	0.0001252	0.00000162	0.00000507
	9-6-2	0.0078921	0.0008234	0.0002284	0.00000143	0.00000304
	9-9-2	0.0070232	0.0009022	0.0002320	0.00000138	0.00000302
	9-11-2	0.0070091	0.000689	0.0006542	0.00000232	0.00000205
Breast Cancer (Prognostic) 1995	9-3-2	0.0060090	0.0006363	0.0001983	0.00000292	0.00000205
	9-6-2	0.0006374	0.0000321	0.0003432	0.00000270	0.00000107
	9-9-2	0.0006513	0.0009121	0.0002123	0.00000170	0.00000507
	9-11-2	0.0004195	0.0008871	0.0001092	0.00000140	0.00000304
Breast Cancer (Diagnostic) 1995	9-3-2	0.0010430	0.0009123	0.0001009	0.00000110	0.00000307
	9-6-2	0.0001023	0.0006564	0.0001004	0.00000194	0.00000204
	9-9-2	0.0001022	0.0006342	0.0008232	0.00000195	0.00000203
	9-11-2	0.0001324	0.0004254	0.0007334	0.00000173	0.00000105

Table 14.5 Average MSE (Testing) on Out-of-Sample Data for Breast Cancer Classification

Data set	NN Structure	ABC	Global ABC	Guided ABC	GGABC	HGABC
Breast Cancer (Original) 1992	9-3-2	0.0020289	0.0012091	0.0017344	0.0001031	0.0000261
	9-6-2	0.0090141	0.0012022	0.0093429	0.0002022	0.0000348
	9-9-2	0.0042029	0.0009821	0.0049022	0.0001021	0.0000122
	9-11-2	0.0020906	0.0004891	0.0091920	0.0001931	0.0000198
Breast Cancer (Prognostic) 1995	9-3-2	0.0011291	0.0008798	0.0002756	0.0002101	0.0000206
	9-6-2	0.0020174	0.0005920	0.0003437	0.0001569	0.0000129
	9-9-2	0.0010220	0.0002345	0.0038961	0.0001104	0.0000129
	9-11-2	0.0095201	0.0018633	0.0034272	0.0001031	0.0000165
Breast Cancer (Diagnostic) 1995	9-3-2	0.0091600	0.0021981	0.0092103	0.0002082	0.0000148
	9-6-2	0.0049001	0.0003452	0.0020911	0.0003021	0.0000125
	9-9-2	0.0020128	0.0007362	0.0060812	0.0001304	0.0000192
	9-11-2	0.0013491	0.0001009	0.0001211	0.0001015	0.0001201

Table 14.6 Average RMSE on Out-of-Sample Data for Breast Cancer Classification

Data set	NN Structure	ABC	Global ABC	Guided ABC	GGABC	HGABC
Breast Cancer (Original) 1992	9-3-2	0.045723	0.022116	0.095875	0.0138960	0.0044517
	9-6-2	0.033602	0.029661	0.016601	0.0144951	0.0045395
	9-9-2	0.044915	0.024331	0.018539	0.0125262	0.0035921
	9-11-2	0.031969	0.015313	0.062419	0.0105074	0.0035921
Breast Cancer (Prognostic) 1995	9-3-2	0.097571	0.043166	0.058542	0.0101540	0.0040626
	9-6-2	0.095708	0.046884	0.095971	0.0144292	0.0038475
	9-9-2	0.070001	0.018584	0.045729	0.0173810	0.0035364
	9-11-2	0.044864	0.027133	0.077982	0.0114191	0.0043823
Breast Cancer (Diagnostic) 1995	9-3-2	0.036731	0.010045	0.011005	0.0100750	0.0109592
	9-6-2	0.088843	0.090663	0.099104	0.0045181	0.0045181
	9-9-2	0.031986	0.030065	0.031337	0.0021031	0.0021031
	9-11-2	0.097587	0.096546	0.095306	0.0031217	0.0031217

Table 14.7 Average Classification Accuracy for Breast Cancer Classification

Data set	NN Structure	ABC	Global ABC	Guided ABC	GGABC	HGABC
Breast Cancer (Original) 1992	9-3-2	96.36%	96.43%	94.23%	99.98%	100%
	9-6-2	97.83%	96.08%	93.83%	99.99%	100%
	9-9-2	98.23%	97.79%	94.23%	100%	100%
	9-11-2	98.74%	98.44%	95.74%	100%	100%
Breast Cancer (Prognostic) 1995	9-3-2	90.92%	91.34%	96.92%	99.99%	100%
	9-6-2	91.42%	92.82%	97.42%	100%	100%
	9-9-2	95.51%	95.83%	96.51%	100%	100%
	9-11-2	97.23%	96.36%	96.08%	100%	100%
Breast Cancer (Diagnostic) 1995	9-3-2	94.74%	93.83%	91.79%	99.9%	100%
	9-6-2	95.92%	95.23%	93.44%	100%	100%
	9-9-2	96.42%	97.74%	95.34%	100%	100%
	9-11-2	98.51%	98.92%	96.82%	100%	100%

point with smallest RMSEs compared to other learning algorithms. The performance became stable with very small errors through the proposed HGABC and GGABC algorithms.

The accuracy obtained by above learning algorithms for breast cancer classification is given in Table 14.5. Efficient breast cancer prediction results can be obtained by increasing the number of hidden nodes and using the proposed learning GGABC algorithm for training MLP. The classification accuracy of the proposed GGABC and HGABC algorithms are compared with the ABC, GABC, and Guided ABC algorithms using accuracy percentile ratios. The highest classification accuracy was achieved by the proposed HGABC and GGABC algorithms, which was better than standard algorithms. ABC had less classification accuracy from proposed. Moreover, it can be noted from the data that the prediction accuracy of global ABC is better than standard ABC and guided algorithms. Overall, from Table 14.7, it can be seen that the MLP structure played an important role in getting a high accuracy, meaning that when the hidden nodes were increased, the accuracy also increased.

The learning techniques demonstrated that the predicted and original signals of GGABC and HGAC are very close to each other except for ABC, which failed to perform on breast cancer classification. Using the proposed techniques GGABC and HGABC, the predicted points are going to overlap in some signals, which clearly demonstrates the prowess of these learning approaches on nonlinear time-series data. The learning curve of ABC, Guided ABC, Global ABC, and proposed GGABC and HGABC algorithms are plotted in Figures 14.3 to 14.5. The proposed learning algorithm HGABC has small testing MSE value on out of samples and fast convergence compared to ABC, Guided ABC, and Global ABC algorithm, as indicated in Figure 14.3. The convergence speed of GGABC is fast for breast cancer (original) 1992 classification from standard algorithms.

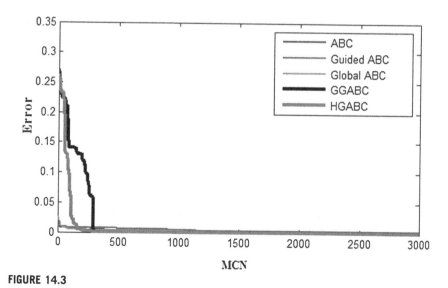

FIGURE 14.3

Learning curve for breast cancer 1992 classification by all training algorithms.

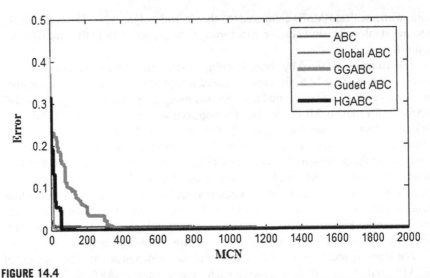

FIGURE 14.4

Learning curve for breast cancer (Prognostic) 1995, by all training algorithms.

The convergence speed of proposed HGABC is faster than other learning algorithms for breast cancer (Prognostic) 1995 classification (Figure 14.4). The convergence speed of GGABC is also faster for breast cancer classification than ABC, Guided ABC, and Global ABC algorithms.

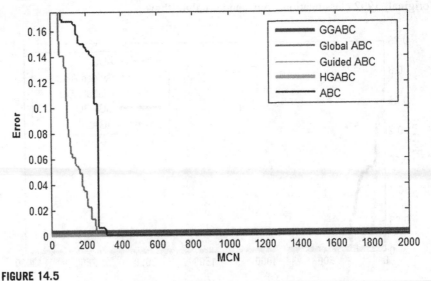

FIGURE 14.5

Learning curve for breast cancer (Diagnostic) 1995, by all training algorithms.

Again, the proposed learning algorithms HGABC and GGABC have small testing MSE values on out of samples and fast convergence compared to ABC, Guided ABC, and Global ABC algorithms on breast cancer (Diagnostic) 1995 as shown in Figure 14.5. The convergence speeds of HGABC and GGABC are faster for breast cancer classification compared with other bio-inspired algorithms. The MSE is continuously decreasing using GGABC and HGABC on breast cancer (Diagnostic) 1995, whereas the ABC fails to decrease MSE with high magnitude. Comparative simulation studies have been presented to show the effectiveness of our new algorithms. In terms of the convergence rate, the simulation results on learning depicted in Figures 14.3 to 14.5 demonstrate the effectiveness of the GGABC and HGABC learning algorithms.

CONCLUSION

Bio-inspired learning algorithms with ANN have great potential for accurate medical disease classification and prediction tasks. Swarm-based learning algorithms are famous because of the efficient exploration and exploitation processes through intelligence behaviors for achieving high performance in different problems. In this research work, the two hybrid algorithms, namely, GGABC and HGABC, are proposed for breast cancer classification tasks. The simulation results on the breast cancer data set demonstrate that the proposed algorithms are able to classify female breast cancer with a high accuracy and efficiency from standard algorithms. Furthermore, the proposed GGABC and HGABC algorithms are successfully used to balance the high amount of exploration and exploitation processes. Besides breast cancer classification, the proposed methods may also be used for breast cancer diagnosis and medical image processing and so on.

REFERENCES

[1] Zhang L, Wang L, Wang X, Liu K, Abraham A. Research of Neural Network Classifier Based on FCM and PSO for Breast Cancer Classification. In: Corchado E, Snášel V, Abraham A, Woźniak M, Graña M, Cho S-B, editors. Hybrid Artificial Intelligent Systems, vol. 7208. Berlin: Springer; 2012. p. 647–54.
[2] Chauhan NC, Kartikeyan MV, Mittal A. Soft Computing Methods. In: Soft Computing Methods for Microwave and Millimeter-Wave Design Problems, vol. 392. Berlin: Springer; 2012. p. 9–23.
[3] Sivakrithika V, Shanthi B. Comparative Study on Cancer Image Diagnosis using Soft Computing Techniques. Int J Comput Appl 2011;19(5).
[4] Nabili Siamak N. What are the most common diseases and conditions seniors face as they age? 2015, 2 January.
[5] Jun L, Xiaohong Q. A Novel Hybrid PSO-BP Algorithm for Neural Network Training. In: International Joint Conference on Computational Sciences and Optimization; 2009. p. 300–3.

[6] Tao G. Artificial immune system based on normal model and immune learning. In: IEEE International Conference on Systems, Man and Cybernetics; 2008. p. 1320–5.

[7] Yan H, Jiang Y, Zheng J, Peng C, Li Q. A multilayer perceptron-based medical decision support system for heart disease diagnosis. Expert Syst Appl 2006;30:272–81.

[8] Chen L-F, Su C-T, Chen K-H, Wang P-C. Particle swarm optimization for feature selection with application in obstructive sleep apnea diagnosis. Neural Comput Appl 2011: 1–10.

[9] World Health Organization. The top 10 causes of death. 2015, 29 November. Available: http://www.who.int/mediacentre/factsheets/fs310/en/.

[10] Daoudi R, Djemal K, Benyettou A. An Immune-Inspired Approach for Breast Cancer Classification. In: Iliadis L, Papadopoulos H, Jayne C, editors. Engineering Applications of Neural Networks, vol. 383. Berlin: Springer; 2013. p. 273–81.

[11] Khuwaja G, Abu-Rezq AN. Bi-modal breast cancer classification system. Pattern Anal Appl 2004;7:235–42.

[12] Jamshed A, Syed AA, Shah MA, Jamshed S. Improving cancer care in Pakistan. South Asian J Cancer 2013;2:36–7.

[13] Banning M, Hafeez H. A Two-Center Study of Muslim Women's Views of Breast Cancer and Breast Health Practices in Pakistan and the UK. J Cancer Educ 2010;25:349–53.

[14] Quinlan E, Thomas-MacLean R, Hack T, Kwan W, Miedema B, Tatemichi S, et al. The impact of breast cancer among Canadian women: Disability and productivity. Work 2009;34:285–96.

[15] American Cancer Society. Cancer Facts and Figure 2013.

[16] Şengelen M, Kutluk T, Fırat D. Cancer statistics in Turkey and in the World (1996–2003). Turkish Association for Cancer Research and Control. Ankara: İZ Press; 2007.

[17] Cianfrocca M, Goldstein LJ. Prognostic and Predictive Factors in Early-Stage Breast Cancer. The Oncologist 2004;9:606–16.

[18] Saritas I. Prediction of Breast Cancer Using Artificial Neural Networks. J Med Syst 2012;36:2901–7.

[19] Parikh P, Patil V, Agarwal JP, Chaturvedi P, Vaidya A, Rathod S, et al. Guidelines for treatment of recurrent or metastatic head and neck cancer. Indian J Cancer 2014;51:89–94.

[20] Chou S-M, Lee T-S, Shao YE, Chen IF. Mining the breast cancer pattern using artificial neural networks and multivariate adaptive regression splines. Expert Syst Appl 2004; 27:133–42.

[21] Roskell DEBID. Fine needle aspiration cytology in cancer diagnosis. BMJ 2004;329: 244–5.

[22] Haykin S. Neural Networks: A Comprehensive Foundation. 2nd ed. Upper Saddle River, NJ: Prentice Hall; 1999.

[23] Jung I-S, Thapa D, Wang G-N. Neural Network Based Algorithms for Diagnosis and Classification of Breast Cancer Tumor. In: Hao Y, Liu J, Wang Y, Cheung Y-m, Yin H, Jiao L, et al., editors. Computational Intelligence and Security, vol. 3801. Berlin: Springer; 2005. p. 107–14.

[24] Connor JT, Martin RD, Atlas LE. Recurrent neural networks and robust time series prediction. IEEE Trans Neural Netw 1994;5:240–54.

[25] Fahlman S. An empirical study of learning speed in backpropagation networks. 1988. Technical Report CMU-CS-88–162.

[26] Azmi B, Mohd Z, Cob C. Breast Cancer prediction based on Backpropagation Algorithm. In: 2010 IEEE Student Conference on Research and Development (SCOReD); 2010. p. 164–8.

[27] Burke HB, Rosen DB, Goodman PH. Comparing artificial neural networks to other statistical methods for medical outcome prediction. In: Presented at the IEEE World Congress on Computational Intelligence; 1994.

[28] Visioli F, Poli A. Current issues on probiotics in human health. Nutrafoods 2011;10: 9–15.

[29] Mori C. High-risk group and high-risk life stage: Key issues in adverse effects of environmental agents on human health. Reprod Med Biol 2004;3:51–8.

[30] Rashid MU, Muhammad N, Faisal S, Amin A, Hamann U. Deleterious RAD51C germline mutations rarely predispose to breast and ovarian cancer in Pakistan. Breast Cancer Res Treat 2014;145:775–84.

[31] Sivak A. Human Exposure to Radiofrequency Radiation—Public Health Issues. In: Carlo G, Supley M, Hersemann S, Thibodeau P, editors. Wireless Phones and Health. New York: Springer; 1998. p. 197–202.

[32] Dekker JWT, Gooiker GA, Bastiaannet E, van den Broek CBM, van der Geest LGM, van de Velde CJ, et al. Cause of death the first year after curative colorectal cancer surgery; a prolonged impact of the surgery in elderly colorectal cancer patients. Eur J Surg Oncol (EJSO) 2014;40:1481–7.

[33] Lee S, Saraswati H, Yunihastuti E, Gani R, Price P. Patients co-infected with hepatitis C virus (HCV) and human immunodeficiency virus recover genotype cross-reactive neutralising antibodies to HCV during antiretroviral therapy. Clin Immunol 2014;155: 149–59.

[34] de Martel C, Franceschi S. Infections and cancer: established associations and new hypotheses. Crit Rev Oncol Hematol 2009;70:183–94.

[35] Bhattacharyya M, Nath J, Bandyopadhyay S. MicroRNA signatures highlight new breast cancer subtypes. Gene 2015;556:192–8.

[36] van Kruijsdijk RCM, van der Graaf Y, Bemelmans RHH, Nathoe HM, Peeters PHM, Visseren FLJ. The relation between resting heart rate and cancer incidence, cancer mortality and all-cause mortality in patients with manifest vascular disease. Cancer Epidemiol 2014;38:715–21.

[37] Dokter J, Felix M, Krijnen P, Vloemans JFPM, Baar MEv, Tuinebreijer WE, et al. Mortality and causes of death of Dutch burn patients during the period 2006–2011. Burns 2015;41:235–40.

[38] Ferlay J, Soerjomataram I, Dikshit R, Ervik M, Mathers C, Elser S, Parkin DM, Rebelo M, Forman D, Bray F. (2013,13/12/2013). GLOBOCAN 2012 v1.0, Cancer Incidence and Mortality Worldwide. Available: http://globocan.iarc.fr.

[39] McCulloch WS. A logical calculus of the ideas immanent in nervous activity. Bull Math Biol 1943:5.

[40] Desylva C. Hyper-threading: Perfect for Neural Networks. In: Colin Johnson GCR, editor. SlashdotMedia.com, vol. 2015; 2012.

[41] Rosenblatt F. A Probabilistic Model for Information Storage and Organization in the Brain. Cornell Aeronaut Lab 1958;65:386.

[42] Rosenblatt F. The Perceptron: A probabilistic model for information storage and organization in the brain. Cornell Aeronaut Lab 1958;65:386–408.

[43] Fangyue C, Guanrong C, Guolong H, Xiubin X, Qinbin H. Universal Perceptron and DNA-Like Learning Algorithm for Binary Neural Networks: LSBF and PBF Implementations. IEEE Trans Neural Netw 2009;20:1645–58.

[44] James K, Russell E. Particle swarm optimization. Proc IEEE Int Conf Neural Netw 1995;4:1942–8.

[45] Mohammadi A, Jazaeri M. A hybrid particle swarm optimization-genetic algorithm for optimal location of svc devices in power system planning. In: 2nd International Universities Power Engineering Conference; 2007. p. 1175−81.

[46] Carvalho T, Ludermir B. Particle Swarm Optimization of Feed-Forward Neural Networks with Weight Decay. In: Sixth International Conference on Hybrid Intelligent Systems; 2006. HIS '06; 2006. p. 5.

[47] Dorigo M, Stützle T. The Ant Colony Optimization Metaheuristic: Algorithms, Applications, and Advances. In: Glover F, Kochenberger G, editors. Handbook of Metaheuristics, vol. 57. New York: Springer; 2003. p. 250−85.

[48] Shah H, Herawan T, Naseem R, Ghazali R. Hybrid Guided Artificial Bee Colony Algorithm for Numerical Function Optimization. In: Tan Y, Shi Y, Coello CC, editors. Advances in Swarm Intelligence, vol. 8794. Springer International Publishing; 2014. p. 197−206.

[49] Karaboga D, Akay B, Ozturk C. Artificial Bee Colony (ABC) Optimization Algorithm for Training Feed-Forward Neural Networks. In: Torra V, Narukawa Y, Yoshida Y, editors. Modeling Decisions for Artificial Intelligence, vol. 4617. Berlin: Springer; 2007. p. 318−29.

[50] Karaboga D, Gorkemli B. A combinatorial Artificial Bee Colony algorithm for traveling salesman problem. International Symposium on Innovations in Intelligent Systems and Applications (INISTA), 2011; 2011. p. 50−3.

[51] Karaboga D, Akay B. A comparative study of Artificial Bee Colony algorithm. Appl Math Comput 2009;214:108−32.

[52] Zhang D, Guan X, Tang Y, Tang Y. Modified Artificial Bee Colony Algorithms for Numerical Optimization. 3rd International Workshop Intelligent Systems and Applications (ISA), 2011; 2011. p. 1−4.

[53] Shah H, Ghazali R. Prediction of Earthquake Magnitude by an Improved ABC-MLP. Developments in E-systems Engineering (DeSE). 2011. p. 312−17.

[54] Tarun K, Sharma, Pant M, Bhardwaj T. PSO ingrained Artificial Bee Colony algorithm for solving continuous optimization problems. In: IEEE International Conference on Computer Applications and Industrial Electronics (ICCAIE), 2011; 2011. p. 108−12.

[55] Narasimhan H. Parallel artificial bee colony (PABC) algorithm. World Congress on Nature & Biologically Inspired Computing, 2009. NaBIC 2009; 2009. p. 306−11.

[56] Zhu G, Kwong S. Gbest-guided artificial bee colony algorithm for numerical function optimization. Appl Math Comput 2010;217:3166−73.

[57] Peng G, Wenming C, Jian L. Global artificial bee colony search algorithm for numerical function optimization. In: Seventh International Conference on Natural Computation (ICNC), 2011; 2011. p. 1280−3.

[58] Karaboga D, Basturk B. On the performance of artificial bee colony (ABC) algorithm. Appl Soft Comput 2008;8:687−97.

[59] Ozturk C, Karaboga D. Hybrid Artificial Bee Colony algorithm for neural network training. IEEE Congress on Evolutionary Computation (CEC), 2011; 2011. p. 84−8.

[60] Shah H, Ghazali R, Herawan T, Nawsher K, Muhammad S, Khan. Hybrid Guided Artificial Bee Colony Algorithm for Earthquake Time Series Data Prediction. Presented at the IMTIC '13. 2013.

[61] Tuba M, Bacanin N, Stanarevic N. Guided artificial bee colony algorithm. In: Presented at the Proceedings of the 5th European Conference on Computing, Paris, France; 2011.

[62] Yang SD, Yi YL, Shan ZY. Gbest-guided Artificial Chemical Reaction Algorithm for global numerical optimization. Proc Eng 2011;24:197−201.

[63] Rumelhart DE, Hinton GE, Williams RJ. Learning representations by back-propagating errors. Nature 1986:323.

[64] Rumelhart DE. Parallel Distributed Processing: Exploration in the Microstructure of Cognition. Boston: MIT Press; 1986.

[65] Von Lehmen A, Paek EG, Liao PF, Marrakchi A, Patel JS. Factors influencing learning by backpropagation. IEEE International Conference on Neural Networks, 1988; 1988;1: 335—341.

[66] Yao Z. Updating learning rates for backpropagation network. Proceedings of 1993 International Joint Conference on Neural Networks, 1993. IJCNN '93-Nagoya; 1993; 1:569—572.

[67] Gardner MW, Dorling SR. Artificial Neural Network (Multilayer Perception)—A review of applications in atmospheric sciences. Atmos Environ 1998:32.

[68] Seong W, Lee. Multilayer cluster neural network for totally unconstrained handwritten numeral recognition. Neural Netw 1995;8:783—92.

[69] Suganthan PN, Teoh EK, Mital DP. Multilayer backpropagation network for flexible circuit recognition. Proceedings of the International Conference on Industrial Electronics, Control, and Instrumentation, IECON '93. 1993;3:1645—1650.

[70] Wolberg WH, Mangasarian OL. Multisurface method of pattern separation for medical diagnosis applied to breast cytology. Proc Natl Acad Sci USA 1990:9193—6.

Index

Note: Page numbers followed by "f" and "t" refer to figures and tables respectively.

Printed in the United States
By Bookmasters